Bargaining for Change

Bargaining for Change

UNION POLITICS IN NORTH AMERICA AND EUROPE

Edited by
Miriam Golden
and Jonas Pontusson

CORNELL UNIVERSITY PRESS
Ithaca and London

First published 1992 by Cornell University Press.

International Standard Book Number 0-8014-2647-2 (cloth)
International Standard Book Number 0-8014-9948-8 (paper)
Library of Congress Catalog Card Number 91-57901

Printed in the United States of America

Librarians: Library of Congress cataloging information appears on the last page of the book.

♾ The paper in this book meets the minimum requirements of the American National Standard for Information Sciences—Permanence of Paper for Printed Library Materials, ANSI Z39.48-1984.

Contents

Preface

This volume contains eight case studies of union politics in Western Europe and North America in the era since the second oil shock of 1979. Some of the case studies discuss the experiences of confederal peak organizations, others deal with specific industrial unions, and two focus on firm-level unionism. Most of the case studies are paired comparisons of union experiences in different countries. The Introduction sets out a framework for the comparative examination of union politics. The concluding chapter develops the analytical themes of the preceding essays and situates the volume in the context of the existing literature on union politics in the advanced capitalist countries. Although the Conclusion is primarily aimed at a professional audience, we hope that the introductory chapter will be useful for advanced undergraduates as well as graduate students.

All but two of the case-study chapters are based on papers that were presented at a conference held at Cornell University in the spring of 1986. The conference was made possible by a Workshop Grant from the Council on European Studies and by additional support from the Center for International Studies at Cornell. Peter Lange participated in organizing the conference and has continued to support this project. We thank him for his encouragement and his many contributions. We also thank the following conference participants: David Cameron, Michael Goldfield, Peter Hall, Niamh Hardiman,

Stephen Herzenberg, Harry Katz, Peter Katzenstein, Randall Kindley, George Ross, Sidney Tarrow, and Lynne Wozniak.

We both acknowledge the German Marshall Fund of the United States for research fellowships during part of the time that we worked on this volume, and Miriam Golden also thanks the National Endowment for the Humanities for its support. Finally, we are, of course, most grateful to the contributors to this volume—among other things, for their patience.

MIRIAM GOLDEN AND JONAS PONTUSSON

Los Angeles, California
Ithaca, New York

Bargaining for Change

Introduction: Organizational and Political-Economic Perspectives on Union Politics

Jonas Pontusson

In this volume we explore the challenges currently confronting organized labor in Western Europe and North America and the responses different unions have elaborated. From 1974 to 1983, the advanced capitalist countries experienced a deep economic crisis, and unemployment rose sharply in all but a couple of them. Organized labor weathered this crisis remarkably well, at least through the 1970s. Indeed, the recession of the mid-1970s enhanced the political influence union leaders had acquired during the postwar boom. As international demand contracted, the containment of labor costs emerged as the key to government efforts to promote economic recovery, yet all governments, conservative as well as socialist, were wary of allowing unemployment to rise beyond a certain point. Hence they were more or less forced to enter into some form of social contract with union leaders.

When a group of scholars affiliated with Harvard's Center for European Studies investigated European union responses to the economic crisis at the beginning of the 1980s, they found that union perceptions and responses varied greatly across countries.[1] In each

For comments on previous drafts of this chapter, I am indebted to Peter Lange, Lowell Turner, and especially Miriam Golden.

1. Peter Lange, George Ross, and Maurizio Vannicelli, *Unions, Change and Crisis* (London: Allen & Unwin, 1982); and Peter Gourevitch et al., *Unions and Economic Crisis* (London: Allen & Unwin, 1984).

country, however, unions were essentially acting within established traditions. Union officials and intellectuals associated with labor movements believed that unions could remain successful simply by modifying the approaches, programs, and practices they had developed during the postwar boom. In this book we offer a different picture, one of unions very much on the defensive, divided among themselves, and lacking a coherent programmatic response to far-reaching changes in their political-economic environment.

Curiously, this apparent sea change in the situation of organized labor has occurred during a period of renewed economic growth. There are reasons to doubt the long-term viability of the world-economic boom of the second half of the 1980s, but to claim that capitalism is in crisis today seems counterintuitive, and to sustain such a claim would require a rather elaborate analysis. On the other hand, it seems increasingly apposite, though perhaps a bit shrill, to speak of a crisis of organized labor throughout the advanced capitalist countries.

As public subsidies to uncompetitive producers have been cut, drastic workforce reductions have occurred in industries that have traditionally been union strongholds—coal, steel, and shipbuilding, to mention only the most striking examples. Frequently, unions have been asked to accept wage cuts in order to forestall, postpone, or minimize workforce reductions. While mass unemployment and the expansion of unorganized or less organized sectors have weakened labor's economic and political leverage, the size of the public sector has emerged as an issue of contention between private-sector and public-sector unions. At the same time, private- and public-sector employers alike have challenged the traditional parameters of collective bargaining in the name of flexibility, demanding that unions agree to temporary employment contracts or increased subcontracting, more flexible working hours and working practices, and greater emphasis on incentive pay in wage determination.

It should be noted at the outset that it is only in the United States that the "employer offensive" of the 1980s has involved a direct and sustained attempt to eliminate unions altogether—and, in the United States, this part of the employer offensive actually predates the current period of economic restructuring.[2] As a rule, European employers

2. See Michael Goldfield, *The Decline of Organized Labor in the United States* (Chicago: University of Chicago Press, 1987).

have sought not to abolish collective bargaining but rather to redefine its parameters and procedures. Union membership figures held steady in West Germany and Scandinavia in the 1980s, and the decline of union membership in Britain appears to be primarily due to changes in the sectoral and geographic makeup of the labor force.[3] Insofar as there is a general crisis of organized labor, it is not a crisis of unionism as such, but rather a crisis of national union organizations—a crisis of national unions and confederal peak organizations purporting to represent broadly defined wage earner interests. In most countries, such organizations did not assume a prominent role until the interwar or even the postwar period. From the vantage of the early 1990s, the national character of bargaining between labor and capital emerges as a distinctive feature of the postwar boom and its immediate aftermath.

The crisis of national union organizations can be interpreted in at least two ways. To begin with, it can be viewed as a consequence of decentralizing and internationalizing trends in the political economy of advanced capitalism. This interpretation holds that the role national union organizations assumed in the postwar era depended on (a) wages being the central issue of contention between labor and capital, and (b) national governments being able to regulate their associated economies. The postwar strategies of West European labor movements and, to a lesser extent, of their North American counterparts sought government intervention not only to ensure that wage increases would not translate into unemployment but also to compensate workers for their acceptance of economic restructuring.

Since the mid-1970s, nonwage issues, pertaining to job security, new technologies, and working practices, have assumed increased salience for employers and workers alike and have prompted employers to push for decentralization of collective bargaining. At the same time, the internationalization of capital and, more generally, the growing interdependence of the advanced capitalist economies have undermined the regulatory capacities of national governments. In sum, the strategies of national unions have been undermined by a twofold shift toward local or perhaps regional bargaining, on the one hand, and economic regulation by international actors (including private banks and multinational corporations as well as intergovernmental organizations such as the European Community), on the other.

3. Philip Bassett, *Strike Free: New Industrial Relations in Britain,* rev. ed. (London: Papermac, 1987), chap. 3.

In a somewhat different vein, the crisis of national union organizations may be viewed as an expression of the fragmentation of wage earner interests.[4] As I argue at greater length below, the restructuring of the advanced capitalist economies since the mid-1970s has intensified traditional conflicts of interest and generated new conflicts among wage earners. I advance this interpretation as a complement to the notion of a twofold shift toward international and subnational structures.

The fragmentation of wage earner interests renders the challenges of internationalization and decentralization more serious by calling into question the organizational viability of labor movements as currently constituted. From the point of view of the twofold shift, the problem confronting unions is to develop a strategy for multilevel bargaining. Along these lines, Kathleen Thelen argues in her contribution to this volume that the challenge to national unions is to coordinate local-level bargaining over workplace issues within a unified framework and in pursuit of goals that encompass the interests of their entire constituency. Similarly, we might say that European unions must begin to articulate demands and coordinate their strategies at a Europe-wide level. But this is easier said than done; the problems involved here are organizational as well as programmatic. Organizational fragmentation renders programmatic innovation an increasingly difficult and possibly futile exercise.

In the essays in this volume we consider the experiences of organized labor in eight advanced capitalist countries (Belgium, Britain, Canada, France, Italy, Sweden, the United States, and West Germany) and address a wide range of issues pertaining to wage bargaining and economic restructuring. Apart from a common focus on the period since the mid-1970s, the editors and contributors share certain analytical concerns, discussed more fully by Miriam Golden in her concluding essay. As political scientists, we are disappointed with the industrial relations literature insofar as it reduces organized labor to an economic actor on a par with corporations or treats industrial relations as a system of procedural rules and norms that evolves according to its own logic. Yet, we are also critical of the common tendency

4. See Scott Lash and John Urry, *The End of Organized Capitalism* (Madison: University of Wisconsin Press, 1987), chap. 8.

among political scientists to treat organized labor as a more or less unitary national actor. This tendency is particularly pronounced in the literature on corporatist policymaking, but it also appears in the two volumes that issued from the aforementioned research project at Harvard's Center for European Studies. These two collections have greatly influenced the contributors to this volume, but nonetheless our research represents a shift in the focus of analysis away from confederal peak organizations (such as the AFL-CIO) to national unions and subnational union organizations. More important, however, we want to stress that the process whereby unions aggregate interests and mobilize their members for collective action is a conflict-ridden and inherently political one.

Like the Harvard Center volumes, this book adopts a comparative approach to union politics. In seeking to account for cross-national variations and, in some cases, variations across firms or regions within a country, virtually all our contributors emphasize the importance of the organizational structures of labor movements. This approach is informed by and resonates with several "neoinstitutionalist" arguments within our discipline.[5] For our purposes, institutional arrangements matter in two specific ways. First, the way unions are organized affects the extent and nature of their current difficulties. Second, organizational structures affect the strategic options available to unions and their preferences among different strategic options.

Although the labor movements of the advanced capitalist countries confront broadly similar problems, the extent of their difficulties clearly varies a great deal. In particular, our case studies suggest that the salience of different kinds of intraclass conflict varies and that these variations are related to the organization of labor. As Golden demonstrates in her conclusion, the proposition emerging from our case studies is that intraclass conflicts tend to become a source of politicization and organizational fragmentation when they coincide with (preexisting) organizational boundaries. A few examples suffice

5. See Peter Hall, *Governing the Economy* (New York: Oxford University Press, 1986), esp. chap. 9. Other major works in the institutionalist tradition include John Zysman, *Governments, Markets, and Growth* (Ithaca: Cornell University Press, 1983); Peter Katzenstein, *Small States in World Markets* (Ithaca: Cornell University Press, 1985); and Peter Evans, Dietrisch Reuschemeyer, and Theda Skocpol, eds., *Bringing the State Back In* (London: Cambridge University Press, 1985).

to illustrate this theme. Peggy Kahn shows how the coincidence of material conflicts of interest and organizational cleavages of a regional character split Britain's National Union of Mineworkers in 1984–85. In my own essay, one sees that conflicts of interest between skilled and unskilled workers have been a more important source of disunity in Britain than in Sweden. And Peter Swenson's comparison of Sweden and West Germany suggests that some labor movements are more vulnerable to conflicts of interest between public- and private-sector workers than others.

We do not wish to imply that organizational variables provide a sufficient explanation of variations in the importance of different kinds of intraclass cleavages. As Swenson points out, the size of the public sector must feature in any explanation of why divisions between private- and public-sector unions are more prominent in some countries than in others. Similarly, the importance of declining industries to the economy as a whole is greater in some countries than in others and obviously affects the pressures on organized labor. But, within these parameters, the organizational politics of labor seem to be an important explanatory variable.

To the extent that we can hold the pressures on unions constant, organizational structures also seem to affect their strategic capacities and inclinations. Charlotte Yates's essay on the responses of American and Canadian autoworkers to employer demands for concessions illustrates this theme most clearly. Yates shows that the tradition of rank-and-file participation in union decision making within the Canadian section of the United Auto Workers made it both possible and necessary for Canadian union leaders to adopt a militant response. Similarly, Anthony Daley's comparison of union responses to the decline of the steel industry in France and the United States suggests that different organizational structures led to the adoption of different strategies.

By way of introduction, the following discussion takes on two tasks. First, I identify the principal ways the organization of labor varies across the eight countries treated here and discuss the significance of such variations. Second I address the question of how and why the political-economic environment of organized labor has changed in the 1970s and 1980s. These analytical perspectives are meant to complement each other. Whereas in the first section I deal with labor movements, in the second I consider the political-economic environment of organized labor. And whereas the first emphasizes cross-national variations, the second emphasizes general trends that cut across the advanced capitalist countries. In the third and last section, I introduce each of the essays to follow.

COMPARATIVE LABOR MOVEMENTS

We can distinguish among the labor movements of the advanced capitalist countries in terms of the extent to which they organize, represent, and mobilize wage earners. We can also distinguish among them in terms of *how* they organize, represent, and mobilize wage earners, that is, in terms of their organizational structures. As indicated above, the research presented in this volume is primarily concerned with the latter problematic.

In addressing the topic of cross-national variation in organizational structures, political scientists have focused primarily on the centralization of authority within unions and, more specifically, on the authority wielded by confederal peak organizations. Thus they have sought to measure the extent to which confederal officials have the authority to make decisions and enter into agreements on behalf of affiliated unions (and union members) and to rank national labor movements according to this criterion.[6] In my view, the authority of confederal peak organizations represents but one aspect—indeed, a secondary one—of how national labor movements differ in their organizational structures.

I propose two arguments as to the secondary status of confederal authority. First, history suggests that the centralization of authority within national unions (in some countries known as federations) is a necessary precondition for the emergence of strong peak organizations. Second, the centralization of authority within national unions itself depends in large measure on the absence (or attenuation) of competition among unions. When unions compete for the same potential

6. See, for example, Philippe Schmitter, "Interest Intermediation and Regime Governability in Contemporary Western Europe and North America," in *Organizing Interests in Western Europe*, ed. Suzanne Berger (Cambridge: Cambridge University Press, 1981), pp. 287–330; and David Cameron, "Social Democracy, Corporatism, Labour Quiescence, and the Representation of Economic Interest in Advanced Capitalist Society," in *Order and Conflict in Contemporary Capitalism*, ed. John Goldthorpe (Oxford: Oxford University Press, 1984), pp. 143–78.

membership, they are likely to take full advantage of favorable bargaining conditions at the local level, and power tends to gravitate toward union officials most closely in touch with the rank and file. This argument brings out the importance of distinguishing among labor movements in terms of their degree of fragmentation or concentration as well as their degree of centralization.

Table I-1 provides a list of confederal peak organizations in the eight countries treated in this volume and specifies the number of unions affiliated with each (as well as their total membership). These data provide a rough idea of cross-national variation in degrees of labor movement concentration, but they do not add up to a straightforward concentration index. If we count peak organizations, Britain has only one, whereas Sweden has three. Yet the number of unions affiliated to the British Trades Union Congress is far greater than the total number of unions in Sweden. What weight should we assign to confederal fragmentation relative to the number of individual unions? There is no obvious answer to this question. Indeed, the significance of confederal fragmentation very much depends on the organizational basis of peak organizations. Whereas French peak organizations compete directly for the allegiance of wage earners, the two major Swedish peak organizations, the Landsorganisation and the Tjänstemannens Centralorganisation, represent two mutually exclusive constituencies (blue-collar and white-collar employees). At this stage, numerical exercises become somewhat pointless; clearly, the French labor movement is more fragmented than the Swedish.[7]

The following discussion proceeds in three steps. First, I briefly address the significance of cross-national variation in union membership level and develop my case for attending to organizational variables. Second I distinguish among national labor movements in terms of the degree and sources of organizational fragmentation. Finally, I return to the role of peak organizations and the centralization of authority. It should be noted at the outset that the question of why different labor movements have come to be organized differently lies beyond the

7. Rather than simply counting unions and peak organizations, we should perhaps measure union concentration in the way economists measure industrial concentration, that is, in terms of the five or ten largest unions' share of total union membership in each country. But the question of the weight to be assigned to confederal fragmentation remains under this procedure. My discussion of centralization and concentration draws extensively on Miriam Golden, "An Institutional Analysis of Trade Unions" (Paper presented at the Conference on The New Institutionalism at the University of Colorado, Boulder, January 12–13, 1990).

Table I–1 Major union confederations, 1988

	Affiliates	Membership (000's)
Belgium		
Confédération des Syndicats Chrétiens (CSC): confederation of Christian unions	18	1,336
Fédération Générale du Travail de Belgique (FGTB): Belgian confederation of labor	11	1,098
Centrale Générale des Syndicats Liberaux de Belgique (CGSLB): Belgian confederation of liberal unions	NA	250
Canada		
Canadian Labor Congress (CLC)	90	2,200
Confédération des Syndicats Nationaux (CSN): confederation of national unions	NA	235
Canadian Federation of Labor	14	225
Federal Republic of Germany		
Deutscher Gewerkschaftbund (DGB): German confederation of trade unions	17	7,600
Deutscher Beamtenbund (DBB): civil servants confederation	45	800
France		
Confédération Générale du Travail (CGT): confederation of labor	40	1,402
Confédération Générale du Travail–Force Ouvrière (CGT-FO): confederation of labor–workers strength	30	1,150
Confédération Française Démocratique du Travail (CFDT): French democratic confederation of labor	22	900
Confédération Générale des Cadres (CGC): confederation of executive staff	71	300
Confédération Française des Travailleurs Chrétiens (CFTC): French confederation of Christian workers	48	265
Italy		
Confederazione Generale Italiana del Lavoro (CGIL): Italian confederation of labor	NA	4,600
Confederazione Italiana dei Sindicati Lavorati (CISL): Italian confederation of workers' unions	NA	2,980
Unione Italiana del Lavoro (UIL): Italian labor union	30	1,447

Table I–1 Major union confederations, 1988 (continued)

	Affiliates	Membership (000's)
Sweden		
Landsorganisationen (LO): confederation of labor	24	2,280
Tjänstemännens Centralorganisation (TCO): central organization of salaried employees	20	1,212
Sveriges Akademikers Centralorganisation/ Statstjänstemännens Riksförbund (SACO/SR): confederation of professional associations	26	300
United Kingdom		
Trades Union Congress (TUC)	102	9,127
United States		
American Federation of Labor–Congress of Industrial Organizations (AFL-CIO)	90	14,400

Source: Trade Unions of the World, 2d ed. (Harlow: Longman, 1989).
Note: Membership figures refer to membership claims by the confederations themselves in the 1985–88 period. It is a commonplace that French and Italian unions claim to have more members than they actually have, and this may be true in other cases as well. In the French case, the numbers of affiliated unions refer only to industrial union federations (they do not include regional and departmental unions).

scope of this discussion. The questions before us are whether organizational variables matter, which organizational variables matter, and how or why they matter.[8]

The Case for an Organizational Approach

As Table I-2 demonstrates, union membership levels vary markedly across the eight countries. Assuming that the extent to which unions organize the labor force affects their bargaining leverage vis-à-vis employers and government officials, such data may be used as a rough measure of cross-national variations in the power of organized labor. In other words, the figures in Table I-2 may be invoked to support propositions such as "the Swedish labor movement is more powerful than the American labor movement" or, more elaborately, "the power

8. On the historical origins of cross-national variations in labor organization and strategy, see Aristide Zolberg, "How Many Exceptionalisms?" in *Working Class Formation,* ed. Ira Katnelsen and Aristide Zolberg (Princeton: Princeton University Press, 1986), pp. 397–456; and James Fulcher, "On the Explanation of Industrial Relations Diversity: Labour Movements, Employers and the State in Britain and Sweden," *British Journal of Industrial Relations* 26, no. 2 (1988): 246–74.

Table I–2 Union members as percentage of the total labor force 1955–85

	1955(%)	1970(%)	1980(%)	1984–85(%)
Sweden	70	79	90	95
Belgium	NA	75	75–80	NA
Italy	NA	50–55	55–60	NA
Britain	46	52	57	53
West Germany	46	37	42	42
Canada	32	32	36	37
France	23	22	28	NA
United States	34	31	25	18

Source: Adapted from Michael Goldfield, *The Decline of Organized Labor in the United States* (Chicago: University of Chicago Press, 1987), p. 16.

of the Swedish labor movement increased while the power of the American labor movement declined in the 1970s." The assumption involved here seems quite reasonable, but two problems with using membership data as a measure of power must be noted. First, the meaning of union membership varies from one country to another. In France or Italy, belonging to a union tends to imply a fairly high level of commitment and activism. This is less true of Sweden, where virtually everyone belongs to a union. In a conflict with management, French or Italian unions are often able to mobilize support beyond their membership. Relative to Swedish unions, the power resources of French and Italian unions may be greater than Table I-2 suggests.

Second and perhaps more important, we must keep in mind that labor's power relative to employers depends on the power resources of employers as well as of labor. According to Table I-2, Swedish unions have much greater power resources than do American unions, but perhaps this is also true of Swedish employers. Indeed, there is some evidence to suggest that union membership levels are positively correlated with economic concentration; that is, that union organizing tends to be more successful in economies made up of a few large firms than in economies made up of many small firms.[9] Insofar as concentration also strengthens the power resources of employers, we would expect countries with strong unions to also have strong employers.

Our concern with the question of how unions organize, represent, and mobilize wage earners is in part a reaction to the manifest inadequacies of various attempts to explain union strategies and

9. John Stephens, *The Transition from Capitalism to Socialism* (London: Macmillan, 1979), chap. 4.

achievements ments strictly in terms of power resources, measured by membership data and in some cases by electoral support for labor parties. We simply cannot treat these labor movements as if they were the same, except for the fact that some are more powerful than others. The empirical focus of the research presented here underscores this point, for our research is heavily biased toward traditional manufacturing industries. Within these industries, cross-national variations in unionization rates are much smaller than the economy-wide variations reported in Table I-2. Simply put, the huge difference between Swedish and American membership levels is primarily due to the fact that Swedish unions have been so much more successful in organizing services, white-collar employees, public-sector employees, and women, and not so much to greater success among steelworkers or autoworkers. If we restrict ourselves to traditional manufacturing industries, the question of how unions organize wage earners—that is, how their organizational structures differ—tends to overshadow the question of the extent to which unions organize wage earners.

Our approach proceeds from the recognition that wage earners, like any social class, and perhaps to a greater extent than other social classes, have multiple and partly contradictory interests. As a group, they have an interest in maximizing their share of national income, but they also have an interest in securing noninflationary growth (to avoid inflation and unemployment). Which of these interests will prevail? Since labor's share of national income is determined by economic conditions beyond its exclusive control, different categories of wage earners inevitably end up competing with each other for their share of labor's share. This competition has traditionally focused on wages, but it also involves job security and other benefits. Although intraclass competition is inevitable, the forms it assumes vary depending on how unions are organized. Do white-collar and blue-collar employees belong to the same unions? Do skilled craft workers belong to the same union as unskilled workers? Arguably, organizational structures affect more than the way union members and officials define wage earner interests; they also impinge on the strategic options available. In particular, organizational structures seem to have a direct bearing on the question, continuously confronted by all unions, of whether to rely on the exercise of marketplace power through collective bargaining or to pursue their interests by legislative means, that is, through the exercise of political power.

Let us dwell for a moment on the topic of how organization affects the trade-off between maximizing one's share of national income and securing noninflationary growth. Following Mancur Olson, it seems plausible to suppose that unions are more likely to take the macroeconomic consequences of their wage demands into account the larger a segment of the labor force they represent.[10] Narrowly based unions have less incentive than encompassing unions to sacrifice short-term distributive gains in order to achieve long-term growth, for they stand to gain only a small share of the benefits of growth, and they can always hope for a free ride on the sacrifices of others (note that this argument applies to all interest groups, not just to unions).

The logic of Olson's argument is compelling, but unionization rates alone do not provide an adequate predictor of how unions order their preferences with respect to the trade-off between their short-term interest in maximizing their share of national income and their long-term interest in maximizing national income. Consider the British and German cases. As Table I-2 shows, British unions organize a significantly larger segment of the labor force than do West German unions. Yet everyone would agree that West German unions have been more inclined to exercise wage restraint in order to secure noninflationary growth. This apparent paradox dissolves once we take into account the organizational structure of the two labor movements. There are more than 400 unions in Britain (102 TUC affiliates), as compared to less than 70 unions in West Germany (17 DGB affiliates). By comparative standards, the British *labor movement* is quite encompassing, but British *unions* represent narrow constituencies.

The more centralized authority structure of West German unions may also be invoked to explain their greater willingness and ability to engage in voluntary wage restraint. This line of argument holds that national union officials are more likely to take macroeconomic consequences into account than are local officials (or activists), and that center-periphery relations within union organizations therefore affect the trade-off between redistribution and growth. Such an argument represents a modification of rather than a departure from Olson's logic, for national officials are here identified with large constituencies and local officials or activists with narrow constituencies. But it is not clear that we need to introduce the centralization variable to account

10. Mancur Olson, *The Rise and Fall of Nations* (New Haven: Yale University Press, 1982).

for the contrast between the West German and British cases. And, again, the centralization of authority may be viewed, at least in part, as a derivative of concentration.

Organizational Boundaries

As long as we restrict our concerns to the trade-off between redistribution and growth, the degree of union fragmentation or concentration may provide an adequate explanation of divergent union strategies. But if we are interested in union responses to economic restructuring and corporate efforts to reorganize work, as most of our contributors are, the nature of organizational fragmentation is at least as important as the degree of fragmentation. As suggested above, moreover, some forms of organizational fragmentation appear to be more conducive to wage rivalries than others.

Leaving white-collar unions aside for the moment, we can easily distinguish three types of labor movements: craft-fragmented labor movements, politically fragmented labor movements, and unitary labor movements.[11] The British case provides the most obvious example of a labor movement organized on the basis of craft divisions within the working class. In some British plants, there are as many as fifteen unions representing different categories of blue-collar workers (machinists, electricians, plumbers, assembly operators). By contrast, the French, Italian, and Belgian labor movements are organized on the basis of political or religious divisions within the working class. In the Belgian case, such divisions also have an ethnic-linguistic component.

French and Italian unions seek to organize workers according to the principles of industrial unionism rather than those of craft unionism; that is, they seek to organize workers on the basis of who they work for rather than on the jobs they do. But in each industry there are at least two, and often three, unions that seek to organize all the workers of that industry. These unions belong to separate confederations and compete on the basis of ideological appeals and political affiliations as well as their abilities to deliver material gains. In both countries, workers with socialist and Catholic sympathies have traditionally been organized by separate unions. In France, the Communist party's

11. See George Ross, "What is Progressive about Unions?" *Theory and Society* 10 (1981): 609–43. Adolf Sturmthal, *Comparative Labor Movements* (Belmont, Calif.: Wadsworth, 1972) presents a similar typology couched in terms of party-union relations.

growing domination of the principal union confederation (CGT) led moderate socialists to establish a separate confederation (CGT-FO) in 1948. Yet another split occurred in 1964 when the majority of the Catholic confederation (CFTC) formed a new, nondenominational and increasingly socialist confederation (CFDT). In Italy, socialist union activists chose to remain within the Communist-dominated CGIL, and the split between the CGIL and its Catholic counterpart (CISL) remains the principal organizational divide within the labor movement, though there is a smaller confederation (UIL) with a non-denominational and nonsocialist orientation. (During the 1970s, the three Italian confederations set up joint organizations in several industries, but this effort to forge a unitary labor movement fell apart in the 1980s.)

The Swedish and German cases clearly fit the category of unitary labor movements. In both countries, blue-collar unions organize industries rather than crafts and belong to a single confederal peak organization. Needless to say, this does not mean that there are no craft divisions or political-religious divisions within the Swedish and German working classes. The point is rather that union organizations cut across or encompass such divisions. In the German case, a unitary labor movement was not formed until the 1940s. Prior to its destruction by the Nazis, the German labor movement was fragmented on political-religious grounds, much as the French and Italian labor movements are today.

The American and Canadian cases do not fit so neatly within this typology of labor movements, but they seem to have more in common with the British case than with any of the others. It must first be noted that the British case is by no means one of pure craft unionism. In some sectors of the British economy, most notably coal, we do find industrial unions. More important, the British labor movement is characterized by the coexistence of craft unions and so-called general unions, which organize unskilled and semiskilled workers across a wide range of industrial sectors. Beginning in the 1890s, general unions emerged because craft unions refused to organize unskilled workers in new mass-production industries. In response to this challenge, craft unions broadened their organizing efforts. The fragmented character of the British labor movement derives not only from the craft basis of many unions but also, and perhaps more important, from the absence of clear jurisdictions among unions. Not only do craft and general unions compete with each other for the same potential membership; general unions also compete among themselves.

In the United States, craft unions dominated the early labor movement to a greater extent than they did in Britain, but they failed to gain a firm foothold in the new mass-production industries. When these industries were finally organized in the 1930s, they were organized by industrial unions. The merger of the AFL and the CIO in 1955 brought an end to the struggle between craft unions and industrial unions and institutionalized the dualism that distinguishes the American case (and the Canadian case as well). In some sectors of the American economy, unions are organized on craft lines in a way that resembles the British pattern minus general unions. In other sectors, they are organized on industrial lines in a way that resembles the Swedish-German pattern. I return to the significance of this dual structure in the next section.

In all the advanced capitalist countries, the postwar period was characterized by the expansion of white-collar employment (both in absolute terms and in relation to the labor force as a whole). At the same time as the working conditions of many white-collar employees became more akin to those of blue-collar employees, the wage demands of blue-collar unions prompted white-collar employees to defend their position in the wage hierarchy by joining unions and engaging in collective action. With few exceptions, white-collar employees were organized by separate white-collar unions. Some white-collar unions pursued craft-like organizing strategies (for instance, restricting their membership to people with certain kinds of professional degrees); others opted for the model of industrial unionism. For our present purposes, however, it is sufficient to consider cross-national variations in the relationship of white-collar unions to blue-collar unions.

In most of the countries treated in this volume, white-collar unions are either independent or affiliated with confederal peak organizations that include and tend to be dominated by blue-collar unions. In France and Italy, confederal peak organizations include white-collar unions, which compete with each other on the same basis as blue-collar unions, but there are also unaffiliated white-collar unions such as the French teachers' union, Fédération de l'Education Nationale. In Britain, the major white-collar unions joined the TUC in the postwar period.

The most notable exception to this pattern is the Swedish case. Whereas LO remains exclusively a peak organization for blue-collar unions, two separate peak organizations for white-collar unions (TCO and SACO-SR) emerged in the postwar period. One of these organizations primarily represents civil servants with university degrees. In Germany, there is also a separate peak organization of civil servant unions, but the DGB includes unions that organize public- as well as private-sector white-collar employees.

Intraorganizational Hierarchies

Returning now to the role of confederal peak organizations and their authority vis-à-vis affiliated unions, we might consider the Swedish and American cases to be the poles of a continuum from strong to weak peak organizations. Whereas the AFL-CIO remains a lobbying organization, representing the political interests of independent unions and lacking any involvement in collective bargaining, the Swedish peak organization of blue-collar unions, LO, became a bargaining organization in the postwar period, engaging in direct negotiations with its employer counterpart over wage increases and other benefits. In most West European countries, peak organizations have been drawn into collective bargaining through various government-initiated incomes policy deals, but their involvement has been more intermittent and less authoritative than LO's.

Most accounts of the Swedish labor movement tend to exaggerate the formal powers of LO vis-à-vis its affiliates. Arguably, what really sets the Swedish case apart is the centralization of authority within the national unions affiliated with LO. LO's ability to coordinate wage bargaining in the postwar period rested on a consensus about wage policy norms among its principal affiliates, a consensus which held that the LO unions should together seek to boost the relative standing of their least-paid members. As Swenson's contribution to this volume documents, LO's role diminished as the consensus among its affiliates fell apart in the 1980s.

Again, I believe that our explanation of the centralization of authority within the LO unions must proceed from the fact that Swedish workers are almost exclusively organized on an industrial basis, and that a high degree of union concentration follows from the consistent application of industrial unionism in the absence of political fragmentation (LO's five largest unions account for more than 70 percent of its total membership). The case for a causal linkage between industrial unionism and the centralization of authority can be argued in at least two ways.

First, the value craft unions typically assign to the autonomy of union locals may be linked to the fact that their marketplace power depends on unilateral control over the supply of certain skills. All workers with these skills must comply with whatever sanctions the union imposes on particular employers. Industrial unions neither can nor need to control the supply of labor in this manner. Instead, they rely on collective bargaining, backed up by the threat of temporary disruptions of production. In short, craft unions depend on the commitment and participation of individual members to a greater extent than do industrial unions, and this dependence represents a constraint on the centralization of authority (a different argument along such lines would be that skilled workers are more inclined to demand a say in union affairs than are unskilled workers).

Second, and perhaps more straightforward, industrial unionism can be said to facilitate the centralization of authority to the extent that it eliminates competition among unions. To repeat, competition forces unions to take advantage of favorable bargaining conditions at the local level, and under these circumstances power gravitates toward union officials most closely in touch with the rank and file. From this perspective, the split between blue-collar and white-collar unions that characterizes the Swedish labor movement is compatible with the centralization of authority because these unions organize completely distinct constituencies. Indeed, the argument here implies that pure craft unionism would also be compatible with the centralization of authority. The constraints on the centralization of authority are greatest where general unions compete with craft unions or among themselves, as in the British case, and where industrial unions compete with each other, as in the French and Italian cases.[12]

I hasten to note that craft unions do, in a sense, compete with each other even if they organize distinct constituencies. When workers in the same plant are organized by different unions, they likely compare their own union's performance with that of other unions. By the same token, wage comparisons across the blue-collar/white-collar divide

12. On the relation between interunion competition and the weakness of national unions in France, see Martin Schain, "Corporatism and Industrial Relations in France," in *French Politics and Public Policy*, ed. Philip Cerny and Martin Schain (New York: St. Martin's Press, 1980), pp. 191–217. On the Italian case, see Miriam Golden, *Labor Divided: Austerity and Working-Class Politics in Contemporary Italy* (Ithaca: Cornell University Press, 1988).

may be a source of rank-and-file militancy, weakening the centralization of authority. In the Swedish case, wage rivalries between blue-collar and white-collar unions became much more prominent in the 1970s than they had previously been and contributed to the subsequent erosion of LO's internal cohesion. It should also be noted that the introduction of new computer-based manufacturing technologies has, in some instances, blurred the distinction between blue-collar and white-collar employees.

My claim is that interunion competition represents a constraint on the centralization of authority within national unions. It does not follow that the absence or attenuation of interunion competition necessarily implies centralization of authority. To explain why centralization occurs, we must resort to some other argument. For instance, we might resort to Robert Michels's classic notion of an "iron law of oligarchy."[13] Thus, we would argue that there is an inherent tendency for power to be centralized in union organization, and that this tendency becomes operative when the constraints of interunion competition are removed.

The Swedish experience suggests an alternate argument. In this case, employers actively pursued industry-wide collective bargaining in order to prevent unions from using favorable local labor market conditions to whipsaw employers and, in effect, forced the LO unions to centralize their internal decision-making procedures in the period immediately prior to World War II.[14] Employer strategies appear to be relevant in other cases as well. Be that as it may, we can affirm, with some confidence, that the absence or attenuation of interunion competition is a necessary but not sufficient condition for the centralization of authority within national unions.

Similarly, the centralization of authority within national unions seems to be a necessary but not sufficient condition for the emergence of strong peak organizations. In the United States as well as in Sweden, plant-level bargaining occurs within the parameters of detailed and legally binding contracts agreed at the level of the firm or the industry, and local union officials are directly dependent on the national leadership. This pattern stands in marked contrast to that in Britain,

13. Robert Michels, *Political Parties: A Sociological Study of the Oligarchical Tendencies of Modern Democracy* (New York: Free Press, 1962).

14. See Geoffrey Ingham, *Strikes and Industrial Conflict: Britain and Scandinavia* (London: Macmillan, 1974), chap. 4; and Peter Swenson, *Fair Shares: Unions, Pay, and Politics in Sweden and West Germany* (Ithaca: Cornell University Press, 1989), chap. 2.

where collective bargaining is largely carried out by shop stewards elected by workers within a small part of the plant, and national union officials have had little ability to direct the activities of shop stewards (a similar system of decentralized shop-floor bargaining emerged in Italy in the late 1960s). By comparison to British unions, American unions—at least, American industrial unions—must be considered quite centralized in their internal structure. Yet the AFL-CIO seems to be a weaker peak organization than the TUC. Also, German industrial unions seem to be as centralized as their Swedish counterparts, but the DGB is manifestly weaker than LO.

In the Swedish case, employer pressures again played an important role in the second phase of centralization, that is, in the transfer of bargaining authority from national unions to LO (a process that began in the 1930s and was completed in the 1950s). But this time around, pressures from the Social Democratic government also played a crucial role. LO's role in the postwar period must be understood in the context of the logic of class compromise in Sweden. In effect, LO exercised wage restraint in order to enable the Social Democratic party, to which LO has always been closely linked, to remain in government and carry out various policies beneficial to LO members. In other words, LO came to assume such a prominent role because the LO unions were, more or less consciously, engaged in political exchange.[15]

The question of why the role of peak organization varies thus appears to be linked to the question of why some unions tend to rely on the exercise of marketplace power to achieve gains for their membership while others look to government legislation to achieve similar objectives. The latter is a big and complicated question which I do not attempt to resolve here. I do suggest, however, that organizational structures can be invoked to explain the extent to which unions are *inclined* to pursue economism or political exchange as well as the extent to which they are *able* to exercise the wage restraint that constitutes an essential component of successful political exchange. Again,

15. I am here using the term "political exchange" in the sense used by Peter Lange, "Unions, Workers, and Wage Regulation," in *Order and Conflict,* ed. Goldthorpe, p. 109, and by Walter Korpi and Michael Shalev, "Strikes, Power and Politics in the Western Nations, 1900–1976," *Political Power and Social Theory* 1 (1980): 301–34. Alessandro Pizzorno's original usage is slightly different; see Pizzorno, "Political Exchange and Collective Identity in Industrial Conflict," in *The Resurgence of Class Conflict in Western Europe since 1968,* 2 vols, ed. Colin Crouch and Alessandro Pizzorno (London: Macmillan, 1978), vol. 2, pp. 277–98.

my argument turns on the distinction between craft unionism and industrial unionism and on the issue of interunion competition.

To the extent that they are able to control the supply of certain skills, craft unions wield a great deal of marketplace leverage. At the same time, it is both possible and necessary for craft unions to focus their energies on the provision of benefits restricted to their own members. The situation of industrial unions is entirely different, for they organize large numbers of unskilled and semiskilled workers. These workers have less marketplace leverage to the extent that their skills are less valuable, and they themselves are more replaceable than the workers organized by craft unions. On the other hand, they may constitute a significant electoral constituency. Most important, perhaps, the pursuit of comprehensive legislative solutions to issues such as old-age pensions is consistent with the ambition of industrial unions to organize all workers. Indeed, the material gains industrial unions seek can rarely be restricted to their own members, for employers have an interest in providing the same benefits to nonunion employees.

In sum, we should expect industrial unions to be more inclined to engage in political exchange, and much empirical evidence could be invoked in support of this expectation. The above characterization of the situation of industrial unions applies equally to British-style general unions, but the competitive nature of general unionism undermines the prospects for durable political exchange. Arguably, the prospects for durable political exchange are even worse in the case of politically fragmented labor movements, for here interunion competition not only undermines the ability of unions to exercise wage restraint but also resonates with a competitive form of leftist politics that may weaken labor's political influence in the first place.

From the perspective of this discussion, American industrial unions appear to be uniquely economistic in their orientation. Perhaps this manifestation of American exceptionalism can be explained by the dual structure of the labor movement and the large size of the nonunion sector of the American economy. Arguably, these features of the American political economy, along with the absence of a labor party, make it both possible and necessary for industrial unions to act according to a logic akin to that of craft unionism.

To conclude, the way unions are organized varies greatly among the advanced capitalist countries, and these variations profoundly affect union politics. They affect the political salience of different wage-earner interests as well as the strategies unions pursue. The role of confederal peak organizations is a secondary issue in this context. The crucial structural differences among national labor movements have to do with the extent to which, and the terms on which, unions compete with each other.

THE POLITICAL ECONOMY OF POSTWAR CAPITALISM

Having identified the principal variations among national labor movements, we can now proceed to a discussion of cross-national commonalities in the postwar evolution of labor politics. As I suggested at the outset, we can generalize across our eight countries to say that the period from World War II through the 1960s, and in several cases through the 1970s, is distinguished by the national character of bargaining between labor and capital and by the prominence assumed by national unions and confederal peak organizations within national labor movements. Though less centralized than their Swedish counterparts, British national unions and the TUC, for example, assumed a more prominent role, relative to local union actors, in the 1940–70 period than they did before or after.[16] The two countries that do not quite fit this generalization are France and Italy, where trends toward national coordination of wage bargaining and growing union influence over government policy did not appear until the 1960s.

The prominence assumed by national union organizations can be related to certain institutional features of postwar capitalist development in Western Europe and North America. It is commonplace to argue that the unprecedented economic boom of the 1950s and 1960s rested on an accommodation between labor and capital, sometimes referred to as the "postwar settlement." The timing and durability of this accommodation varied from one country to another, and so did the exact terms of accommodation. To a greater or lesser extent, however, postwar capitalist development in all these countries involved two common elements: the spread of Fordist mass production and the

16. See Colin Crouch, *The Politics of Industrial Relations*, 2d ed. (London: Fontana, 1982).

growth of the Keynesian welfare state. If we restrict ourselves to our Western European cases, we might say that the emergence or the extension and reinforcement of corporatist patterns of interest mediation represents another commonality of postwar capitalist development.

I use the term "corporatism" here to denote a situation in which (a) the interests of wage earners, employers, and other producer groups are represented by a relatively small number of organizations, and (b) the leaders of these organizations are involved in the formulation and implementation of government policy on a more or less permanent basis, interacting with each other as well as with government officials. With Britain as a partial exception, Western Europe has a long tradition of close, interdependent relations between government officials and organizations representing different sectoral interests. What is distinctive about the postwar era in Western Europe, at least in its northern regions, is the fact that organized labor increasingly came to be included in corporatist arrangements. Thus, we might speak of a shift from bipartite to tripartite corporatism (that is, from government-business corporatism to government-business-labor corporatism).

Due to the weakness of left-wing parties as well as the fragmentation of labor, the development of tripartite corporatism has been less pronounced in France and Italy than in Sweden, Germany, and Britain. Let me emphasize at the outset that I am here concerned with tendential rather than static commonalities across countries. In focusing on common trajectories, I do not wish to deny the specificity of national experiences. Rather, I believe that this exercise may enable us to specify more precisely, and appreciate more fully, what is specific or exceptional about the experiences of particular countries.

In most countries, the postwar settlement began to come undone in the late 1960s. Broadly speaking, we can divide the 1970s and 1980s into three distinct periods. The first, roughly from 1968 to 1974, was characterized by rising working-class militancy and a consequent resurgence of shop-floor power and a marked radicalization of union demands. The sharp economic downturn of 1973–74 marks the beginning of the second period, characterized by stagflation and the emergence of mass unemployment. At least in Western Europe, the economic crisis initially enhanced the political influence of national union leaders and contributed to a recentralization of collective bargaining under the auspices of government-initiated incomes policies. The period since the early 1980s, finally, has been characterized by a weakening of labor's economic and political power and by the fragmentation of working-class interests as well as the decentralization of collective bargaining. I treat the first and second of these post-1968 periods only briefly. My principal aim is to show how the political-economic conditions of the 1980s differ from those of the "golden era" of postwar expansion.

The Postwar Settlement

When students of Western European politics speak of a postwar settlement between labor and capital, they are usually referring to the introduction of Keynesian demand management, the expansion of public welfare programs, and the development of tripartite corporatism.[17] We might say that labor abandoned its socialist ambitions to nationalize industry and to institutionalize democratic planning in return for redistributive welfare reforms and active government efforts to promote full employment. In a second phase, tripartite corporatism developed in response to the inflationary pressures of full employment. Committed to the maintenance of full employment, government officials had to rely on the cooperation of unions to keep inflation under control. To achieve this cooperation, they granted union leaders regularized representation in policy making, including representation on the boards of various state agencies. Over time, the logic of political exchange thus became institutionalized and increasingly implicit.

The inflationary consequences of full employment pose a threat to international competitiveness. It follows that different economies are more or less vulnerable to the problem of inflation, depending on the relative importance of international trade. This analysis seems to explain why tripartite corporatism developed earlier and more fully in smaller European countries such as Sweden and Belgium.[18] It might

17. For a comprehensive overview along these lines, see Stephen Bornstein, "States and Unions: From Postwar Settlement to Contemporary Stalemate," in *The State in Capitalist Europe,* ed. Stephen Bornstein, David Held, and Joel Krieger (London: Allen & Unwin, 1984), pp. 54–82.

18. See, for example, Katzenstein, *Small States.* Other important contributions to the analysis of national variations in the extent and character of corporatist arrangements can be found in Berger, ed., *Organizing Interests;* Goldthorpe, ed., *Order and Conflict;* Philippe Schmitter and Gerhard Lehmbruch, eds., *Trends toward Corporatist Intermediation* (Beverly Hills, Calif.: Sage, 1979); and Gerhard Lehmbruch and Philippe Schmitter, eds., *Patterns of Corporatist Policy-Making* (Beverly Hills, Calif.: Sage, 1982).

also be invoked to explain the accentuation of the corporatist trends in the large countries during the 1960s, for this decade witnessed a far-reaching liberalization of trade, brought on by the Kennedy round of GATT negotiations as well as the formation of the European Community. In a sense, the large countries became smaller in the 1960s. It should also be noted that this accentuation of corporatist trends coincided with the political ascendancy of labor-affiliated parties in Britain and West Germany. To the extent that wage restraint requires that unions sacrifice short-term gains to achieve long-term objectives, it presupposes an element of trust. In other words, union leaders—and, ultimately, union members as well—must be convinced that the government will fulfill its end of the bargain. For obvious reasons, unions are more likely to trust labor governments.

The literature on the development of Keynesian economic policy, the welfare state, and tripartite corporatism tends, however, to overlook a crucial dimension of the politics of class compromise in the postwar era, namely, the spread of Fordist mass production. This term refers to the system of production pioneered by Henry Ford at his famous Model T assembly plant in Dearborn, Michigan, which started production in 1913. For our purposes, Fordist mass production can be defined in terms of three features. First, it rests on the principle that management should minimize the opportunities for workers to exercise discretion in the production process by defining in advance, and as precisely as possible, their job assignment, including the sequence in which tasks should be performed and the time allowed to perform them. Second, Fordist mass production involves the pursuit of productivity gains through the division of labor—in other words, by minimizing the number of tasks assigned to each worker. Third, it involves the mechanization of production. Going beyond the management principles of Fredrick Taylor and Adam Smith's insights about the division of labor as a source of productivity gains, Ford organized his plant around a mechanized conveyor belt, setting the pace of assembly workers, and pursued further productivity gains by introducing special-purpose machinery at various stages in the production process.

Ford's system of production made possible rapid productivity growth and was quickly adopted by other U.S. car manufacturers. In the 1940s and 1950s, Fordism spread to other sectors and other countries. As Michael Piore and Charles Sabel emphasize, the success of Fordist mass production depended on stable demand for standardized products.[19] The essential logic of Fordism is to lower production costs per unit by producing large quantities of the same product. If consumers want customized products, Fordist producers lose their distinctive advantage over producers that rely on a more skilled and flexible labor force. Also, Fordist producers incur high fixed costs by investing in machinery dedicated to the production of a specific product. If demand for this product drops, their losses are greater than those of more labor-intensive producers, who can cut their costs by laying off workers.

It is not accidental, then, that the rise of Fordist mass production coincides with the emergence of active government efforts to counteract fluctuations in demand (Keynesian macroeconomic demand management) and, in some countries, active government efforts to promote the purchasing power of the working class (the Keynesian welfare state). Piore and Sabel downplay the significance of active government intervention in stabilizing the postwar U.S. economy, however, emphasizing instead the stabilizing effects of the system of wage determination that emerged after the war. Linking wage bargaining to productivity improvements and providing for automatic annual wage increases indexed to economy-wide changes in consumer prices, the historic agreement signed by General Motors and the UAW in 1948 formed the keystone of this system. The GM-UAW agreement in effect ensured that the purchasing power of GM workers would grow at the same rate as the productive capacity of the economy as a whole. The diffusion of this effect occurred through pattern bargaining within the unionized sector and nonunionized employers keeping up with union wages to avoid unionization. At the same time, a nationally legislated minimum wage checked the tendency for competition from unorganized, unskilled workers to drive wages down.

The GM-UAW agreement marked the end of the era of militant workplace struggles in the U.S. auto industry. In return for institutionalized collective bargaining, including seniority rules and grievance procedures, and a wage-setting formula that effectively guaranteed real wage growth, the UAW accepted short job cycles, machine pacing, and management's right to manage. This kind of Fordist

19. Michael Piore and Charles Sabel, *The Second Industrial Divide* (New York: Basic Books, 1984). Other works that emphasize the Fordist foundations of postwar growth include Michel Aglietta, *A Theory of Capitalist Regulation* (London: New Left Books, 1979); and David Harvey, *The Condition of Postmodernity* (Oxford: Basil Blackwell, 1989).

bargain can be said to have accompanied the spread of mass production in other countries as well.[20]

The state came to play a more important role in regulating the business cycle and compensating workers for their acceptance of Fordist working conditions in Western Europe than in the United States. Beyond Keynesian macroeconomic management in the narrow sense of deficit spending and interest rate manipulations, the postwar expansion of the welfare state served to stimulate and stabilize demand, especially for consumer goods. Redistributive policies increase aggregate demand to the extent that lower-income strata consume a larger share of their income. More important, perhaps, redistributive policies increase demand for mass-consumption goods. Also, welfare programs tend to have more or less automatic, countercyclical effects: as the economy begins to sag, welfare spending increases because more people become eligible for benefits.

At the same time as the expansion of the welfare state promoted mass consumption and hence mass production, the productivity growth realized by the introduction and diffusion of Fordist production methods facilitated the expansion of the welfare state (if employment and productivity grow, government revenues increase at a given rate of taxation). In this sense, Fordism and the Keynesian welfare state can be seen as reinforcing each other. Both had important implications for organized labor.

Workers and unions benefited from the postwar expansion of the welfare state in several ways. To begin with, workers benefited insofar as the welfare state redistributes income from salaried wage earners to workers. The welfare state may also be said to have brought about a partial "decommodification" of labor power in the sense that it attenuated the compulsion to work by providing workers with the option to stay home if they did not feel well or to quit their job in order to look for another.[21] Related to this, welfare reforms attenuated competition among workers and thereby reinforced the positive effects of

20. See, for example, Robert Boyer, "Wage Labor, Capital Accumulation, and the Crisis," in *The French Workers Movement,* ed. Mark Kesselman (London: Allen & Unwin, 1984), pp. 17–38. The term "Fordist bargain" is taken from Samuel Bowles and Herbert Gintis, "The Crisis of Liberal-Democratic Capitalism," *Politics and Society* 11 (1982): 9–45. On Fordist mass production and industrial relations, see also Steven Tolliday and Jonathan Zeitlin, eds., *The Automobile Industry and Its Workers* (Cambridge: Polity Press, 1986).

21. See Gösta Esping-Andersen, *The Three Worlds of Welfare Capitalism* (Princeton: Princeton University Press, 1990).

full employment for labor's bargaining leverage in the postwar era. We could also cite instances in which welfare reforms directly strengthened union organization. Most notably, the public unemployment insurance system introduced by the Swedish Social Democrats in 1934 subsidized union-administered unemployment funds and thereby provided a direct incentive for wage earners to join unions.[22]

The implications of Fordist mass production for organized labor are perhaps even more important than the implications of welfare state expansion, for the spread of Fordism provides an explanation for the prominence of national union organizations in the postwar era. The industrial working class of the late nineteenth century was characterized by a sharp split between craft workers and unskilled workers. The new mass-production industries of the twentieth century generated a large intermediary group of semiskilled workers, which came to constitute the core constituency of organized labor in most countries. At the same time as the spread of Fordism served to homogenize the working class in an objective sense, the new industrial relations that accompanied it facilitated the aggregation of working-class interests by restricting collective bargaining almost entirely to quantifiable issues—wages, benefits, and working hours.

The 1970s: From Militancy to Crisis

In some countries, the postwar settlement was accompanied by a marked decline of strikes and other forms of industrial conflict. In others, strikes remained a regular part of the process of collective bargaining, and the level of strike activity fluctuated without any secular trend in the 1950s and 1960s. Irrespective of preceding conditions, a significant increase in strike activity occurred throughout the advanced capitalist countries in the late 1960s. The scope and duration of this strike wave varied by country, but most countries recorded unusually high levels at least until the economic downturn of 1973–74.[23]

Especially in its early stages, the strike wave of 1967–73 was distinguished by two features. First, many of the strikes were wildcat strikes or, in British terminology, unofficial strikes: they occurred during a contract or were initiated by rank-and-file activists rather than

22. See Bo Rothstein, "Marxism, Institutional Analysis and Working Class Strength: The Swedish Case," *Politics and Society* 19, no. 3 (1990): 317–45.
23. Korpi and Shalev, "Strikes, Power, and Politics."

union officials. In some instances, union officials actually opposed the strikes and brought sanctions against their instigators. Over time, however, union officials either became more militant or were replaced by militants, and unions began to assume leadership in the strike wave. The second distinctive feature was that many of the early strikes involved qualitative as well as quantitative demands: the strikers not only demanded higher wages and more benefits but also protested against bad working conditions and the arbitrariness of managerial authority, demanding a say in management decisions if not the introduction of some form of "workers' control."[24]

Why did industrial workers become more militant in the late 1960s? And why did this militancy assume broadly similar forms and goals across Western Europe and North America, despite national variations in industrial relations institutions? An adequate answer to these questions lies beyond the scope of the present discussion, but I can suggest three relevant considerations. From a historical perspective, the militancy of the late 1960s can be seen as a manifestation of worker resistance to the stress and boredom of assembly line work. Arguably, full employment and welfare reformism had gradually undermined the cultural or societal conditions for the Fordist model of development. Simply put, workers were no longer willing to put up with working conditions they had previously considered acceptable. But why did militancy erupt so uniformly at this particular time? As Golden, too, notes, in her concluding essay, two other considerations must be invoked at this point. First, employers responded to the intensification of international competition in the 1960s, and to the recession of 1966–67 in particular, by seeking to further rationalize production and to speed up work. In this sense, the strike wave was not simply a manifestation of the gradual exhaustion of the Fordist model but also a response to renewed employer efforts to perfect that model. At the same time, the inflationary pressures of this period brought about various incomes policy experiments in Western Europe. Rank-and-file militancy resulted from employers seeking to increase the rate of exploitation at the shop floor at the same time that government and national union leaders sought to restrain wage demands.[25]

24. On these and other aspects of the 1967–73 strike wave and the experiences of particular countries, see Crouch and Pizzorno, eds., *The Resurgence of Class Conflict*.

25. See David Soskie, "Strike Waves and Wage Explosions, 1968–70," in ibid., vol. 2, pp. 221–46.

In most countries, union leaders responded to the strike wave of 1967–73 not only by adopting a more militant stance in wage negotiations but also by advancing more radical political demands. Most notably, organized labor now began to demand legislation that would introduce or extend industrial democracy by strengthening the rights of workers and unions at the workplace and providing them with direct influence over corporate decision making. Going beyond codetermination, unions began to push for more extensive and detailed government intervention in industrial restructuring in the 1970s. Their advocacy of an active industrial policy (Sweden) or an alternative economic strategy (Britain) included calls for the nationalization of banks and industry. In Sweden, the LO congress of 1976 endorsed a proposal for collective profit sharing, which, had it been implemented, would have lead to a gradual yet inexorable transfer of ownership from private individuals and institutions to so-called wage earner funds. Similar schemes were discussed by unions elsewhere in Western Europe in the 1970s.

By challenging managerial authority at the workplace and the power of private capital in society at large, these various reform initiatives represented a break with the terms of the postwar settlement. Since the mid-1970s, conservative political forces have gained electoral support in many countries, and the political agenda has, in any case, shifted toward more market-oriented policies. In the end, very little came of labor's radical reform initiatives in the 1970s.[26]

The protracted economic slump of 1974–83 provides the most obvious explanation for the erosion of labor's bargaining power and its loss of political initiative, but, again, it is only from a retrospective point of view that the political impact of the crisis becomes apparent. In the short run, the economic downturn of the mid-1970s enhanced the political influence union leaders had acquired in the preceding period. As international demand contracted, the containment of labor costs emerged as a critical component of government efforts to promote economic recovery; yet moderate and conservative as well as labor-affiliated governments were initially unwilling to allow unemployment to rise beyond a certain point. Hence all were more or less forced to enter into some form of social contract with organized labor.

26. On the Swedish experience, see Jonas Pontusson, *The Limits of Social Democracy: Investment Politics in Sweden* (Ithaca: Cornell University Press, 1992).

In other words, domestic political actors responded to the international recession of the mid-1970s within the framework of tripartite corporatist arrangements institutionalized in the postwar era.[27]

In the context of slack labor markets, government-initiated incomes policies served to recentralize wage bargaining processes. At this point, it seems useful to distinguish between, on the one hand, cyclical or conjunctural changes in the locus of collective bargaining and, on the other, structural or institutional changes of a long-term nature. As suggested above, tight labor markets make the exercise of wage restraint imperative and thus enhance the political influence of union officials. At the same time, however, tight labor markets make it difficult for national union officials to discipline local union actors. During economic upswings, the significance of wage drift at the local level tends to increase relative to wage settlements at the national, sectoral, or regional level. From this perspective, the decentralization of collective bargaining in the 1980s might be viewed as yet another phase in a cyclical pattern (centralization in the 1950s and the first half of the 1960s, decentralization 1967–73, centralization 1973–80, and decentralization since 1980). Alternatively, one might argue that the decentralization of collective bargaining in the 1980s has occurred within a fundamentally new context and has been accompanied by institutional changes of an enduring character, changing the parameters of cyclical variations in the locus of collective bargaining. Let me try to develop, however briefly, the case for this alternative interpretation.

The New Political-Economic Environment of the 1980s

Since 1983, most of the advanced capitalist countries have experienced fairly high rates of economic growth. But the pattern of growth in the 1980s appears to be different from that of the postwar boom. To begin with, it is less conducive to full employment. Despite a rapid expansion of output in recent years, unemployment remains high in most countries. In those countries where growth has been accompanied by a significant expansion of employment, notably the United States and Britain, most of the newly created jobs have been relatively low paying, typically in the service sector, and frequently of

27. See Lange, Ross, and Vanicelli, *Unions, Change and Crisis;* and Gourevitch et al., *Unions and Economic Crisis.*

a temporary nature or involving irregular working hours (part-time, for example).[28] The growing number of such jobs may come to represent a new historic opportunity for organized labor, but there are obvious, immediate obstacles to the unionization of this new labor force, and unions may have to change their internal organization as well as their conception of workers and their interests in order to overcome these obstacles. In any case, it seems clear that changes in the structure of employment, along with persistent mass unemployment, have thus far weakened labor's leverage vis-à-vis governments as well as employers.

As Golden emphasizes in her conclusions, the accelerated internationalization of capital in the period since the mid-1970s has also tipped the scale to the advantage of capital. The rise of multinational corporations is hardly something new, even in the European context, but the motives and mechanisms of multinationalization have changed. Following the American pattern, large European firms became multinational in the postwar era by establishing marketing organizations and production facilities abroad. Corporate headquarters and research-and-development facilities remained firmly embedded in the home country. To the extent that multinationalization took the form of mergers, smaller competitors were absorbed as part of the effort to penetrate particular national markets. In the 1980s, by contrast, we have seen a spate of mergers among multinational corporations, and multinationalization has been driven largely by financial considerations. The upshot has been the formation of giant and truly global holding companies without national bases in the traditional sense.

The increasing interdependence of the world economy, and the internationalization of capital markets in particular, imposes constraints on deficit spending and more generally restricts the capacity of national governments to regulate or direct economic activity. The erosion of labor's economic and political power in the 1980s is closely related to this development. Whether or not they purported to transform society, the traditional reformist projects of Western European labor movements hinged on expanding the scope of government involvement in the domestic economy and presupposed that national economies could be effectively regulated as separate and sovereign entities.

The political climate became overtly hostile to organized labor in Britain and the United States in the 1980s, but the rise of the new

28. See Bennet Harrison and Barry Bluestone, *The Great U-Turn* (New York: Basic Books, 1986).

right in these countries is only the most obvious manifestation of a more widespread rightward policy drift in the advanced capitalist countries. To some degree, neoliberalism corresponds to the imperatives of the new world economy since, in the absence of an internationally coordinated effort at reflation, each national government must pursue policies of fiscal retrenchment, deregulation, and high corporate profits in order to keep or attract internationally mobile capital.

The experience of the French Socialists in the early 1980s brought home the new limits on "Keynesianism in one country." When the Socialists came to power in 1981 (forming the first leftist government in France since 1948), they were committed to combating unemployment by stimulating domestic demand. They soon discovered that increased domestic demand meant increased German and Japanese imports, and hence balance-of-payments difficulties. Unwilling to allow the franc to continue to fall, they were forced to abandon their reflationary strategy.

When the Swedish Social Democrats returned to power in 1982, they adopted a more market-oriented approach to economic policy. While keeping the lid on unemployment, they allowed corporate profits to rise to unprecedented levels and thereby undermined the ability of the unions to pursue a coordinated wage policy based on the solidaristic principles. Even in the stronghold of social democracy, then, organized labor found its existing repertoire of policy and strategy overtaken by events in the 1980s.

From the point of view of organized labor, the strengthening of the institutions of the European Community in the 1990s upholds the promise of resurrecting the Keynesian welfare state at a Europe-wide level. But the obstacles to such a project are formidable indeed. The social charter drafted by the European Commission in the fall of 1989 is a much watered-down version of the charter originally proposed by the European Trade Union Confederation, and most of its provisions are, in any case, unlikely to become legally binding directives.[29]

As the experience of the social charter suggests, it is unreasonable to suppose that organized labor could wield more political influence at the level of the European Community than it can at the level of national governments. Indeed, there are at least two strong reasons to suppose that organized labor is particularly disadvantaged at the

29. See Stephen Silvia, "The Prospect of a Unified European Union Movement as a Result of 1992" (Unpublished paper, 1990). My discussion here also draws on Wolfgang Streeck, "The Social Dimension of the European Firm" (Unpublished paper, 1989).

European level. First, the concrete interests of national labor movements diverge with respect to many of the issues involved in Europe-wide social regulation. Although all unions agree that the Community should establish minimum social security standards, for instance, they are likely to disagree on the level at which such standards are set. Second, the emerging Community polity differs from national polities in that the "government," that is, the European Commission, is not elected. This removes what is arguably the unions' principal asset in corporatist bargaining at the national level, namely, their capacity to mobilize voters.

Turning now to collective-bargaining developments, we can note that employers in most of the advanced capitalist countries have pushed for decentralization as a means to promote the productivity and flexibility of their labor force since the late 1970s or early 1980s. For instance, many employers have sought to substitute plant-level profit-sharing schemes for traditional cost-of-living adjustments, tying wage increases more closely to plant performance and often creating a situation in which plants compete with each other for a finite amount of bonus payments.

Documented by most of our contributors, this employer offensive is partly explained by a shift in the balance of power in the labor market to the advantage of employers. In the tight labor markets of the postwar era, employers competed with each other for labor and looked to unions to secure the aggregate wage restraint necessary to maintain international competitiveness. The rigidities of centralized wage bargaining were the price they had to pay for successful and enduring wage restraint. In the new conditions of the 1980s, employers can rely instead on market forces to keep wage levels in check.

The new bargaining strategies of employers can also be seen as a response to changes in product markets.[30] The proposition that demand for mass-produced goods has been exhausted is surely an exaggeration, but it quite clear that demand for some products, such as automobiles, has become more differentiated, and that fluctuations in demand have become greater. As suggested above, the advantages of the Fordist model of mass production turn into liabilities under such circumstances. The uncertainties of the marketplace have forced Ford-

30. See Wolfgang Streeck, "The Uncertainties of Management in the Management of Uncertainty," *International Journal of Political Economy* 17 (1987): 57–87, as well as Piore and Sabel, *Second Industrial Divide*.

ist mass producers to pursue more flexible production and marketing strategies. At the same time, the microelectronics revolution has made flexible production commercially feasible by lowering the costs of programmable, multipurpose machinery. Frequently, new technologies require a more flexible deployment of labor as regards working hours as well as craft demarcations.

As Thelen argues in her contribution to this volume, many of the issues surrounding the introduction of new technology and working practices simply cannot be handled through centralized collective bargaining. Again, the centralization of collective bargaining in the postwar era rested on a Fordist bargain, which meant that wages and benefits constituted the central issue of contention between unions and employers. As employment and the organization of production itself have emerged as issues of contention, the locus of collective bargaining has inevitably shifted to a lower level.

The success of employers' new strategies appears to be closely related to the fragmentation of wage earner interests. While traditional conflicts of interest within the broad constituencies of national labor movements have become more intense, new conflicts of interest have emerged since the mid-1970s. At the same time, employers and, in some cases, governments as well have become more willing and more able to exploit these conflicts to their advantage. The essays in this volume provide a great deal of evidence for these propositions. Rather than summarizing the evidence, I propose a framework for understanding conflicts of interest among wage earners in which the stories told by our contributors might be situated.

Arguably, all conflicts of interest among wage earners revolve around three basic issues: (a) jobs and job security, (b) skills and occupational status, and (c) wages and other benefits. These issues are closely intertwined, for skilled workers typically enjoy better wages and greater job security than do unskilled workers, but they are distinguishable and their relative prominence varies. Leaving gender, race, and ethnicity aside, intraclass conflicts over jobs, skills, and wages have traditionally been fought along three lines of cleavage: white-collar versus blue-collar, skilled versus unskilled, and regional or sectoral cleavages.[31] As I indicated above, national union movements

31. We leave gender, race, and ethnicity aside for three reasons: (a) they overlap with the categories elaborated below, (b) they are sources of nonclass conflict in their own right, and (c) they hardly figure at all in the essays that follow.

have been organized on the basis of these cleavages. We can identify five other lines of cleavage that have emerged or become more prominent in the period since the mid-1970s.

First, employment versus unemployment has obviously become a sharper cleavage within the working class. Presented with a direct trade-off between higher wages and new employment, employed workers are likely to opt for the former. Second, the distinction between primary and secondary employment conditions has become both sharper and more prominent. In an immediate sense, core workers benefit from labor-market dualism and are unlikely to engage in industrial action on behalf of less privileged workers. At the same time, workers in the secondary labor market have distinctly different interests and concerns from those in the primary labor market. For instance, they may well be more concerned with day-care facilities than with promotional prospects within the firm.

Third, the parameters of the plant or firm appear to have become increasingly important lines of demarcation dividing core workers. As Jeanette Money demonstrates in her essay, interfirm labor mobility declined markedly in the 1970s, and has subsequently remained much lower than it was in the postwar era. In part, this is a consequence of unemployment and limited job opportunities, but it is also due to deliberate employer efforts to develop internal labor markets, that is, to promote from within and to use internal promotion to encourage hard work and initiative among employees. As I noted above, many employers have also sought to tie wage increases more directly to plant performance and to involve local union representatives in plant-level consultation schemes. At least in some cases, plant- or firm-level corporatism of this sort has undermined tripartite corporatist arrangements at the national level.[32] Fourth, the introduction of new technologies has generated new conflicts over the allocation of skills among craft workers as well as between craft workers and production workers. And, fifth, the postwar expansion of the public sector and the fiscal constraints precipitated by the economic crisis have brought conflicts of interest between private- and public-sector employees to the fore of union politics.

These conflicts of interest impinge on all the labor movements considered in this volume, but the salience of particular conflicts varies

32. See Wolfgang Streeck, "Neo-Corporatist Industrial Relations and the Economic Crisis in West Germany," in *Order and Conflict*, ed. Goldthorpe, pp. 291–314.

from one country to another. To repeat, our case studies suggest, and Golden argues at length, that different labor movements are more or less vulnerable to different types of intraclass conflict or, more specifically, that intraclass conflicts tend to become a source of politicization and organizational fragmentation to the extent that they coincide with preexisting organizational boundaries. But we do not wish to imply organizational variables provide a sufficient explanation of variation in the salience of different intraclass cleavages. The particular configuration of national political economies must also be taken into account. For instance, job security legislation and welfare programs have effectively curtailed the development of labor market dualism, and active labor market policy has arguably reduced the salience of regional and sectoral cleavages in Sweden. By the same token, however, the size of the public sector in Sweden has, as Swenson's essay demonstrates, rendered the conflict between private- and public-sector unions particularly acute in the Swedish case.

To summarize, I have argued here that the prominence national union organizations came to assume during the postwar boom depended not only on full employment but also on a particular pattern of capitalist development, one characterized by the spread of Fordist mass production and welfare state expansion. The spread of Fordist mass production facilitated the expansion of welfare programs that strengthened labor solidarity and power and also had homogenizing effects on the industrial working class. Since the mid-1970s, the political-economic environment of organized labor has undergone far-reaching changes. On the one hand, the internationalization of capital and the growing interdependence of the advanced capitalist countries have undermined the regulatory capacities of national governments. On the other hand, mass unemployment and new corporate strategies emphasizing flexibility have led to a fragmentation of wage earner interests. Both developments have contributed to the decentralization of collective bargaining and the declining significance of tripartite corporatism.

THE CASE STUDIES

All the essays in this volume are case studies, most of them comparative, but they address different issues. In Chapter 1, Peter Swenson compares the politics surrounding the distribution of wage increases between the private- and public-sector employees in Sweden and West Germany. In the Swedish case, the powerful metalworkers' union joined forces with private employers and the government in seeking to prevent public-sector employees from keeping up with private-sector wage increases in the 1980s. In the German case, by contrast, the metalworkers' union allied itself with public-sector unions in defense of wage militancy. Swenson's explanation of this divergence in the metalworkers' attitude toward public-sector wages takes into account the fact that the public sector is larger and taxes higher in Sweden than in West Germany. But Swenson argues further that the politics of private-public conflict in the 1980s must be situated in the context of prior pay-distributional alignments within the two labor movements.

In the Swedish case, the low-wage unions within LO prevailed over the metalworkers in the postwar era, insisting that centralized wage bargaining be linked to a compression of intersectoral wage differentiations. For the Swedish metalworkers, support for decoupling private- and public-sector wage bargaining became necessary in order to claim a share of the huge profits enjoyed by export-oriented manufacturing firms in the 1980s. In the West German case, by contrast, the metalworkers successfully resisted efforts by other unions to pursue coordinated wage bargaining on a solidaristic basis in the 1960s and 1970s and enjoyed relatively higher wages. As the issue of public-sector wage restraint came to be couched explicitly in terms of wage restraint by (or for) well-paid government employees, the metalworkers naturally feared that such a policy would ultimately be turned against them.

Chapter 2, by Jeannette Money, also deals with country cases: France, Belgium, and the United States. Money demonstrates that national wage bargaining has increasingly been displaced by firm-level bargaining in all three countries, despite very different industrial relations systems. She argues that this shift in the locus of wage bargaining can be traced back to the 1960s and linked to the decline of labor mobility. The militancy of the late 1960s was a result of rank-and-file dissatisfaction with bargains negotiated at the national level and resulted in increased shop-floor control of the bargaining process. Money argues further that the decentralization of wage bargaining accounts for the increasing salience of sectoral, regional, and firm-based cleavages within national labor movements.

The three essays that follow Money's take industrial sectors as their unit of analysis. In each case, the analysis focuses on the response of industrial unions to sectoral decline or restructuring. In Chapter 3, Charlotte Yates compares the responses of the Canadian and U.S. sections of the UAW to employer demands for concessions. Yates argues that the leadership of the Canadian section adopted a more militant strategy than did its American counterpart, and that the Canadians successfully resisted concessions the Americans accepted. She attributes this strategic divergence to the democratic structure of the Canadian section, which broke off to establish itself as a separate union in 1984.

Anthony Daley's analysis of French and United States union responses to the crisis of the steel industry in Chapter 4 is similar to Yates's analysis. Like Yates, Daley focuses on divergent union responses to similar market pressures and seeks to evaluate different union strategies in terms of the material interests of union members and the unions' mobilizational capacity. Contrary to the conventional view of France as the archtypical case of an organizationally weak and politically excluded labor movement, Daley argues that the beleaguered French steel unions achieved better compensation for workforce reductions than did their American counterpart, the United Steel Workers. He links their relative success to government intervention in restructuring. The French steel unions struck a better deal because they relied on community mobilization to put pressure on the government, whereas the United Steel Workers relied on the exercise of (rapidly waning) marketplace power through collective bargaining.

In Chapter 5, Peggy Kahn analyzes the politics of the restructuring of the British coal industry since the 1960s. Kahn shows how the regional differences within the National Union of Mineworkers, along with the government's hard-nosed tactics, contributed to the defeat of the union's strategy of militant resistance to pit closures. Kahn also compares the strategies pursued by the National Union and the breakaway Union of Democratic Mineworkers in the aftermath of the dramatic and disastrous national strike of 1984–85. She shows how the uneven impact of the restructuring of the industry has favored the latter, thereby institutionalizing rival unionism.

The final three case studies address the relation between national unions and local union organizations at the level of the firm or plant.

In part because they introduce firm- or plant-level analysis, these essays are focused on different substantive issues. Whereas the first five chapters are primarily concerned with wages and employment, these last three are mainly focused on new technologies and new working practices. Kathleen Thelen traces the response of the German metalworkers' union to the changes and challenges of the 1980s (Chapter 6). Her analysis addresses the union's efforts to combat unemployment through working-time reduction as well as its efforts to shape the deployment of new technologies and other aspects of the ongoing reorganization of work, but her treatment of both issues revolves around the tension between national and local concerns within the union. To be successful in the new era, Thelen argues, unions need to develop new strategies that combine central coordination with decentralized, plant-level mobilization. At least in part, she suggests, the German metalworkers' union has remained powerful because it has recognized this imperative and begun to reorient its organization accordingly.

Richard Locke compares the politics of the reorganization of production at Fiat and Alfa Romeo in Italy in Chapter 7. At Fiat, relations between management and unions had always been conflictual, and the unions resisted management's proposals for workforce reductions and reorganization in 1980. Their strike ended in failure, and the company subsequently imposed its own vision of flexible work practices, tightly controlled by management. At Alfa Romeo, by contrast, management and unions cooperated in the introduction of shop-floor changes. Seeking to explain different management as well as union strategies, Locke emphasizes the different social structures and political traditions in Turin, Fiat's main location, and Milan, Alfa's main location.

Much like Locke's essay, my own contribution (Chapter 8) focuses on new technology and work reorganization and takes the form of a comparison of two auto firms; but in this case the comparison is cross-national. My two firms are Volvo and British Leyland. Whereas British Leyland provides an example of confrontation between unions and management and imposition of change by management, Volvo illustrates extensive union involvement in the process of reorganizing production. I argue, however, that the role of labor does not provide an adequate explanation of these changes in workplace organization. To understand the politics of new technology and working practices, we must consider corporate strategies as a variable that is not simply derivative of union influences. Specifically, I argue that Volvo's emphasis on upgrading assembly can be seen as a response to Swedish labor market conditions—most notably, high rates on labor turnover due to full employment and solidaristic wage policy. Operating under very different conditions, British Leyland has been under much less external pressure to break with traditional assembly line principles.

It should be clear from this presentation that our volume does not purport to offer anything like a comprehensive overview of the current situation of organized labor in the advanced capitalist countries. Most of the essays are organized around sectors, unions, or firms rather than around countries, and they are focused on quite specific issues. Also, the selection of cases is clearly biased toward the manufacturing industries, especially autos. Except for Swenson's discussion of relations between private- and public-sectors unions, we barely touch on the problems and strategies of unions in the service sector.

Most of the contributors rely on a method of comparative case studies to establish causal claims. Most engage in paired, cross-national comparisons; Kahn instead compares regions within the British coal industry, and Locke compares firms within the Italian auto industry. The methodological problems with comparative case studies are well known. Apart from the question of how representative the cases are, paired comparisons are particularly prone to the problem of overdetermination. If two cases vary on several counts, how do we know which variable accounts for the divergence of outcomes? We can hardly expect generalizations based on the experiences of declining industries, such as steel and coal, to be applicable to a mature but reasonably stable industry, such as autos.

Nonetheless, the essays do seem to converge on the importance of organizational variables in union politics and suggest certain tentative generalizations in this regard. Above all, perhaps, they illustrate an approach to union politics that combines concerns with organizational and political-economic variables. In her concluding essay, Miriam Golden situates this approach in relation to the existing literature on union politics and summarizes the substantive findings of the essays in a way that enables her to generate broad hypotheses.

Part 1

NATIONAL CONFEDERATIONS AND WAGE COORDINATION

1 Union Politics, the Welfare State, and Intraclass Conflict in Sweden and Germany

Peter Swenson

Does control of state power by the left always help it strengthen working-class organization? Does social democracy's progress, measured by welfare state development, necessarily help reinforce the unity of its organized constituency?[1] If not, and if in fact the economics and politics of the growing welfare state were to divide the working class, would the resulting disunity and decentralization of labor organizations always impair allied left-wing political parties?[2] Conflicts within Swedish and West German labor about the costs of the welfare state in the 1980s, analyzed here in historical perspective, suggest some answers.

Recent Swedish and German politics show that the large and growing welfare state tends to divide organized labor, its core organizational constituency. But events also show that this very division can provide the opportunity for a realignment of political forces enabling

I wish to thank Fred Block, Miriam Golden, Peter Lange, Andrei Markovits, Andrew Martin, Jonas Pontusson, Werner von der Ohe, Michaela Wenninger-Richter, and anonymous reviewers for their generous criticism and encouragement.

1. Gøsta Esping-Andersen, in *Politics against Markets: The Social Democratic Road to Power* (Princeton: Princeton University Press, 1985), argues a strong connection between the universalistic welfare state and the reproduction over time of social democracy's broad electoral base in a changing society.

2. Many writers on social democracy and corporatism make an empirical case that labor's organizational unity strengthens leftist parties; see especially David Cameron, "Social Democracy, Corporatism, Labour Quiescence, and the Representation of Economic Interest in Advanced Capitalist Society," in *Order and Conflict in Contemporary Capitalism*, ed. John H. Goldthorpe (Oxford: Clarendon Press, 1984), pp. 143–78.

the left to regain or maintain political power though it loses forward momentum as a transformative force. The evidence and argument presented here about those events suggest that the organizational pillars of the welfare state, social democratic labor unions and parties, are likely to impose limits on the welfare state. They are likely to do so in conflict with themselves, and in alliance with outside interests.

In the tradition of Max Weber, capitalism's anxious intellectuals such as Joseph Schumpeter repeatedly ask whether in the long run capitalism can maintain its political, institutional, and ideological defenses in the era of the democratic welfare state.[3] Even before coming to fruition, reform movements in the Soviet bloc have stirred worries among conservatives that dissipating fear of communism will weaken right-wing solidarity against state encroachments. But contrasting analyses, like the following, of the contradictions of the welfare state show capitalism to be more robust and likely to outlive those who see only progressive cultural and political delay.[4]

Labor's intraclass conflict, a source of capitalism's political vitality (and one of the mechanisms confining the welfare state), is curiously neglected in comparative studies of the capitalist political economy. This observation holds especially for the study of "class compromises" between the left and capitalist accommodationists that bring labor into government and policy making. One school sympathetic to social democracy tends to depict labor, when it is successful, as an undifferentiated and unified bloc. Incentives for compromise with capital are specified as collective or broadly beneficial payoffs (growth, low unemployment, social programs) for the generalized short-run sacrifices of wage restraint.[5] Capital, often depicted as comparatively divided

3. See Weber, *Gesammelte politische Schriften*, 2d ed. (Tübingen: J. C. B. Mohr, 1958); Schumpeter, *Capitalism, Socialism, and Democracy* (New York: Harper & Brothers, 1942). For a more recent statement, see Daniel Bell, *The Cultural Contradictions of Capitalism* (New York: Basic Books, 1976).

4. On the contradictions of the welfare state, see also John Logue, "The Welfare State: Victim of Its Success?" *Daedalus* 108, no. 4 (1979): 69–87, and "Will Success Spoil the Welfare State," *Dissent* (Winter 1985): 96–104; Rudolf Klein, "The Welfare State: A Self-Inflicted Crisis?" *Political Quarterly* 51 (1980): 24–34; Claus Offe, *Contradictions of the Welfare State* (Cambridge: MIT Press, 1984); and Massimo Paci, "Long Waves in the Development of Welfare Systems," in *Changing Boundaries of the Political: Essays on the Evolving Balance between the State and Society, Public and Private in Europe*, ed. Charles S. Maier (Cambridge: Cambridge University Press, 1987), pp. 179–99.

5. Peter Lange speculates on how to deal with the obvious rational-choice objections to this kind of model in "Unions, Workers, and Wage Regulation: The Rational Bases of Consent," in *Order and Conflict*, ed. Goldthorpe, pp. 98–123.

and politically disadvantaged, is motivated to release political power in class compromises with labor for similarly undifferentiated and therefore vaguely specified payoffs. The model neglects to specify the distributional results of collaboration that pit union against union and make it look suspiciously like divide-and-rule by capitalists.[6]

Marxists, on the other hand, do not hesitate to focus on division. Their critiques of social democracy's use of state power to promote centralized capital-labor collaboration identify deep hierarchical conflicts of interest between leaders and the rank and file as a defining feature of social democratic corporatism—and a cause of its instability.[7] They overlook, however, intersectoral distributive conflict within the working class, which is conducted by leaders at odds with each other on behalf of distinct member groups. These material conflicts too can destabilize social democratic power and cross-class collaboration. But labor's intramural distributional conflicts can also activate the cross-class alliance making that *helps* social democracy. Intramural opponents to the alliances can be disarmed and material conflict neutralized by leaders wielding powerful ideological as well as coercive resources. The stability of Swedish social democracy from the 1930s onward is an important case in point.[8]

To argue here for including intraclass distributional conflict in the comparative study of social democracy, I first analyze the logic of cross-class realignments that labor's internal conflicts over the welfare state engender. Then in the case studies I analyze events in the 1970s

6. The following important works, among others on the foundations of social democracy, class alliances, and labor-inclusive corporatism, all neglect analysis of decisive labor divisions: Francis G. Castles, *The Social Democratic Image of Society* (London: Routledge & Kegan Paul, 1978); John Stephens, *The Transition from Capitalism to Socialism* (London: Macmillan, 1979); Peter Katzenstein, *Small States in World Markets: Industrial Politics in Europe* (Ithaca: Cornell University Press, 1985); Gregory M. Luebbert, "Social Foundations of Political Order in Interwar Europe," *World Politics* 39 (July 1987): 449–78. See also Esping-Anderson, *Politics against Markets;* and Cameron "Social Democracy." By contrast, Peter Gourevitch sometimes includes intraclass divisions of a different sort than analyzed here, in his *Politics in Hard Times: Comparative Responses to International Economic Crises* (Ithaca: Cornell University Press, 1986).

7. See for example, Leo Panitch, "The Development of Corporatism in Liberal Democracies," *Comparative Political Studies* 10 (April 1977): 61–91, and "Trade Unions and the Capitalist State," *New Left Review* 125 (January-February 1981): 21–43. The argument need not be explicitly Marxist, of course. See Charles Sabel's excellent treatment of the issues in "The Internal Politics of Trade Unions," in *Organizing Interests in Western Europe: Pluralism, Corporatism, and the Transformation of Politics*, ed. Suzanne Berger (Cambridge: Cambridge University Press, 1981), pp. 209–44.

8. For greater detail, see Peter Swenson, *Fair Shares: Unions, Pay, and Politics in Sweden and West Germany* (Ithaca: Cornell University Press, 1989), pp. 31–70.

and 1980s in light of past alliances that helped secure social democratic parliamentary power in Sweden since the 1930s and in West Germany in the 1960s and 1970s. The case studies show that the big welfare state in these two countries sowed the seeds of division in its most important constituency, the leadership of social democratic unions. In the 1980s, recent (Sweden) or incipient (West Germany) cross-class alliances against government employees' pay, security, and protection from market forces were accompanied by bitter conflict within labor movements' leadership corps. Normally reticent about internal squabbles, union leaders accused each other and social democratic leaders of nothing less than parasitism and treachery. Old labor movement taboos against airing disagreements on collective bargaining issues in public debate were defiantly violated. Opening divisions signaled opportunities for social democratic leaders to try refashioning tacit alliances with powerful employer interests that would help them consolidate or recapture parliamentary control. The terms of these cross-class settlements were clear: a halt to the growth of the welfare state, especially of government pay and employment, and even revamping of public-sector employees' privileged immunity from disciplinary market forces.

My analyses of events in Sweden and West Germany show broad similarities in the politics of cross-class alliances, but also intriguing differences. In Sweden, for example, the metalworkers' union played a leading role in a successful alliance against the public-sector unions, while in West Germany the leadership of the metalworkers rallied aggressively behind the public sector against the threat of a cross-class alliance of business, party, and union forces. The threat was implied in the strategies and ambitions of a rising contender for leadership of the Social Democratic party, Oskar Lafontaine. In a separate section, I analyze how the two metalworkers' unions differ because of widely divergent historical experiences with cross-class alliances and the varying size and relative advantages of the public-sector workforce in the two countries. These differences are probably key to understanding the future possibilities of their respective Social Democratic parties.

I conclude with a discussion of the implications of labor's intraclass conflict both for capitalism and for social democracy. In response to doubts about the sufficiency of capitalism's political resources in the era of the welfare state, I argue that social democracy's successes in transforming capitalism are self-limiting. Like the peasants' revolution in eighteenth-century France, whose very success "tended to undermine the . . . solidarity that had made the revolution possible in the first place," the advanced welfare state can brake organized labor's forward momentum as a unified force behind government growth and antimarket principles of welfare state administration.[9] Division fostered by welfare state growth, I argue, prepares the way for a powerful countervailing politics of capitalist defense.

Finally, on the implications for social democracy: The conventional logic of unity as the basis of power would lead one to predict that division within labor over the welfare state will weaken it in future parliamentary politics. My analysis of intraclass conflict and cross-class alliances modifies both the conventional picture of labor's compromises with capital and any summary prediction that internal conflict—at least within politically unified labor movements like the Swedish and German—inevitably means political weakness.[10] If the contradictions of the welfare state undermine social democracy's transformative prospects, they do not necessarily limit its more immediate political ones.

LABOR'S CONFLICTS AND ALLIANCES IN THE WELFARE STATE

In much of the world, organized labor has contributed to the success of reformist left-wing parties; thus to the growth of nationalized social, educational, and health services; and so to the employment of millions in the public sector. Private-sector unions have also asserted public employees' associational rights and their claim to good pay and working standards. Government employment can tighten labor markets and improve private-sector unions' bargaining power. Welfare's "safety nets" can save unions as well as workers from the injuries of unemployment. Only weakly constrained by market forces, the practices of a large public sector regarding pay, benefits, promotion, and job protection can be a strong normative and market force improving the conditions private employers must provide to attract and pacify labor.

9. Theda Skocpol, *States and Social Revolutions* (Cambridge: Cambridge University Press, 1979), p. 127.

10. On the special and deeper problems of ideologically divided labor movements, see Miriam Golden, "Interest Representation, Party Systems, and the State: Italy in Comparative Perspective," *Comparative Politics* 18 (April 1986): 279–301.

But latent conflicts grow with expansion of the welfare state, for private-sector unions have material cause to reduce the well-staffed, well-organized, and well-paid service state. Public financing is the private sector's loss. Highly progressive taxes can break the link between nominal and real disposable pay increases, since pay raises can also bring tax rate increases. Pay raises high enough to overcome the effects of "bracket creep" may bring so much inflation that real wages or employment suffer and may tend to push pay in the public sector up in step as well. Tax increases, inflation, or budget deficits follow, all potentially costly for workers in the private sector. High pay for comfortable jobs in the public sector may attract a skilled and productive workforce away from industry where it is needed for quality and price competitiveness and for the expansion of shares in world markets to maintain employment levels as productivity steadily rises.

Economic stagnation or a crisis of competitiveness on one side and government growth on the other can turn latent conflicts within labor into open rivalry, making private-sector unions available for external alliances. Zero-sum conflict among unions over shares of national income can disrupt previously stable relations within their confederations. Intramural unity and power balances, once stabilized by a static distribution of pay and benefits across unions, is disturbed in crises by tectonic shifts in supply and demand in domestic and international markets.[11] And so follows a reappraisal of existing political-economic alliances. In pursuit of their own political or economic gains, politicians and organized business groups can exploit the opening divisions.

These divisions concern structures of pay or other benefits and working conditions, and in particular their distribution across unions' jurisdictional boundaries. Distributional divisions are especially subject to political manipulation when different unions' bargaining power in their respective sectors rapidly diverges. Only under restrictive conditions (such as full employment and unsegmented labor markets) is one vanguard union's independent bargaining success in setting wages, benefits, or working hours likely to boost others automatically by activating market forces in the same direction. Normally, however, and especially during crisis, a union can isolate itself politically if its

11. This unity is cemented by consensual norms of distribution and collective bargaining arrangements that can enforce them against market disturbances; see Swenson, *Fair Shares*, pp. 11–30, 71–108. On wage norms, see Jon Elster, "Wage Bargaining and Social Norms," *Acta Sociologica* 32, no. 2 (1989): 113–36.

bargaining success is not readily matched by others. In so doing, it invites the formation of an antagonistic coalition of other unions with external interests.

The cross-class alliance of organizational and governmental interests against the vanguard union or unions may be informal, but none the less decisive, for labor parties, which practically never achieve electoral or even parliamentary majorities.[12] Employers in alliance may retreat from active political opposition and quietly accept (or even favor) governments dominated or monopolized by Social Democrats. They may be willing to trust Social Democrats because of their leverage over labor confederations dominated by union factions that in turn have leverage over the vanguard. The tacit alliances also help Social Democrats maintain open lines of communication with centrist partners in cabinet or ad hoc legislative coalitions.

Union leaders can be tempted to join these political-economic alliances to restrain the vanguard if the alternative of keeping up brings unemployment and sour relations with strong employers. The remaining alternative of falling behind means members and activists grow impatient with their leaders as they compare their contracts against those of unions luckily facing more forgiving markets and employers. For example, discontent with leadership may surface within restrained unions in internationally traded goods sectors by successful militancy in home or protected industries. Similarly caught between constrained employers and critical members, leaders of private-sector unions may join alliances to hold back their public-sector counterparts who face a softer employer front due to government vulnerability to strikes and ability to tax and borrow to meet payrolls.

Also, the bargaining success of one sector of labor can directly undermine the success of others. Unions negotiating high wages in primary or intermediate goods industries might raise costs and reduce ability to pay in finished goods. Similarly, high pay increases negotiated for the public sector may come out of other workers' paychecks; if profits suffer instead, employers resist granting raises. Private-sector workers pay twice with absolute and relative earnings. Leaders of private-sector unions inhibited by exposure to intense international competition—where employers cannot turn pay into price increases—

12. See Adam Przeworski, "Social Democracy as a Historical Phenomenon," *New Left Review* 122 (July–August 1980): 27–58, and *Capitalism and Social Democracy* (Cambridge: Cambridge University Press, 1985).

are likely to sympathize with private employers and politicians challenging the power of public employees.

In Sweden, for these and other reasons, employers and Social Democratic politicians formed a cross-class alliance with large private-sector unions to reduce government deficits, relieve pressure for tax increases, and promote export competitiveness. The alliance against public-sector unions probably improved the Social Democrats' medium-term prospects of holding power, relying as they did on minority control in the Riksdag after returning to government in 1982. This is not to say that a backlash of strikes and strike threats of public-sector unions cannot weaken the party, as they did by bringing on the government crisis of February 1990 and the early resignation of the finance minister who helped engineer the alliance. At this time, it remains to be seen how successfully a militant backlash from within the public sector can injure the Social Democrats in the long term.

"PAY PARASITES" IN THE LABOR MOVEMENT: SWEDEN IN THE 1980s

Long-simmering conflict within Landsorganisationen (LO), the blue-collar Swedish trade union confederation, between its public- and private-sector wings first came to a boil in the heat of stalled public-sector pay negotiations. In September 1986, the leader of LO's metalworkers' union (Metallindustriarbetareförbundet, or Metall for short) attacked the confederation's two public-sector unions for their "irresponsible" wage demands. "We have a gang of cuckoo chicks in the nest. Now that we've fed them, they're eating up the mother too," chairman Leif Blomberg wrote in Metall's magazine, which circulated at the LO congress in session. LO's state employees' union (Statsanställdas Förbund), and its municipal workers' union (Svenska Kommunalarbetareförbundet) had recently rejected a mediated offer that Blomberg insisted was 3 percent too high compared to his own contracts. Leaders of the public-sector unions were naturally outraged at Metall and its most outspoken ally, the Swedish factory workers' union (Svenska Fabriksarbetareförbundet, or Fabriks). With members in chemicals, plastics, pharmaceuticals, and other export sectors, the leadership of Fabriks had declared in 1982 that it was time to "stop the pay parasites"—public-sector and white-collar workers who demanded contract clauses guaranteeing increases to match wage drift for blue-collar workers in the private sector.[13]

The private-sector unions' attack on public-sector pay enjoyed solid moral support from outside LO. Kjell Olof Feldt, the Social Democratic finance minister, reorganized Statens Avtalsverk, the agency responsible for negotiating central government pay, putting it under direct supervision of a "minister of pay" in the finance ministry, the tough and abrasive Bengt Johansson. In 1986, Feldt, Johansson, and Statens Avtalsverk issued warnings that public pay settlements even at the level suggested by the independent government-appointed mediators would bring retribution in the form of either tax increases or personnel cutbacks, or perhaps even both.

Private-sector employees confederated in Svenska Arbetsgivareföreningen (SAF) actively facilitated the union-party alliance against public-sector unions. Capitalizing on conflict within LO, engineering employers in Verkstadsföreningen (VF) offered extra-high increases to Metall in 1982 to entice the union away for the first time from the peak-level bargaining system developed in the 1950s. For reasons indicated below, by breaking up centralized bargaining employers helped reduce the relative pay growth of the public sector.[14]

This realignment of the mid-1980s confirmed predictions of a prominent expert from the employers' side in 1982 that future distributional problems "will probably tend to unite wage-earners against the public sector, not against corporate profits."[15] LO's leadership probably had mixed feelings about the newly shaping alignment because it would mean a weakening of LO's central bargaining and political role.[16] In public, the confederation tried to appear neutral, and it even sided with the public-sector unions by criticizing the Social Democrats' and Metall's violation of the strong norm against public criticism of separate union demands, especially during ongoing negotiations. But in fact by 1986 official LO policy began advocating more

13. *Dagens Nyheter,* September 25, 1986; *Fabriksarbetaren* 20 (December 8, 1982).

14. *SAFtidningen,* December 16, 1982; *Dagens Nyheter,* September 22 and April 23, 1983.

15. Karl-Olof Faxén, "Wages, Prices and Taxes in the 1980s," in *Sweden: Choices for Economic and Social Policy in the 1980s,* ed. Bengt Rydén and Villy Bergström (London: Allen & Unwin, 1982), pp. 195–96.

16. Decentralization partially divides employers, too; see Hans De Geer and Hans L. Zetterberg, *Mål, motiv och verksamhet: En SIFO-undersökning om delägarnas syn på Svenska Arbetsgivareföreningen och dess förbund* (Stockholm: SAF, 1987).

than limits to the supply of resources to the public sector. It also advocated a rethinking of the public sector's fundamental administrative principles and therefore change in the way it uses the resources it gets.[17]

The Realignment in Historical Perspective

The realignment in response to the crisis of the 1980s followed two earlier institutionally secured cross-class alignments of interwar and postwar Sweden, set in motion by world depression in the first case and internationally induced inflation in the second. All three alliances included Social Democratic governments and export-oriented employers dominant in SAF. All three brought changes in the structure of authority within LO (increasing centralization in the first two, decreasing in the third). Equally important, all three entailed pay-distributional settlements favoring the LO faction joining the alliance at the expense of other unions.[18]

The first realignment followed the depression era Social Democratic breakthrough to power. A left-center alliance with the Agrarian party was made possible by their 1933 compromise package of deficit-financed public construction and farm price supports. It was followed in 1935 by a royal commission advocating public policy and industrial relations reforms promoting Swedish export capital. Next came the famous Saltsjöbaden agreement of 1938, a procedural peace agreement between LO and SAF that export-oriented employers in engineering had favored for years. Finally came revision of LO's own statutes in 1941, which secured LO's centralized control over the strike funds and tactics employed by its constituent unions, and therefore over their autonomous power to set wages far out of line with other unions in structurally weaker bargaining positions.

All four policy and institutional changes aimed in part to weaken one large and militant bloc of unions—in the building industry. Con-

17. See LO's congress reports *Fackföreningsrörelsen och välfärdsstaten: Rapport till 1986 års LO-kongress från LOs utredning om den offentliga sektorn* (Stockholm: LO, 1986), and *Gemensamt ansvar för arbete: Rapport till 1986 års LO-kongress från LOs utredning om arbete* (Stockholm: LO, 1986).

18. The following discussion draws on Swenson, *Fair Shares,* pp. 42–60, and differs markedly from Gourevitch's *Politics in Hard Times,* which occasionally argues the importance of labor divisions (especially union versus nonunion) in other domestic alliances and ignores divisions in Sweden altogether.

struction unions were a "constant thorn in export industry's side" because building workers' militancy and rising wages infected metalworkers with similar militancy and frustration with Metall's leadership.[19] Also, engineering had to compete for skilled craftsmen and laborers with the seasonal, trade-sheltered, and for those reasons well-paying construction industry. For export manufacturers concerned about price and delivery performance in world markets, plant building costs and completion problems associated with militancy in construction probably added to their motives. Metall, constrained by its industry's vulnerability, stood to gain by controlling the construction unions via centralized LO control. The Social Democrats, finally, felt strong pressure from the Agrarian party to end the rampant militancy (and a ten-month strike in 1933) in the building sector in exchange for support of public housing projects, which after all had to be built by construction workers paid out of government funds.[20]

Whereas Metall was an insider in the farmer-labor-export industry alliance of the 1930s, it opposed the realignment response to the inflationary, full employment economy of the 1950s. The new alliance brought peak-level centralization of collective bargaining, giving LO a degree of control exceeding even what it acquired in the 1930s. Centralized bargaining made possible Sweden's famous solidaristic wage policy, which restrained metalworkers' relatively high wages along with Metall's bargaining autonomy, in favor of the much weaker low-pay unions in woodworking, textiles, garments, and agriculture. Profits in high-paying engineering benefited from solidaristic wage policy, and the Social Democratic government benefited from employers' continued political quiescence. Combined threats of Social Democratic intervention and economy-wide lockouts by SAF in response to inflationary free-for-all wage rivalry had persuaded Metall's leaders to submit to LO's peak-level control. In addition, LO leaders forged broad-based support by granting solidaristic wage policy to low-pay unions who otherwise would not have accepted peak-coordinated wage

19. Sven Anders Söderpalm, *Direktörsklubben: Storindustrin i svensk politik under 1930- och 40-talet* (Stockholm: Zenit/Rabén & Sjögren, 1976), p. 21.

20. See Olle Nyman, *Svensk parlamentarism, 1932–1936* (Uppsala: Almqvist & Wiksell, 1947); Feiwel Kupferberg, "Byggnadsstrejken 1933–34," and Hartmut Apitzsch, "Byggnadsbranschen: Produktionsförhållanden och organisationsstruktur," both in *Arkiv för studier i arbetarrörelsens historia* 2 (1972); and Sven Anders Söderpalm, *Arbetsgiarna och Saltsjöbadspolitiken* (Stockholm: SAF, 1980).

restraint. Metall's leadership, at least initially, did not welcome the new institutional and distributional settlement favoring export employers in SAF and low-pay unions in LO.[21]

The Recent Realignment

Although Metall's leadership would come to accept and affirm LO's peak-level control and egalitarian wage policy in the 1960s and 1970s, latent discontent remained below the surface. In the meantime, Social Democratic rule gave public-sector workers the right to strike, and egalitarian wage policy in the private sector legitimated their efforts to achieve intersectoral pay parity—and even to exceed it for low-pay groups. As the public sector grew, both labor and income were diverted from the private sector. Internal strains built until economic crisis in the early 1980s once again threw export-oriented employers and Metall into each others' arms, as in the 1930s. This time the shared opponent was different—not the building workers but government employees. But now, unlike the past two alignments, the new distributional and institutional settlement brought more pay inequality and less centralization of union power in LO.

The Social Democratic government joined Metall and employers, especially the big export manufacturers in VF, in the new distributional alliance. Controlling payroll costs and increasing pay differentiation in the public sector was key to the government's efforts to reduce budget deficits. Also, by influencing the intra- and intersectoral pay structure, the government wanted to help industry adapt to the hostile international economy: by reducing tax costs (for price competitiveness), to improve the supply of skilled labor and legitimate greater private-sector pay differentiation (for productivity, flexibility, and quality competitiveness), and to reduce production and delivery interruptions caused by disruptive and infectious public-sector militancy (for customer loyalty and world market shares).

The evidence suggests that the new alliance succeeded in restructuring pay. Pay for manual workers in local government relative to industry reached a plateau in the early 1980s after increasing in the 1970s, but it then fell rapidly from about 95 percent of the average industry

21. See Jörgen Ullenhag, *Den solidariska lönepolitiken i Sverige* (Stockholm: Läromedelsförlagen, 1971); Axel Hadenius, *Facklig organisationsutveckling* (Stockholm: Rabén & Sjögren, 1974).

wage to about 89 percent in 1985. Their counterparts in the central government reached their plateau in the late 1970s, falling from about 109 percent of the average industry wage in 1977 to 97 percent in 1985. Very few other LO unions slipped as much. Salaried government workers represented by unions outside LO and less loyal to the Social Democrats (and therefore more militant) defended themselves better, but after peaking around 1981 their pay fell between 1 and 4 percent with respect to white-collar personnel in private industry by 1986.[22]

Success for the alliance can in part be accounted for by public-private employer collaboration initiated around 1980 by the non-socialist coalition government. Cross-sector collaboration only intensified under the Social Democrats after their return to power, when the intergovernmental employer organization Offentliga Arbetsgivares Samarbetsorgan coordinated strategies and objectives with SAF during the 1984 wage round.[23] In 1984, the Social Democratic government hoped that by holding back public-sector pay agreements they could set the pattern for subsequent private-sector agreements. The LO leadership joined in by supporting limits on the wage drift clauses in public contracts that compensated government workers for private-sector pay drift (market-driven, extracontractual pay increases).

LO's own two public-sector unions, like those in Tjänstemännens Centralorganisation, the white-collar confederation, opposed all limits on drift compensation.[24] LO leaders took a stand against their own public-sector affiliates in 1984 only after engineering employers had managed two years earlier to wean Metall from similar wage drift clauses. With an extra-high offer, VF had bought Metall's defection from peak-level bargaining conducted by LO and abstinence from the automatic pay drift compensation clauses for its own members who

22. Landsorganisationen, *Statistisk sammanställning av löneutveckling och lönestruktur: Lönepolitisk delrapport* (Stockholm: LO, 1987); for white-collar pay, see Statistiska Centralbyrån, *Statistisk årsbok* (1984–88).

23. Björn Rosengren, "En unik samverkan," in *Storkonflikten på den svenska arbetsmarknaden 1980,* ed. Anders Broström (Stockholm: Arbetslivscentrum, 1981), p. 69; Nils Elvander, *Den svenska modellen* (Stockholm: Almänna Förlaget, 1988), pp. 144–47. Peter Walters also notes the broad continuity between the Social Democratic government and its predecessors in efforts to reduce government expenditures in "Distributing Decline: Swedish Social Democrats and the Crisis of the Welfare State," *Government and Opposition* 20 (Summer 1985): 366.

24. Elvander, *Den Svenska modellen,* pp. 145, 147, 150.

did not benefit from wage drift. With the unitary front in defense of these automatic clauses broken, the rest of the unions were to lose theirs starting in 1986.

Although solidaristic wage policy lived on in the form of extra-high average increases for low-pay industries in the private sector, which SAF then conceded in order to buy off LO demands for pay drift guarantees,[25] the distribution of pay *within* industries and firms was no longer guaranteed in any way to be egalitarian. Intraindustry distribution remained to be negotiated in sectoral negotiations, when the unions were bound by a no-strike clause in the peak-level agreement. Employers thus regained the upper hand in bargaining at subpeak levels for the first time since the early 1970s.

By allowing for greater market determination of wage differentiation within and across industries, the 1986 agreements for the private sector helped deflate the public sector's moral claim to full intersectoral parity without regard to economic consequences. Consequently, the two-year public-sector settlements for 1986 and 1987 spelled the end of automatic adjustments to keep government pay upwardly drifting along with the private sector. During these negotiations, conflict within LO between private- and public-sector unions came to a head (the "cuckoo" controversy), as Finance Minister Feldt openly threatened either tax increases or public-sector layoffs—a clear attempt to exploit the divisions between and within the unions.

The 1988 contracts brought increasing pay differentiation, but not as much as employers hoped. Feldt publicly opened ceremonies by playing off the unions against retirees and families with children, promising improvements for those groups only if unions held wage increases to 4 percent rather than the 11 percent being demanded by some, including the low-pay public-sector unions. He also explicitly rejected the idea that public-sector pay should increase in lock-step with pay in the private sector. The alternative he threatened was the "dismal road" of unemployment, traveled elsewhere in the world, to bring inflationary wage rivalry and union militancy under control.[26]

Without a fight, intimidated public-sector unions accepted contract increases amounting to about 6 percent compared to up to 8 percent

25. *Dagens Nyheter,* October 22, 1986.
26. *Dagens Nyheter,* January 12, 1988.

for the private sector.[27] For managing even that well, they could thank local governments' acute need to match private-sector pay in tight, shared labor markets. Morale, recruitment, and turnover crises festered in some of the most important sectors of the Swedish welfare state. Those affected most were women in moderate and low-pay occupations, who received considerable sympathy in the press: nurses, nurse's aides, day-care and preschool teachers, and social workers. Regional governments had recently begun pirating labor from each other and the private sector, bidding up nurses' benefits and bonuses to get around rigid nationwide pay standards.[28]

Contract increases had to provide for these personnel needs without increasing total payrolls. Taking cues from the private sector, government employers therefore sought substantial flexibility for pay differentiation from department to department, region to region, and individual to individual. This allowed for high pay raises where labor market forces mandated, even if *average* government pay failed to keep up with private-sector pay (only limited movement in this direction had been made in 1986). Despite his 1988 promise that "we can never abandon the solidaristic wage policy—it's the precondition for the trade union movement's survival," chairman Sigvard Marjasin of LO's union of local government workers was forced less than a week later to back down. The 1988 agreement he signed allowed for considerable departmental and regional pay differentiation geared to recruitment needs, especially of the health sector.[29]

Dissemination of a draft party program for public debate by the Social Democrats the following year indicated how far the coalition of forces against public-sector costs could lead. A key chapter of the document dealt with "renovation" of the public sector.[30] It is telling that

27. *Dagens Nyheter,* February 23, April 23, and June 18, 1988. In 1985, the government showed its muscle and nerve by locking out 20,000 white-collar (non-LO) public-sector workers in response to a limited but unpopular strike.

28. *Dagens Nyheter,* March 28, 1988.

29. *Dagens Nyheter,* April 13, April 18, 1988. The attack on rigid pay standardization in the public sector had begun in the late 1970s under bourgeois governments, but it gained full momentum under the Social Democrats. On earlier developments, see Maivor Sjölund, *Statens kaka: Lönepolitik i förändring* (Stockholm: Allmänna Förlaget, 1987).

30. See Anna-Greta Leijon et al., *90-tals programmet: En debattbok om arbetarrörelsens viktigaste frågor under 90-talet* (Stockholm: Tidens Förlag, 1989). See also Casten von Otter, *Kan man rationalisera folkhemmet?* (Stockholm: LO, 1986). For an English version of these ideas, see Richard B. Saltman and Casten von Otter, "Re-vitalizing Public Health Care Systems: A Proposal for Public Competition in Sweden," *Health Policy* 7 (February 1987): 21–40.

among the authors were three individuals with official or research backgrounds in Metall. None came from public-sector unions. According to the draft, government employees were too protected by rigidly centralized, rule-bound personnel and service delivery practices at the expense of citizens as taxpayers and "users" of the welfare state. Public interests would be better served with more citizen choice and political oversight via comparative performance evaluation. Consequently, units in the welfare state bureaucracy should be subject to budgetary rewards and punishments according to performance and client loyalty. The draft program maintained that collective incentives, along with a more flexible promotion process and individually differentiated salary structure, were necessary to promote more cost-efficient government and check growing interest in privatization among local governments, business, and the public.

A reform of the welfare state initiated and promoted by private-sector union interests can reinforce the cross-class comity that has so benefited Social Democrats in the past. Business quiescence was a normal condition since the 1930s, with temporary mobilizations that unnerved Social Democratic governments and sometimes (but not always) imposed immediate electoral costs.[31] The new programmatic shift on the part of Social Democrats represents in part an attempt to assure themselves political quiescence from the right as the basis for enduring control of government.[32] There was good reason at the time to think that they could still renew the tacit coalition. According to Peter Wallenberg of Sweden's largest financial empire, Sweden's economic success in the 1980s could be accounted for by the "constructive attitude of Swedish labor." Surveys of corporate executives found that a substantial proportion were favorable to the Social Democratic party and even preferred its rule over that of the opposition.[33]

31. In 1948, the Social Democrats appeared to have lost a large share of votes to the bourgeois parties after intense attacks from the right on their postwar planning and nationalization program. They managed to hold ground, however, probably by recovering votes lost to the Communists in the 1944 election; see Diane Sainsbury, *Swedish Social Democractic Ideology and Electoral Politics, 1944–1948* (Stockholm: Almqvist & Wiksell International, 1980); and Leif Lewin, *Planhushållningsdebatten* (Stockholm: Almqvist & Wiksell, 1967), pp. 213–347. On VF's and SAF's role during this period and since then, see Söderpalm, *Direktörsklubben*, pp. 114–25, and Sven Ove Hansson, *SAF i politiken: En dokumentation av näringslivsorganisationernas opinionsbildning* (Stockholm: Tidens Förlag, 1984), pp. 12–14.

32. For more on the conservative shift, see Jonas Pontusson, "Radicalization and Retreat in Swedish Social Democracy," *New Left Review* 165 (September–October 1987): 5–33.

33. A survey of 450 firms found 70 percent of managers (95 percent in the largest companies) favorable to the Social Democratic party. Although only 18 percent of the one hun-

Recent events are illustrative. In February 1990, Volvo's chief executive, Pehr Gyllenhammar, exhorted the conservative parties not to take advantage of the Social Democrats' strife with public-sector and white-collar unions preparing to strike. Threatening new elections, the government had proposed a wage freeze and strike ban along with other things attractive to employers, even if a price and dividend freeze were also included. Gyllenhammar recommended voting for the package, or at least abstention.[34] Interestingly, whereas the municipal workers' union rejected the package completely, LO and Metall endorsed it, albeit grudgingly.[35] Gyllenhammar's failure to persuade the bourgeois parties resulted in the government's temporary resignation (and Finance Minister Feldt's permanent resignation). The conservative parties probably counted on early elections, which would have strengthened them in the Riksdag. But instead of calling elections, the Social Democrats returned to power with the help of Communists in the Riksdag. They then proceeded, to employers' satisfaction, with a dramatic tax reform and cutbacks or postponements of planned vacation and parental leave improvements. In doing so, the government openly courted the Liberal party's future support for a possible coalition, something Gyllenhammar had advocated.

That the Social Democrats could not reverse their substantial electoral decline with these maneuvers can in part be explained by growing strife within the party and throughout the labor movement. Chances of staying in power were somewhat better than of gaining votes, but only because their cross-class strategy made majoritarian center-left coalitions possible. Despite their fall from power in 1991, Social Democrats' recently declared openness to joining the European Community and their foot dragging on the dismantling of nuclear power stations—combined with intense divisions among the bourgeois parties—improve their prospects of repairing the cross-class alliance in the not-too-distant future.

---

dred top executives favored a Social Democratic government, 39 percent believed the party to be better for business than the opposition; see Henry Milner, *Sweden: Social Democracy in Practice* (Oxford: Oxford University Press, 1989), p. 137. Wallenberg quoted in *Inside Sweden* 2 (May–June 1988).

34. Pehr Gyllenhammar, "Regeringen får inte falla," *Dagens Nyheter,* February 13, 1990.

35. Jonas Pontusson, "Austerity, Government Crisis, and Political Realignment in Sweden, 1989–90" (Paper presented at the 1990 meeting of the American Political Science Association, San Francisco, August 29–September 1).

TREACHERY: WEST GERMANY IN THE 1990s

In Sweden, problems of reducing government debt and adapting to international competition united Social Democrats with unions and employers in export sectors in a broad coalition against government workers' share of national income and against the current distribution of government pay. In West Germany, economic crisis set in motion attempts at a similar refashioning of alliances, potentially suited to return the Social Democratic party to power. Led by an ambitious maverick in the Sozialdemokratische Partei Deutschlands (SPD), the initiative played several popular themes, including reduction of the relative pay of civil servants. But an intense struggle ensued within the labor movement, when in stark contrast to its Swedish counterpart the union of metalworkers rallied in defense of existing inter- and intrasectoral pay structures. By doing so, Industriegewerkschaft Metall (IG Metall) fought the revival of a union-party alliance with leanings to the political center and accommodationist approaches to private employers.

Latent distributional conflict within the German unions invited an ambitious politician to fashion a politically rewarding alliance against public-sector unions. Oskar Lafontaine, premier in the Social Democratic government of the Saarland, proposed that salaried civil servants abstain from pay compensation enjoyed by others for progressive work-time reduction. Guaranteed publicity because the 1988 nationwide public-sector wage negotiations were under way, Lafontaine's proposal resonated with a common public hostility toward civil servants' relatively high salaries, pensions, and job security. His ostensible aim was not to level pay for its own sake but to finance additional public jobs when budget deficits spoke against other solutions to high unemployment. In other words, the civil servant was to pay the tab; the lower-paid government employee, even if fortunate enough to have a job, should not be called on to do so.

Lafontaine, an ambitious protégé of Willy Brandt and strong contender for the party leadership and chancellorship should the SPD ever return to power, triggered a fierce intramural debate closely covered by the press and television. Particularly enraged was Franz Steinkühler, leader of Germany's enormous union of both blue- and white-collar workers in the steel, machinery, auto, and electronics industries. A relatively high-pay union, IG Metall had been a leader in a campaign since 1978 for job creation through negotiated work-week reductions. A key demand of IG Metall's 35-hour work-week campaign was full pay compensation or no simultaneous reductions in weekly earnings. Although Lafontaine only suggested relative, not real, reductions—and only for civil servants—Steinkühler rushed to attack in the harshest of terms. Lafontaine's initiative, he said, was "like a stab in the back (*wie ein Dolchstoss*)." To propose work-time reduction without compensation during the wage round in progress was, he said, like throwing "the famous Austrian hand grenade, which doesn't explode but has a terrible effect on morale."[36]

Like leaders of other unions and the DGB (the German trade union confederation), Steinkühler attacked Lafontaine for violating labor's taboo against mobilizing external public support for results unwanted by unions presently engaged in negotiations. He attacked on substantive grounds, too, arguing that progressive taxation, not collective bargaining and differential wage restraint, was the suitable device for redistributing income within the working class, and that tax-financed job creation was more appropriate for creating jobs. If collective bargaining should in any way redistribute employment, only negotiated work-time reductions were appropriate. Lafontaine's progressive wage restraint for redistribution of income and jobs, as "socialism within one class," was to be rejected. Steinkühler thus denounced anything like Swedish solidaristic wage policy, following in the tradition of his predecessors.[37]

IG Metall and Lafontaine in Historical Perspective

Lafontaine touched sensitive nerves with his proposal. The acrimony he aroused can only be understood in light of the West German labor movement's postwar interest alliances and internal distributional conflict. In trying to advance himself and revive the SPD politically, Lafontaine threatened to recreate a previously successful cross-class alliance of union, employer, and party forces that had checked IG Metall's more radical influence in politics and collective bargaining for over twenty years. In the 1960s and 1970s, the stifling of IG Metall's influence in the DGB and SPD made the SPD *koalitionsfähig*, or

36. *Frankfurter Allgemeine Zeitung*, March 7, 1988.
37. Franz Steinkühler, "Angst vor den Freunden: Zerbricht das Bündnis von Gewerkschaften und Sozialdemokraten?" *Die Zeit*, March 25, 1988, p. 13.

suitable as a coalition partner for the centrist Liberal Party (FDP). It also fostered stable corporatistic relations between employers, unions, and government.[38] While this alliance ruled, IG Metall was eclipsed within the DGB by more conservative unions. Steinkühler's bellicose response was therefore a preemptive strike against a return of the alliance and IG Metall's return to weakness.

IG Metall has experienced two periods of relative dominance, one before its long period of weakness from about 1960 to 1984 and another since the mid-1980s. Its two periods of dominance in the labor movement appear, at least in time, closely associated with Social Democratic parliamentary weakness. In the immediate postwar period, under the leadership of Otto Brenner, IG Metall's domination in the labor confederation resulted in the DGB's endorsement of IG Metall's militant or "expansive" wage policy for redistributing income between labor and capital. The idea was that high wage increases would increase labor's share of national income and at the same time stimulate demand, growth, and employment. IG Metall economist Viktor Agartz, who introduced the notion, headed the DGB's research and policy institute.

But like employers and the postwar conservative government, the leadership of other important unions differed and hoped to reorient the DGB—in part to undermine IG Metall's ideological influence over militants in their own ranks. Among them were the construction and allied workers' union (IG Bau-Steine-Erden), the union of mining and energy workers (IG Bergbau und Energie), and at least two unions in the public sector, the government and transport workers' union (ÖTV, Gewerkschaft Öffentliche Dienste, Transport und Verkehr), and the union of postal employees (DPG, Deutsche Postgewerkschaft).

One reason they differed was that a militant IG Metall "had repeatedly broken union solidarity by dictating a tempo and program which most other unions simply could not follow.[39] Unemployment in construction and chronic structural decline in mining hindered IG Metall's union critics in the private sector. Also weak were the relatively low-pay public-sector unions in the face of a conservative government and high unemployment. The ÖTV and the DPG, unlike in later

38. On the "accommodationist" unions' politics in postwar union-party-government relations, in contrast to IG Metall's, see Andrei S. Markovits, *The Politics of the West German Trade Unions: Strategies of Class and Interest Representation in Growth and Crisis* (Cambridge: Cambridge University Press, 1986), esp. pp. 83–157.

39. Ibid., p. 90.

years, therefore supported the conservative mining and construction unions in their ambitions in the 1950s for the DGB to exercise some peak-level coordination over member unions' bargaining strategies. DGB control in the hands of these conservative unions would check IG Metall's autonomy, wage militancy, and presumably relative pay.

Although the conservative unions never succeeded in empowering the DGB with formal control over IG Metall's bargaining autonomy, they did acquire control over the DGB's programmatic positions by the early 1960s. The radical voice of IG Metall was muffled by the accommodationist faction that supported doctrines of productivity-oriented, "distributionally neutral," and "cost-neutral" wage policies that employers, the government, and its economic advisers advocated. Consequently, the conservative unions were at least able to prevent use of the confederation for strong moral and material backing of IG Metall to counteract the power of more tightly centralized and coordinated employers. With the DGB so neutralized, the SPD gained in attractiveness as a coalition partner with the employer-friendly Freie Demokratische Partei (FDP).

In spirit, then, the conservative unions endorsed the employer confederation Bundesvereinigung der Deutschen Arbeitgeberverbände with its strategy of economy-wide standards for pay increases oriented to average productivity increases. These increases would generally stay below those for the engineering sector and so help it maintain profits and international competitiveness. With theirs and the DGB's passivity during IG Metall offensives, these unions implicitly backed the employer confederation and its strongest affiliate Gesamtmetall (Gesamtverband der Metallindustriellen Arbeitgeberverbände) against IG Metall. IG Metall contracts would then become the pattern for the rest of industry, and the conservative unions could then boast to members of agreements equal to those gained by the powerful IG Metall.[40]

An indicator of IG Metall's weakness in the 1960s was the replacement of IG Metall's Agartz by Bruno Gleitze as head of the DGB's research institute. Gleitze was the author of a plan for "collective capital formation," a major source of inspiration for LO's Rudolf Meidner, who authored a similar proposal for wage earner funds. The Gleitze plan, and later versions of collective capital formation that it

40. On the employer confederation and Gesamtmetall versus IG Metall, see Claus Noé, *Gebändigter Klassenkampf: Tarifautonomie in der Bundesrepublik Deutschland* (Berlin: Duncker & Humblot, 1970), pp. 49–54, 256–60.

spawned, was the accommodationists' programmatic answer, adopted by the DGB, to the militant "expansive wage policy" of IG Metall. As IG Metall saw it, Gleitze's plan was a backdoor attempt to control its militancy and relative wages.

Gleitze cleverly appealed to the DGB unions wanting limits on IG Metall's militancy, for it dealt at least in principle with the same wealth-concentration problem that IG Metall proposed to remedy with confrontational wage bargaining. According to IG Metall, profits secured by wage restraint and retained for self-financed investment only contributed to an advancing concentration of ownership and thus economic and political power. Gleitze countered that when disposable wages cut into profits one sees either (a) price increases and an inflationary reinstatement of previous functional income distribution, or (b) disinvestment and unemployment. Instead of high wages, he proposed a tax on profits to capture a portion of value added for labor on top of productivity-linked pay increases. This share would be skimmed off into collective funds controlled by the unions. It would be kept in circulation as investment capital for socially and distributionally desirable economic development.[41]

IG Metall saw collective capital formation as a way of legitimating restraint by making it seem distributionally progressive rather than regressive, thus broadening the ideological appeal of its opponents in the DGB. Ironically, IG Metall's most important allies in its vigorous opposition to collective capital formation in the 1970s were to be three unions in the public sector (ÖTV, DPG, and the railroad workers' union); the first two had once openly allied with IG Metall's detractors in the generally lower-pay or structurally handicapped construction, mining, textile, garment, and food industries. By the mid-1970s, Social Democratic control of government, full employment, and growth of public-sector union membership helped wages in the public sector catch up. Between 1970 and 1976, public-sector pay rose by about 87 percent. The average increase for industry was only 77 percent.[42] Public-sector unions could now sometimes match and even surpass IG

41. See Bruno Gleitze, ed., *Sozialkapital und Sozialfonds als Mittel der Vermögenspolitik*, WWI-Studie zur Wirtschaftsforschung no. 1, 2d ed. (Cologne: WWI, 1969).

42. Gerhard Weiss, *Die ÖTV: Politik und gesellschaftspolitische Konzeptionen der Gewerkschaft ÖTV von 1966 bis 1976* (Marburg: Verlag Arbeiterbewegung und Gesellschaftswissenschaft, 1978), p. 201; Projektgruppe Gewerkschaftsforschung, *Rahmenbedingungen der Tarifpolitik: Band I: Gesamtwirtschaftliche Entwicklung und Organisationen der Tarifparteien* (Frankfurt: Campus, 1979), p. 244.

Metall's successes, as in the 1974 strike, which even upset IG Metall's leadership held at bay by the 1973 oil price shock. Thus in 1975 the public-sector unions departed from their 1950s policy by not endorsing a renewed effort at DGB-coordinated restraint, led by the low-pay Gewerkschaft Textil und Bekleidung (the textile and garment workers' union).[43]

As IG Metall and now its public sector allies saw it, the 1970s idea of collective capital formation was a subtle challenge to autonomous militancy. The intense split within the DGB, uniting the unions in the two largest sectors (metals and government) against most of the rest, had helped ensure that collective capital formation would die in 1974 before becoming a serious item on the legislative agenda, just as the split and stalemate had obstructed DGB "coordination" of IG Metall. Meanwhile, employers benefited from the impasse within the DGB, whose net effect was to isolate IG Metall, undermine public support for its militancy, and weaken it against Gesamtmetall, its powerful opponent in the employer confederation. The balance of power within the DGB therefore helped the liberal FDP to accept a coalition with the SPD during the 1970s.[44]

The Nascent Alliance and IG Metall's Defense against Lafontaine

After the Social Democrats lost power in 1982, IG Metall recovered leadership in the DGB with the support of public-sector unions. Together they easily held comfortable and growing majority control in the 1980s, approaching even the two-thirds majority necessary for reform of the DGB's rules and structure. Ernst Breit from Gewerkschaft Post, one of the allies, was elected DGB chairman in 1982 to replace the retiring Heinz-Oskar Vetter (who had been a leader of IG Bergbau und Energie, the miners' union, a supporter of DGB coordination and collective capital formation). Indicative of IG Metall's leadership was the DGB's endorsement of a militant campaign for the 35-hour work week as a remedy for double-digit unemployment, which IG Metall,

43. Deutscher Gerwerkschaftsbund, *Protokoll: 10. ordentlicher Bundeskongress 1975* (pp. 199, 324–25).

44. The FDP supported a conservative version of the DGB's Gleitze plan that gave distributional legitimation to wage restraint but left out union control of the capital funds and was therefore potentially acceptable to employers; see Wilfried Höhnen, "Zwanzig Jahre vermögenspolitische Diskussion," in *Das Nein zur Vermögenspolitik,* ed. Karl Heinz Pitz (Reinbek bei Hamburg: Rowohlt, 1974), pp. 25–55.

along with printers in IG Druck und Papier (now IG Medien), independently struck for in 1984.

Until that time, the conservative unions' nonconfrontational response to unemployment was negotiated, government-subsidized early retirement, which business did not strongly oppose. The conservative Christian Democratic–Liberal government obliged with legislation, hoping this would take the wind out of IG Metall's sails.[45] Initially, the tactic appeared successful in fostering deep divisions between IG Metall and the accommodationists, with Günter Döding of the low-pay food, beverage, and restaurant industry workers' union leading the faction for early retirement. IG Metall loudly agitated against early retirement in the DGB and public debate, hoping to mobilize pressures inside other unions for following in IG Metall's steps. The unwillingness of the other unions to keep pace would hold IG Metall back in its campaign for a rapid reduction of the work week and isolate it politically.

Strong pressure indeed built up inside accommodationist unions to follow IG Metall's lead. But instead of enlisting external political forces to hold IG Metall back, by the spring of 1988 even such solidly conservative unions as IG Chemie, IG Bau, and the textile and garment workers' union chose to join rather than beat the vanguard. For one thing, it turned out that there were few remaining workers still eligible for early retirement. Döding, one of the most prominent accommodationist opinion makers, began insisting in 1986 that early retirement and the reduced work week were not mutually exclusive but rather complementary approaches.[46]

Thus, earlier distributional conflict within the DGB at IG Metall's expense and IG Metall's desire to protect a new and fragile unity behind work-week reduction help explain both the intensity of Steinkühler's attack against Lafontaine and the milder manner in which other DGB unions opposed him.[47] By endorsing differentiated wage restraint—if only for high-paid government employees as an act of solidarity with the unemployed—Lafontaine's proposal threatened to le-

45. Wolfgang Spieker, "Verbände und Institutionen in der Arbeitszeitpolitik," in *Perspektiven der Arbeitszeitverkürzung*, ed. Hans Mayr and Hans Janssen (Cologne: Bund-Verlag, 1984), pp. 297–98.

46. See Günter Döding, *Die neuen Aufgaben der Gewerkschaften* (Stuttgart: Bonn Aktuell, 1986), p. 27.

47. *Frankfurter Allgemeine Zeitung*, March 10, 1988. Lafontaine actually received support from the generally accommodationist ex-DGB chairman Heinz-Oskar Vetter; *Frankfurter Allgemeine Zeitung*, March 8, 1988.

gitimate a distributional principle that could be wielded at the expense of IG Metall's ascendance in the DGB, its militant bargaining strategies, and maintenance of its members' relatively high wages.[48] It might therefore help revive the same kind of union coalition that once dominated the DGB and supported coordination and collective capital formation. This coalition included low-pay unions and those compelled by strong employers and weak markets to let their members' relative pay slide.

Ideas about redistribution of wages, whether across or within industries, have always made IG Metall leaders nervous. Debates at IG Metall's congresses since the 1970s show that the large and heterogeneous union is perennially haunted by its own intramural conflicts over pay distribution. At times the union tries to raise pay for low-pay members faster than for others, but most of the time it neglects leveling for other objectives—such as work-week reduction. The leadership therefore probably fears that proposals like Lafontaine's might also arouse opposition within the union by providing low-pay groups and their spokespersons the grounds for restraining wages of higher-pay workers, including white-collar members in IG Metall, for their own benefit.[49]

These speculations about Steinkühler's fears of the class-splitting and cross-class alliance Lafontaine could forge are bolstered by a striking similarity between Lafontaine's pronouncements and the employers' campaigns for *Flexibilisierung* in, among other things, the distribution of reduced working hours. In 1989, Lafontaine announced his support for allowing routine work on Saturday and Sunday, which IG Metall (and its closest ally on the issue, IG Medien) wanted to keep free for family, community, and leisure.[50] In doing so, Lafontaine

48. Responding to IG Metall's concerns, the DGB asserted that higher civil servants in the Deutscher Beamtenbund (the federation of German civil servants) should get just as large a pay increase as the DGB unions were getting in 1987; *Frankfurter Allgemeine Zeitung*, January 21, 1987. The DGB leadership feared that extra pay restraint for high earners in the public sector "would set precedents for contract trends in other areas and would thereby encroach on bargaining autonomy [of private-sector unions]"; *Frankfurter Allgemeine Zeitung*, April 23, 1988.

49. In the late 1970s, IG Metall chairman Loderer even prevented the distribution to union officials of a book on (and favorably disposed to) solidaristic wage policy, written by his own researcher, economist Hans-Adam Pfromm. The book, which included an analysis of Sweden, was *Solidarische Lohnpolitik: Zur wirtschaftlichen und sozialen Problematik tariflicher Lohnstrukturnivellierung* (Cologne: Europäische Verlagsanstalt, 1978).

50. On employers, see Bundesvereinigung der Deutschen Arbeitgeberverbände, *Zwanzig-Punkte-Programm: Für mehr Beschäftigung* (Cologne: BDA, 1985); Gesamtmetall, *Bericht*

provocatively joined forces with the conservative IG Chemie-Papier-Keramik (IG Chemie, the union of chemical and allied industry workers) in endorsing weekend work, a gesture of independence that sat well with centrist, swing voters hostile to "union" (meaning in particular IG Metall) control of the SPD agenda.

Hermann Rappe of IG Chemie was, along with Günter Döding, a leader of the group of five DGB unions generally advocating nonconfrontational relations with employers and frequently challenging IG Metall's agenda.[51] Lafontaine therefore probably saw Rappe as a potential ally whom he had to split off from IG Metall, after Rappe had uncharacteristically supported Steinkühler's response to Lafontaine's "Austrian hand grenade." IG Chemie also had a reputation of antagonism to the ecology agenda Lafontaine promoted. By siding with IG Chemie on the weekend work issue, he showed his recognition of the union's pivotal importance in the game of cross-class alliances.[52]

To broaden his support, Lafontaine also toned down his antigrowth image and openly endorsed market-oriented rather than statist policies in the course of the decade. But even as early as 1985 he asserted, much like LO and Swedish Social Democrats, the need to "decentralize, debureaucratize, and democratize" welfare state administration.[53] These themes made him increasingly palatable to both industry and the FDP, even if his leadership in the ecology debate made him an uncertain friend.[54] Lafontaine's strategy appeared to lie in patching to-

der Geschäftsführung, 1983–1985 (Cologne: Gesamtmetall, 1985), p. 114; Erich Ott, "Arbeitszeitflexibilisierung und Beschäftigungswirkung," in *Perspektiven der Arbeitszeitverkürzung*, ed. Hans Mayr and Hans Janssen (Cologne: Bund Verlag, 1984), pp. 137–39; Arbeitsgruppe Alternative Wirtschaftspolitik, *35 Stunden sind genug! Abbau der Massenarbeitslosigkeit und Verbesserung der Arbeits- und Lebensbedingungen durch Arbeitszeitverkürzung* (Cologne: Pahl-Rugenstein, 1987), pp. 32–37.

51. In this regard, they have replaced Georg Leber of IG Bau-Steine-Erden, the union of construction workers; see Christian Zentner, *Das Verhalten von Georg Leber—analysiert unter dem Aspekt seiner macht-politischen Bedeutung für die deutsche Gerwerkschaftsbewegung und die Sozialdemokratische Partei Deutschlands* (Mainz: V. Hase & Koehler, 1966).

52. On Rappe vis-à-vis employers, Steinkühler, and Lafontaine, see *Frankfurter Allgemeine Zeitung*, August 4 and December 29, 1988; and *The German Tribune*, August 6, 1989. For more on IG Chemie's swings and shifts, see Markovits, *West German Trade Unions*, pp. 267–326; and Swenson, *Fair Shares*, pp. 212–16.

53. Oskar Lafontaine, *Der andere Fortschritt: Verantwortung statt Verweigerung* (Hamburg: Hoffman & Campe, 1985), p. 109.

54. On Lafontaine vis-à-vis business and the FDP, see "Unternehmer sind auch Wähler, Ein Zeit-Gespräch mit Oskar Lafontaine über Wirtschaftspolitik und Gewerkschaften," *Die Zeit*, September 23, 1988. See also *The German Tribune*, March 6, 1988; *Der Spiegel*, no. 41 (1988); *The Economist*, March 19, 1988; *Der Spiegel*, November 20, 1989; and *Der Tagesspiegel*, August 15, 1989.

gether support from diverse groups by promising more with one hand than he threatened with the other. Metal and government workers got the opposite treatment. Lafontaine borrowed popular elements from IG Metall's strategy against unemployment, but he attached new conditions pleasing to other potential supporters and unacceptable to IG Metall. The strategy promoted public perception of him as a figure unusually unintimidated by two powerful but politically isolated labor aristocracies, making him look highly electable as a candidate for chancellor.[55]

By lashing out against Lafontaine and temporarily preventing him from displacing party leader Hans-Jochen Vogel at the 1988 SPD conference, IG Metall lined up behind its old public-sector allies and their high-pay members.[56] Concern for unions and pay in the public sector added to fear for its own autonomy, militancy, and ultimately the relative pay of its own members. The desire to protect itself against a coalition of outsiders—unions, parties, and employers—was the same motive for criticizing DGB coordination and collective capital formation earlier. In other words, IG Metall fought Lafontaine's revival of an accommodationist cross-class coalition against IG Metall. The union opposed a contender for leadership of the party who, given a chance, was likely to form a government on terms threatening to IG Metall's recently recovered programmatic leadership within West Germany's dominant labor confederation. If (plausibly it seemed at the time this was written) Lafontaine's leadership is the SPD's only immediate chance at regaining power, IG Metall's success in obstructing Lafontaine may come at the party's expense.

Recent German reunification of course overwhelms other issues in determining the course of electoral and coalition politics in the near future. At present, Lafontaine has probably been hurt more by his criticism of Helmut Kohl's popular rush to unification than by internal party disputes. The distributional implications of reunification are also as yet unclear, as capital moves eastward and labor moves westward. As frustration inevitably sets in with the problems of

55. In September 1989, Lafontaine was more popular than SPD leader Hans-Jochen Vogel and was favored 49 to 41 percent over CDU-chancellor Helmut Kohl for the future chancellorship; *Der Spiegel,* September 25, 1989. Lafontaine cultivates an image as a daring thinker in three recent books, including the latest, *Die Gesellschaft der Zukunft* (Hamburg: Hoffman & Campe Verlag, 1988).

56. "Boosts for Women and Vogel but not for Lafontaine," *The German Tribune,* September 11, 1988.

reunification, Lafontaine's apparent creativity at recasting alliances may yet prove decisive in bringing the Social Democrats back to power.

METALWORKERS AND THE CROSS-CLASS ALLIANCES IN COMPARISON

When he attacked the SPD's Oskar Lafontaine and defended the material interests of high-pay government employees, IG Metall's Franz Steinkühler was trying to stall a cross-class political realignment in West Germany at the union's expense. In Sweden, by contrast, Metall's Leif Blomberg was part of just such a realignment against the public sector, which included engineering employers and Social Democratic politicians. In both cases, the two large unions of metalworkers were decisive players. They moved, however, in opposite directions. How can their differences be accounted for?

Both were motivated by the desire to control the inter- and intrasectoral pay structure to their benefit. Both therefore shared a desire to enhance their collective bargaining autonomy or power. Sweden's Metall (representing about 20 percent of LO's members) achieved this by agreeing with employers who wanted more decentralized collective bargaining; Germany's IG Metall (about 30 percent of the DGB) tried to protect its power against employers by neutralizing political forces that would strengthen its conservative opposition within the DGB and therefore demobilize a confederation only recently supportive of IG Metall's vanguard role.

Similar motives interacted with markedly different intersectoral trends in pay and working conditions to produce deviating alliance patterns. In Sweden, public-sector pay had advanced much further with respect to the private sector, while in Germany, rapid growth in relative pay in the early 1970s had already been reversed in the late 1970s by a conservative government. For Sweden's Metall, the prevailing interest lay in containing public-sector wages and costs to stop the drain on private-sector income and labor, which undermined their industry's ability to compete in world markets. IG Metall's dominant problem was the opposite one of ensuring that other unions like those in the public sector kept pace with its militancy, especially toward the shorter work week, for fear of isolating itself politically. The two countries also differed dramatically in terms of public employment levels: in Germany, the public sector accounted for 15.8 percent of total employment in 1986; in Sweden, 36.6 percent. High taxes were therefore more of a concern for Swedish workers, who pay a larger share of their earnings in taxes than workers in any other country of the world.[57] Sweden's Metall thus had a stronger motivation to support an alliance against public-sector costs and inefficiency.

For IG Metall in Germany, defense of the public sector amounted to self-defense against the same kind of coalition that imposed peak-level centralization, a loss of autonomy, and relative pay stagnation on Sweden's Metall in the 1950s and 1960s. At that time in Sweden, low-pay unions had joined the Social Democratic government and employers in forcing through peak centralization with egalitarian wage policy, or interindustrial leveling at the expense of metalworkers. Lafontaine's proposal, it will be recalled, threatened to legitimate the Swedish idea of extra pay restraint for high-pay unions such as IG Metall. The German unions potentially friendly to Lafontaine's threat against high earners in the public sector tended also to be the same structurally weaker, low-pay unions that had supported DGB coordination, collective capital formation, and early retirement as ways of restraining IG Metall. Their temptation to do so was (and is) probably strong. In 1984, blue-collar workers in German engineering earned about 116 percent of what food industry workers did and 143 percent of what garment workers earned. In Sweden, engineering workers earned only 102 percent and 118 percent, respectively.[58]

The two unions' contrasting positions on public-sector pay parallels another difference between them on the issue of collective capital formation. In Sweden, the metalworkers' union supported Rudolf Meidner's famous wage earner funds, largely borrowed from the DGB's Bruno Gleitze,[59] since it offered justification for the wage restraint it had been compelled to exercise on behalf of the solidaristic policy of wage leveling across and within industries. Collective profit sharing promised to skim off so-called excess profits (associated with

57. Walters, "Distributing Decline," p. 65. Employment figures from *Statistisches Jahrbuch 1987* and *Statistisk årsbok 1987*.

58. Swedish Employers' Confederation, *Wages and Total Labour Costs for Workers: International Survey, 1974–1984* (Stockholm: SAF, 1986).

59. Meidner, "Deutsche Einflüsse auf die Schwedische Debatte über überbetriebliche Vermögensbeteiligung," in *Die Freiheit des Anderen: Festschrift für Martin Hirsch*, ed. Hans Jochen Vogel, Helmut Simon, and Adalbert Podlech (Baden Baden: Nomos Verlagsgesellschaft, 1982), pp. 377–88.

restraint by high-pay workers in high-profit firms) that appeared responsible for disruptive wage drift and wildcat strikes in the 1970s. But the relatively high-pay German metalworkers' union reacted vehemently against the other DGB unions' ambitions for collective capital formation. The leadership of IG Metall feared that collective profit sharing would help solidify and empower a coalition of union and government support behind employers' efforts to contain IG Metall's militancy. Collective capital formation would improve the chances for the DGB to encroach on IG Metall's bargaining autonomy by providing an egalitarian justification for wage restraint.

To put it succinctly, Swedish metalworkers sought wage earner funds as compensation for a loss of autonomy and related wage restraint, whereas German metalworkers opposed collective capital formation in *defense* of its militancy and autonomy because it lent egalitarian justification to the opposite. In both countries, "fund socialism" failed due to united business and conservative opponents who were never won over to the idea that its threats were outweighed by the advantages of the overall wage restraint it promised to foster. Intimidated by intense business opposition, Swedish Social Democrats passed a heavily watered-down version in the Riksdag. An unusual coalition of IG Metall and employers killed the issue in Germany. Ironically, the conservative unions could not count on the employer support they needed for their distributional challenge against IG Metall, for they were simultaneously challenging the power and privileges of capital as well.[60]

CONCLUSION: LABOR STANDS DIVIDED

Even in comparison to their West German counterparts, workers in the Swedish welfare state are numerous and well paid. For this reason, it is no surprise that private-sector unions in Sweden are at this time leading advocates of containing and reforming the welfare state. And, more immediately exposed and vulnerable to harsh international competition than their public-sector counterparts, Swedish private-sector unions such as Metall and Fabriks share compelling economic and political interests in joining outside groups interested in limiting the welfare state.

60. For an analysis of the wage earner funds debate in both countries, see Swenson, *Fair Shares*, pp. 129–223.

The Swedish case proves that capitalism's intellectuals such as Joseph Schumpeter have fretted all too much about the decay of capitalism's political defenses. Echoing Max Weber, Schumpeter longed for politically robust and charismatic bourgeois leadership from the ranks of the entrepreneurial class, which he thought modern capitalism destroys when it substitutes the corporate bureaucrat for the entrepreneur. Schumpeter may have been right in trusting oligopoly capitalism's indefinite economic vitality, but he was wrong in thinking that capitalism would not take care of itself politically in the postwar world.[61] For it seems that the politics of alliance formation, even when it includes the main organizational constituency of the welfare state, are part of its immune system. Leadership from a strong entrepreneurial class appears politically as well as economically dispensable. As a social basis for leadership, the allied officialdom of corporate capitalism, Social Democratic parties, and organized labor proves to be an effective substitute. The recent Swedish alliance led by export industry interests shows that national political processes set in motion by world market forces can check the forward movement of social democracy's international vanguards. Politically isolated, groups benefiting from the growth of the welfare state and opposing the alliance offer weak resistance.

Writing more recently from a different ideological vantage point, Claus Offe has argued that the state in capitalism responds to capitalism's changing needs, and therefore to its own, by creating an extensive "decommodified" realm of production, the welfare state. On the other hand, he argues, the welfare state weakens capitalism by draining resources from the commodified sector and undermining it ideologically by diffusing values antithetical to possessive individualism—capitalism's "normative or moral infrastructure."[62] Offe's dialectics are more open-ended than Schumpeter's, and they never quite guarantee the demise of capitalism. Rightly so, it seems; in the very country where capitalism should have suffered the most ideological decay, Swedish Social Democrats have led the way with moves to impose competition, incentives, and other marketlike disciplinary mechanisms

61. In *Capitalism, Socialism, and Democracy,* pp. 59–163, Schumpeter argued that capitalism could take care of itself economically (it would not collapse from its own crisis tendencies) but ultimately corroded its own political, cultural, and ideological foundations. See also Daniel Bell in *Cultural Contradictions,* pp. 77–80, on the "abdication of the corporate class."

62. Claus Offe, "Theses on the Theory of the State," in *Contradictions of the Welfare State* (Cambridge: MIT Press, 1984), pp. 119–29. In contrast, Schumpeter maintained that capitalism was politically strengthened by precapitalist culture and "protective social strata"—and hurt by capitalist values.

on the public sector. This ideological reaction has come from within the modern welfare state's own traditional constituency. Unions representing workers in the private sector have not only accepted for themselves a partial return to less egalitarian pay and employment practices as recommended by competitive individualism; they have also led the effort to impose partial "recommodification" on the welfare state itself.

Oskar Lafontaine's similar ideas for West Germany suggest that, if Social Democrats manage to regain power, they might also reform the welfare state on social democracy's own terms—that is, without privatization and by upholding traditions of quality and equality in the provision of health, education, and welfare.[63] If so, they will succeed only in alliance with outside pressures as they oppose their own constituents' relative income, bureaucratic unresponsiveness, and insulation from market discipline. This conclusion finds historical evidence in past labor politics in Sweden and West Germany, which show that social democracy's success measured in terms of parliamentary control is not necessarily foreclosed and may even be facilitated by intramural conflict.

"Labor-inclusionary" politics appear to result when labor movement factions are able to assert control over other unions on distributional terms suiting not only themselves but also powerful business groups and adroit leftist politicians with a keen eye for shifting coalitional possibilities. Comparative case analysis shows that internal power and distributional conflicts within labor movements structure opportunities for class-splitting, cross-class alliances through which labor movements most effectively bring their power to bear in parliamentary politics. Labor has acquired power, not only because of sheer numbers of votes or ideological unity, but because of internal distributional conflict that union leaders, politicians, and business groups can exploit. In that manner, labor turns apparent organizational adversity into political advantage. Though it divides labor, the crisis of the welfare state is not necessarily a crisis for social democracy.

63. Lafontaine, *Der andere Fortschritt*, pp. 103–13.

2 The Decentralization of Collective Bargaining in Belgium, France, and the United States

Jeannette Money

"History has not forged nor men invented a better instrument for struggle than organization."

—VICTOR SERGE, *Conquered City*

In this essay I examine the transformation of relations among the levels of union organization in France, Belgium, and the United States. Since the 1960s, much collective bargaining in these countries has been displaced from confederal and sectoral jurisdictions and relocated to the firm.[1] My analysis of this phenomenon focuses on a factor previously excluded from analyses of internal trade union politics: labor mobility. I argue that declining interfirm labor mobility created greater heterogeneity of rank-and-file bargaining demands. To manage this diversity, unions and employers selected a strategy of decentralization.

Conventional analyses of trade union movements in industrialized countries identify three stages of institutional change between the 1960s and the 1980s. In the first stage, trade unions witnessed a transfer of power and influence to the shop floor. Between 1974 and 1980, national confederations attempted to regain control of bargaining initiatives and to recentralize negotiations. Then, in the 1980s, a new phase of decentralization was introduced. In partial contrast to this periodization, I suggest that there is substantial continuity between the

I wish to acknowledge the useful comments and criticisms of Miriam Golden, Sanford Jacoby, Peter Lange, Jonas Pontusson, George Tsebelis, and Michael Wallerstein.

1. The three primary levels of union organization are the union local, the national union, and the confederation. To avoid terminological confusion, I adopt the following conventions: a national union is any organization that groups workers of a particular trade or industry on the national level; a confederation is the intersectoral, national organization to which national unions adhere.

1960s and the 1980s. Although union elites attempted to regain centralized control over the rank and file during the 1970s, their incomplete success can be understood in part as a product of secular trends in labor market structures.

To explain union and employer strategies, I propose a new way of modeling union bargaining demands. Rather than positing the traditional goal of maximizing union wages and employment, I assume that union leaders maximize membership. To retain union members, bargaining platforms incorporate the demands of union members at the extreme ends of the frequency distribution rather than those of the average union member. Consequently, growing diversity of member interests expands union demands for *both* employment and wage levels. To successfully conclude an agreement, unions and employers' organizations decentralize the process of collective bargaining to the level where worker demands are more homogeneous. Union leaders are than able to retain union members while moderating bargaining demands sufficiently to successfully conclude negotiations. I attribute growing fragmentation of member interests to a secular decline in interfirm labor mobility, although the cyclical decline in mobility during the economic recessions of the 1970s and the 1980s clearly aggravated these longer-term trends.

Variables other than declining labor mobility can universally or selectively contribute to decentralization of collective bargaining. Much of my argument is thus congruent with existing interpretations of trade union politics. Economic, political, institutional, sociological, and technological factors can each affect labor market structures as well as independently affect internal union politics. I am not attempting to refute these various accounts. Rather, where such factors affect my primary explanatory variable, labor mobility, I seek to incorporate them. My purpose, however, is less to offer a complete description of the causes of bargaining decentralization over the past few decades than to draw attention to a hitherto unnoticed contributory factor: the fall in rates of labor mobility.

To emphasize the decentralist trends in Western industrial relations is not to suggest that national unions and confederations have withered away. Both levels of union hierarchy continue to condition firm-level outcomes to a greater or lesser extent. Beginning from different levels of central control, the process of decentralization is less firmly rooted in some nations than in others. The firm's environment has, however, become increasingly important to the interaction between unions and employers. An understanding of this institutional evolution is critical in part because structure shapes union demands, strategies, and successes. Unions have long sought to take wages out of competition. Fragmentation of the bargaining apparatus through decentralization reintroduces wages into the competitive equation of the firm, thereby fragmenting the labor movement.

The essay is divided into four sections. I first sketch the argument theoretically. I then define the concept of labor mobility, differentiate between cyclical and secular trends, present some empirical evidence, and speculate about the sources of declining labor mobility. Next I analyze decentralization in Belgium, the United States, and France, weaving together labor market conditions, union responses, managerial strategies, and the transformation of collective bargaining structures; this is a "most different case" analysis in which the union movements considered vary along dimensions of unionization, centralization, concentration, and ideology. Finally, I address the implications of this decentralization and fragmentation for collective bargaining in the 1980s.[2]

THEORY

The flavor of collective bargaining in the 1980s is conveyed by Richard Edwards and Michael Podgursky's characterization:

> The bargaining structures built up over many years are crumbling and collapsing. Interindustry bargaining has given way to industry-by-industry crisis bargaining. Industry-wide agreements are yielding to company-by-company bargaining. And in the face of plant closure threats, company-wide agreements have been superseded or supplemented by plant-level concessions. Unions now find themselves negotiating with increasingly centralized corporations at an increasingly decentralized level.[3]

2. Although the scope of this article is limited to three nations in the industrialized West, evidence is growing that decentralization of the collective bargaining function is spreading to other nations. See the introduction to this volume as well as Wouter van Ginneken, "Wage Policies in Industrialised Market Economies from 1971 to 1986: Between Controls and Free Bargaining," *International Labour Review* 126 (August 1987): 379–404.

3. Richard Edwards and Michael Podgursky, "The Unraveling Accord: American Unions in Crisis," in *Unions in Crisis and Beyond,* ed. Richard Edwards, Paolo Garonna, and Franz Tödtling (Dover, Mass.: Auburn House, 1986), pp. 15–60; quotation from p. 46.

These comments were written in reference to the United States, but similar descriptions characterize the bargaining process in France and Belgium.[4] These three countries, as well as many other industrialized market economies, had carefully constructed regional, industrial, or intersectoral bargaining structures, structures that had emerged earliest in Belgium and become visible in the United States and France during the 1950s and 1960s. But by the 1980s, observations of decentralist trends were commonplace. To explain why collective bargaining agents selected centralized strategies in the 1960s and decentralized strategies in the 1980s, I start with the assumption that unions and employers are rational, utility maximizing actors and then explore changes in labor market conditions that caused employers and unions to modify their collective bargaining strategies.

Mobility and membership demands. Union members desire both high wages and employment security, but they confront a trade-off between the two. Higher wages cause employers to hire fewer workers; higher employment levels and greater job security accompany lower wages. Fluid labor markets, by equalizing wage and employment conditions, tend to compress the variance in worker demands for a particular wage/employment trade-off. Declining interfirm mobility, on the other hand, increases the diversity of conditions members face and therefore the diversity of demands for wage and employment levels.

If workers are mobile, they are indifferent to the economic conditions of the firm. In perfectly competitive labor markets, where workers are perfectly mobile, firms offer the going wage: a lower wage offer attracts no workers; a higher wage offer inundates the firm with qualified applicants. If the firm cannot cover its production costs at this wage, it goes out of business. Workers, however, are unaffected by the demise of an individual firm. Because they are by definition mobile, they can move to another firm if the first one fails. Mobility tends

4. For Belgium, see Thérèse Beaupain, "Vers un glissement des niveaux et du contenu de la négociation," in *L'évolution des relations industrielles en Belgique* (Louvain: Institut des sciences du travail, dossier no. 7, Catholic University of Louvain, 1985), pp. 115–31. For France, see François Eyraud and Robert Tchobanian, "The Auroux Reforms and Company Level Industrial Relations in France," *British Journal of Industrial Relations* 23 (July 1985): 241–59; Bernard Moss, "After the Auroux Laws: Employers, Industrial Relations and the Right in France," *West European Politics* 11 (January 1988): 68–80; and François Sellier and Jean-Jacques Silvestre, "Unions' Policies in the Economic Crisis," in *Unions in Crisis and Beyond*, ed. Edwards, Garonna, and Tödtling, pp. 173–226.

to equalize employment conditions and thus the demand for a specific wage/employment level.

If workers are immobile, their preferences for specific wage and employment levels become more closely tied to the economic fortunes of the individual firm in which they are employed rather than to the state of the economic sector or of the economy as a whole. The inability to move freely from one firm to the next makes the worker sensitive to a firm's specific conditions. If the firm is close to bankruptcy, workers become willing to lower relative wages in order to ensure continued employment. Workers in a successful firm, on the other hand, are optimistic about continued employment and therefore prefer higher wages. Immobility increases the diversity of working conditions and therefore the diversity of worker interests.

In practice, as I show below, evidence suggests that union labor mobility in the three countries investigated here—and perhaps in general as well—underwent substantial declines in the 1950s and 1960s. The impact of declining labor mobility was quite dramatic with time. As workers' ability to seek alternative employment fell, firms' specific circumstances came to condition worker interests in wages, employment security, and other working conditions. A variety of other factors contributed to the same outcome; widely different rates and types of technological innovation across firms and industries, for instance, also helped generate increasingly diverse employment conditions.

The result was a substantial widening of the material conditions workers confronted. While in one firm they might face relative employment security and stable wages, down the street men and women with the same skills, doing the same jobs, might find themselves confronting technological unemployment. The interests of similarly positioned groups of workers thus came increasingly to diverge, as different firms offered different combinations of wages, working conditions, and job security.

I argue that the pressure for bargaining decentralization arose as union leaders sought to manage the greater heterogeneity of the rank-and-file working conditions created by increasingly immobile labor markets. Diversity of worker interests affects union strategies in two ways. First, it increases the uncertainty associated with communicating rank-and-file interests to union leadership. Second, it expands the scope of demands incorporated in the union bargaining platform.

Uncertainty and union institutions. Union leaders seeking to remain in office develop a bargaining platform representative of union members' demands.[5] Efficient leaders develop methods of polling union members which require the least resources at an acceptable level of accuracy. Statistically, the greater the variance in the population, the greater the degree of uncertainty about union member demands, holding the polling technique constant. As diversity of member interests increases, union leaders develop different or expanded polling techniques to reduce the growing uncertainty.

Empirically, this does not mean that union leaders select a statistically valid sample of union members and send them survey questionnaires. I simply suggest that whatever methods were previously in use—word of mouth, annual conventions—no longer provide as accurate a picture of union membership when the variance in member interests increases. In response to indicators of member discontent over union contracts—wildcat strikes, membership losses—rational leaders modify polling methods to reduce uncertainty and to maintain membership support.

Demands and union strategies. Given the voluntary nature of trade unions, I assume that union leaders, in formulating bargaining demands, seek to maximize union membership; that is, rather than using the median trade union member as the basis for formulating demands, union leaders consider the preferences of members at either end of the frequency distribution. Bargaining demands are formulated to ensure that members are indifferent between the union program and defection from the union. The distance between the ideal position of the extreme members and the proposed bargaining platform selected by union leaders represents the "exit" costs to union members. These costs are a function of individual bargaining strength or the existence of alternative collective bargaining organizations.

Figure 2–1, part A, illustrates the scenario in which union member *A* prefers lower wages and higher employment, member *B* prefers higher wages and lower employment, and median member *C* lies between the two. In this case, the union leadership selects point *C*, and

5. This claim assumes that union officials are subject to some type of competition. Although the level of competition varies across unions and across countries, because union membership in industrialized nations is voluntary, union movements are all subject to some degree of either internal or external competition.

the distances *AC* and *CB* represent the exit costs to members *A* and *B* should they leave the union. Since here union member demands are relatively homogeneous and exit costs large, bargaining demands coincide with those of the median voter.

In part B, the distribution of union members' demands is wider. In evaluating the union bargaining platform, member *B* will resign if he can individually negotiate wages higher than those provided by the union, or if a second union (which may already exist or which he may organize) offers to present his higher wage demands. Member *A*, confronting the possibility of unemployment if her firm is uncompetitive at the union-supported wage rate, will resign in order to offer her services at lower than negotiated rates. Given this distribution of demands, in order to ensure that members *A* and *B* do not resign from the union, union leaders select point *X*, where both wage and employment demands are greater than those of the median union member *C*.

Two propositions follow from this model of demand formulation: First, as the diversity of union member interests increases, bargaining demands proposed by the union move farther from the median union member; all other factors being equal, greater diversity of member interests increases the scope of bargaining demands formulated by union leaders. Second, those unions whose members face higher exit costs present more moderate bargaining demands than unions whose members can resign with few consequences. Again, this is because the latter unions are under more pressure to formulate demands responsive to member interests in order to stave off resignations. Unions in the former category, knowing they are likely to retain members at both ends of the frequency distribution, conclude a bargain that is closer to the position of the median union member and is more acceptable to employers. Empirically, this suggests that, in nations with trade union pluralism, members experience lower exit costs and unions therefore formulate more extreme bargaining demands, whereas nations without trade union pluralism are characterized by more moderate union demands.

LABOR MOBILITY

Turnover at the level of the firm includes both voluntary (quits) and nonvoluntary (layoffs) separations from the firm. For my purposes,

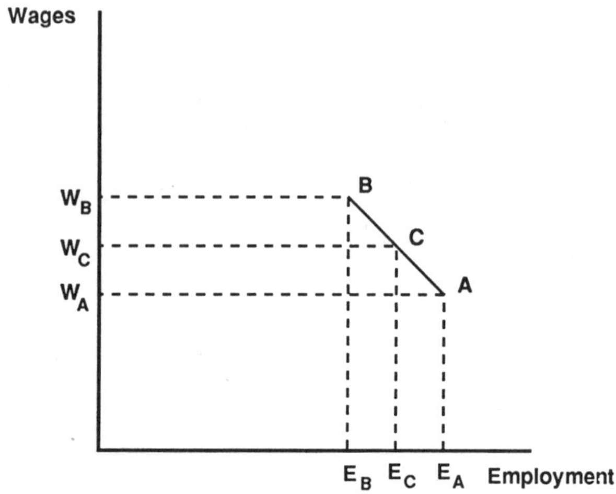

A. Bargaining demands with homogeneous member interests: the bargaining platform is identical to the demands of the median union member.

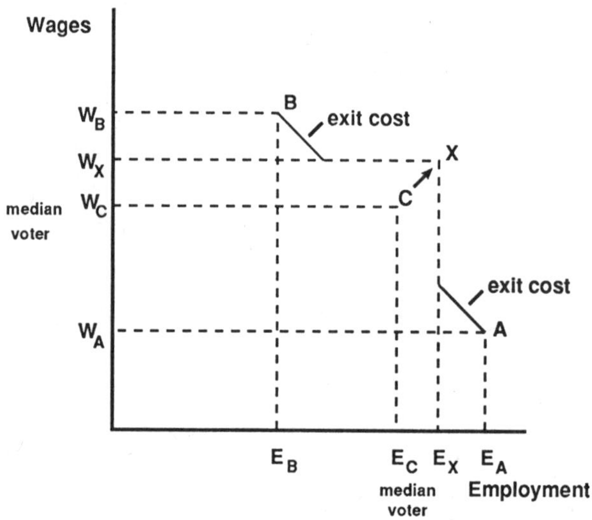

B. Bargaining demands with diverse member interests: the bargaining platform exceeds the demands of the median union member

Figure 2–1. Formulation of bargaining demands

labor mobility is confined to the former category, the voluntary departure of workers from firms. Mobility varies both among workers and over time. For example, younger workers tend to be more mobile than older workers; all workers are less mobile in economic recession than during periods of economic growth.

To understand how frequently workers change jobs, labor economists use a "search and information" model, which posits that workers attempt to maximize expected income in an environment where their knowledge of job opportunities is imperfect.[6] In such circumstances, the worker incurs search costs in an effort to determine whether other, more remunerative employment opportunities exist. Most simply, the employee quits only when the expected income from alternative employment is greater than the sum of current earnings plus search costs. Several implications follow from this simple model of labor mobility. The smaller the value of alternative employment, the less likely a worker is to move. On the other hand, the lower the current wage, the more likely the employee is to quit. Finally, reductions in search-and-move costs improve the likelihood of worker mobility.

Cyclical and secular variations in mobility. Conventional wisdom, as well as economic reasoning, suggests that workers are less likely to change jobs during a recession; fewer, less lucrative, employment opportunities are available. Empirical evidence supports the contention that labor mobility in advanced industrial countries fell during the recessions of the 1970s and 1980s. Such evidence, however, fails to explain the timing of union decentralization that originated in the 1960s. My argument requires attention to longer-term, secular changes in labor mobility which predate the oil crisis as well as to the usual cyclical patterns.

Evidence on labor mobility. The evidence on secular trends in labor mobility is speculative at best. Our concern with labor mobility really requires cross-national time series data on union labor mobility, but such a data set does not exist. Even where time series data on mobility are available, as in the United States, they encompass manufacturing employment in the economy as a whole rather than employment in firms where union bargaining occurs. Still, the primary and secondary

6. Donald O. Parsons, "Quit Rates over Time: A Search and Information Approach," *American Economic Review* 63 (1977): 390–401.

sources that do exist provide data congruent with the hypothesis of a secular decline in labor mobility.

Secondary analyses of U.S. labor mobility indicate a decline in union labor mobility after 1958. James Ragan examined labor mobility in the manufacturing sector between 1950 and 1978. After controlling for business cycles and changes in youth and female employment (those segments of the labor force least likely to be unionized), he found that mobility rose between 1950 and 1958 and declined thereafter.[7]

French mobility statistics exist only as of 1969, so it is impossible to trace the rise in mobility rates prior to the recorded decline experienced since 1969. But given the massive movement from agriculture into manufacturing in the early postwar period as well as the absolute growth of manufacturing employment, the assumption that union labor mobility increased in the 1950s and 1960s is at least reasonable. For the period after 1969, labor mobility for men, the most unionized segment of the workforce, declined every year except 1972 and 1978, when small increases occurred (0.6 and 0.2 quits per 100 workers per year).[8] This information, to be sure, gives only a small clue about unionized labor mobility, because unionization rates in France have never exceeded about 25 percent of the workforce. But French mobility statistics, although incomplete, are at least congruent with the hypothesis of declining labor mobility preceding the economic recessions of the 1970s and 1980s.

Belgians also started collecting mobility data only in the 1970s, under the auspices of the European Statistical Office of the European Communities. Time series data, however, are not publicly available.[9] Rising unemployment rates in key heavy industrial sectors of the economy provide an indirect indicator of increasing labor market rigidity.

7. James F. Ragan, Jr., "Investigating the Decline in Manufacturing Quit Rates," *Journal of Human Resources* 19 (1984): 53–71. Although the manufacturing segment of the economy is the most unionized, unionization rates varied from 51.3 percent in 1956 to 39.7 percent in 1978, making overall mobility rates an imperfect indicator of union labor mobility. Ragan's analysis, however, controls not only for the business cycle but for youth and female employment as well. Because those segments of the labor force are least likely to be unionized, the remaining variation in manufacturing labor mobility is the closest available to union labor mobility.

8. Michel Cézard and Daniel Rault, "La crise a freiné la mobilité sectorielle," *Economie et statistique* 184 (January 1986): 42.

9. The sole published source of Belgian mobility statistics is European Communities, Statistical Office, *Social Indicators for the European Community 1960–1975* (Luxembourg: Statistical Office of the European Communities, 1977). Only one year is published.

Whereas unemployment in the economy as a whole was low throughout the 1960s, unemployment in the coal industry began to rise in 1964, shortly after the collapse of the Belgian coal industry, and indicates the inability of miners to move from coal to other parts of the economy. Other sectors of heavy industry were also affected. Although the leap from this observation to a secular decline in labor mobility may be large, additional indirect evidence is suggested by the fact that, on a cross-national basis, Belgium had the lowest mobility rates in the European Community in 1977.

Timing and sources of declining mobility. Although the empirical evidence points to internal union changes in the late 1960s and early 1970s for the cases in question (1968 for France, 1970 for Belgium, and 1972 for the American United Mine Workers), my argument does not require a uniform and dramatic drop in labor mobility just prior to these institutional changes. As I illustrate through the three case studies, numerous other factors mediate between declining mobility and union strategies. For example, the mobility of United Mine Workers members declined dramatically during the 1950s, but worker discontent exploded only in 1964. This circumstance can be attributed in part to the timing of contract negotiations as well as to the national and international stature of the union's president, John L. Lewis, who retired only in 1960. After Lewis's departure, a decade-long struggle ensued before a grass roots movement seized control from an entrenched union leadership. Institutional reform immediately followed the 1972 victory of the Miners for Democracy. Hence, a variety of intervening variables helps explain the lag between declining mobility and union strategic reorientation.

If substantial uncertainties exist regarding the existence and timing of declining labor mobility, the sources of that decline are no less controversial. Many argue that the advent and spread of "internal labor markets" reduced labor mobility by removing hiring, training, and the allocation of personnel from market forces, instead subjecting those decisions to a set of administrative rules and regulations.[10] The sources of internal labor markets are, in turn, disputed: some scholars attribute them to a cost-conscious personnel management attempting to lower the costs of personnel turnover, others, to defensive managers

10. Sanford M. Jacoby, "Industrial Labor Mobility in Historical Perspective," *Industrial Relations* 22 (Spring 1983): 261–82.

responding to the rise of unionism. In support of the internal labor market hypothesis, Ragan argues that an increase in fixed costs relative to wages made labor turnover more costly to employers.[11] In response, employers raised the costs of quitting for employees. The rise of seniority-based fringe benefits serves as an example of such a strategy. In support of such an argument, U.S. evidence shows that employee benefits grew from 23.2 percent of payroll costs in 1959 to 42.5 percent in 1979. Evidence from the U.S. coal industry also supports the internal labor market hypothesis; the creation of the Welfare and Retirement Fund shortly preceded the decline in coal miner labor mobility.

A complementary hypothesis focuses on the shift from an industrial to a postindustrial society in which shrinking job opportunities in manufacturing generate declining union labor mobility. According to this view, relative employment in manufacturing is "the most satisfactory measure of the factory worker's opportunity to change jobs."[12] In Europe, manufacturing employment increased or remained stable relative to agricultural and service employment during the 1950s and 1960s, declining thereafter. In the United States, a similar line of reasoning applies to absolute levels in manufacturing employment rather than to relative employment levels. Although the transition to a service economy had been ongoing since well before World War II, the absolute number of jobs in manufacturing continued to increase until the 1960s despite its decline relative to other segments of the economy.[13] The increasing availability of jobs provided the alternative job offers necessary to induce mobility from one firm to another, from one industry to another. Once the absolute number of jobs began to level off, however, there were fewer offers and therefore declining mobility. Blue-collar workers were both unwilling and unable to shift to the tertiary segment of the economy which was undergoing expansion. The trend in declining union labor mobility was then aggravated by the absolute decline in manufacturing employment experienced more recently.

In sum, the empirical evidence on declining union mobility is somewhat speculative. The available data are congruent with the hypothesis

11. Ragan, "Investigating the Decline," pp. 62–64.
12. Ibid., p. 66.
13. Ibid. In the United States, manufacturing employment declined from 33.7 percent of total nonagricultural payroll employment in 1950 to 23.4 percent in 1979.

of secular decline but are not decisive. Theoretical work on internal labor markets and labor mobility tends to reinforce my interpretation of the evidence.

I have thus far proposed that the secular decline in labor mobility in the 1950s and 1960s had, by the 1970s, restructured the strategies chosen by union leaders to maximize union membership and by unions and employers to conclude collective bargains.[14] Confronting the uncertainty associated with increased heterogeneity of membership interests, union leaders installed more effective mechanisms to communicate with the rank and file. Better informed union leaders then more accurately incorporated demands of members at the extreme ends of the frequency distribution (after accounting for exit costs) into bargaining platforms, thereby expanding the scope of demands for both wages and employment. In response, employers simply rejected these demands. The inability to reach agreement on the national level then forced bargaining to the level at which union demands could be disaggregated. My focus on labor market conditions and labor mobility does not preclude the possibility that other, country-specific factors intervened to facilitate or hinder the decentralization of collective bargaining. Labor mobility, however, provides a common factor that explains a shared feature of the industrial relations landscapes in the three countries in question.

EVIDENCE

The level of institutional centralization is defined by the locus of trade union decision making and can reside anywhere from the shop floor to the national union confederation. The concept of centralization has been operationalized in part by the level of collective bargaining.[15] Determining the true level of collective bargaining may be difficult, however, because formal rules and existing structures do

14. In this essay I explicate union decentralization. Although I have not worked out an explicit parallel argument for employers, a similar logic should hold.

15. Bruce W. Headey, "Trade Unions and National Wages Policies," *Journal of Politics* 32 (1970): 407–39; Jelle Visser, "The Unification and Centralisation of the Trade Union Movement," (Florence: European University Institute, 1983); and John P. Windmuller, "The Authority of National Trade Union Confederations: A Comparative Analysis," in *Union Power and Public Policy*, ed. D. B. Lipsky (Ithaca: New York State School of Industrial and Labor Relations, Cornell University, 1975), pp. 91–107.

not always reflect actual practices. Shop-floor collective bargaining can be directed by the national union through the centralized appointment of shop-floor representatives, for instance. Conversely, national bargains may require membership approval. Therefore, I consider not only the actual arena of collective bargaining but also the level of union hierarchy in control of the bargaining process.

For each case, I first present information on collective bargaining institutions and the national bargaining framework that predated decentralization. I then link the indicators of growing labor immobility described in the previous section to leadership strategies to control the level of internal uncertainty through institutional changes in trade union structures. Finally, I describe the devolution of collective bargaining.

Belgium

With approximately 70 percent of the workforce unionized, Belgium has the strongest union movement of the three cases under review. Collective bargaining has also been historically more centralized there than in France or the United States. The locus of industrial relations shifted from the confederal to the national sectoral jurisdiction during the 1950s, and the national level began being displaced by firm-level bargaining in the 1980s.[16]

Collective bargaining structures. Employee representation in the firm dates from the immediate postwar period. Works councils and health and safety committees were established in 1948 and 1953, respectively. Employee representatives to these institutions are elected solely from union lists. Unions were also able to obtain shop-floor bargaining representation in 1947 by virtue of an agreement authorizing union delegates. The methods of selecting union delegates vary from union to

16. The discussion on Belgium is based on Etienne Arcq, *Les relations collective du travail en Belgique* (Brussels: Dossiers du CRISP no. 17, 1982); Etienne Arcq and Pierre Blaise, *Les organisations syndicales en Belgique* (Brussels: Dossiers du CRISP no. 23, 1986); Pierre Blaise, "L'accord interprofessional du 7 novembre 1986," *Courrier hebdomadaire du CRISP,* no. 1137 (December 5, 1986); Roger Blanpain, "Recent Trends in Collective Bargaining in Belgium," *International Labour Review* 104 (July-August 1971): 111–29; B. S. Chlepner, *Cent ans d'histoire sociale en Belgique* (Brussels: Editions of the Free University of Brussels, 1956); Thérèse Klein-Beaupain, *Deux systèmes de relations industrielles en Belgique* (Brussels: Editions of the University of Brussels, 1979); and Guy Spitaels, *Le mouvement syndicale en Belgique* (Brussels: Institute of Sociology, Editions of the University of Brussels, 1967).

union and have also been modified over the course of time. Each of these three firm-level institutions performs a different role: works councils serve as a conduit for enterprise information and employee consultation; health and safety committees ensure safe working conditions; union delegates perform grievance and collective bargaining functions. The first two bodies are legally required, subject to minimum firm size, whereas the third is optional. In fact, the extension of shop-floor bargaining representatives proceeded slowly. By 1955, eight years after they were recognized, only a few firms had union delegates.

At the national, sectoral level, the bipartite collective bargaining commissions that developed directly after World War I acquired legal status in 1945. These bipartite commissions constituted the locus of collective bargaining for much of the interwar and postwar periods. Directly before and after World War II, trade union confederations, representing all sectors of the economy, temporarily acted as the primary bargaining agents. Nationwide, intersectoral bargaining was invoked originally in 1936 at the height of the great depression, then in 1939–40 to regulate issues of wage indexation, and subsequently during the economic reconstruction of Belgium after World War II. Whatever tenuous control the confederations maintained over their national unions after 1936 had dissolved by the early 1960s, and collective bargaining devolved to the national, sectoral arena. This is not to suggest that Belgian industrial relations practices are completely uniform; customs vary across economic sectors. The chemical industry, for example, has always reserved core negotiations for the firm, whereas the textile industry conducts prototypical national level negotiations.

Labor mobility, uncertainty, and institutional change. Strike statistics provide evidence of the growing uncertainty confronting union leadership during the 1960s as labor mobility declined.[17] Spontaneous and wildcat strikes became common and the shape of industrial conflict changed. In comparison to the more volatile 1950s, the number of

17. Materials on Belgian strikes are drawn from Kim Dai Won, "Au delà de l'institutionalisation des rapports professionnels: Analyse du mouvement spontané ouvrier belge" (Doctoral thesis, Catholic University of Louvain, 1977); *Annuaire statistique de la Belgique* (Brussels: National Institute of Statistics, multiple years); and *Année sociale* (Brussels: Institute of Sociology, Editions of the University of Brussels, multiple years).

days lost due to strike activity actually declined, while the number of strikes almost doubled. Strikes in the 1950s involved whole sectors of the economy for relatively short periods, whereas in the late 1960s and 1970s strikes involved firms or regions and lasted longer. Between 1950 and 1959, 1,227 strikers participated in each strike, with 8.1 days lost per striker on average. Between 1970 and 1980, 372 strikers participated per strike, with an average of 10.6 days lost per striker. The structure of strike activity suggests the growing differentiation between and within sectors; the spontaneous or unauthorized nature of strikes confirms the growing uncertainty facing union leaders in formulating bargaining platforms.

The distance separating the rank and file from the union's leadership reached crisis proportions less than two years after the 1968 French social upheaval. Autonomous shop-floor action by miners, circumventing union leadership and denouncing a newly signed agreement, resulted in violence and led to a governmental crisis. Although the strike originated in a single sector without spreading to others, it mirrored member discontent with union leadership across the entire economy. The 1970 miners' strike acted as a catalyst for institutional changes that improved communication between the rank and file and union officials through a reinforcement of union presence in the firm. A 1971 agreement between unions and employers provided an increased number of union representatives in the firm, additional union training, and additional hours for union delegates to perform their duties. Informal shop-floor control over the contents of collective agreements was also extended: a systematic process of consultation and approval of agreements was established. These changes improved communications between the rank and file and union officials by allocating supplementary resources to that function and by formalizing the process of consultation.

The devolution of national bargaining. The most visible aspect of the collapse in union centralization was the termination of national, intersectoral bargaining. Unions and employers had met biannually since 1960 at the national, intersectoral level to negotiate indirect wages (vacation days, vacation bonuses, hours worked). The last agreement between the trade union confederations and the employers' association was drafted in 1974 and promulgated in 1975. Thereafter, as union demands began to reflect the extreme ends of the membership distribution, incorporated through the newly established procedures for membership consultation, employers became intransigent. A major issue was the reduction of the work week. Unions called for a 36-hour work week as a means of augmenting job opportunities. At the same time, however, members also demanded the maintenance of weekly wages. The socialist union confederation in particular, fearing defection of its powerful industrial unions, maintained its minimum demands at the national level and further rejected all policies limiting improvements in sectoral collective bargaining agreements.[18] In response, employers characterized union appetites as "insatiable," bitterly denouncing the demise of "social consensus."[19] In contrast to earlier periods when negotiations and concessions were the rule, industrial relations degenerated into "intransigent monologues."

Unable to reach agreement for more than seven years, unions and employers finally "agreed to disagree" at the national level. At this point, the government threatened to legislate wage scales if employers and unions failed to reach an accommodation. The outcome was a settlement that decentralized collective bargaining to lower levels. The most recent intersectoral agreement, concluded in 1986, also devolves issues of working hours and wages to lower levels.

This most visible aspect of collapse was reproduced on the sectoral level. One observer of Belgian industrial relations dates the decentralization of collective bargaining to 1971 (the year of union institutional change) and describes a process of regionalization, the proliferation of subcommissions and regional bipartite commissions, and their developing autonomy to conclude collective bargaining agreements.[20]

The practical result of this change, reinforced by government sanctions for failure to conclude collective agreements, has been the decentralization of the process of collective bargaining. Whereas the sectoral levels served as the primary negotiating arena in the early postwar period, now the firm is gaining in prominence. The process of decentralization is clearly demonstrated by the change in the number

18. *Année sociale* (1978), p. 139.
19. Jacques Moden and Jean Sloover, *Le patronat belge: Discours et idéologie, 1973–1980* (Brussels: Center for Research and Socio-Political Information, 1980).
20. Kim "Au delà de l'institutionalisation," p. 121.

of agreements concluded outside intersectoral and sectoral forums, from just under 9 percent in 1970 to more than 90 percent in 1985.[21]

In summary, Belgian industrial relations in the postwar period have undergone a continuous process of decentralization, moving from the confederal to the sectoral and then to the firm level. Union leadership responded to the growing heterogeneity of union member demands, created by declining interfirm mobility, by strengthening shop-floor institutions and developing procedures for polling members. Incorporating the demands of those who sought job security as well as those who demanded higher wages expanded the overall scope of union demands. Employers and unions then agreed to disagree at the national level and proceeded to conclude firm-level agreements. As a consequence, as Thérèse Beaupain observes, "the reinforcement of firm-level agreements is an accomplished fact.... On the whole, local contracts tend to reflect local bargaining strength, labor market conditions, and management policy, making for considerable disparities in actual earnings and terms of employment."[22]

United States

Those familiar with collective bargaining in the United States know the distinctiveness of the American system compared with the European. The requisite bargaining unit elections to win union recognition and the continuous role of the National Labor Relations Board (NLRB) in shaping the industrial relations landscape are foreign to the European experience. Despite these significant differences in industrial relations structures, a similar pattern of national wage parity developed in the United States during the 1950s and 1960s, only to be eroded in the 1970s and 1980s.

Collective bargaining structures. The 1935 National Labor Relations Act forms the legal basis for union representation and collective bargaining in the United States. It establishes workers' rights to organize

21. These statistics should be digested with a healthy dose of caution. As both Beaupain and Blaise note in presenting the figures, before 1983 there was no requirement to record firm-level collective bargaining agreements with the Conseil National du Travail. Still, the increase in agreements concluded outside intersectoral and sectoral forums is startling and is widely interpreted in Belgium as a sign of the growing significance of firm-level negotiations; see Beaupain, "Vers un glissement," p. 118, and Pierre Blaise, "L'accord interprofessionnel," pp. 24–28.

22. Beaupain, "Vers un glissement," p. 124.

and employers' responsibility to bargain in good faith. The structure of collective bargaining in the United States is in part a function of union recognition practices. Union representation is not universally granted, as in many European countries; rather, a majority vote of the workers themselves determines the union's status and the employer's responsibilities. Critical to the question of union structure is the size of the bargaining unit within which the workers vote. Legally, the bargaining unit is defined as "a group of workers who have a 'community of interests'."[23] The NLRA legislation does not specify the size of the bargaining unit; NLRB decisions have variously interpreted the legislation to include the plant, the firm, multiple employers, or even an entire industry. In practice, though, the requirements of collective bargaining are subservient to the requirements of union organizing. The union must first demonstrate that 30 percent of the members of the bargaining unit want a union (showing of interest), then win a majority vote in an election. Typically, the result is small bargaining units, due in large part to the organizational capacity of the union. Far from being the last part of the union structure put in place, firm-level representation constitutes the core of U.S. industrial relations.

The legal apparatus of the American industrial relations system centers at the plant or firm level. Four-fifths of workers covered by collective agreements (in firms of 1,000 employees or more) are covered by firm- or plant-level agreements.[24] Even where wage bargains have risen to higher levels, supplemental agreements are frequently negotiated in the firm. In contrast to Belgian and French practices, where working conditions are customarily regulated by legislation or form the subject of intersectoral agreements, central wage agreements, where they exist, are often complemented by agreements that govern shop-floor issues of job control.

Despite, or perhaps because, the locus of union recognition resides in the firm, unions in the United States developed and maintained strong national structures and tools for disciplining union locals and shop-floor representatives.[25] Union organizers and officials are often appointed by the national union, and the legal device of trusteeship allows national officials to take control of dissident union locals. These

23. William B. Gould, *A Primer on American Labor Law* (Cambridge: MIT Press, 1983), p. 43.

24. Edwards and Podgursky, "Unraveling Accord," p. 23.

25. Lloyd Ulman, *The Rise of the National Trade Union* (Cambridge: Harvard University Press, 1955).

practices allowed bargaining to rise to higher, even national (sectoral) levels, although the methods of achieving industry-wide parity varied. The United Automobile Workers, for example, made famous the system of pattern bargaining. Compensation parity across companies was achieved by targeting an individual firm each bargaining round to set the standard for agreements that followed. The "big-four" settlement, (Chrysler, General Motors, Ford, and American Motors) was gradually accomplished by diminishing intercompany differentials in the 1950s and 1960s. A similar pattern developed in the steel industry. Unions in regulated industries, communications and transportation, also achieved national agreements in the 1960s, as did other unions.

The coal industry. Although the coal industry is unrepresentative of U.S. industrial relations in many ways, an examination of the bargaining structures that developed there allows a clear comparison between Belgium and the United States and provides a substantial amount of detail on labor mobility, uncertainty, institutional changes, and employers' strategies.

Throughout its history, the United Mine Workers (UMW) has sought to achieve national wage bargaining in the coal industry, a goal finally realized in 1950.[26] Enterprise agreements were superseded by local, then regional, interregional, and finally national contracts. As early as 1898, the UMW concluded a "Central Competitive Field Compact" that included all workers in Indiana, Illinois, western Pennsylvania, and Ohio. This agreement collapsed under the weight of various factors in 1927 but was revived in an enlarged form in 1933 in the "Appalachian agreements." These settlements included coal operators in western Kentucky, northern Tennessee, West Virginia, and Virginia. Although Indiana and Illinois were no longer parties to the contract, they followed the pattern set in the Appalachian agreements. The decade of the 1940s was a period of bargaining disarray, but in 1950 the National Bituminous Coal Wage Agreement, covering all members of the Bituminous Coal Operators Association (BCOA), was signed. In 1950, the BCOA was "virtually industrywide, [a] multiemployer bargaining association that represented all but a small percentage of coal production capacity in the United States."[27]

26. Charles R. Perry, *Collective Bargaining and the Decline of the United Mine Workers* (Philadelphia: Industrial Research Unit, University of Pennsylvania, 1984).
27. Perry, *Collective Bargaining*, p. 113.

Under the leadership of John L. Lewis for the union and Harry Moses for the employers, national bargaining continued for almost a decade and a half. But declining labor mobility during this period began to attach miners to individual coal producers or specific regions, placing stress on national policies that exchanged wage increases for productivity increases while halving the mining workforce over the course of the decade. Again, there are no mobility statistics for union members only, but for the period in question 90 percent of coal was UMW-mined coal. The Bureau of Labor Statistics series indicates a dramatic decline in mobility to one-tenth of levels previously achieved, from 3.3 quits per 100 workers per month in 1949 to 0.3 quits per 100 workers per month in 1960.[28]

Following these declines in labor mobility, uncertainty about acceptable contract demands erupted in the early 1960s. Wildcat strikers in 1964 and 1966 protested the contents of the National Bituminous Coal Wage Agreement. This protest was followed in 1968 by an unauthorized strike when no agreement was reached prior to contract expiration. Tony Boyle, who inherited the Lewis mantle in 1963 after a short interim reign under Thomas Kennedy, failed to implement institutional changes to improve communication and was replaced by Arnold Miller in 1972 after a bitter and violent struggle. Miller immediately instituted constitutional changes that protected the autonomy of union districts and established a new procedure for contract ratification. Henceforth contracts required the approval of the rank and file. Both changes were critical to the bargaining process. District presidents sat on the bargaining board, providing a channel of communications to individual districts, and membership ratification procedures assured that one district's demands would not be traded against those of a second district.

These procedural changes preceded a qualitative change in the scope of miners' demands at the bargaining table. A coal industry observer noted that the "return to democracy . . . brought a visible expansion in the size and scope of the union's bargaining demands." In the 1974 contract negotiations, the union sought "*both* a sizable economic package and a host of changes in work rules designed to protect the 'health and safety' of miners," rules that expanded the workforce and provided

28. Although turnover data have been collected since 1930 for some manufacturing sectors, statistics on coal mining began to be tabulated in 1943; see the U.S. Bureau of Labor Statistics, *Monthly Labor Statistics*.

higher employment levels.[29] The operators' response to union demands was swift. BCOA members with western surface mining operations negotiated a distinct regional agreement in 1975, the Western Surface Mining Agreement. In the east, the BCOA attempted to stand firm against union-negotiated demands. When the operators' organization caved in to union demands, BCOA members began to defect. In 1978, both Pittsburgh and Midway abandoned the association. 1979 saw the temporary withdrawal of Consolidated Coal, the second largest coal producer in the United States, whose leadership was instrumental in the formation of the BCOA in 1950.

Withdrawal of coal operators from the BCOA, competition from rival unions, and the inability to organize new mines contributed to the collapse of national bargaining. A substantial decline in coal production covered by the national contract resulted. By 1970, only 70 percent of U.S. coal was produced under BCOA/UMW contract, and this percentage fell below 50 percent by 1980.[30] The UMW has now become a regional coal mining union representing primarily Appalachian miners.

This transformation of collective bargaining in the coal industry shows remarkable similarities to the Belgian experience: declining mobility, tension between the rank and file and union leadership, internal institutional changes, expansion of union demands, and employer intransigence. The type of decentralization is distinctive: although the UMW continues to sign "national" agreements, those agreements are now effectively regional. Non-UMW miners have found alternative representation with the International Union of Operating Engineers or the International Brotherhood of Electrical Workers, or they remain unrepresented. In contrast to the Belgian (and other European) experience, the lack of universal union recognition in the United States often amounts to nonbargaining rather than decentralized bargaining.

Other sectors of the economy. A similar pattern is reflected in other sectors of the American economy, albeit with some structural variation. Because most collective bargaining is traditionally located in the firm, national wage bargains were attained partly by dispossessing union locals of control over bargaining activities. The change in union institutions therefore took a different form than in Belgium; in the

29. Perry, *Collective Bargaining,* p. 98.
30. Ibid., p. 113.

United States, bargaining decentralization is reflected in the demands for internal union democracy. One early assault on national union control over firm-level representatives occurred with the Landrum-Griffin Act of 1959. Despite the official position of the AFL-CIO against the proposal many members of the labor movement supported its passage.[31] The Landrum-Griffin Act reinforced membership control over the activities of union leaders. The ability of national offices to discipline union locals which had developed over the previous decades was undermined by provisions that ensured union members' right to elect union officials every three years. These provisions aided grass roots groups within some unions to assume control of the national apparatus, in some cases inaugurating further decentralization and democratic reform. The provisions of the act posed a potential, if not immediate, threat to the entrenched leaders and ensured that greater attention would be paid to rank-and-file demands. Marten Estey provides only one of many reports that suggest that institutional change expanded union demands at the bargaining table. He describes employers as "wishing for a return to one-man rule in unions—to 'responsible' union leaders with final authority to make a binding decision which management can be confident will not be rejected by the membership."[32]

The demise of national coal agreements was therefore not unique. Shop-floor input into the collective bargaining process expanded the scope of negotiating demands, and employers slowly began to withdraw from national bargains in various other sectors as well. Parity in the automobile industry broke down when American Motors, facing bankruptcy in 1977, failed to follow the established pattern. Shortly thereafter, the "big three" became the "big two" with the Chrysler collapse of 1979. The structures of collective bargaining in the automotive industry, as elsewhere, did not merely reflect the changed position of individual firms. When labor markets provided sufficient

31. The Labor-Management Reporting and Disclosure Act, also known as the Landrum-Griffin Act, was actively opposed by the AFL-CIO. But some members of the labor movement itself were concerned with the protection of trade union democracy. According to the National Lawyers Guild, a "number of members of the labor movement, as well as traditional allies of the labor movement, became disturbed at the extent to which some union officials were abusing their power"; see National Lawyers Guild, National Labor Committee, *Employee and Union Member Guide to Labor Law* (New York: Clark Boardman, 1985), section 8, p. 4.

32. Marten Estey, *The Unions: Structure, Development, and Management* (New York: Harcourt Brace Jovanovich, 1976), pp. 53–63.

mobility for workers to find alternative employment in the face of firm bankruptcy, unions refused to acknowledge individual defections. Firms went out of business (Studebaker) and national bargains were maintained. In the 1970s, unions began to negotiate separate agreements with defectors, indicating that unions themselves had modified their bargaining strategies and were responding to a diversity of membership interests through decentralized bargaining. This was true in other industries as well. National agreements in transportation (trucking, air traffic controllers, intercity buses, airlines), communications, and steel, among others, also broke down in the late 1970s and early 1980s.

In summary, many U.S. unions achieved national wage parity in the 1950s and 1960s, despite the firm-level focus of the American industrial relations system. Collective bargains varied from the company-by-company pattern bargaining established by the United Auto Workers to the comprehensive national agreements of the UMW. Union leadership responded to changing labor market conditions by modifying internal union structures to ensure enhanced communication between members and union officials. Employers only then began to miss "responsible" union leadership and withdrew from national bargains. Timing of the demise of national bargaining varied but, as the case of the UMW illustrates, it followed a period of declining labor mobility and preceded the recession of the 1970s.

France

Industrial relations in France have generally been codified and transformed through legislation. My examination of French collective bargaining therefore centers on the legislative history of industrial relations. The requirement for unions and employers to bargain annually at the firm level was initially enacted in 1982, under the first majoritarian Socialist government in French history. This industrial relations reform is attributable to the changed political scene, but pressure for decentralization arose earlier and had a longer history of legislative lobbying efforts.[33]

33. The discussion on France draws from Guy Caire, "Recent Trends in Collective Bargaining in France," *International Labour Review* 123 (November-December 1984): 723–41; Paul Durand, "The Evolution of Industrial Relations Law in France since the Liberation," *International Labour Review* 74 (December 1956): 515–40; Eyraud and Tchobanian, "Au-

Collective bargaining structures. Historically, firm-level union structures were poorly developed in France. The lowest organizational unit of the trade union was the union local (*syndicat*), which organized trade union members by trade and by city; union representatives had no authorized role or presence in the firm. The development of worker representation in the firm was a source of continuous conflict between unions and employers as both sought to control the institutions that developed. The earliest form consisted of "personnel delegates," a product of the Matignon agreement that followed the 1936 strikes. The agreement was legally replicated in 1946 when the presence of personnel delegates was required in firms of more than 10 employees. The second major post–World War II industrial relations reform was the creation of works councils, formally installed in firms of more than 100 employees in 1945 and immediately extended to firms of more than 50 employees in 1946. The degree of union control over works councils as well as personnel delegates is ambiguous because representatives for both are selected by secret elections in which all employees, not just union members, vote. Election lists are presented by "representative" unions in the first round, but in the second round nonunion employees are also able to stand for election. Unlike developments elsewhere, these firm-level institutions rarely served as bargaining sites. Personnel delegates are authorized to present employee grievances to management, and works council representatives manage the firm's social works and serve as a conduit for management information to employees regarding the organization of work.

Collective bargaining developed slowly and reflected union and employer organizational structures. Prior to World War II, collective bargaining was relatively undeveloped. In the postwar period, the national level was initially privileged. A 1946 law designed a hierarchical system of bargaining that required the conclusion of a national agreement before regional or local negotiations could commence. In 1950, unions and employers were freed from a predetermined hierarchical

---

roux Reforms"; Peter Lange et al., *Unions, Change and Crisis* (London: Allen & Unwin, 1982); René Mouriaux, *Les syndicats dans la société française* (Paris: Presses of the National Foundation of Political Science, 1983); Organisation for Economic Co-operation and Development, "France," in *Collective Bargaining and Government Policies in Ten OECD Countries* (Paris: OECD, 1979), pp. 38–57; Jean-Daniel Reynaud, *Les syndicats, les patrons, et l'état: Tendances de la négociation collective en France* (Paris: Workers Editions, 1978); Adolf Sturmthal, "Collective Bargaining in France," in *Contemporary Collective Bargaining in Seven Countries*, ed. Adolf Sturmthal (Ithaca: Institute of Industrial and Labor Relations, Cornell University, 1959), pp. 127–67.

bargaining process: local, regional, and national agreements could coexist. Firm-level agreements were not prohibited, but neither were they acknowledged. In practice, emphasis quickly shifted from the national level to the departmental or regional subunits, determined in large part by the scope of the employers' organizations.

Gradually, national bargains became important, in part through the process of extending agreements to firms in the same industry or in similar industries. The concept of extending the scope of collective bargaining agreements originated in 1936 legislation and was maintained in subsequent industrial relations legislation. The practice slowly spread. Although even now collective wage bargaining plays a smaller role in France than elsewhere in the industrialized West, due partly to the weakness of the French labor movement, national wage agreements achieved through extension do affect wage structures. Collective wage agreements usually set minimums rather than actual wage increases. These are often unilaterally determined by employers. Still, minimum wages often require the readjustment of the wage hierarchy in order to maintain appropriate wage/skill differentials. Wage agreements therefore affect a large portion of the workforce.

Labor mobility, uncertainty, and institutional change. Increasing uncertainty created by growing worker heterogeneity is evident in the rapid growth of the Confédération Française Démocratique du Travail (CFDT) to the detriment of the Confédération Générale du Travail (CGT). A transformation of the Christian Confédération Française des Travailleurs Chrétiens (CFTC) established in 1964, the CFDT not only presented a nonconfessional alternative to the communist CGT but traditionally emphasized strong shop-floor union representation and continuously fought for union presence in the firm.

Uncertainty regarding the nature of union member demands was confirmed by the 1968 upheavals in France. Although union confederations were quick to overtake the general strike and provide leadership and direction, a major outcome contained in the Grenelle agreement and formalized in legislation was the institution of union sections within the firm itself. Union sections alone are empowered to sign a collective agreement. Shortly thereafter, firm-level bargaining was specifically recognized. Moreover, shop-floor input is guaranteed by provisions for submitting draft agreements negotiated by trade union representatives to a general assembly of the firm employees, a practice established since the 1968 strike.

Unlike the Belgian and U.S. cases, union institutional changes in France appeared to have little effect on the conclusion of national agreements. In 1981, only 10 percent of French firms were covered by company agreements, whereas 77 percent were covered by industry-level agreements—basically because employers found a moderate opponent in one representative union, Force Ouvrière (FO). FO was able to moderate its demands in part because its ties to the shop floor are minimal. Formed by scission from the CGT in 1947 and 1948, FO's membership was and continues to be concentrated in the public sector. Few of its members are manual workers. But the legislative definition of "representative" union allows FO to negotiate and sign agreements even in sectors where it regularly polls less than 10 percent of the workforce. In contrast, those unions with strong shop-floor ties, the CGT and CFDT, refused to sign most national agreements.[34]

The devolution of national bargaining. Because moderate national agreements continued to be negotiated in France, sustained pressure emanated from radical unions to decentralize collective bargaining. That pressure is reflected in the different lobbying positions of the three major trade union confederations. All three unions sought to reinforce the labor movement through legislation. FO, the union with the fewest shop-floor ties, adamantly opposed shop-floor bargaining. In contrast, both the CGT and the CFDT supported the reinforcement of unions in the firm. The CFDT developed a philosophical justification for *autogestion,* or self-management, and began campaigning on behalf of employees' right of expression in the firm in 1973. Even prior to 1968, the CFDT made strong demands for the legal recognition of trade union branches in firms. The CGT focused on politics in hopes of obtaining a political majority of the left, but when that strategy failed in the 1978 legislative elections it also adopted a platform of *autogestion* in the firm.

Union pressure on the government to decentralize collective bargaining was continuous after 1968. The conservative government of

34. For example, the March 17, 1975 agreement was signed by the FO, CFTC, and CFE-CGC (the managerial union). Both the CGT and the CFDT refused to sign. The same is true of the 1971 Paris metalworking industries agreement. But both the CGT and the CFDT do sign some agreements. In general, the CGT is more contestatory than the CFDT.

Giscard d'Estaing surveyed industrial relations structures and recommended the firm as a locus for collective bargaining in the 1975 Sudreau report. Employers who benefited from moderate national wage agreements negotiated with FO opposed the devolution of bargaining and were sufficiently strong to ward off reform efforts under the conservatives. They were unable to maintain their influence when the Socialist government was elected in 1981. Union lobbying finally resulted in the Auroux laws of 1982. For the first time in France, there is a requirement to bargain in good faith. The new legislation requires firms and unions to bargain annually over wages, hours, and working conditions and gives workers the right of collective expression. The Auroux laws also reinforce the representativeness of bargaining structures: trade unions that obtain a majority in works council elections are given veto power over agreements. Two "representative" organizations can veto the extension of collective agreements.

The Auroux laws provide for industry-wide bargaining in which firm-level agreements reside. But institutional structures within the trade unions themselves allow shop-floor militants to shape firm-level bargaining. Because "grass-roots support is never guaranteed . . . trade union officials within firms tend to support the immediate aspirations of their members."[35] Union leaders promote firm bargaining in order to maximize membership support and prevent the defection of members to other unions.

The results of the Auroux reforms are only now being reaped. By June 1984, more than 3,500 enterprise agreements had been reached. Bernard Moss confirmed the decentralization of bargaining in a 1988 article where he reported a continuing increase in firm agreements accompanied by decreased industry wage accords.[36]

In summary, union structure and collective bargaining processes in France traditionally centered on the industrial sector. Agreements were negotiated on the departmental or regional level and extended to the national level, or they were negotiated at the national level. Declining labor mobility led to greater uncertainty in collective bargaining, an uncertainty reflected in strike statistics and the changing relative power of union confederations. Union leaders, seeking to control the level of uncertainty, obtained the establishment of union sections in the firm and implemented a shop-floor review of draft

35. Eyraud and Tchobanian, "Auroux Reforms," pp. 251–52.
36. Moss, "After the Auroux Laws," p. 75.

agreements. The ability of employers to find a moderate bargaining partner at the national level forced the two unions with greatest shop-floor ties to demand the legislative reinforcement of collective bargaining at the plant level. Employers and their moderate trade union partner were able to fend off this decentralist pressure under the conservative government, but a decentralist reform was implemented in 1982 under the Socialists. François Eyraud and Robert Tchobanian conclude: "The obligation to negotiate imposed on firms by the state has indeed led to a change in the nature of bargaining, despite the hostility of employers towards such institutional intervention in the organization of work and the unions' fears that forms of representation and redress over which they had no control would develop.[37]

MOBILITY, UNION POLITICS, AND CLASS CONFLICT IN THE 1980s

I have proposed a model of union demand formulation to explain features of internal union politics and collective bargaining strategies. Changes in strategy arise from rising diversity of worker demands, in turn attributed to declining labor mobility. Pressures for decentralization are, however, mediated by the exit costs of workers from the union. Exit costs, in turn, are a function of the worker's individual bargaining power and alternative possibilities of collective representation. If these arguments are correct, they illuminate several dilemmas union leaders confronted in the 1980s.

If the proposed model of demand formulation clarifies the sources of intraunion conflict, it also explains the tension that arises between trade unions and contributes to the vertical fragmentation of the labor movement. In a world of imperfect information, union leaders are likely to miscalculate the exact point X that would prevent all defections. Therefore, a small stream of defections to alternate organizations, or the creation of a new organization of collective action, can be anticipated. As time passes, however, defections are likely to increase the homogeneity within each union but decrease the homogeneity between unions. Suppose uncertainty causes leaders of union A to propose X' rather than the true value X that would prevent all defections.

37. Eyraud and Tchobanian, "Auroux Reforms," p. 252.

This choice of *X'* emphasizes employment security over wage levels, so those union members who prefer higher wages defect and join union *B*. Similarly, union *B* officials confront the same uncertainty and select *Y'* rather than the true value *Y* that would prevent defections. Union *B* officials, however, err on the side of wage demands, so their defectors are those who favor employment security. At the end of the period, both unions are more internally homogeneous, but ideal bargaining positions diverge more, making coordination of bargaining more difficult. This dynamic, which intensifies vertical cleavages within the trade union movement, is visible in the three case studies, mediated through union institutional structures.

In Belgium, institutional fragmentation increased in the 1980s while coordination and cooperation decreased. Historically, three trade union confederations (socialist, Christian, and liberal) were granted "representative" status in the early postwar period, reinforcing their monopoly of representation. But, union leadership in all three unions miscalculated, to a greater or lesser extent, the ideal strategy to prevent defection of unionized managerial personnel; the formation of a distinct managerial confederation followed. This new confederation gained representative status in 1986, the first to obtain such a grant for forty years. This success was perceived as a serious defeat and further fragmented power within the Belgian working class. Now, bipartite and tripartite boards that abound at all levels of the Belgian economy require coordination of four, rather than three, confederal policies, a heroic task. This episode illustrates the growing cleavages between managerial and nonmanagerial personnel in a nation where such differences were previously encompassed within the existing trade union structures.

The model also suggests that cooperation between confederations reinforces the tendency for dissatisfied workers to defect to alternative organizations, thereby constraining the ability of confederations to form a common front. In Belgium, this tension is visible in the devolution of cooperation from the national to the regional, sectoral, subregional, or firm levels, where labor market conditions are more similar.[38] The most important of these was the adoption of a common program by the Wallonian socialist and Christian regional unions in 1981, which facilitated and reinforced solidarity at lower levels but so-

38. Arcq and Blaise, "Les organisations syndicales," p. 23.

lidified the diversity between regions and increased interunion conflict at higher levels.

The effects of this phenomenon are not limited to the economic arena. Belgian unions have traditionally cemented national unity across the linguistic differences that divide the country. When Belgian political parties split into Wallonian and Flemish branches during the 1960s and 1970s, unions promoted labor solidarity across this division. Now, decentralized bargaining reinforces territorial divisions and promotes intraregional solidarity. One of the last barriers to territorial divorce in Belgium is rapidly disintegrating.

In France, trade union pluralism has been a continuous obstacle to the labor movement. Yet, when mobility was sufficiently high, the communist CGT was able to negotiate a common position with the socialist CFDT. The collapse of political cooperation surrounding the 1978 legislative elections undoubtedly affected the prospects for trade union unity, but the "unity in action" agreement between the two largest French trade union confederations was never renewed despite the accession to power of a leftist government in 1981. Declining mobility has reinforced rather than relieved union competition, as witnessed by the continuously shifting balance of power between the trade union confederations and the remarkable success of FO in the 1980s. Although demographics of union membership are nonexistent or unavailable, there is a general perception that each confederation represents a particular type of worker: CGT is a predominantly blue-collar union, whereas CFDT represents white-collar workers, FO, public-sector workers, and CFE-CGC, managerial employees.

In the United States, the self-exile of the UMW from the AFL and the CIO facilitated the rise of dual unionism in the coal industry. The cleavage is most clearly visible between underground and surface mining, representing the declining and expanding segments of the coal industry, respectively. While the UMW has maintained its dominance in representing underground miners, it faces stiff competition in surface mining from the International Brotherhood of Electrical Workers and the International Union of Operating Engineers. Further, the electric workers' union organizes "captive" surface mines owned by the electrical utilities, whereas the union of operating engineers organizes surface mines that sell coal on the open market.

In other sectors of the economy, where AFL-CIO arbitration has limited jurisdictional disputes, internal union politics have grown more divisive, the dissident movement within the United Auto Workers being only one prominent example. Here, high exit costs limit but do not preclude defection; the disadvantage of high exit costs is growing internal union conflict, as the more diverse members voice their opposition to bargaining platforms.

The American example suggests that, although trade union pluralism reinforces fragmentation under conditions of labor market rigidity, a centralized union movement confronts its own distinct problems when coping with declining labor mobility. In highly centralized systems where union confederations control the bargaining apparatus, they risk the defection of entire sectoral unions, as witnessed by the Swedish metalworkers' defection during the late 1970s and 1980s. They also face eventual competition from new or previously marginal unions.

But perhaps the most common response to declining mobility in either type of union structure is the departure of union members whose skills allow them to strike a better individual bargain with employers. As bargaining becomes more decentralized and lower-level bargains begin to reflect *either* employment *or* wage concerns, the benefits of defection accruing to workers with individual labor market power begin to exceed exit costs. Thus, the most talented and capable workers, who previously formed the core of union membership and replenished the ranks of union leadership, are deserting the union movement.

The model presented here may help clarify the dilemmas confronting union leaders as well as their successes and failures in the 1980s. It explains why nations with trade union pluralism have developed a reputation for profligate demands and have been unable to overcome labor movement fragmentation. In turn, it suggests that nations with centralized trade union movements are more effective in the pursuit of solidaristic policies, although they are not completely immune to the eventual creation of alternative organizations of collective action. In those nations where institutional structures present high exit costs, however, internal union conflict can be expected to grow as union members begin to voice dissatisfaction with the bargains struck. Both types of union movements face the defection of the most talented workers, who are striking out on their own to negotiate more favorable bargains with individual employers. Retaining this group of potential labor leaders and enlisting their resources is surely one of the most pressing issues of the 1990s.

Part 2

INDUSTRIAL UNIONS AND SECTORAL CHANGE

3 North American Autoworkers' Response to Restructuring

Charlotte Yates

The 1980s were a decade of adjustment and restructuring for the North American auto industry. Faced with intensified international competition, declining profits, and shrinking domestic markets, the "big three" automakers (General Motors, Ford, and Chrysler) undertook to increase their competitiveness, thereby ensuring their survival, by rationalizing and restructuring production. This process, not unique to the auto industry, has led to plant closures and demands for concessions from workers and unions in a drive to construct a more flexible labor process, one no longer characterized by the rigidities and inefficiencies associated with old Fordist production techniques. These corporate moves represented an attack on existing regulatory structures of collective bargaining which had served to stabilize labor-management relations in the postwar period and secure for unions a place of prominence and power in the workplace and society. As such, this corporate strategy constituted a threat to the International Union of United Automobile, Aerospace and Agricultural Workers of America (UAW), which until 1984 represented both Canadian and American autoworkers.

In spite of belonging to the same union, confronting identical corporate employers, and working from similar regulatory structures of

I wish to thank Jane Jenson, Rianne Mahon, and Robert Currie for their comments on this essay. Thanks also to the Social Sciences and Humanities Research Council of Canada for financial support of some of the research for this essay.

collective bargaining, the Canadian and American sections of the UAW chose to respond quite differently to the challenge of the 1980s. Canadian union members rejected the automakers' attempts to dismantle the existing regulatory structures of collective bargaining. The Canadian UAW sought to defend existing arrangements and in so doing to secure a position of strength from which it could affect the planning of any new regime of production and collective bargaining. The union did this by pursuing a strategy of mobilizing rank-and-file autoworkers to resist concessions and plant closures. In contrast, the American section of the UAW acquiesced to corporate solutions to the economic and industrial crisis. The union agreed to concessions, entered into profit-sharing agreements, and encouraged participation in labor-management productivity discussion groups. The American union leadership, backed by various industrial relations experts, attempted to sell this cooperative union strategy as the only means to increase the international competitiveness of the American auto industry and hence save jobs and the union.

In this essay I seek to answer two questions. Why did the Canadian and American autoworkers choose such different courses of action in response to capital restructuring in the auto industry? What impact have these different strategies had on the two unions? I argue that union strategy is a matter of choice, circumscribed by limits arising from national political-economic conditions but not *determined* by these external factors. The Canadian UAW's decision to pursue a militant course of action rather than a cooperative strategy similar to that chosen by its American counterpart stemmed from the different internal dynamics of the two unions as well as their divergent historical experiences in dealing with rank-and-file discontent in the late 1960s and early 1970s. These two sets of factors combined to leave open to the two unions different strategic options and resources.

In the first section of this essay I lay out the main theoretical tenets of the argument on the internal dynamics of unions, and in the second I briefly summarize the regulatory structures of collective bargaining in the postwar auto industry. The next two sections are examinations of the particular internal dynamics of the Canadian and American UAW and their effects on the strategic capacity of these two unions. In the fifth section I discuss how the two strategies adopted by the Canadian and American UAW in the 1970s to deal with rank-and-file militancy opened up different subsequent strategic options for these unions. Finally, I draw on earlier sections to explain the different strategies pursued by the Canadian and American unions in the 1980s and assess their implications for the union.

THE INTERNAL DYNAMICS OF UNIONS: A THEORETICAL APPROACH

Unions are strategic actors that make choices about their activities in the political and economic arenas. These choices, although conditioned by external factors such as the state of the economy and the political environment, are not determined externally. Rather, a union's past choices and practices and its analysis of society and organized labor's place within it influence the particular course of action chosen by a union.

Having made their choice, unions must be able to successfully pursue their chosen course of action. Here I refer to this ability as a union's strategic capacity. Different unions have variable strategic capacity, just as one union's strategic capacity differs at various points in time. Union strategic capacity is influenced by two sets of factors. First, it is influenced by existing political-economic conditions; for example, when competition for jobs is intense due to high unemployment, a union's ability to undertake certain activities is restricted. Second, a union's strategic capacity is shaped by the union's available resources and its effectiveness in marshaling these.

The most important resource of industrial unions is their organization of large numbers of workers. The degree to which this resource can be mobilized to enhance the strategic capacity of a union rests on the ability and willingness of these large numbers of workers to engage in united collective action, with the final sanctioning power being the strike. To use effectively the resource of large-scale membership as a basis for power, and ultimately a successful strategic battle with capital and the state, unions are confronted with two contradictory dimensions of power. The first dimension is derived from the collective organization of workers, which ultimately comes down to a question of size. The second dimension rests on the union's ability to mobilize successfully any group of workers into collective action. Whereas the first dimension of power relies on the ability of a union to organize more workers or at least to maintain existing memberships, the second requires that a union articulate and redefine the diverse interests of its membership in such a way as to mobilize this diversity behind a united strategy of collective action. There is obviously a potential contradiction between these two dimensions: a larger and more diverse union generally finds it more difficult to mobilize behind a single project.[1]

Two factors may either facilitate or impede the ability of a union to mobilize successfully its large and potentially diverse membership behind a course of collective action: the union's organizational structure and its collective identity. Traditionally, political scientists have argued that unions, like most large organizations, develop a bureaucracy as they grow larger. This organizational structure tends to separate union leaders from the rank and file and create organizational barriers to the articulation of common interests and to mobilization behind a common course of action. This tendency leads Claus Offe and Helmut Wiesenthal to conclude that there is an optimal size for unions beyond which they become incapable of constructing unity out of the diversity of their memberships.[2]

This analysis is problematic. First, it reduces the complex questions of unions' mobilization capacity to that of size. Second, and for our purposes more important, it reduces the study of organizational structure to one of bureaucracy in general. Although all unions tend to become bureaucratic, the potential variety of structures for and the political dynamics of interest intermediation in unions is lost in this type of analysis. Rather than focusing on the effects of bureaucracy in general, it is more instructive to examine the actual processes and changing structures of representation inside a union and thereby to assess the tensions between leadership centralization and rank-and-file control.

Briefly, there are three aspects of union organizational structure important in determining the actual relation between the rank and file and the leadership. These are (a) those organizational means open to the membership for input into union decision making and effective mobilization of opposition to incumbent leaders; (b) the degree to which union resources are centralized in the hands of the leadership, thereby giving leaders the capacity to impose solutions on the mem-

1. Claus Offe and Helmut Wiesenthal, "Two Logics of Collective Action," in *Disorganized Capitalism: Contemporary Transformations of Work and Politics*, ed. Claus Offe (Cambridge: Cambridge University Press, 1985), pp. 170–220.
2. Ibid., p. 187.

bership rather than forcing them to respond to demands by dissidents; and (c) those avenues of communication that connect the top union leadership to local leaders and the rank and file. By examining a union along the first two dimensions, one can assess the capacity of the membership to mount a concerted challenge to the leadership as well as the capacity of the leadership to either ignore or crush opposition. The third characteristic of organizational structure determines the degree to which the leadership is aware of membership demands and has available the channels to mobilize its membership behind a chosen course of action.

Beyond this schematic framework of analysis, it is crucial also to understand that organizational structures develop out of struggles waged both inside and outside the union, rather than from a blind drive to rational decision making. Consequently, to understand the contribution of organizational structure to mobilizational capacity it is useful to look, not only at the structures themselves, but at the historical struggles that prompted their emergence and continuation.

A second factor contributing to a union's capacity to construct a unity of interest among its membership and to mobilize the rank and file behind a common course of action is the collective identity forged inside the union.[3] "Collective identity" refers to the shared values and interests of a group, those that forge bonds of solidarity among its members such that these members are motivated by their identification with the collectivity to which they belong. A union's collective identity hinges on both objective and ideological characteristics of the membership.

Objective factors include, among others, the diversity of jobs of the rank and file and the geographic concentration and social characteristics of the membership. These objective characteristics shape the nature of the values and interests around which the collective identity is forged. The heterogeneity or homogeneity of objective characteristics also determines (a) possible conflicts over the discourse and symbols that make up the collective identity, (b) the existence of alternate collective identities, and (c) the impetus for change in the dominant identity. The more diverse a membership's characteristics, the more difficult it is to find a common basis on which to articulate shared

3. Alessandro Pizzorno, "Interests and Parties in Pluralism," in *Organizing Interests in Western Europe*, ed. Suzanne Berger (Cambridge: Cambridge University Press, 1981), pp. 249–84.

values and interests for the membership. Moreover, if the objective characteristics of membership change once a collective identity has been forged, the collective identity may alter to incorporate the new groups or the union may become fragmented, thereby reducing its cohesion around the former identity. Such fragmentation creates an obstacle to the capacity of the union to mobilize the rank and file behind a concerted program of collective action.

Objective conditions alone, however, do not forge a collective identity. The ideology of the union membership is also a crucial influence on how these objective conditions are articulated as a collective identity. Ideology provides the membership with a definition of the union's role and place in politics and society and members' relations with one another. An ideology that binds workers to a corporation or ethnic groups in society, rather than to the union or a conception of the working class, is likely to create obstacles for a union that seeks to appeal to workers to mobilize behind a course of union or class action. Workers may instead seek solutions to their problems through nonunion-oriented courses of action.[4]

I have so far focused largely on the internal union determinants of strategic capacity. I have said little about the internal determinants of union choice, that is, about why a union chooses to use strike action, for instance, rather than lobbying or party politics to gain favorable policy decisions. Such choices are obviously influenced by immediate political-economic conditions. They are also influenced by the historical relations and regulations consolidated by unions with key political and economic actors such as political parties, individual corporations, and governments. Beyond these external factors, however, the internal dynamics of unions also shape the choices unions make. At the most basic level, the resources controlled by a union alter the choices open to it. For example, a numerically small union is unlikely to control adequate financial resources to mount a massive television campaign to pressure governments into action. Available resources are by no means, however, the most important determinant of a union's strategic choices. Perhaps most important is the specific ideological expression of the union's collective identity. The ideology influences

4. Mike Davis, "Why the U.S. Working Class Is Different," *New Left Review* 123 (September-October 1980): 3–44; Janine Brodie and Jane Jenson, *Crisis, Challenge and Change: Party and Class in Canada Revisited* (Ottawa, Canada: Carleton University Press, 1988), chap. 1.

how a union employs its resources, whether vast or limited, and shapes whether it sees as viable a strategy based on militant worker action or one based on cooperation with management. A union's organizational structure also influences the perceived strategic choices open to the union by facilitating or blocking rank-and-file input to leadership. As we see in the discussion of the American UAW in the 1980s, when there is weak communication between rank and file and top leadership, strategic choices become limited to those selected by the leaders. Finally, the proven strategic capacity of a union to mount a certain action may also influence future choices.

These, then, are the internal limitations on a union's strategic choices and capacity. Before examining the particular internal dynamics of the Canadian and American sections of the UAW, however, it is important that we also identify the limits imposed on UAW strategy by postwar developments in the regulation of labor-capital relations in the auto industry.

THE POSTWAR PARADOX: UAW BARGAINING POWER AND RANK-AND-FILE DEMOBILIZATION

The immediate postwar struggles between the UAW and the auto corporations put into place a system of collective bargaining and a form of political interest intermediation that encouraged the centralization of union decision making and the abandonment of militant practices in favor of "responsible" union behavior. These developments, while securing a legitimate place for the UAW in postwar Canada and the United States, placed limits on the union's subsequent political strategies by restricting both the perceived choices of strategy and the union's capacity to mobilize its membership.

The combination of the Canadian and American governments' reluctance to regulate their respective economies and the weakness of national labor federations in both countries left the UAW to seek the benefits of postwar prosperity through collective bargaining arrangements with the auto corporations. Out of struggles waged over the first ten years following World War II, a highly structured collective bargaining regime was put into place, one that tended to integrate the Canadian and American sections of the UAW. Such integration, based as it was on virtually identical bargaining structures, was not surprising given that the main employers in the auto industry were the same in both countries, as was the union that represented Canadian and American autoworkers.

Wages were calculated on the basis of a rigid formula, which included an annual improvement factor linking wages to productivity and a cost-of-living allowance. A highly structured collective bargaining process characterized by long-term contracts and master and pattern bargaining also emerged. By the 1960s, a system had developed whereby American negotiations were settled first and then applied, with minor modifications, to Canadian contracts.[5]

This institutionalization of collective bargaining was a double-edged sword for the union. On the one hand, it guaranteed substantial and stable wage and benefit increases and a consolidation and stabilization of labor-management relations. Moreover, master bargaining strengthened the union's bargaining position by allowing common strike action by different locals of the same corporation. A master contract also allowed for the establishment of common wage rates, work standards, and benefit packages, which prevented companies from pitting one local against another in an attempt to reduce union gains to a lowest common denominator. Yet, the institutionalization of collective bargaining also tended to demobilize and hence weaken the union. Master and pattern bargaining, in particular, decreased the autonomy of union locals by encouraging the centralization of decision making in the hands of union leaders who were responsible for coordinating activities between various locals. Furthermore, gains made by the UAW through these collective bargaining structures were dependent on a trade-off with the corporations whereby the union agreed to contain the militancy of its membership and to cede to management the right to organize production as it saw fit. One consequence was the gradual elimination of union demands that either infringed on production standards or called for sweeping changes in the workplace. Moreover, this trade-off made the UAW leaders responsible for controlling spontaneous demonstrations of rank-and-file resistance, and in particular for wildcats. In Canada, this role for the union was re-

5. For a discussion of the emergence of these structures in Canada, see Charlotte Yates, "From Plant to Politics: The Canadian UAW, 1936–1984" (Ph.D. dissertation, Carleton University, Ottawa, Canada, 1988), chaps. 3–5; in the United States, see Harry Katz, *Shifting Gears: Changing Labor Relations in the U.S. Automobile Industry* (Cambridge: MIT Press, 1985), chap. 5.

inforced by provincial labor legislation that prohibited *all* strikes during the life of a collective agreement and for a specified period during negotiations. The overall effect of this collective bargaining regime was the demobilization of the rank and file, whose role in the collective bargaining process tended to be reduced to ratifying bargaining demands presented by the leadership and acting as "cannon fodder" in centrally coordinated strikes.

These demobilizing tendencies of the emergent collective bargaining regime were reinforced by the effects of interest group lobbying. Following the rejection by both the Canadian and American governments of wartime UAW demands for tripartite forms of decision making, the UAW found that the only legitimate avenue open for communication of its demands to government officials was via single interest group lobbying. The structure and practice of lobbying tended to encourage the centralization and professionalization of interest representation, thus reinforcing the union leadership's dominant role in the union. Moreover, lobbying, based as it is on the pluralist discourse of compromise and cooperation, tended to support the move toward "responsible" union behavior and discourage more radical forms of action.

Overall then, the postwar regulation of labor-capital relations, despite its real gains for workers, had a demobilizing effect on unions. Consequently, it tended to reduce the strategic capacity of unions and to restrict strategic choices. Nonetheless, while the political practices and collective bargaining structures of the Canadian and American UAW converged in the postwar period, the organizational structures and collective identities of these unions developed quite differently. In Canada, these internal dynamics mitigated against demobilization, while in the American section of the union they reinforced this tendency. It is therefore to a discussion of organizational structure and collective identity that we now turn.

MOBILIZATIONAL VERSUS BUREAUCRATIC ORGANIZATIONAL STRUCTURES

The organizational structure of the Canadian region of the UAW provided opportunities for membership (and in particular oppositional caucus) influence over the direction of the union and for ongoing communication between the rank and file and the leadership. The centerpiece of the unique Canadian structure was a constitutionally chartered district council, (also referred to as the Canadian council) which provided a forum for membership debate and input on union policy and set the priorities of the Canadian union. The structure of the council ensured it a high degree of autonomy from the union leadership. It met quarterly and was financed independently of the union administration through per capita levies allocated directly to the district council. Locals elected council delegates, who in turn elected executive members for the council. The regional director and staff had voice but no vote in the council's proceedings, an arrangement that increased the capacity for membership control. Whereas district councils were constitutionally restricted from establishing union policy, the one in Canada, because of its role in representing the interests of autoworkers from a separate country, developed a policy-making capacity in such areas as partisan politics, national economic policy, and internal union affairs. Although collective bargaining agenda were determined at international conferences, the Canadian district council provided a forum through which Canadian concerns were voiced and organized into a unified program.

This body was important for at least two reasons. First, it provided oppositional caucuses with an organizational structure through which to mobilize and coordinate the activities of supporters, who otherwise would have been isolated at the local level, as they were in the United States. It was, for example, through the Canadian council that a leftist caucus mobilized support to resist the full-scale purges of militants attempted by Walter Reuther in the late 1940s and maintained left-wing influence in the Canadian region. The combination of this organizational support for opposition caucuses with the council's importance for policy making and consensus building in the Canadian region reduced the union leadership's capacity to impose strategic solutions on Canadian autoworkers. Moreover, the role of the Canadian council as a forum for ideological and strategic debate within the union curbed the tendency toward demobilization associated with the emergent collective bargaining structures.[6]

6. Charles Sabel makes a similar argument concerning the relations between organizational structure, leadership, and ideological debate inside unions; see "The Internal Politics of Trade Unions," in *Organizing Interests in Western Europe,* ed. Berger, pp. 209–44.

Second, the district council acted as a communication link between union leaders and the membership. As I illustrate in the discussion of the 1980s, debates at Canadian council meetings kept leaders' fingers on the pulse of membership reaction to such issues as plant closures and concessions. At the same time, the council also provided the leadership with a means of mobilizing the rank and file behind a chosen course of action and monitoring local conformity with union policy.

In contrast to the Canadian union structure, the American section of the UAW had no such independent intermediary structures of interest representation. Although district councils once existed throughout the UAW, by 1945 most of these bodies in the United States had been disbanded. Union leaders stayed in touch with the rank and file through administrative caucuses first set up by Reuther. Members of these caucuses were handpicked by the administration, however, a process that minimized input from Reuther's opponents. Moreover, these administrative caucuses were entirely dependent on the incumbant leadership for their survival.[7] This dependence minimized the possibility for strategic debate and instead focused the energies of these caucuses on the means for ensuring passage of leadership policy.

Other forums of debate and decision making, such as international conventions and economic collective bargaining conferences, were structured to further minimize the possibility of a successful challenge to leadership policy.[8] Consequently, in contrast to the Canadian experience, the organizational structure of the American UAW secured the leadership a disproportionate share of union resources and provided few organizational opportunities for independent rank-and-file mobilization. These structures therefore tended to reinforce the demobilizing tendencies of the postwar collective bargaining regime and to limit the strategic choices available to the union.

The demobilization of Canadian autoworkers was further hampered by the limited development of the union's bureaucracy and the skeletal professional staff assigned to the Canadian region. Because the Canadian region was only one of many, the international executive was unwilling to allocate much greater than proportional resources to it. At the same time, the need by Canadian autoworkers to meet the challenge of Canadian political and economic conditions required that this region act independently of the international office on several issues.

7. Jack Steiber, *Governing the UAW* (New York: Wiley & Sons, 1962), pp. 67–73.
8. Ibid., chap. 2.

In the absence of professional staff to handle such matters as research and policy formation and educational forums, the Canadian council assumed this role. This, in turn, had the unanticipated effect of further entrenching a tradition of rank-and-file activism within the union. Moreover, once this tradition was established, Canadian autoworkers struggled to prevent the centralization of union affairs in the hands of leaders and experts. This situation was a considerable contrast to the professionalization of lobbying activities in Washington by the UAW, its corporate running of the Black Lake education center in Michigan, and its massive bureaucratization under Reuther. American autoworkers were one step farther removed from the activities of their union. The effect of this organizational crystallization has been aptly summarized by George Ross and Jane Jenson: "Ordinary workers learned to perceive their unions less as collectives for mutual struggle than as distinct and separate agencies which acted *for* them, to be sure, but more often than not *in their place*."[9]

COLLECTIVE IDENTITIES OF AMERICAN AND CANADIAN AUTOWORKERS

The American UAW emerged deradicalized from the cold war. Its syndicalist past was replaced by an orientation whereby the union implicitly accepted capitalist growth criteria as a basis for its demands and managed its membership in ways not unlike the corporations with which it bargained.[10] Little or no ideological debate took place within the union, and strategic choices, although ratified by the membership at international conventions, were carefully planned and executed by the leadership. Strategic challenges to the leadership, such as the 1953 demand for a shorter work week, were discredited as communist

9. George Ross and Jane Jenson, "Post-War Class Struggle and the Crisis of Left Politics," *Socialist Register, 1985/86,* ed. Ralph Miliband et al. (London: Merlin Press, 1986), p. 25.

10. For a discussion of this deradicalization of the UAW, see Nelson Lichtenstein, "Auto Worker Militancy and the Structure of Factory Life, 1937–1955," *Journal of American History* 67 (September 1980): 335–53; William Andrew, "Factionalism and Anti-Communism: Ford Local 600," *Labor History* 20 (Spring 1979): 227–55. A particularly excellent view of the UAW's use of capitalist growth criteria in articulating its collective bargaining goals can be found in Walter Reuther's arguments in 1958 in favor of profit sharing; for example, see transcript of Mike Wallace Interview ("60 Minutes") with Walter Reuther, January 25, 1958.

plots.[11] In particular during the Reuther years, a challenge to Reuther's leadership became synonymous with a challenge to the UAW and tantamount to treason.

This ideological transformation of the union provided a weak basis for the identification of individual members with their union. This weakness was likely reinforced by a declining sense of community among autoworkers which accompanied the dispersion of auto production outside Detroit. Ties to the union were even weaker among blacks due to an exclusively white leadership which, until the late 1960s, determined UAW ideas and practice.[12] The development of a weak and conservative collective identity limited the perceived strategic options available to the union and tended to exclude those that would have relied on the militant mobilization of the rank and file.

In contrast, the Canadian UAW maintained a militant syndicalist orientation with a strong tradition of rank-and-file activism and democracy. The development and survival of this syndicalist orientation was the result of several related factors. It was partly the result of the peculiarities and influence of the left-wing caucus, which maintained a strong presence in the Canadian region until the late 1950s. The caucus that emerged victorious from the struggles with Homer Martin in 1939 was a loose coalition of communists, left-wing members of the social democratic Cooperative Commonwealth Federation, and militants with little or no interest in party politics. Due to the need to maintain itself by compromise in the prevailing political and economic conditions of the 1940s, this caucus steered the Canadian UAW onto a course of workplace-based action rather than party politics. The success of this strategy during and immediately following the war, combined with Canadian autoworkers' bitter experience with party meddling in union affairs, encouraged support for a trade union–centered strategic orientation and reinforced the syndicalist tradition inside the union.

Reuther's attempted purges of militants from the Canadian region in the late 1940s were less successful than similar moves in the United States, for they were perceived as a challenge to Canadian autoworkers' control over their own union. Thus, the syndicalist tradition and

11. Steiber, *Governing the UAW*, pp. 45–46.

12. Steve Jefferys, *Management and Managed: Fifty Years of Crisis at Chrysler* (Cambridge: Cambridge University Press, 1986), chaps. 8–9; Charles Denby, "Black Caucuses in the Unions," in *Autocracy and Insurgency in Organized Labor*, ed. Burton Hall (New Brunswick, N.J.: Transaction Books, 1972), pp. 138–46.

the options for alternate strategies based on militancy survived the 1950s. For similar reasons, the tradition and commitment to rank-and-file activism and democracy persisted in Canada. Whereas Reuther subverted these traditions in the United States with his establishment of the "one-party union," the commitments to rank-and-file activism and democracy were reinforced in Canada by this region's organizational structures and the continued influence of left-wing militants inside the union.[13]

At the same time, Canadian autoworkers were sensitive to the possible damage to their union of continuous internal rivalry between left and right. Consequently, a tradition of internal debate and struggle developed within the Canadian UAW, following which all union members were expected to abide by the decisions and support the adopted course of action. Opponents of the union's course of action or leadership were therefore expected to act as a loyal opposition, thus producing a tradition of unity in diversity.

One final factor facilitated the development of a union-centered collective identity in Canada. In contrast to U.S. autoworkers, Canadian autoworkers were, until the mid-1960s, culturally relatively homogeneous. They were predominantly white, English-speaking males concentrated in auto plants in the southern part of Ontario. This homogeneity reduced the basis for the organization of competing sectoral groups, such as regional caucuses, and provided a common basis of cultural identity among autoworkers. Thus, ideological divisions in the union were not overshadowed by regional, gender, or racial divisions.

Overall, the collective identity of Canadian autoworkers, combined with the Canadian region's organizational structure, encouraged rank-and-file activism and mobilization. It tended to leave open the possibility of adopting militant forms of action.

ECONOMIC INSTABILITY AND RANK-AND-FILE MILITANCY, 1967–78

In the late 1960s, the UAW in both Canada and the United States found itself caught in what appeared to be a no-win situation. The UAW saw its position in the auto industry as dependent on its struc-

13. On Canada, see Yates, "From Plant to Politics." On the one-party union, see Frank Marquart, *An Auto Workers' Journal* (University Park: Pennsylvania State University Press, 1975); Lichtenstein, "Auto Work Militancy," pp. 350–52.

tured relationship with corporations. To maintain this relationship, the UAW had to live up to its side of the wage-productivity trade-off whereby it controlled membership militancy and left production decisions to management. At the same time, the UAW's position of strength vis-à-vis the corporations depended on support from its membership and the maintenance of its position as representative of autoworkers. These two tasks became virtually irreconcilable.

In the late 1960s, auto corporations experienced declining productivity and profitability. Corporations responded to these problems with a strategy based on increasing the exploitation of the existing workforce through speedups of the assembly line and compulsory overtime. Pressure increased on individual workers, who, given the lack of union support for resisting these changes to production standards, wildcatted in protest. Corporations then looked to the UAW to control these unauthorized work stoppages. The union was thus in a position of either taking up the membership's cause or squelching the militancy in order to preserve the union's relationship with the corporations.

These pressures on the UAW were aggravated by the expansion and growing diversity of UAW membership. The prosperity of the North American auto industry in the early 1960s had brought with it an expansion of production and hence of the workforce. For both the American and Canadian UAW, this occasioned massive increases in union membership. These membership additions strengthened the UAW by enlarging the number of workers it represented while maintaining its monopolistic position in the auto industry. At the same time, this expansion complicated the tasks of representing the interests of the membership, whose demographic characteristics and demands had changed.

In the United States, greater numbers of young workers, a large proportion of whom were black, entered the ranks of the union. These young workers demanded more than the high wages and benefits the union had succeeded in securing in the postwar years. Black workers, spurred on by the civil rights movement, demanded redress of their ghettoization in the worst jobs in auto plants and their lack of representation in the UAW itself.[14] The Canadian region experienced similar pressures from younger workers as well as a new group of nationalist Quebecois workers. The Quebecois, like the blacks in

14. Jefferys, *Management and Managed*, pt. 4; Stanley Aronowitz, *False Promises* (New York: McGraw-Hill, 1973).

the United States demanded proper representation in the union, in particular French-language services, as well as wage and working condition parity with their English-speaking brothers and sisters in Ontario.[15]

These new workers had little or no attachment to the historical traditions and practices of the union, which had been defined by the older, more conservative white males who had hitherto dominated the UAW. The combination of this lack of historical identity with the union and the different objective characteristics of these members erected barriers to their mobilization behind existing union goals. Moreover, these new workers were unwilling to accept the terms of the wage-productivity trade-off and instead demanded action on issues of production standards and working conditions. These workers therefore joined other autoworkers in wildcats and various forms of workplace protest. Although these acts of resistance were initially aimed at corporate attempts to intensify work on the assembly line, they soon took aim at the UAW itself, which often played an active role in squashing these demonstrations of militancy.

Discontented American autoworkers were unable to mount a concerted opposition to the UAW's leaders. They lacked the organizational means through which to mobilize support and coordinate their activities and were ideologically and racially divided. The combination of the fragmented nature of the opposition and the leadership's commitment to cooperation with management meant that the American UAW's leaders were neither forced nor ideologically predisposed toward the strategic possibility of mobilizing membership discontent to make greater gains from management and in this way reconstruct internal unity. Rather, the union leaders responded with a strategy of divide-and-rule and open coercion.[16] The effect was demobilization of the union membership and suppression of ideological and strategic debate.

The Canadian UAW initially followed the lead of the International, disciplining workers involved in wildcats, bargaining away the varied workplace and language demands of Canadian autoworkers, and staying close to the pattern settlements negotiated in the United States.

15. Yates, "From Plant to Politics," chaps. 6–7.

16. Jefferys, *Management and Managed*, chaps. 8–9; Nelson Lichtenstein, "UAW Bargaining Strategies and Shop Floor Conflict: 1946–1970," *Industrial Relations* 3 (Fall 1985): 360–81; William Serrin, *The Company and the Union* (New York: Alfred Knopf, 1973).

This position, however, spawned the development of a new opposition caucus led by left-wing militants who had survived the 1950s Reuther purges. This caucus found in the Canadian council a means of coordinating its platform and organizing membership support across various union locals. Furthermore, it articulated its program in nationalist, ideological terms at a time when Canadian nationalism was on the rise. Nationalism garnered the caucus more widespread membership support and provided the basis for ideological unity among an otherwise diverse group of militants, including young and old autoworkers, liberals, social democrats, and communists. In this way, militants in the Canadian UAW mounted a concerted challenge to union leaders and forced them to act on many caucus demands.

In 1971, the Canadian UAW began using collective bargaining and the strike weapon to force companies to address workers' concerns over compulsory overtime and speedups. The union also responded to rank-and-file pressure for increased Canadian autonomy within the international union structure with the creation of a Canadian research staff, separate Canadian UAW affiliation to world bodies, establishment of a national newsletter, and, most important, the spending of dues collected from Canadian UAW members in the Canadian region.

Although the left-wing caucus took up some of the Quebecois' demands, Quebec workers posed a different challenge to the Canadian UAW leadership. Although Quebec autoworkers constituted a small and relatively isolated group within the union, they could not be easily ignored or divided, as could blacks in the United States. The reason for this lay in their higher degree of ideological unity and the historical tradition of Quebec's labor movement to organize into Quebec-based unions. The UAW could ill afford to lose its presence in Quebec, for this would destroy its monopolistic position in the auto industry and raise the possibility of union competition and variability on issues of wages, benefits, and so on. The UAW therefore struggled for and won wage and benefit parity for Quebec autoworkers with their Ontario counterparts. The union also gradually extended French-language services in union affairs. After heated debate, the Canadian council came out in favor of the two-nation concept of Canada and of the Parti Quebecois, a nationalist independentist party supported by an increasing number of Quebec autoworkers.[17] The Canadian UAW had succeeded

17. Yates, "From Plant to Politics," chap. 7.

in reconstructing internal unity through internal reform and a willingness to take up many of the demands of militants and other discontented autoworkers.

At the moment internal harmony was restored by both unions, however, Canadian and American autoworkers were confronted with a more serious economic downturn and new political-economic challenges. Inflation soared, partly due to the 1973 oil crisis, consumer spending dropped, and international competition from more fuel-efficient cars increased. The short-term corporate solution to these problems was massive layoffs. The long-term solution, however, lay in increasing worker productivity through quality-of-worklife projects and in shifting production to low-wage nonunionized locations. For General Motors, the latter included shifting American production to the southern states.

The American UAW was ill prepared to respond to these new corporate initiatives with militancy and membership mobilization. Rather, it relied on its well-established relationship with the corporations to negotiate leadership-inspired solutions. A deal struck between the UAW and General Motors in the mid-1970s epitomized the union's strategic orientation. In exchange for promoting and participating in quality-of-worklife projects, the UAW ultimately gained the right to automatic recognition in new General Motors plants.[18] Thus, rather than having to mobilize workers in these new plants, and in so doing build membership support, the UAW effectively imposed its organization on new workers and committed autoworkers to new forms of labor-management cooperation. In the short-term, this strategy strengthened the UAW organizationally by maintaining its monopolistic position in the auto industry. At the same time, this strategy, combined with the decision of the early 1970s to squash militants, further eroded any strong collective identification of autoworkers with their union and reinforced the tendency of the union to identify ideologically its interest with those of the corporation.

Canadian autoworkers faced many of the same problems as their American brothers and sisters. Although they were not confronted with a southern strategy, the growing trend of disinvestment from the Canadian auto industry begun in 1976 threatened not only jobs of au-

18. Thomas Kochan et al., *The Transformation of American Industrial Relations* (New York: Basic Books, 1986), p. 60.

toworkers but the survival of the entire Canadian auto industry.[19] Nonetheless, corporate initiatives to respond to the recession were eclipsed by the federal government's introduction in 1975 of mandatory wage controls. The fight against these controls became the primary focus of Canadian UAW activity between 1975 and 1978.

The wage control program was structured to encourage corporations and unions to negotiate voluntarily wages within guidelines established by government. To enforce the guidelines, however, a specially established government agency examined all collective agreements and had the right, subject to union appeals to a final arbiter, to order rollbacks of excessive wage settlements. The Canadian UAW rejected the wage control program and fought it with strikes and mass demonstrations. It mobilized its members through the Canadian council, educational forums, and the Canadian edition of the newspaper *Solidarity*.[20]

Dennis McDermott, Canadian regional UAW director until 1978, was initially leery of mass protests, and in particular of the proposal made by militants in his and other Canadian unions for a general strike. Rank-and-file autoworkers' enthusiastic response to planned demonstrations on Parliament Hill combined with mounting grass roots pressure for visible action by labor to protest government policy forced McDermott to change his tune. He took up the call for a one-day general strike and became instrumental in obtaining the Canadian Labour Congress's endorsement of the plan. Thereafter, the Canadian UAW pulled out all the stops in mobilizing its membership behind the call for a general strike. When the strike was finally staged in October 1976, the Canadian UAW had one of the highest participation rates of any union in Canada. Regardless of threats by corporations to discipline workers absent from work, many auto plants were completely shut down thanks to autoworkers' participation in the strike.

Although the general strike had no perceivable effect on government policy, it, along with contract strikes, worried the corporations enough to encourage them to cooperate with Canadian autoworkers in sidestepping wage controls. Managements used loopholes in the

19. Ross Perry, *The Future of Canada's Auto Industry* (Ottawa: Canadian Institute for Economic Policy, 1982), chap. 3.

20. For a more detailed discussion of the wage control policy and some discussion of the UAW response, see Allan Maslove and Gene Swimmer, *Wage Controls in Canada, 1975–78* (Montreal: Institute for Research on Public Policy, 1980). For a more detailed account of Canadian autoworkers, see Yates, "From Plant to Politics," pp. 399–426.

government's wage control order to increase autoworkers' pay above government guidelines. A second effect of this militant strategy was internal to the union. The struggles and mass demonstrations against wage controls cemented autoworkers' ties with their union and fanned the left-wing fires that had been rekindled in the late 1960s. Thus the viability of strategic choices based on direct worker action increased.

Membership commitment to the Canadian UAW was also reinforced by the union's experience in the late 1970s with a series of violent and bitter strikes that reminded union members of the fragility of any rapprochement with management. To win these strikes, the UAW had to move into waters uncharted since the 1940s. For example, in a strike at Fleck Manufacturing, where a small group of women fought to gain their first contract as part of the UAW, strikers were met with massive police support for the company and brutal physical attacks. In retaliation, the UAW called out its biggest and most militant workers from a nearby auto plant to "man" the barricades and meet force with force. These experiences reinforced the growing militant tradition among Canadian autoworkers. Thus, while the American UAW remained locked in a strategy of cooperation and compromise, the Canadian UAW reentered the terrain of militant, mobilizational politics and in so doing opened the door to future militancy.

UNION DIVERGENCE IN THE FACE OF RESTRUCTURING

The economic uncertainty of the 1970s became worldwide recession in the 1980s, with continued high inflation, double-digit unemployment, and a severe drop in productivity. The North American auto industry was particularly hard hit. In the short term, it suffered an immediate drop in profitability owing to declining consumer incomes and the increased penetration of foreign cars into the North American market. More serious, however, was the prospect of the North American producers' loss of their position of world dominance in auto production. The root of this problem lay in the industry's failure to meet the Japanese challenge of more efficient utilization of resources and organization of production. Fordist and Sloanist solutions to profitability were called into question in the 1980s. North American auto producers therefore began searching for alternative means to restore their competitiveness.

In the short term, auto and parts makers responded with plant closures and layoffs. To increase long-run efficiency and competitiveness, corporations automated their plants, introducing robots and computer technology. Streamlined production and lower costs were obtained by using fewer parts in cars, producing standardized car designs that could be sold in any market, shifting production to cheap labor zones in third world countries, and entering into joint ventures with foreign corporations. Corporations also downsized their cars in the hopes of competing with the Japanese in the small, more fuel-efficient car market.[21]

This rationalization of the production process was accompanied by corporate attempts to reduce labor costs and restructure relations with the UAW. The restructuring process constituted a move to dismantle existing collective bargaining arrangements and replace them with a system characterized by flexibility in the allocation of labor and variability in wage and benefit calculations. These moves were seen as imperative by management, who saw master and pattern bargaining, seniority arrangements, and structured wage and benefit increments as fetters on corporate initiatives to restore their competitiveness. Concessions from workers became the means to achieve both goals.

While auto corporations used threats of plant closure and job loss as a means of forcing workers into accepting concessions, they also attempted to mobilize ideologically workers and the UAW behind corporate restructuring strategies. A new management discourse of teamwork, joint decision making, and "equality of sacrifice" accompanied demands for concessions, heightened pressure for quality-of-worklife programs, and the reorganization of production. The auto corporations were intent on making workers and the UAW their allies in the struggle to restore industry competitiveness.[22]

21. For a discussion of restructuring in the American auto industry, see Alan Altshuler et al., *The Future of the Automobile*, Report of MIT's International Automobile Program (Cambridge: MIT Press, 1984); on Canada, see Patrick Lavelle and Robert White, *An Automotive Strategy for Canada*, Report of the Federal Task Force on the Canadian Motor Vehicles and Automotive Parts Industries (Ottawa: Minister of Industry and Commerce, 1983); Marc Van Ameringen, "The Restructuring of the Canadian Automobile Industry," in *Le Canada et la Nouvelle Division Internationale du Travail*, ed. Duncan Cameron and Françoise Houle (Ottawa: University of Ottawa Press, 1985), pp. 267–87.

22. For an excellent example of this new corporate discourse, see Lee Iacocca with William Novak, *Iacocca: An Autobiography* (New York: Bantam Books, 1984).

This reformulation of labor relations, aimed at tying wages and worker interests to corporate productivity, constituted a threat to the relationship between the union and its members. In the not-so-long run, the union could find itself defending measures that would ensure the profitability of the company at the expense of wages and the protection of union members. Furthermore, union locals could become tied to the interests of the corporations, resulting in a weakening of the union organization itself. Second, proposed labor-management committees could lead to a devolution of the union's role as a protector of workers' interests. Third, in negotiating and selling concessionary agreements to their members in the absence of guarantees of job security, unions could find themselves the object of growing membership discontent; this would lead to divisions among the membership, thereby threatening the capacity of the union to pursue a strategy of collective action. Finally, since the late 1940s, the UAW had relied on the existing collective bargaining regime for its organizational strength. By accepting the reformulation of labor relations, the UAW faced the possible erosion of its established organizational position and an accompanying loss of power in the workplace and ultimately the political arena. On the other hand, if the UAW did not accept concessions, it was possible that corporations would either shift production to cheap labor zones or face possible bankruptcy, thus threatening the jobs of autoworkers and leading to a decline in union membership.

The Canadian and American sections of the UAW finally chose quite different strategic responses to concessions and management's strategy for restructuring. The Canadian UAW pursued a strategy of militant mobilization of its membership in an attempt to resist concessions and plant closures and to force the adoption of a new strategy for recovery. In contrast, the American UAW leadership opted for a strategy of cooperation with management in the hope that helping the company today would ensure jobs and a place for the union tomorrow.

The Canadian UAW's first major act of resistance came in response to plant closures. After failing in its lobbying efforts to gain government action to protect workers thrown out of work due to closures, the UAW Canadian council formulated a strategy of plant-level sitdown strikes. Rank-and-file autoworkers were eager for action and rushed to offer their plants as the first sites for a sitdown.[23] With the

23. Minutes of meeting of Canadian UAW council, June 21, 22, 1980.

pending closure of several small, older plants and the poor severence packages offered to workers, the Canadian UAW decided to fight back. On August 9, 1980, two hundred autoworkers occupied the Houdaille plant in Oshawa. They held fast until August 21, when a settlement was reached. The union declared victory. Severence pay was to be increased to almost six times the amount originally offered by the company and pensions were improved and extended to include workers of 55 years of age.[24] By September, autoworkers at Beach Appliance and the Bendix plant had also staged sitdowns, meeting with similar successes.[25] As a result of these union actions and the publicity they generated, the Ontario government passed severence pay legislation to protect workers faced with plant closures.

The importance of this victory for Canadian autoworkers was not only in the tangible rewards won for workers directly affected by the closures. The union had successfully mobilized its rank and file at a time when unions were in retreat, thereby cementing rank-and-file solidarity. Moreover, this course of action revealed to union leaders the extent of membership willingness to fight against corporate decisions and mobilize behind a militant course of action.

This victory for the union was all the more important since it coincided with early company demands for concessions. In 1979, the financially troubled Chrysler corporation first asked for concessions from its workers. Both Canadian and American autoworkers accepted these demands. Nevertheless, by 1980, Chrysler, seemingly on the verge of bankruptcy, appealed to the U.S. government for help. Congress offered to bail out the corporation if Chrysler could gain further concessions from its workers and loans from other governments, in particular the Canadian one. The American members of the UAW international executive board accepted concessions as the only way to save the corporation (and hence jobs), but Robert White, Canadian director of the UAW, refused to go along with the deal. He rejected the notion that Canadian collective bargaining should be determined by a foreign government.[26] The hand of Canadian autoworkers was strengthened by the Canadian government's position on the Chrysler loan negotiations. Contrary to the U.S. government position and

24. *Globe and Mail*, August 9, 21, 1980.

25. Canadian regional director's report to Canadian council, September 14, 15, 1980, pp. 4, 10.

26. Canadian regional director's report to Canadian council, January 26, 27, 1980.

largely as a result of the dependent nature of the Canadian economy, the Canadian government made any loans to Chrysler conditional on corporate guarantees of increased investment and jobs in Canada.[27]

Although this move by White represented the first step toward what would become major strategic differences between the Canadian and American sections of the UAW, neither section of the union had yet determined a long-term strategy for dealing with corporate demands. This fact was illustrated when the Canadian director, along with the American UAW, agreed to a third round of concessions demanded by Chrysler. White argued that these concessions were imperative—that they were based on the very real possibility of bankruptcy and loss of jobs and were not the result of pressure from Congress.[28]

The dangers of accepting these and other concessionary deals became quickly apparent on both sides of the border. In Canada, only 2,921 Chrysler workers voted in favor of the agreement containing concessions while 2,664 rejected it.[29] Open criticism of UAW leaders mounted. The union was being divided.[30]

In the face of this growing internal discontent and the prospect of a flood of concessions demanded by other corporations following Chrysler's lead, White announced that the Chrysler contract was the last Canadian one to be reopened. The Canadian council then voted to resist future concessions.[31] The American UAW appeared bent on a similar strategy of resistance when in July 1981 the international executive board voted not to reopen other contracts for concession bargaining. This coincidence of strategy was short-lived, however. When General Motors demanded concessions late in 1981, the board agreed. Backed by the 1981 Canadian council decision to resist concessions, White cast the lone dissenting vote against the decision.[32] Thereafter, the Canadian and American UAW followed different courses of action.

The Canadian UAW's no-concessions policy appeared at one level to be a strategy of bargaining as usual. Rather than reopening contracts

27. Canadian regional director's report to Canadian council, June 21, 22, 1980, p. 16; *Globe and Mail,* May 1, 1980.

28. Canadian regional director's report to Canadian council, January 31 and February 1, 1981, p. 8.

29. *Globe and Mail,* January 30, 1981.

30. Interview with Robert White, Canadian UAW regional director, 31 December 1985.

31. Minutes to meeting of Canadian council, January 31 and February 1, 1981, p. 8.

32. Canadian regional director's report to Canadian council, September 12, 13, 1981; January 30, 31, 1982.

to pave the way for concession bargaining, the Canadian UAW entered negotiations with an agenda of demands and the threat of a strike. The union aimed to protect structured wage and benefit increases, seniority arrangements, and master and pattern bargaining. It therefore rejected profit sharing and lump sum payments in lieu of wages, the drastic reduction of job classifications in existing plants, and the two-tier wage system whereby new workers were paid on a lower scale than older workers. Although Canadian autoworkers experimented with quality-of-worklife projects, their scope was automatically restricted by the union's hard line against such accompanying changes as reduced job classifications.[33] For Canadian autoworkers, these programs were seen as a possible means of improving life on the assembly line, not as a vehicle for joint decision making, of which autoworkers were highly suspicious.

For this strategy to work in the face of corporate and international union opposition, the Canadian UAW had to mobilize membership support and present a united front. This was a difficult task; although large numbers of autoworkers were against concessions, others were afraid of the possible loss of jobs should their union fight the corporations. Moreover, by fighting concessions the Canadian UAW was asking members to abandon their historical practice of abiding by international union policy. The Canadian UAW therefore had to construct a unity of interest among the membership. The union disseminated information on both the effects of concessions and the union's strategy through its educational forums, the Canadian council, shop stewards, and the communications network of newspapers and fact sheets. To ensure compliance with the no-concessions policy, the union carefully monitored all negotiations, a practice that was facilitated by the centralized collective bargaining system. Finally, autoworkers voted to set up a no-concessions fund based on special membership levies that increased the level of strike pay and provided resources for the union to mount its anticoncessions campaign. This mobilization of unity in the ranks was facilitated by the early victories over plant closures and the growing success of the union's resistance to concessions.[34]

To bolster its position, the Canadian UAW sought and received widespread union and community support for its no-concessions

33. Yates, "From Plant to Politics," chap. 8.
34. Ibid.

policy. This support was important, for if the UAW remained alone in its no-concessions stand it might become the target of criticism from the public, governments, and corporations and be vilified for its unwillingness to sacrifice in the name of economic recovery. This, in turn, could have generated pressure on the part of the rest of the Canadian labor movement for the UAW to reverse its position and retreat with other unions. Canadian UAW leaders also adopted a policy of openness and availability to the media in order to place the union's agenda before the public and in national debates on economic restructuring.

Alongside this workplace strategy, the Canadian UAW stepped up its lobbying efforts to have the federal government adopt a trade policy that dealt more adequately with the question of international competition. Rather than advocating protectionism, the Canadian UAW demanded that the Autopact be extended to cover all automakers. The Autopact, a Canadian-U.S. trade agreement signed in 1965, had provided tariff-free access to the Canadian market in exchange for guaranteed levels of investment and production in the Canadian auto industry. Canadian autoworkers anticipated that extending this agreement would ensure investment in Canada by non-U.S. auto producers and hence jobs.[35]

The no-concessions stand paid off for the union. In negotiations with General Motors and Ford in 1982 and 1984, the Canadian UAW successfully resisted the replacement of regular wage increases and cost-of-living allowances with profit sharing and lump sum payments and maintained master bargaining and seniority. Although it lost paid personal holidays and certain other benefits, the basic structure of bargaining remained intact. Perhaps the most important victory came during the 1983 Chrysler negotiations. In the face of corporate threats of job loss and plant closure, Canadian autoworkers went on strike for five weeks to recoup some of their losses from earlier concessions and begin the move toward regaining wage parity between Chrysler and other autoworkers. This strike not only resulted in a substantial wage increase for Canadian workers but led the way for wage increases in the stalled American Chrysler negotiations. This success demonstrated the viability of the Canadian UAW's militant strategy and highlighted

35. Lavelle and White, *An Automotive Strategy.*

the possibilities for American autoworkers had a similar strategy been adopted by their union. Canadian successes also suggested that restructuring through concessions was not the only corporate strategy available.[36]

The Chrysler negotiations were difficult and a landmark for the Canadian UAW, but strikes in some of the smaller plants also proved the metal of the union and the importance of its no-concessions fight. In 1983, UAW members employed by Hussman Store Equipment struck to resist company demands for twenty-eight concessions, including zero wage and benefit increases, major changes to seniority provisions, elimination of voluntary overtime, and termination of paid lunch breaks. After nine months of strike, the strikers defeated almost every company demand and won wage and benefit increases.[37]

As a result of such victories, the Canadian UAW, and in particular Robert White, became the darling of the media and a symbol for all Canadian workers of the militance and justness of labor's fight to protect its position in the workplace. The cost of this militancy was high, however. Following internal union struggles over the 1984 General Motors negotiations, Canadian autoworkers found themselves forced to move toward independence. In 1985, the founding convention of the new National Automobile, Aerospace and Agricultural Implement Workers Union of Canada (CAW) was held and a new chapter in the history of Canadian autoworkers began.

In contrast to the Canadian UAW, the American UAW leadership took it on itself to sell concessions to workers as the only means to increase the competitiveness of the American auto industry and hence save jobs and the union. In negotiations with the "big three," the American UAW accepted profit sharing and lump sum payments in lieu of the annual wage increase and cost-of-living allowances. In many local negotiations, job classifications were reduced, two-tier wage systems came into effect, and seniority was modified to include provisions recognizing know-how and education. Implicit in these changes was the effective dismantling of master and pattern bargaining. In their place, contracts became tailor-made to different corporations, re-

36. Yates, "From Plant to Politics," chap. 8.

37. List of company's major concessions presented to Local 397 membership by local bargaining committee, n.d.; Proposed contract between Local 397 UAW and Hussman Store Equipment, n.d.

gional economic conditions, and individual plants. The Saturn contract epitomized this new era of tailor-made contracts.[38]

Alongside the negotiation of these concessions, the American UAW accepted management's introduction of the team concept and the extension of programs such as quality circles. In the new spirit of cooperation, then-UAW president Douglas Fraser accepted a position on the Chrysler board of directors. Although some UAW leaders remained suspicious of the benefits of this work reorganization and of concessions, their fear of foreign competition and strong identification with the American auto companies prevented them from seriously considering an alternate no-concessions strategy. Other UAW leaders were more enthusiastic about the changes accompanying restructuring and wholeheartedly accepted the corporate discourse of joint decision making and teamwork. Donald Ephlin, vice-president of the UAW's General Motors section, described the 1984 Ford agreement in terms of equality of sacrifice and evaluated the union's strategy as follows: "While we still disagree from time to time and will likely continue to do so, we are trying to develop "win-win" solutions. . . . That spirit of communication and joint decision-making is increasingly present in the day-to-day efforts of the union and the company on the shop floor."[39]

This strategy met with growing rank-and-file discontent. Contract ratification votes became tight races between those in favor and those against concessions. For example, when in early 1982 UAW president Fraser recommended reopening the General Motors contract to negotiate concessions, 46 percent of the U.S. General Motors local leadership voted against this proposal. Nevertheless, the slightly favorable majority was taken as a mandate to reopen the contract and the renegotiated agreement made $3 billion in concessions. Discontent and splits within the American rank and file were reflected in the ratification vote: only 52 percent of the workers voted for the contract.[40]

38. Kochan et al., *Transformation;* Jane Slaughter, *Concessions and How to Beat Them* (Detroit: Labor Education and Research Project, Labor Notes, 1983), chap. 1; Katz, *Shifting Gears,* chaps. 3–4; Peter Meyers, "General Motors' Saturn Plant: A Quantum Leap in Technology and its Implications for Labor and Community Organizing," *Capital and Class* 30 (1986): 73–96.

39. Donald Ephlin, "The UAW Ford Agreement—Joint Problem Solving," *Sloan Management Review* 24 (Winter 1983): 64–65.

40. Minutes to meeting of Canadian council, January 30, 31, 1982, p. 32; *Globe and Mail,* April 16, 1982.

New anticoncession caucuses began to emerge aimed largely against the union leadership's unwillingness to coordinate a no-concessions strategy.[41] Some disenchanted American UAW locals went as far as to apply for membership in the newly formed CAW.[42]

As in the 1970s, the UAW leadership ignored membership calls for an alternate course of action based on militancy and instead actively opposed union militants. Rather than mobilizing the membership, the American UAW once again adopted a top-down strategy of selling management solutions to the rank and file and of disciplining dissidents. Ironically, the latter became more difficult as the centralized institutions, which in the postwar years had given leaders the organizational resources to force membership compliance with union policy, became undone as a consequence of the leadership's own strategy. The result was a union deeply divided and hence weakened in both its appeal to workers and its capacity to effectively win concessions from management.

The question remains as to why the Canadian and American branches of the UAW chose different responses to corporate pressures in the 1980s. Both unions faced similar situations. On one hand, they were confronted with corporate threats of plant closures and bankruptcy and the economic realities of the deepest economic downturn since the 1930s. On the other hand, both unions felt mounting pressure from their members to protect them from corporate assaults, including concessions. Canadian autoworkers felt the additional pressure from their international union to conform with union policy. Why did the two unions diverge in strategy?

A popular explanation for the different strategies pursued by Canadian and American autoworkers rests on the different economic conditions facing the two countries' auto industries in the 1980s. Some argue that, due to the lower value of the Canadian vis-à-vis the American dollar, automakers were under less pressure to reduce labor costs in Canada. Therefore, they were less concerned with concessions and the rationalization of production to increase productivity. Consequently, Canadian autoworkers had greater economic maneuverability than did their American brothers and sisters.

This argument is based on hindsight and has several problems. First, it ignores the fact that the drop in the value of the Canadian

41. Slaughter, *Concessions*, pp. 79–81, 96, 98.
42. *Globe and Mail*, April 16, 1986, p. A10.

dollar was initially seen as temporary and not the basis for long-term corporate strategy. Second, arguments regarding the importance of the lower Canadian dollar fail to take into account the dependent nature of Canada's auto industry. For the first years of recession, the "big three" automakers made it impossible for Canadian branch plants to take advantage of the lower Canadian dollar by instituting internal transfer pricing policies that increased the price of parts for cars assembled in Canada to the point where production became equally if not more expensive in Canada than in the United States. Third, in the early 1980s corporate investments in small car production were destined for the United States, leaving Canada with the production of large and possibly obsolete cars and specialty vehicles. Although with hindsight we know that the Canadian auto industry recovered more quickly than the American, in the depths of the recession the reverse seemed possible given these investment decisions.[43]

Only since 1983 has the Canadian auto industry regained some of its economic viability. This renewed prosperity no doubt bolstered the Canadian autoworkers' position in its negotiation with Chrysler in 1983 and General Motors in 1984 and in subsequent negotiations with other corporations. Nonetheless, the state of the economy alone cannot account for the Canadian UAW's choice of militant action. At best, it helps explain the union's success.

The fact that the auto industry constituted the heart of Canada's industrial complex indirectly increased the UAW's strategic capacity due to the support given certain union strategies by the Ontario and federal governments. The conditions attached to the Canadian Chrysler loan is one example. Given the absence of a Canadian or Ontario industrial strategy for the auto industry, however, this government support was ad hoc and often only followed the UAW's articulation and pursuit of a militant strategy. Conversely, the fact that American autoworkers faced a more hostile government under Ronald Reagan no doubt weakened the position of their union.

These political-economic factors provide us with some of the reasons for the variable strategic capacity of the two unions, but they give us little insight into the reasons for the two unions' different choice of strategy. To understand the choices, we must examine the internal dynamics of the two unions. The militant syndicalist tradition of the Ca-

43. Perry, *Future of Canada's Auto Industry*, chap. 3.

nadian UAW, which had been rekindled by the union's experience in the 1970s, provided a necessary ideological space for the articulation of union strategies based on militant forms of workplace action. Canadian autoworkers maintained a trade union–centered worldview in which the interests of the trade union were understood as independent of, if not in opposition to, those of the corporations. This interpretive framework made Canadian autoworkers and their leaders suspicious of the new 1980s management discourse of teamwork and of attempts to define the interests of workers with those of individual corporations. Moreover, such a trade union–centered view alerted Canadian UAW leaders to the dangers of concessions to the union's credibility among the rank and file.[44]

Two other factors reinforced the likelihood that Canadian autoworkers would choose a militant strategy rather than the cooperative one advanced by the international union. In 1978, Robert White was elected director of the Canadian region of the UAW. Although White had been pro-international and a one-time Reuther man, he came out of the syndicalist tradition of the UAW. His election brought this tradition back into the top leadership of the union and bolstered the position of those staff, local leaders, and members who supported militant tendencies in the union. Furthermore, the success of militant action in the 1970s proved the viability of such a course of action in the face of demands for workers to bear the brunt of economic recovery.

In contrast, the American UAW leadership had developed, since the 1950s, a worldview that emphasized consensus and the commonality of interest between the union and the corporations. The language once used by Walter Reuther to encourage profit sharing in the 1950s was not so different from the corporate arguments used in favor of these arrangements in the 1980s. Moreover, the postwar years of a "civilized" relationship with management in which mass picketing during strikes became a thing of the past encouraged this identification of union with corporate interests.[45] This ideological heritage laid the groundwork for the American UAW's acceptance of management's promise of a new era of labor-management relations based on teamwork and equality of sacrifice and for management's strategy to recruit

44. Canadian regional director's report to Canadian council, January 30, 31, 1982, p. 23.

45. William Serrin's discussion of the 1970 General Motors–UAW negotiations in *The Company and the Union* provides tremendous insight into the union's identification of its interests with corporations.

the union to its side in its drive to restore competitiveness and productivity through concessions from union members.

This interpretation of labor-management relations had been reinforced by the American UAW's experience and strategy in the 1970s. After squashing rank-and-file discontent, the American UAW pursued a strategy of concerted cooperation with management to reformulate shop-floor relations and increase productivity through quality-of-worklife projects. When faced once again in the 1980s with rank-and-file dissent and renewed calls for more militant action, American UAW leaders responded as they had ten years earlier. Thus, even though militant action was seen as a viable strategy by many autoworkers, it was outside the worldview of the top union leadership.

The differing internal structures of the two branches of the UAW further contributed to the strategic differences of the union. The Canadian UAW's organizational structure kept leaders in touch with rank-and-file sentiments and enhanced the union's capacity to mobilize members behind a united course of action. In contrast to the experience of the early 1970s, in which the Canadian council provided the means for dissidents to organize a concerted opposition to the incumbent leadership, in the 1980s struggles this same council became a means for the leadership to mobilize membership support for its strategy. In this capacity, the council served as the leadership's means for mobilizing unity behind two highly divisive issues—concessions and the move toward independence. White used the council as a means for gaining decisions on concessions and independence rather than relying on other measures such as referenda. In so doing, he restricted the forums open for opponents to mobilize and protected the Canadian UAW from attacks by the hawks of the labor movement. Furthermore, because the Canadian council is a rank-and-file body, White was able to legitimize his opposition to the international union and his position as representative of Canadian autoworkers, calling the council "the parliament of the union."

The educational and communications network of the union further augmented the efforts by the union leadership to mobilize support. The Canadian UAW's educational thrust is not limited to training shop stewards and administering collective agreements but includes sessions on party politics, economic issues, and government policy. Furthermore, the Canadian Region holds sessions for families of active trade unionists in order to teach them the principles of trade unionism and holds seminars for retirees on how to budget and prepare emotionally for retirement. This policy has provided the union with a well-informed membership able to become actively involved in the community and willingly mobilized behind issues central to the union. Finally, by involving families and retirees in the education process, the union has provided the basis for a union culture based on solidarity and pride in the union's commitment to the membership. In this way, the Canadian UAW blunted the tendency for members to see their union as a bureaucratic organization servicing their needs and encouraged a vision for the union as a crucial link in membership struggles.

This structure distinguishes the Canadian UAW from its American counterpart, in which centralized bureaucratic control and "expertise" have replaced union initiative through mobilization of the rank and file. The historical legacy of these characteristics is leadership-dominated decision making with few organizational channels for membership influence on strategy or for concerted opposition by militants. The lack of a widespread network of local activists with links to union leaders further impeded mobilization of American autoworkers. Thus, whereas the militant syndicalist collective identity and the unique organizational structure of the Canadian UAW contributed to both its choice and its strategic capacity to reject concessions, the American UAW's ideological heritage and centralized organizational structure eclipsed this option.

Both the Canadian and the American UAW strategies are risky. Both unions see their strategies as a means for assuring their place in the future. The American UAW strategy, however, threatens to destroy the very organization it is intended to protect—the UAW. In agreeing to and promoting concessions and management's vision of reformulated labor relations, the American UAW has unwittingly weakened itself. Concessions and cooperation with management have failed to deliver the wages and benefits workers have come to expect of the UAW, thus undermining existing members' attachment to their union and limiting the appeal of the union to new workers. Furthermore, the devolution of collective bargaining to the local level has fractured the membership on local and corporate lines. Competition among autoworkers and between union locals undermines the union's capacity to engage in collective action. Moreover, it erodes the centralized organizational structure that had served as a basis for union power since the immediate postwar years. The prospects for the American UAW appear bleak, and its marginalization in the new economy emerges as a real possibility.[46]

Although the Canadian UAW, now the CAW, emerged from its struggles united and more powerful than ever, it too faces serious challenges. Recent mergers with other unions and successful organizing drives by the CAW have increased its numerical strength; they have also increased the diversity of union membership. In so doing, these membership additions may have created future obstacles to the articulation of a unity of interest among Canadian autoworkers and hence the capacity of the union to engage in united collective action. Moreover, certain organizational changes to the union since its independence have led to increased bureaucratization and a possible loss of independence of the Canadian council. Finally, the CAW continues to face the challenges of restructuring. New Japanese auto plants in Canada pose an organizational challenge to the CAW; although the CAW has been successful in its bid to represent workers in the new CAMI Automotive plant, a joint venture between General Motors and Suzuki, the future of the union remains uncertain in the new Honda, Toyota, and Hyundai plants.[47] Unless it is successful, the CAW will lose its monopolistic position in the auto industry and face the prospect of wage competition. Moreover, it remains unclear how the CAW will mesh demands for Japanese-style labor-management relations with those existing in the older auto plants. At the moment, however, the CAW is operating from a position of strength. This is certain to have an impact on how restructuring is effected. What remains to be seen is whether this union has the power to effect a qualitatively different form of restructuring in which unions continue to play a pivotal role.

The Canadian and American autoworkers' unions appear bent on two different courses of action with the likelihood that the former will survive while the latter withers. Yet, this prediction is premature. As economic restructuring proceeds, it becomes more and more evident that corporations are unsure of the best strategy for economic survival.

46. Jane Slaughter and Mike Parker, "The Team Concept in the U.S. Auto Industry: Implications for Unions" (Paper presented to Annual Meeting of the Canadian Political Science Association, Windsor, June 9, 1988); Helen Zia, "UAW: Broken Ranks," *Monthly Detroit*, January 1984, pp. 43–44; David Milton, "Late Capitalism and the Decline of Trade Union Power in the U.S.," *Economic and Industrial Democracy* 7 (August 1986): 319–339.

47. *Globe and Mail*, October 29, 1988, p. A15.

Such corporate uncertainty increases the space for debate and struggle over restructuring and consequently the place for unions to shape the economic future. To take advantage of this opportunity, unions must have the power to make their voices heard and to back their proposals with action. At the moment, the CAW appears better prepared to take up this challenge. Nonetheless, the growing support for the rank-and-file New Direction Movement in the United States may promise a revitalization of the American UAW. The task confronting this and other rank-and-file movements in the United States is monumental, however, for it requires not only a restoration of the collective bargaining strength of unions but a fundamental ideological transformation and a remaking of workers' history.

4 The Steel Crisis and Labor Politics in France and the United States

Anthony Daley

New technologies and organizational forms confronted workers and their unions with particular force in the 1980s. In the steel industry, such changes restored profit margins after a decade of decline in the advanced countries. Following the leads of the Japanese and Germans, producers in Britain, France, and the United States adopted continuous casting, automated controls, and other new technologies to improve product quality while lowering production costs. Years of low-capacity utilization, however, forced producers to close plants, and no steel industry has saved jobs since the mid-1970s (see Table 4–1). While the business press heralds labor market flexibility, sympathetic analyses bemoan the loss of union power.[1]

In this essay I compare the mobilization and organization of steelworkers in France and the United States. Unions in both steel industries have histories of antagonism with capital. Yet they have had very different strategic orientations—class-based in France and apolitical in the United States. Consequently, the two movements have diverged in their willingness to mobilize members. Two configurations of political and market institutions have also offered the union movements dif-

I owe a special debt of gratitude to the two editors of this book, who helped sharpen my analysis. Special thanks as well to Peter Hall, George Ross, and Sidney Tarrow for their comments on an earlier draft.

1. See, for instance, Martin Rhodes and Vincent Wright, "The European Steel Unions and the Steel Crisis, 1974–84: A Study in the Demise of Traditional Unionism," *British Journal of Political Science* 18 (April 1988): 171–95.

Table 4–1 Employees in the steel industry, 1967–87 (000's)

	Japan	United States	Italy	West Germany	France
1965	321.9	584.5	69.7	255.6	158.8
1970	345.2	549.6	74.4	237.7	145.7
1974	323.8	525.0	93.6	230.6	155.7
1976	320.0	469.7	97.0	220.3	154.5
1978	287.8	471.4	96.3	205.1	135.9
1980	271.0	429.3	101.0	201.0	114.0
1982	268.5	323.6	97.0	181.0	97.0
1984	264.8	267.4	81.7	156.5	87.1
1987	232.3	210.0	64.9	137.3	62.9

Source; OECD, *The Steel Industry* (Paris: OECD, various years).
Note: Employees include process workers, technicians, office staff, workers in auxiliary services, and apprentices.

ferent sets of challenges. This combination of strategic orientation and institutional constraints led to significantly different outcomes for steelworkers after the crisis in international steel markets.

French steelworkers received protection from market forces, whereas their American counterparts were defenseless when producers streamlined operations. While American steelworkers were laid off in increasing numbers after 1974, no French workers received pink slips. Labor shedding took place in the French industry via negotiated social plans in which workers received transfers to other activities, early retirement, or training programs. Material payoffs are important for the individuals involved, but the critical issue in comparing these movements is strategic capacity. Because of their organizational weaknesses, French steel unions pursued a political strategy while their American counterpart followed a more economistic one. Consequently, French unions seemed more interested in protecting jobs and Americans more concerned with wages. This divergent "dependent variable" can be explained largely with two sets of "independent variables": the relative capacity of unions to mobilize their constituencies in attempts to alter industrial decision making, and the willingness of unions to invoke state aid to constrain firm-level decisions.

American steelworkers sought to regulate class conflict "privately," acquiescing to the demands of employers to marginalize state influence. Confinement within the traditional boundaries of industrial relations offered American unions influence in industrial government during periods of growth. This coresponsibility became dysfunctional, however, when management withdrew its consent in the 1980s. Market-led industrial transformation in the United States, in which key investment decisions remained with the companies, enabled American employers to turn the competitiveness issue back against the union.

The French movement, in contrast, sought state intervention against the steel employers because its organizational pluralism and the backwardness of the mill owners could not lead to a situation of cogovernance. State-led adjustment in France fit snugly with state intervention in the social sphere, and both incited a divided union movement to appeal to the political sphere to delay job cuts and soften the impact of job loss. State tutelage forced the French companies to bargain with the unions and rebuild the steel regions.

In this essay I lay out these two country cases. We begin with an investigation of industry and labor politics in the postwar years. Then, we examine the confluence of business and labor strategies in the 1970s; it becomes clear that the massive labor shedding of the 1980s flowed from decisions made earlier. How displacement occurred reflects the strategic capacity of organized labor. I argue that such capacity rests not simply on the organizational strength of trade unions but on the linkages to other actors in the political economy.

INDUSTRIAL POLITICS BEFORE THE CRISIS: 1950–73

How a firm confronted the depressed international steel market in the 1970s depended in large part on decisions made earlier. Market downturn became a crisis to those steelmakers already weak financially or without a strategy in place to adapt to sluggish demand. Here the French and the American industries had much in common. Both invested late in the technologies that would define competitiveness—oxygen converters (BOF) and continuous casters. Both entered the 1970s focusing on carbon steel production (instead of more sophisticated, profitable, and less demand-sensitive alloys). Both feared state intervention would reduce management autonomy. Yet, given the different institutional possibilities, these two industries pursued very different industrial and political strategies. The two adjustment processes had markedly different consequences for labor.

It is easy to forget that the American steel industry introduced many important technical innovations (open-hearth conversion and wide-strip rolling mills) before 1945, and it remained at the forefront of technical research well into the postwar period.[2] The industry enjoyed comparative advantages in plant scale, raw material costs, and technology through the 1950s. In spite of the slow growth in domestic consumption, U.S. steelmakers increased their capacity substantially.[3] They assumed that foreign demand for steel would be relatively inelastic. Capacity expansion in the 1950s took place almost entirely within old plants, however. When the industry invested in the 1950s, it chose the proven technologies (for instance, open-hearth furnaces) over new processes (BOF).

American producers thus pursued conservative investment strategies in the first thirty years of the postwar period. Only one new integrated plant was constructed after 1945.[4] In contending with the depletion of iron ore reserves, they exploited reserves outside the United States—in South America, Africa, and Canada—but heavily favored the Canadian ore because of proximity. They also spent considerable sums on pelletizing plants to upgrade Great Lakes ore.[5] Technically successful, the program introduced an expensive inflexibility into the cost structures of American firms. No sooner were the pelletizing plants finished than imported ore dropped in price. As ore carriers increased in size, shipping became cheaper. By the mid-1960s, the African and Australian ores were more competitive than the Canadian, and American firms experienced a permanent cost disadvantage.[6]

2. See Bela Gold, William S. Pierce, Gerhard Rosegger, and Mark Perlman, *Technological Progress and Industrial Leadership: The Growth of the U.S. Steel Industry, 1900–1970* (Lexington, Mass. Lexington Books, 1984).

3. Apparent consumption grew only 0.4 percent annually between 1950 and 1960; Donald F. Barnett and Louis Schorsch, *Steel: Upheaval in a Basic Industry* (Cambridge, Mass.: Ballinger, 1983), p. 23. Consumption would grow faster during the 1960s—4.3 percent annually. Still, the American market, obviously the largest in the capitalist world, was comparatively slow growing; see Anthony Cockerill, *The Steel Industry: International Comparisons of Industrial Structure and Performance* (London: Cambridge University Press, 1974), p. 11.

4. The Benjamin Fairless Works of U.S. Steel was the only "greenfield" plant built in the 1950s.

5. This meant taking ore with 20–35 percent iron content and making pellets with 60–65 percent iron; see Kenneth Warren, *World Steel: An Economic Geography* (New York: Crane, Russak, 1975), p. 219.

6. See Robert W. Crandall, *The U.S. Steel Industry in Recurrent Crisis: Policy Options in a Competitive World* (Washington: Brookings Institution, 1981), pp. 20–21.

A stable oligopoly facilitated sectoral unity without a powerful trade association. The American Iron and Steel Institute served more as a statistical agency than as a dominant actor. Within that oligopoly, U.S. Steel served as price leader. Price stability enabled the firms to control competition and coordinate collective bargaining efforts. The Coordinating Committee of Steel Companies assembled the twelve integrated firms in 1956 to negotiate industry-wide contracts with labor;[7] it continued to negotiate industry contracts, allowing firms to bargain on local issues.

Management culture also favored clubbish, noncompetitive market-sharing arrangements. At their origin, steel firms were pioneers in corporate organization and were among the first to exploit ruthlessly economies of scale. Yet, by the 1950s, they had developed a serious market myopia—hence the failure to develop export strategies and an increasing vulnerability to imports.

Although below the manufacturing average, profits accrued to American producers through the 1960s because of transport costs to the American market. After 1959, however, the United States became a net importer of steel. By the mid-1970s, the price differential between American and imported steel threatened profitability in the industry.

To control inflation, U.S. presidents repeatedly bargained publicly with industry executives over price increases with little concern about industry economics. Such ad hoc political control of prices may have prevented even more imports from outpricing American steel products. Nonetheless, domestic steel prices rose faster than both world steel prices and domestic wholesale prices. Higher prices compensated for low-capacity utilization rather than ensuring extraordinary profits.[8]

With creeping imports in the 1960s, producers portrayed themselves as victims of international market forces and sought protection. The industry convinced the White House and Congress that protection would strengthen the industry. Voluntary restraint agreements were negotiated with both the European Community and Japan in 1968 and renewed in 1972. Trade protection and (admittedly diminishing) market position enabled American producers to define the

7. Coordinated bargaining had taken place earlier, with U.S. Steel setting the wage pattern, but the smaller producers felt whipsawed when they had difficulty absorbing wage costs (by raising prices) if they were targeted first by the union.

8. Since the domestic steel market is not a free market, oligopolistic firms do not set prices according to market demand. The United States is not unique in this respect.

terms of adjustment at least until international surplus capacity after 1974. The integrated majors invested in new technologies, but at a rate much slower than their international rivals. That lag became serious when markets contracted after 1974.

State policy consequently developed into protection of industry interests without altering the arms-length and adversarial character of business-state relations. The industry had long been the target of antitrust investigations, and its pricing policies had invoked presidential wrath. To industry actors, government labor policy seemed to favor union positions by protecting the machinery of collective bargaining. Truman's seizure of the industry in 1952 constituted simply the most overt expression of presidential displeasure with industry pricing policies and collective bargaining practices.

As a result of the historical sequencing of business-state relations, public policy makers could not intervene directly into company strategy when the crisis hit international markets. The porous political process would permit multiple points of access for societal actors to influence policy.[9] In steel as well as elsewhere, policy makers utilized the hands-off approach of tax incentives and trade policy. A profound distrust continued to exist between big business and its state.[10]

French steelmakers did not enjoy similar strategic options. Protection of the national market was impossible after 1953 with the European Coal and Steel Community, although the latter negotiated Community-wide orderly marketing agreements with Japan and the newly industrializing countries from the early 1970s onward. The policy tools of the French state would erode self-governance once the financial situation of the firms became acute.

The French industry was more bifurcated than its American counterpart. Marshall Plan funds had facilitated the construction of new integrated strip mills (Usinor-Denain and Sollac) in the 1950s. A coastal plant at Dunkirk was finished in 1963. Yet the bulk of tonnages came from plants constructed before 1914. These plants were located inland, mostly in the Lorraine near iron ore deposits whose

9. The result is a pluralism of national purpose; see Stephen D. Krasner, "United States Commercial and Monetary Policy: Unravelling the Paradox of External Strength and Internal Weakness," in *Between Power and Plenty: Foreign Economic Policies of Advanced Industrial States*, ed. Peter J. Katzenstein (Madison: University of Wisconsin Press, 1978), pp. 51–87.

10. David Vogel, "Why Businessmen Distrust Their State: The Political Consciousness of American Corporate Executives," *British Journal of Political Science* 8 (1978): 45–78.

quality eroded during the postwar period. Thus, efficient operations subsidized inefficient ones—much like the American case.

Price controls aggravated low profitability. While the American executive sought to control post hoc price increases announced by the firms, the French government used controls on thousands of goods to direct the course of industrialization. Consequently, French steel prices remained below those of other European industries. The Ministry of Industry compensated for artificially low prices and subsidized credits. The major difference between the French and American cases, however, rested in their respective competitive positions in the 1950s, the decade the price controls most hurt the French industry. The French were high-cost producers while the Americans still enjoyed cost advantages.

Still, the French industry invested more per ton of steel produced than any European producer between 1953 and 1973.[11] Investments, however, kept decrepit plants and machinery functioning. The Lorraine producers replaced machinery in old plants without a view to the structure of production; blast furnaces might be disproportionate to converters and the latter to rolling mills. The French producers achieved the economies of scale reached by the Americans in the 1920s only in the 1960s!

Within this context, the French state intervened to maintain the industry. It has had tools to influence corporate behavior, alter the policy agenda, and generate support.[12] Its capacity to intervene selectively derived from several sources. Through active discrimination it rewarded favored firms with relief from price controls and corporate taxes as well as access to below–market rate investment credits from the Fonds de Développement Economique et Social (FDES, economic and social development fund). By administratively setting prices in securities markets, it could allocate the distribution of privately raised capital.[13] Parapublic banking facilities separated the pro-

11. Jean-Pierre Marger, "La situation et l'avenir de la sidérurgie" (Report presented to the Economic and Social Council, July 3–4, 1979).

12. See Peter Hall, *Governing the Economy: The Politics of State Intervention in Britain and France* (New York: Oxford University Press, 1986), as well as John Zysman, *Political Strategies for Industrial Order: State, Market, and Industry in France* (Berkeley: University of California Press, 1977). See also John H. McArthur and Bruce R. Scott, *Industrial Planning in France* (Boston: Harvard Graduate School of Business, 1969).

13. See John Zysman, *Governments, Markets, and Growth: Financial Systems and the Politics of Industrial Change* (Ithaca: Cornell University Press, 1983).

cess of borrowing from lending and inserted state leverage into the allocation of funds.

State-led adjustment could not remain divorced from the electoral concerns of French politicians. Prestige projects crept into the planning process from the political sphere. The exclusion of the unions brought active disdain from the left before 1981 and a consequent delegitimization of industrial policy. Especially as politics became polarized after 1958, the very success of intervention politicized industrial policy making. If leaders could take credit for success, they could also be blamed for failure.

Until the 1960s, the trade association, the Chambre Syndicale de la Sidérurgie Française (CSSF), played a critical role in protecting industry interests. Membership was compulsory for steel firms. During the postwar shortages, the CSSF allocated raw materials. It continued to process sales of steel products for members, thereby gaining independent knowledge of the industry. It facilitated capital issues by operating a collective borrowing agency, the Groupement des Industries Sidérurgiques.[14] Because the agency board approved applications, it was privy to confidential financial information. Thus, the CSSF had intimate knowledge of the industry.

The financial deterioration of the firms in the 1960s upset the cozy relationships. The increasing drag of the smaller, inefficient Lorraine firms meant a decreasing capacity to finance the new projects necessary to compete with European rivals. Usinor's investment in Dunkirk dried up funds for other plants. Surplus capacity first arose in the early 1960s. Overexpansion led to European price slashing. Debt accumulation accelerated, and the French producers found themselves unable to undertake new investments and facing bankruptcy.[15]

The policy response was a state-financed aid package in 1966. The Convention Etat-Sidérurgie constituted a comprehensive plan to finance investments and restore profitability. Its centerpiece was Fr 2.7 billion in FDES credits and an equal amount of state-guaranteed loans to be used for plant-level modernization and debt reduction. The

14. By pooling guarantees, this agency could raise more funds for the industry than the firms could individually. Given its strategic position, it could affect investment plans, although it was ultimately dependent on the ministries of Finance and Industry for authorization.

15. For a lengthier discussion of the competitive difficulties of French steel, see Anthony Daley, "Labor and Industrial Change: The Politics of Steel in France" (Ph.D. dissertation, University of California, Berkeley, 1988), chap. 4.

Convention responded to the state's concern for national champions by merging several companies into two—Usinor and Wendel-Sidélor (which assumed the name Sacilor in 1973). It transfered some investment control to the ministries of Industry and Finance, but this simply transformed passive oversight into an active one. These ministries would negotiate and monitor firm-level commitments, the latter negotiated by the CSSF. The trade association transformed its detailed understanding of the industry into a position of leadership.

The new role for the CSSF was reinforced by the changing political character of the industry and the dynamism of its president. Industrial concentrations weakened the power of the old steel families whose reputations created legends of paternalism and autocracy. The orientations of the new managers, schooled at the *grandes écoles,* fit well the perspective of state officials. Jacques Ferry, who became head of the CSSF in 1963, argued passionately for the virtues of state-led modernization.

The trade association also acquiesced to a clause in the Convention which required negotiations with the steel unions over the terms of 15,000 job losses. It also accepted the minimum terms stipulated by the state—no layoffs. Here began a cycle of state-imposed negotiations in exchange for financing. While state actors feared the outcome of industrial militancy, especially in periods of close electoral contests, the industry needed funding. Ferry appealed successfully to this mutual dependence.

The CSSF became an active player by utilizing the "productivism" of its membership. Success was gauged by raw tonnages and not by profitability or market insertion. This policy meshed well with the prestige mentality of state planners. Negotiations over a new coastal plant at Fos-sur-Mer in the late 1960s confirmed the merging of industry and state interests. The CSSF accepted the political criteria of the siting. Wendel-Sidélor and Usinor received additional FDES credits to cover costs, overruns, and the phaseout of additional plants in the Lorraine.[16] Wendel-Sidélor also negotiated another 10,000 Lorraine job losses without layoffs, with many workers transferring to Fos.

Thus, institutional arrangements differed dramatically between the American and French cases. Traditional dominance of domestic mar-

16. In 1973 alone, the Ministry of Finance committed 150 percent of the annual FDES budget to the Fos project.

kets permitted America producers to set the terms of adjustment. The hands-off state would intervene through trade policy to protect that market position. The earlier financial crisis in the French industry forced producers to cede mediating authority to the trade association. It also enabled the interventionist state to gain a foothold in industry politics.

LABOR STRATEGY DURING RELATIVE PROSPERITY

The terms of adjustment posed different challenges to unions. At the same time, the internal politics of each labor movement affected their ability to take advantage of institutional possibilities. How the unions perceived and reacted to developments during the years of prosperity structured decision-making possibilities afterward.

Led by Philip Murray and affiliated with the CIO, the Steel Workers Organizing Committee and afterward the United Steel Workers of America (USWA) developed a reputation for confrontational strategy and strong, industrial unionism. Wartime arbitration extended union recognition to all basic steel plants and strengthened the leadership of the union. A high level of organization at the shop floor guaranteed the union human and financial resources. Having accepted a union presence on the shop floor, the companies sought to thwart the disruption of wildcat strikes, enforce labor peace, and enlist the union in productivity bargaining. Indeed, a "benevolent autocracy" protected the infant organization and provided the discipline to confront the oligopolistic industry.[17] For the industry, internal union discipline was a necessary ingredient to successful collective bargaining.

By the late 1940s, industrial relations in steel pitted strength against strength.[18] The USWA developed into a large and prosperous institution capable of bargaining. Industry-wide strikes in 1946, 1949, 1952, 1956, and 1959 showed the militancy necessary to pressure employers unwilling to share profits or shop-floor power. Industrial

17. E. Robert Livernash, *Collective Bargaining in the Basic Steel Industry: A Study of the Public Interest and the Role of Government* (Washington: U.S. Department of Labor, 1961), p. 78.

18. For this period, see also Lloyd Ulman, *The Government of the Steel Workers' Union* (New York: Wiley, 1962).

action in the 1950s targeted primarily wage and fringe issues. This period also marked the institutionalization of collective bargaining. Grievance and arbitration procedures were regularized. Contract negotiations took place at regular three-year intervals, and a plethora of joint boards investigated bargaining issues in the interim. Militancy combined with maturity to fit snugly into the mainstream of American democratic politics. Murray had good relations with Roosevelt and Truman. He was sufficiently anticommunist to appease Washington's political climate. The issue of government intervention pervaded industrial bargaining after 1952.[19] The union perceived arbitration and mediation in positive terms: established rules implied a (limited) partnership. The industry, however, decried pressures on prices combined with leniency in mediating wage disputes.

The national steel strike of 1959 marked a watershed in both industrial relations and adjustment strategies. Previous struggles had secured pension rights in 1949 as well as supplementary unemployment benefits and cost-of-living allowances in 1956. In exchange for the latter, the industry obtained a long-term (three-year) contract with annual increments fixed in advance. Still, the industry sought to gain control over work practices and attempted to roll back a contract clause that protected "past work practices." Although managers claimed the clause resulted in featherbedding, no evidence seems to support the charge. Rather, the issue was symbolic of a struggle over shop-floor management.

The strike and its settlement altered future collective bargaining. The industry dated import penetration to that period and sought to avoid lengthy shutdowns. The dispute also chastised the union. Wage gains were meager (cost-of-living adjustments—COLAs—were seriously weakened), and they combined with four months of lost income to push union officers to seek less disruptive settlements.

By accepting the demonization of imports, the union bought the industry's key argument concerning competitiveness. This acceptance proved increasingly useful to the companies by the late 1960s, when the union could mobilize locals to pressure members of Congress on import protection. More important, however, it facilitated the labor relations sought by the companies. The emphasis on productivity be-

19. Ronald W. Schatz, "Battling over Government's Role," in *Forging a Union of Steel: Philip Murray, SWOC, and the United Steelworkers*, ed. Paul F. Clark, Peter Gottlieb, and Donald Kennedy (Ithaca: ILR Press, 1987), pp. 87–102.

came expedient in the 1960s with higher imports. The union turned its attention away from contesting price increases and company policies in general toward seeking a collaborative relationship to restore competitiveness.

Part of this collaboration consisted of "human relations" bargaining in which quality-of-worklife issues stood on a par with wages. As a result of the 1959 accord, the two sides agreed to meet regularly to iron out differences in contract language. The routinization of contract negotiations, however, effectively eliminated local input into the negotiating process. A negotiating team took positions back to an assembly of local presidents for ratification. Although union officers were appointed by the leadership, they nonetheless needed to be responsive to local issues. Continuous bargaining circumvented even the appointed leadership. The 1962 contract eliminated COLAs and settled on a wage increase well below even government recommendations.

This collaborative relationship depended on the insulation of the leadership ranks. Still, the protection of local work practices meant that dissatisfaction with money issues could be vented elsewhere when management changed staffing. The rumblings from locals contested both the meager wage increases and the modes of decision making within the union.[20]

Previous grass roots action within the USWA had largely ended in failure.[21] Attempts in the 1950s to secure more leadership accountability and greater local autonomy—initially focusing on dues increases—stumbled on weak organization and the leadership's superior organizational resources. The local activists behind the rank-and-file actions depended on their control of local work practices. The industry sought to help the leadership maintain control to provide a more stable collective bargaining.

The 1965 "palace revolt" of I. W. Abel, who defeated the incumbent president David MacDonald, depended on local dissatisfaction with the human relations bargaining. Wages stagnated in the early 1960s, deflecting demands from internal democracy per se toward a more militant stance on the outcome of the bargaining process. Abel

20. Richard Betheil, "The ENA in Perspective: The Transformation of Collective Bargaining in the Basic Steel Industry," *Review of Radical Political Economics* 10 (Summer 1978): 7.

21. John Herling, *Right to Challenge: People and Power in the Steelworkers Union* (New York: Harper & Row, 1972).

mobilized the dissatisfaction for his candidacy but then proceeded to insulate his leadership from pressures from below. Rules changes made strike votes even more difficult. Abel refused to tinker with industry-wide bargaining, thereby continuing to constrain local activists. His leadership also worked with management to thwart local job actions.[22]

Contract rounds in 1965 and 1968 brought higher wages. While the booming economy in 1968 and 1969 encouraged limited wildcatting and wage drift, the union leadership became more assertive in negotiations. A challenger to Abel's candidacy for a second term in 1969 won 40 percent of the vote in the union and a majority among steelworkers[23] (beginning in the 1960s, the USWA had diversified into other industrial activities). Negotiators used a strike threat to reintroduce the COLA in 1971. High wages improved leadership popularity.

By the early 1970s, union-management collaboration had coalesced. The industry conceded wage increases that bought internal union cohesion. Union centralization prevented challenges to industry strategies. The union supported industry attempts to secure the domestic market. It used its political resources to pressure political actors into negotiating trade protection. The protection-employment nexus garnered considerable backing from the 120-member Congressional Steel Caucus that rallied support for an aggressive trade policy.

The French movement, in contrast, challenged the logic of capitalist development. The active exclusion of labor until the late 1960s, however, meant that such challenges long remained on the outside. Therefore, constant demands from the Confédération Générale du Travail (CGT) and the Confédération Française Démocratique du Travail (CFDT) for comprehensive negotiations over the industry and its social issues focused exclusively on the terms of worker displacement. Still, consistent union challenges politicized industrial policy.

French unions had a different set of options in the face of pressures on steel employment. Trade protection was not viable, nor did the unions have the labor market capacity to confront companies head-on in large, protracted strike actions. Because of weak union organizations, the conflict between leadership and members was much less visible. Rather, in a competitive union environment, intraclass conflict

22. Betheil, "ENA in Perspective," pp. 14–16.
23. Herling, *Right to Challenge*, pp. 364–482.

took place *between* unions. Yet, rivalry within certain parameters could encourage mobilization that would challenge industrial decision making. Mobilization combined with state intervention to offer French steelworkers greater protection against fluctuations in the labor market.

French steel unions are shells of their American counterpart. Union density, after a surge in the immediate postwar period, hovered around 25 percent afterward. Organizational competition aggravated low membership rates. Four unions competed for blue-collar loyalties: the CGT, the CFDT, the Force Ouvrière (FO), and the Conféderation Française des Travailleurs Chrétiens (CFTC).[24] The CGT was dominant until the 1960s, although division and secession sprinkled its history.

Throughout the postwar period, the regularity of shop-floor electioneering has compensated for the low union density. Elections have taken place every two years for works councils and every year for shop stewards; both institutions represent the entire workforce and not simply union members. Contests outside the plant for tripartite arbitrators' councils and social security administration boards have been every three years. Electioneering has forced constant contact with rank and file and nonmembers. The task of reelection has spurred union agents to address issues they might otherwise neglect. In steel, the CGT and the CFDT have typically won over 80 percent by themselves.

Steelworkers, like the French working class in general, have suffered from serious political divisions. Whereas the CGT has enjoyed close ties with the Communist party, the other unions have been involved to varying degrees with Socialist and other leftist forces. The CGT–Communist party nexus, however, dominated steel politics. Excluded from the political mainstream during the precrisis period, the Communists provided relentless critiques of state-led capitalist modernization. The CGT developed an "oppositional unionism" that contested the adjustment model in steel as well as elsewhere. Oppositionalism translated into hard collective bargaining positions: demands stretched management while making a statement about

24. The Conféderation Générale de l'Encadrement (CGC) represents supervisors, white-collar employees, and middle management. In other sectors besides steel, "independent" unions play a role in bargaining with employers. Although it did not affect politics in the steel industry, another union broke off from the CGT after the war: the Fédération de l'Education Nationale remains the largest French teachers' union.

class exploitation itself. The other unions articulated their platforms in response to the dominant union discourse. This was especially true for the CFDT, which developed a hypermilitant style of unionism with ties to the Socialist party. For both the CGT and the CFDT, class radicalism would pave the way for the political left to achieve state power.

Still, French steel union activity remained decentralized. Bargaining and militancy took place primarily at the local level. Labor law encouraged decentralization. Unions had few legal requirements for discipline. Labor contracts did not legally bind workers to stay on the job. The same union could strike after signing a wage agreement. Although employers could (until 1982) sign an accord with any "representative" union that applied to the entire workforce, they always risked dissatisfaction leading to strike action.

Union poverty also impeded central mobilization. An absence of strike funds limited the duration of conflict and the leverage of central offices. The latter tended not to instigate industrial conflict. Industrial action relied on the material assistance of municipal government and the left parties. Conflict had much more grass roots support than in the United States. It also depended on the durability of social coalitions.

The absence of social control posed dilemmas for French unions. They seemed to ride the crest of class mobilization, but their interlocutors expected the regulation of behavior. They needed to transform energies into material outcomes. This assumed a party-political flavor in which the organizations seek to implement their program through a left government in or near power. The unions realized that, given their weak organizations, their capacity derived from that very mobilization. Needing yet constraining mobilization produced a strategic duality compounded by competitive unionism. Rivalry raised the stakes of social conflict and consequently empowered the labor movement. It also complicated the duality in ways that would make labor strategy unpredictable.

Two additional factors affected steel politics. Until the construction of Fos, 90 percent of crude steel was produced in the Lorraine and the Nord. As in the American steel regions, steel had a critical part of the local economies of these areas. Thus, adjustment provoked strong local responses. Local mobilization played into the political calendar: electoral contests between left and right after 1965 took place almost annually.[25] To the extent that it depended on a stable electoral majority, the interventionist state was vulnerable to social turbulence. Mobilization would produce substantial and tangible benefits.

Such vulnerability has mattered considerably because the state plays a dominant role in industrial relations. Its minimum wage as well as the legislation on minimum vacations, sick pay, working time, and retirement conditions establish the floor for collective bargaining agreements. The Ministry of Labor can force negotiations through threats of unilateral action. It can extend an agreement to a larger jurisdiction. Several labor market institutions subsidized new jobs and financed retirement, supplementary unemployment benefits, and training programs. The Fonds National de l'Emploi (national employment fund), in particular, facilitated collective bargaining success by financing many of the costs of "private" collective bargaining.[26] It financed each redundancy scheme for French steelworkers between 1967 and 1986.

The appeal of state intervention was all the more powerful because industrial relations in steel had been marked by particularly bitter shop-floor relations. As in other advanced countries, French steel developed in the nineteenth century and pursued paternalistic labor practices to attract skilled workers. Unlike their American counterparts, who recognized unions in the 1940s, French steel employers excluded unions from the shop floor until the post-1968 labor reforms. Exclusion reinforced oppositional unionism. Negotiations before 1966 typically focused on minimum wage rates at the regional level. Managers in individual plants used those minimums to set real wages. Only the threat of class mobilization pressured wage setting. Employment bargaining after the mid-1960s changed industrial relations in steel. The unions used a combination of local mobilization and direct negotiations with the state to protect workers.

The three-week strikes in the Lorraine in April 1967 began a pattern of mobilization for employment protection. The job action originated in a parallel conflict in the iron industry. With iron miners blocking shipments, the steel firms threatened layoffs due to inadequate supplies. The locals of the CGT and CFDT called workers off

25. Presidential elections took place in 1965, 1969, 1974, 1981, and 1988; legislative elections in 1967, 1968, 1973, 1978, 1981, 1986, and 1988; and municipal elections in 1965, 1971, 1977, and 1983. A variety of cantonal and regional elections also tested national political strength.

26. See Daley, "Labor and Industrial Change," chap. 8.

the job to prevent short-term layoffs. The CGT and CFDT cooperated in demonstrations and in meetings with state officials. They coordinated positions for the ongoing bargaining sessions mandated by the Convention signed nine months earlier. As in previous conflicts in the Lorraine, the 1967 strikes became town affairs. Families, local politicians, and the younger clergy took part in the demonstrations and denounced the plans to reduce employment. Communist local government provided facilities for meetings, day care, and soup kitchens.

Demands centered on the guarantees promised by the Convention. Trade union unity facilitated mobilization and bargaining. Unity tapped into regional fears. Oppositional unionism (from both the CGT and CFDT) strengthened mobilization because it articulated sentiments of class injustice. Mobilization changed the course of bargaining. After several months of stalling, negotiations became serious. The strike had apparently prevented the employers from signing less comprehensive accords with only the FO and CGC. The consequent social plan promised a combination of interplant transfers, retraining for other steel jobs, and early retirement. All five unions signed an agreement that avoided layoffs.

Decentralized mobilization and state intervention affected later attempts to reduce staffing. The 1971 job cuts at Wendel-Sidélor (due to the company's overextension at Fos) were preceded by a series of strikes at the plant scheduled to be closed. The unions and the employers reached an agreement whereby the 1967 accord would be extended and all transfers (presumably to Fos) would involve equivalent skilling levels and equal pay.

The internal politics of the French and U.S. labor movements meshed with the adjustment strategies before the crisis in international steel markets. The organizationally weak and divided French unions pursued strategies that targeted the interventionist state. Local mobilization, based on oppositionalist rhetoric, secured state response. Intervention in the social and industrial spheres limited industry maneuverability. The USWA, in contrast, had an ambiguous relationship with the steel companies. It stood as a counterauthority to management, and it had the power to pursue such a confrontation. Yet, it used those resources to secure its share of the economic rents from oligopoly. High wages insulated the union leadership from internal challenges. The USWA sought a common ground with

American steelmakers, outside the purview of state oversight in a joint push for protection, which ignored the evidence of diminished competitiveness.

INDUSTRIAL CRISIS AND INSTITUTIONAL UNCERTAINTY

The dramatic decrease in international demand for steel products after 1974 forced all steelmakers to adjust market strategies. Diminished sales, rising input costs, and declining prices jeopardized balance sheets and threatened even the continued existence of certain firms. Market reorganization demanded response, yet maneuverability was limited by previous investment and production choices. For the unions, the weakening of labor markets disrupted previous assumptions about the nature of market exchange. The trade-off of wages for productivity had earlier guaranteed rising living standards. Market collapse in the steel industry upset that deal. Business-state networks and collective bargaining structures framed the terms of employment bargaining.

The difficult years after 1974 offered no clear guide to market strategy. Producers in both the United States and France recognized the new market conditions slowly. International consumption did not decline smoothly: it perked up in 1976 and 1979. Hoping the upturn was near, producers only reluctantly decreased capacity. The cumulative effect of non–decision making produced enormous instability when drastic solutions to surplus capacity became necessary.

American steelmakers blamed a shrinking competitiveness not on the cost structure of plant organization but rather on surging imports. Competitiveness, however, could not be divorced from labor relations. The attempt to lower unit labor costs, to avoid the disruption of strike activity, and to build a business-labor political coalition dominated adjustment during the 1970s.

Market pressures on the majors came from new domestic sources as well. Minimills precipitated the move out of low-end product lines—bars and structurals. Using electric furnaces and continuous casters, the minimills succeeded where their larger rivals had failed. Specializing in a small range of products for regional markets, they did not invest on the massive scale that the majors claimed correctly to be prohibitively expensive. Consequently, capital costs per ton were much lower. Using nonunion workers, the minimills' wage rates were 25 percent lower than in the integrated firms.

The industry had long argued that shortages caused by the 115-day strike in 1959 ushered in the first wave of imports; it wanted steady production runs to guard against foreign sourcing by domestic consumers during each three-year negotiating round. The producers also sought protection from competitive whipsawing by the union after the high wage settlements of the early 1970s. Thus, uniform wages and labor peace became key industry goals.

The Experimental Negotiating Agreement (ENA) of 1973 marked the culmination of producer strategy for an era of high stable costs. The agreement provided a *framework* by which contract negotiations would take place. The union promised not to strike over industry-wide issues in exchange for a guarantee against lockouts. Unresolved issues would be submitted to binding arbitration. Customers would thereby be assured of steady supplies during negotiations. Workers received the COLA and a minimum annual increase of 3 percent. Both COLA payments and management practices were excluded from arbitration.

The industry purchased union collaboration to increase productivity. The effort marked another attempt to tie wages to productivity to challenge imports. But productivity bargaining became mired in organizational politics. Workers were expected to use the joint committees to eliminate their own jobs. The ENA restored the ability to strike over local issues, although market conditions soon provided new constraints. The agreement also did not tamper with employment practices. The companies retained hiring and firing prerogatives.

The industry seems to have acted on its own propaganda: each disruption of supplies ratcheted up imports. The companies assumed that, with sufficient time afforded by import protection, they could introduce new technologies to regain competitiveness. Most important for the steelworkers, however, management refused to protect employment. Therefore, while management was willing to pay wages far in excess of inflation and productivity and the union leadership sought to reinforce its own position, members experienced plant closings and employment losses. Between 1974 and 1980, employment dropped 20 percent.

As the market continued to stagnate, the deal became costly. In the three contracts governed by the ENA (1974, 1977, and 1980), employment costs spiraled upward such that average hourly employment costs by the early 1980s stood at $23, almost twice the manufacturing average. A high-wage strategy would only succeed if the American industry adjusted rapidly toward new productivity-enhancing technologies.

The no-strike clause of the ENA served as a rallying point for yet another challenge to the union leadership. Ed Sadlowski's Fight Back campaign challenged Abel's appointed successor Lloyd McBride for the presidency in 1977.[27] Although wage issues proved satisfactory, the insurgents demanded member ratification for the relinquishment of such a key tool in the union arsenal. Even McBride hedged during his campaign on the retention of the ENA. Again, however, the leadership depended on USWA workers outside steel to secure its tenure, and McBride beat this challenger. As in 1969, the multijurisdictional nature of the union frustrated the attempts of militants in steel to change the course of bargaining.

The 1974 Trade Reform Act gave the industry an array of tools to continue protection: aggrieved producers could file complaints of sales below average costs and invoke tariff retaliation.[28] The Trigger Price Mechanism in 1977 sought to regularize the process and stabilize import penetration. It was also an admission of competitive erosion: the Japanese were considered the most efficient producers and their costs used as benchmarks for dumping complaints.

The insistence on institutional autonomy by the large integrated companies diverted the only major attempt at industrial policy in steel. In 1977, the Carter administration convened the Steel Task Force, chaired by Undersecretary of the Treasury Anthony Solomon, to study the industry. The task force had recommended the Trigger Price Mechanism to protect the market from imports and tax advantages to enable sufficient profit margins to finance necessary investments in modern equipment. Both trade and tax policy would "enable the industry to compete fairly" without "direct governmental involvement

27. See the discussions in John P. Hoerr, *And the Wolf Finally Came: The Decline of the American Steel Industry* (Pittsburgh: University of Pittsburgh Press, 1988); and Betheil, "ENA in Perspective."

28. See Michael Borrus, "The Politics of Competitive Erosion in the Steel Industry," in *American Industry in International Competition: Government Policies and Corporate Strategies*, ed. John Zysman and Laura Tyson (Ithaca: Cornell University Press, 1983), pp. 60–105.

in the industry's decisions."[29] The pricing floors restored the market sharing threatened by imports. Unlike tripartite committees in the European context, however, the Steel Task Force accepted the industry's argument and imposed few constraints on firm behavior.

Protection gave the industry time. Imports into the American market stagnated until the 1980s, and price levels consequently remained higher than otherwise. High prices, however, simply swelled annual dividends rather than funding badly needed investments. Although the companies introduced BOF and computer-based controls and closed unproductive facilities, the pace proved insufficient to catch up to the productivity levels of international rivals. The integrated firms also began to diversify out of basic steel.

Thus, as the market shrunk around them, the integrated majors continued to accumulate political muscle. They had deflected governmental attempts to direct adjustment. They had purchased labor support. Yet, the utility of political resources depended ultimately on market position. Deterioration would render political gains obsolete. In the meantime, net disinvestment boxed labor into an uncomfortable set of options: high wages with unemployment or the unknown.

Market failure hastened the reorganization of societal interests in the French context. The depression in steel markets hit the French industry particularly hard. Fos began production in 1974, immediately adding capacity to a weak market. Long-term debt had increased with the financing of Fos and a new sectional mill in the Lorraine. Producers were squeezed in 1975 by governmental controls on layoffs for which they received Fr 1.5 billion of FDES credits to meet interest payments. Neither Usinor nor Sacilor would turn a profit until the late 1980s.

A tentative aid package in 1977 poured Fr 1.3 billion of FDES funds into the companies. In return, the companies negotiated with the unions the terms of 17,000 redundancies. Because of the state's increasing mistrust of the industry's unceasing optimism, intensified by the tense political environment, the two companies also had to deposit shares with a state financial concern. An interministerial committee received access to all company data and supervised the holding companies for both firms to prevent active disinvestment. Governmental

29. Anthony M. Solomon, "Report to the President: A Comprehensive Program for the Steel Industry," December 1977, quoted in Borrus, "Competitive Erosion," p. 94.

suspicions of total market failure were confirmed by the companies' performance *with* the infusion of state funds. The following year debt exceeded 100 percent of sales revenue.[30]

The right government's unexpected victory in the March 1978 legislative elections emboldened Prime Minister Barre to assume de facto control of the industry. The state forced the companies to exchange state and bank debt for limited equity. This disguised nationalization temporarily relieved pressure from debt servicing. It also marginalized Ferry and the CSSF, the former forced to resign and the latter reduced to statistical work. The presidents of both Usinor and Sacilor were removed. The government sought to pursue production for the more profitable product niches. It also sought to restore financial equilibrium as quickly as possible. Consequently, production flows were disrupted and industrial siting remained problematic. Once again the bailout insisted on negotiations with the steel unions over the terms of 20,000 redundancies.

Labor mobilization accompanied each successive plan to reorganize the industry. Job actions in 1967 and 1971 had been framed within the context of worldwide growth in steel demand. The French industry suffered serious competitive problems, but unionists showed even more optimism than the CSSF and envisioned a period in which growth would resume and steel employment would even increase. Even after the oil shock and lowered demand in 1973–74, the government prohibited layoffs as a way of increasing purchasing power and preventing social turmoil. Like their American counterparts, French unionists sought to regain a golden age of high production and high wages.

The proposed job cuts in 1977 revived the regional urgency, but accompanying that shock was a new sense of political responsibility within the unions. The 1978 legislative elections were expected to give power to the left, which would revive the industry. The first wave of redundancies was announced in April 1977 immediately after the municipal elections. Both the CGT and the CFDT had met with the owners and with a variety of ministers to argue against the actions. Protests were measured, well disciplined, and careful not to upset the approaching national elections. Both metalworker federations counseled moderation and dampened militancy. Partially as a result, the

30. *Fortune*, June 1978, referred to Usinor and Sacilor as the two most indebted large companies in the world.

early retirement benefits of the social plan used to disengage workers were less generous than those in place from 1971.[31] Given the political climate, only the FO signed the accord. Nonetheless, under state pressures, the companies used early retirement and transfer provisions to ease workers out without resorting to layoffs.

The shock of 1978 altered the strategic orientation of labor. The additional redundancies followed the unexpected electoral loss in March, provoking despair among local activists and a rethinking by union elites. Local actions sought to publicize the plight of the steel regions. Militants from the CFDT occupied the regional television station to broadcast appeals for solidarity. The CGT took over police headquarters in Longwy. FO activists occupied the Bank of France. A few zealous workers blocked the doors of the employer federation with tons of scrap metal. These actions were perpetrated by militants but were seldom conceived through regular decision-making processes in the unions.

Because the actions were directed against the symbols of state and capital, they did not alienate public opinion. Direct actions transcended typical modes of industrial protest. The aim was to damage or destroy property to dramatize the plight of the industry and its workforce. Workers had undertaken equally dramatic actions in the past against the steel employers. The 1978–79 period, however, could not be rivaled for the intensity of actions.[32] For six months the national press covered steel politics on a daily basis.

A cross-class opposition to the redundancies also developed. Local merchants shut their doors. Shopkeepers closed down entire towns. Civil servants used vacation time to join marches. The clergy joined the demonstrations and spoke out from the pulpit. More than at any time in the history of postwar steel politics, this conflict brought together groups of workers that ordinarily did not support each other.

The dashed expectations of March 1978 created serious divisions within the unions, for previous strategy depended on the left assuming power. The CGT and CFDT flirted with a new type of labor market strategy: "counterproposals" would show alternative ways of facing competition. "Propositional" unionism sought policy proposals for competitiveness rather than demands for collective bargaining purposes, "to extend the scope of collective bargaining to include indus-

31. Early retirement, for instance, brought 70 percent rather than 90 percent of previous salaries; see Daley, "Labor and Industrial Change," chap. 7.

32. One author chronicled 183 actions in the Longwy area alone; see Claude Durand, *Chômage et violence: Longwy en lutte* (Paris: Galilée, 1981), pp. 20–23.

trial decision-making."[33] The propositions in the steel industry sought new production strategies to save jobs and restore competitiveness.[34] Because of its insistence on autonomous organization and pragmatic behavior, propositional unionism also implied a diminished role for the Communist party.

Such new-found responsibility created tensions within each federation. The severity of the steel crisis of 1978–79 combined with the swiftness of strategic reorientation to create organizational turbulence. Even weak organizations change strategic course slowly. As both the CGT and CFDT grappled with ways to respond to government initiatives, they created internal confusion. The hard actions of worker violence derived from oppositional and not propositional unionism. The federations supported their members but remained uneasy about the decentralized violence and the broad-based mobilization. The CFDT excommunicated a local in Dunkirk and almost expelled the Longwy section for what it called leftist actions. The CGT had set up a pirate radio station to mobilize broad segments of the population. In the process of mobilization, however, it also lost its union flavor, at least according to union officials, and was closed after the mobilization died down.

Centralization through intellectual direction or organizational coercion meant the gradual demobilization of the steelworkers. Demobilization may have been necessary to secure any advantage from the disturbances. Part of the state's industrial policy was a severence payment of Fr 50,000 to encourage rapid exit from the industry. Foreign workers could also redeem social security contributions. The unions feared that too many workers would bail out and completely diffuse the mobilization the unions were attempting to direct.

Demobilization also resulted from the reentry of party-political forces. The CGT had proposed an interunion march on Paris for March 1979. Yet it organized the show of force in ways that sought to marginalize the other unions. The CGT metalworkers left the preparation to the confederation. The Communists wanted mobilization for their own campaign for the European elections of June. Anger at redundancies became an anti-German, anti-European Community

33. Jean-Pierre Huiban, "The Industrial Counterproposal as an Element of Trade Union Strategy," in *The French Workers' Movement: Economic Crisis and Political Change*, ed. Mark Kesselman with Guy Groux (London: Allen & Unwin), p. 234.

34. For the CGT's position, see "Face à la crise de la sidérurgie: Les solutions de la FTM-CGT pour une négociation immédiate," *Le guide du militant de la métallurgie*, no. 136 (November 1978). The CFDT's ideas were elaborated in "Avenir de la sidérurgie: Propositions de la FGM-CFDT" (Paris: CFDT, 1979).

platform. The CFDT and FO withdrew and ordered militants not to participate. The acquiescence of all but a few locals (Dunkirk and Longwy in particular) broke the union front that existed at the local level. Decentralized labor market mobilization fizzled into explicitly political action.

Nonetheless, the unions used the mobilization to bargain for measures that protected steelworkers. Preretirement dropped to 50 years at 75 percent compensation. Transfer provisions enabled workers to be placed in subsidiaries of Usinor and Sacilor with seniority intact. The companies promised to capitalize reconversion companies that would fund local redevelopment. All five unions signed the social plan of 1979.

The combination of decentralized mobilization and state-led adjustment provided protections for French steelworkers. No layoffs took place after 1966. Yet, this was not a sweet deal for organized labor. It cast the unions into the role of negotiating exit for steelworkers, removing the dynamism from union platforms, and it situated the unions within the web of state social policy, providing the basis for intense interunion conflict in a later period.

Both U.S. and French industries misread long-term market signals. Consequently, adjustment was delayed. In the meantime, adjustment modes became even more solidified. American producers bought time to diversify, but market forces diminished industry stability. Their French counterparts experienced an institutional collapse into state hands, yet state control perpetuated many of the strategic mistakes pursued earlier. Unions in both countries found themselves on the defensive. The cozy relationship with the industry brought higher wages for American steelworkers but it proved incapable of preventing increasing unemployment. State intervention in France first protected jobs, then it provided generous buyouts. Mobilization for French labor became difficult to sustain given the sustained assaults on the industry. Labor market rigidity in the French case and its fluidity in the American one determined the character of employment bargaining in the two countries.

THE HEMORRHAGE OF THE 1980s

If market stagnation produced initial hestitation, the accumulation of company losses forced more decisive action. Factor price increases after the second oil price increase of 1979 and the subsequent international recession compelled even market leaders, such as Germany and Japan, to shrink production, consolidate facilities, and reduce workforces. For the American and French industries, however, previous adjustment decisions necessitated an acceleration of plant and employment reductions. Both labor movements were completely unprepared for the new market solutions.

In the United States, high wages and protection would work only if the companies invested quickly in new technologies. By the early 1980s, however, prices sank below the trigger levels and American producers filed dumping charges against European and third world producers. The new administration's free-trade ideology impeded enforcement of the Trigger Price Mechanism, which was formally abandoned in 1982. In its place, the industry pressed for vigorous enforcement of antidumping legislation. Although the Reagan administration dismissed positive findings of domestic injury, it did negotiate voluntary restraint agreements with the European Community, Japan, and many of the newly industrializing countries from 1982 to 1988.

Trade politics continued to deflect criticism away from the industry's accelerated disinvestment to more profitable ventures. U.S. Steel's development of its energy sector (including its purchase of Marathon Oil) marked the largest producer's move away from steel, symbolized by its name change to USX in 1985. By the late 1980s, steel constituted less than 30 percent of the total USX sales. Armco increased its energy-related activities. LTV remained a diversified holding. Only Bethlehem, among the majors, maintained the core of its activity in basic steel.

Diversification out of steel diminished the importance of labor peace. Import penetration and competition from the minimills encouraged the integrated producers to roll back industry wage rates if they wanted to maintain any presence in steel markets. Here they received important support from academics and government officials who argued that high wages added to competitive erosion.[35]

Although the companies sought to scrap the ENA in the 1980 contract round, they acquiesced to union resistance and bargained under

35. See the strong argument by Robert W. Crandall in "Investment and Productivity Growth in the Steel Industry: Some Implications for Industrial Policy," in *Ailing Steel: The Transoceanic Quarrel*, ed. Walter H. Goldberg (Hants, England: Gower, 1986), pp. 191–204.

the ENA. They were quickly overwhelmed by market forces. After a semblance of stability from 1979 to 1981, profits plunged precipitously: companies affiliated with the American Iron and Steel Institute lost a collective $3.2 billion in 1982.[36] The companies responded with plant closings, arguing that the $23 per hour compensation made their products uncompetitive.[37]

The steel employers demanded midterm contract revisions in 1982. For the union leadership, the evidence of distress was clear: between 1980 and 1982, employment dropped another 25 percent. The Coordinating Committee of Steel Companies demanded a cap on labor cost increases, a moderation of the COLA, and cutbacks on fringe benefits that would have reduced costs by $5 per hour over the next three years. Whereas the union negotiators rejected the first proposals in July, the frustration building within the union encouraged the district presidents to reject the union's own deal in November. Only in March 1983 could a contract be ratified, and the concessions amounted to roughly $2 per hour. Although union negotiators preserved the principle of COLA and extracted a limited early retirement scheme for workers over 60, they also presided over a historic setback without employment protection. The job loss continued unabated the following three years.

The union leadership continued to accept the industry's arguments about competitiveness and believed that the slump in sales was only cyclical. While expressing concern over disinvestment, the union maintained its pressure for import restrictions. The central offices failed to challenge plant closings and even opposed the locals when they confronted management.[38]

Industry-wide bargaining ended with the 1983 negotiations. The subsequent fragmentation of bargaining led to competitive concessions at local plants. At Wheeling-Pittsburgh, management used bankruptcy proceedings to try lowering employment costs by 29 percent. Local mobilization and legal action by the national union (ensuring the strike be defined as a lockout) forced a settlement granting the

36. American Iron and Steel Institute, *Annual Statistical Report,* 1982.

37. *Business Week,* June 13, 1983. It should be added that *cash* wages in steel were only marginally higher than those in other industries. The additional employment costs came from fringe benefits, especially the supplementary unemployment benefits, which mushroomed with the plant closings.

38. Staughton Lynd, *The Flight against Shutdowns: Youngstown's Steel Mill Closings* (San Pedro, Calif.: Singlejack Books, 1982).

union a participative role in management in exchange for only a 17 percent decrease.[39] A settlement with Jones and Laughlin brought changes in job rules in exchange for early retirement. National sold its Weirton plant to employees, who agreed to wage cuts in exchange for collective ownership.

The new competitive environment produced major splits among the producers over both labor and trade issues. Bethlehem protested U.S. Steel's attempts in 1983 to import unfinished slabs from Britain. Bankruptcy-induced wage concessions at Wheeling-Pittsburgh and LTV induced wage competition among the majors. Changes in work rules also showed different approaches to labor relations. USX attempted to move unilaterally to alter skill classifications and work teams. In contrast, Jones and Laughlin, Bethlehem, and National sought negotiated changes.

Within this context the Coordinating Committee of Steel Companies disintegrated.[40] Its negotiating committee consisted of representatives from the largest companies—two from U.S. Steel, one each from Bethlehem and Republic. The smaller producers chafed under its leadership: imports frayed the industry's oligopoly and wage pressure was growing out of control at the local level. Allegheny-Ludlun withdrew from the group in 1983, followed by National the following year. LTV purchased Republic in 1984, merging it with its steel division Jones and Laughlin. The five remaining companies dissolved the coordinating committee in 1985 when USX began using its leadership to further its own hard-line labor relations strategy. Diversification enabled USX to afford such an attitude toward labor. A company such as Bethlehem, whose operations were almost entirely within steel, sought a more negotiated solution.[41]

The 1986 contract renewals took place at the company level. Despite an upturn in economic indicators, depression continued to characterize sales, and the companies pressed for a prolongation of wage concessions. The not-so-veiled threat was shutdown for each company. Still, local negotiations involved important trade-offs for those workers employed. Most contracts imposed restrictions on subcontracting, thereby removing some pressure on union jobs. They also granted

39. For a thorough accounting of the 1983 and 1986 bargaining, see Hoerr, *And the Wolf Finally Came.*

40. Ibid., pp. 474–76.

41. John Strohmeyer, *Crisis in Bethlehem: Big Steel's Struggle to Survive* (Bethesda, Md.: Adler & Adler, 1986).

management greater leeway in local work rule changes. The agreement at National, however, included employment security: those workers displaced would receive jobs elsewhere in the firm. The company also agreed to reinvest savings back into production. Although other agreements did not so explicitly promise employment security and reinvestment, they included local arrangements to trade off higher managerial discretion for some form of employment protection.

Nonetheless, the USWA protected one of the original outcomes of industry-wide bargaining—uniform employment costs. An agreement at LTV served as an informal pattern after which agreements at National, Bethlehem, Inland, and Armco were reached. Only USX held out, believing it could withstand a strike and gain a competitive advantage in concession bargaining; it sought larger savings in salaries, greater shop-floor flexibility, and a reopener clause if bankruptcy led to lower costs in a rival firm. The bitter half-year strike resulted in a limited off-pattern agreement in which the company gained comparable employment cost savings, some advantages on staffing and contracting out, and a longer, four-year contract that would ensure labor peace. In exchange, USX promised to modernize certain facilities and fund a training program for displaced workers.

The USX strike symbolized the transformation from the golden years. The brazen attitude of company negotiators differed only in degree from labor policy elsewhere: the cozy arrangements between big steel and big labor were over. The new competitive environment led to market flexibility—for employment costs if not for product pricing. Although company intransigence enabled the union to sustain the mobilization, this was not the battle of the titans of the 1959 strike. Secondary industries were only marginally affected. Pressures for government intervention were absent. Struggles in steel had been marginalized.

The local agreements in 1986–87 contained several innovative provisions. Yet they did not eliminate arguments for further job reductions. Companies did not need to be explicit to exchange concessions for unguaranteed jobs. The struggle to maintain a "level playing field" for the integrated producers had been severely tested at USX. The union maintained rough uniformity but acquiesced to negotiations along the lines defined by the companies. The latter retained most of their labor market flexibility.

Internal organizational practices again merged with adjustment. The union changed its internal political practices in the midst of concessionary bargaining. Lynn Williams, McBride's successor as president, altered ratification procedures in 1986, enabling rank-and-file approval of contracts. This reversed a half-century of centralization and showed a different leadership ethos. It was also a practical necessity with company bargaining.

American companies achieved profitability and competitiveness in 1987 through stabilized wages, whose savings were magnified by a declining dollar and continued, massive job reductions. Plant closures and work rule changes enabled the industry to halve its workforce between 1981 and 1988. Conceding niches to the minimills and a permanent presence for foreign steel, it reduced capacity 27 percent so production could not meet demand by the late 1980s.[42] With continued pressure in 1989 to maintain the protective blanket of voluntary restraint agreements, foreign companies assumed the paradoxical position of quick acquiescence just to maintain part of the market.

In France, regime change added a twist to state-led adjustment. The new Socialist government formally nationalized Usinor and Sacilor in 1982 and installed new CEOs. It initially revived the industry's productivism. A new industry plan in 1982 sought to return to the production level of 1974 by 1986, so it reduced capacities only minimally. A Fr 20 billion investment program sought to modernize the industry with the newest technologies. It encouraged a further concentration of production and combined steelmaking with higher value-added activity in metalworking. Revitalization took place while international consumption plummeted in the wake of recession.

The expansion induced a financial hemorrhage: the two firms declared Fr 34.5 billion in losses between 1982 and 1984.[43] As industry observers and key actors within the Ministry of Finance argued, the reasoning in 1982 had been unduly optimistic. The 1974 production goal of 27 million tons remained a historical high a decade later. Contradicting its earlier electoral promises, the left government changed course in 1984. State-led modernization emphasized the "modern" for a restricted core of production in line with the

42. *Wall Street Journal,* November 9, 1988.

43. The 1984 losses totaled more than the combined losses of the twenty largest steel firms in the world; *L'expansion,* November 8–21, 1985.

rationalization measures of the European Coal and Steel Community: the issue was not the ability to sell an individual product at a profit but whether other European facilities could produce them more competitively. Investments were canceled. Unprofitable niches were dropped. Production of sectionals and specialty steels were consolidated into joint subsidiaries of Usinor and Sacilor. The two companies merged in 1987.

The cutbacks in the now nationalized steel industry led to demoralization and strategic confusion within the unions. The approval of 30,000 additional redundancies signaled that the left (or at least the Socialist component) would work within a European plan—even more inaccessible to political pressure—to reduce surplus capacity. Ever deepening divisions within the labor movement prevented the generalization of mobilization. The CFDT reluctantly agreed to the Socialists' plans while concerning itself with the terms of the social plan. In contrast, the CGT promised unmitigated opposition. If the two unions had split in 1979, the rift became unmistakable five years later.

Demonstrations, including a march of 150,000 in Paris, accompanied the government announcement. The unions sought centralized control without the willingness to forge common positions. The CGT became more vocal in opposition, especially in its denunciations of trans-European capacity reductions, but it moved reluctantly into oppositional unionism. The Communist party itself emitted mixed signals. Four members remained in the government, but Secretary General Georges Marchais marched in solidarity with the steelworkers. The CFDT moved away from uncritical support for the Socialists, but a new priority on collective bargaining deemphasized mobilization. The tensions between the two confederations filtered down into the federations and locals. Aside from the Paris demonstration, cooperation in organizing mobilization was nonexistent.

Both CGT and CFDT locals pursued guerrilla action, including the destruction of Socialist party offices in Longwy, but the mobilization fizzled. The turbulence within the industry over the previous twenty years had produced a shell-shocked generation. Industrial restructuring by a left government produced a mixture of resignation and disillusion.

Still, a pattern of institutional interaction had been established for reducing employment. The state again set the minimum terms to quell class violence—no layoffs. The social plan of 1984, signed by all the unions except the CGT, utilized a variety of tools to ease workers out. The age measures were retained, although they were losing their effectiveness as the age pyramid flattened. Younger workers could enter state-financed retraining programs for nonsteel skills. Each trainee was guaranteed two job offers on completion. The Socialists strengthened the redevelopment efforts of the companies. The steel regions were also designated eligible for special state subsidies that offered incentives to small- and medium-sized business investment. The commitment to a jobs-based regional reindustrialization was indicated by the appointment of Jacques Chérèque, the former deputy secretary general of the CFDT, as regional coordinator for the reindustrialization of the Lorraine, a subcabinet position.

On their own terms, these measures have been successful. The 1984 social plan was renewed in 1987. Retraining has been largely successful: as of early 1989, 95 percent of the retrainees under the steel redundancy measures have found employment.[44] Between 1984 and 1988, the state created several thousand new jobs in the Lorraine. Most were in small business, and therefore nonunion, although the CFDT made some headway in organizing efforts.

Unionists have sat on a plethora of tripartite committees to ensure the terms of the accords. The administration of collective bargaining agreements and the increased institutional presence, however, has meant a loss of class identity. Officials from the CGT, CFDT, and FO have proven adept at negotiating financing with the Ministry of Labor. They have protected the interests of individual workers as they confront age measures or retraining. Still, they have not wielded power to change industrial decisions. Individual unionists have played the paradoxical role of helping to attract employers to the steel regions and thereby glossing over the legacy of past mobilization.

The French industry gained a competitiveness in the late 1980s that it never enjoyed. Capacity reductions, job cuts, and several billion francs of direct subsidies finally resulted in an industry that in 1988 produced steel more efficiently than any of its European rivals. The same year Usinor-Sacilor swore off state aid and even criticized those companies in the European community still receiving subsidies for distorting competition. With each bailout, governments of the left and

44. Interviews by the author with union leaders and state officials in the Lorraine during January 1989.

the right offered protections to redundant workers. Adjustment in French steel combined the "social" with the "industrial."

The grandeur of French steel and French steelworkers withered with each capacity reduction. The disappearance of a transformative left at a national level removed the anchor of French labor politics. Interunion conflict set labor strategy in steel adrift. With the CGT torn between oppositionalism and propositionalism and the CFDT entrenched in collective bargaining for its own sake, little remained of the dynamic that combined class radicalism with effective negotiating.

POLITICS AND MOBILIZATION

The apparent price of competitiveness in the French and U.S. steel industries has been massive redundancies. The raw numbers, however, obscure the process by which they took place. In the United States, they were imposed by the companies: by collective bargaining agreement, workers received only 90 days notice, although supplementary unemployment benefits eased the labor market transition for workers with seniority. Job cuts in France were imposed much differently. State actors consistently set the minimum terms: redundant workers would not face layoffs. The consequent negotiations between the industry and the unions brought a range of benefits to displaced workers, ranging from intercompany transfers to two-year retraining programs.

Both labor movements faced managements that sought control over local labor markets. After the postwar uncertainty, American steel traded high wages for management autonomy. The concession of a union shop-floor presence in steel meshed with a union movement that wanted recognition as a junior partner in bargaining. This joint strategy culminated in the wages-for-productivity deal of the ENA. Unfortunately, this only enabled producers to escape from an adjustment that would ensure long-term viability. The exclusion of labor in France fueled a class-based, oppositional movement that sought to circumvent the employers and appeal directly to state actors. When the unions received recognition, a model of employment bargaining was already in place. Social conditions were imposed on French employers each time the state intervened.

State intervention strengthened the political capacity of American steel, whereas it weakened the French. Arm's-length state involvement meant ad hoc responses to competitive threats in the American context. Given the porousness of the political process, those responses became increasingly protectionist in nature. Protection *deflected* potential threats to management autonomy and preserved the political independence of firm-led adjustment (and disinvestment). In contrast, the interventionist French state had the policy tools and the political will to intervene directly into industry affairs. The CSSF could not maintain autonomy in the midst of financial collapse. Only the state could restore competitiveness.

French employment bargaining addressed the industry's problems in a comprehensive manner. Employers could not adjust to changing product markets with the labor market destabilization of the Americans. Rather, state constraints forced the industry into investment strategies to meet market challenges. Adjustment in the United States, in contrast, meant greater investment freedom for the firms. The USWA could not resist market strategies aimed at individualizing collective bargaining. The centralized, financially prosperous union responded slowly and inadequately to the industry's restructuring.

Industrial adjustment put different pressures on the internal politics of each labor movement. Maintaining wage uniformity in a stable oligopoly demanded a strong and coherent union. The USWA leadership sought internal discipline to maintain organizational integrity. As negotiating agreements increasingly impinged on member interest, the struggle over internal democracy became entangled with disagreements over the content of collective bargaining. This internalization of working-class conflict undermined the union's capacity to confront adjustment choices. Conflict within the French labor movement, in contrast, took place between labor unions. Competitive unionism forced collective bargaining positions more into the open arena of worker politics. Moreover, labor law prevented the types of rules that constrain local action. Tension and uncertainty existed in both the CGT and the CFDT, especially after 1979, but weak organization permitted a larger degree of consensus building. The externalization of working-class conflict facilitated French mobilization. By the time mobilization had become difficult to sustain, patterns of policy making had already been established.

Because of its wide array of policy tools, the French state has been historically sensitive to labor market destabilization. Although not always in agreement, bureaucratic and political actors sought to calm the effects of unemployment. Labor depended on state intervention to diffuse the social effects of industrial dislocation. The unions have lacked the organizational resources to bargain on their own for the protection workers have received.

American public policy has had the opposite effect. Trade policy has strengthened management control. With its emphasis on unemployment compensation, labor market policy shows the same arms'-length tendency. Intervention in the collective bargaining process centers on arbitrating conflicting interpretations of privately negotiated agreements. The American state lacks the will and the capacity to alter the character of labor markets. Thus, organized labor is left where it has wanted to be—on its own. Business unionism, however, could not muster the resources to confront the severity of adjustment in steel.

In this essay I have stressed the conflation of industrial relations instititions with adjustment patterns. The way each industry confronted international markets affected how it would bargain with labor. Labor market negotiations, in turn, constrained the nature of adjustment. Yet, institutional interaction did not take place in a void. Historical memories structured the responses of labor, capital, and the state. Innovation depended on the *relative* power of each actor.

The results of the employment crisis in steel appear bleak for labor. Joint bargaining has ended in the American steel industry. Class unionism has been weakened, if only by worker attrition, in the French context. Yet, if the analysis here is correct and if the power of labor is relational to other actors, then we should expect new forms of organization and mobilization to appear. Workplace struggles will continue to disrupt the "inevitability" of market forces.

5 Union Politics and the Restructuring of the British Coal Industry

Peggy Kahn

British coal-mining unionism in the late 1980s was marked by a general decline in the strength and effectiveness of organized labor and by an institutional fragmentation of unionism unprecedented in the postwar period. Capacity in the nationalized coal industry declined from approximately 110.3 million metric tons in 1980–81 to 85 million metric tons in 1988–89, and the number of collieries from 211 to 86. The number of workers on the colliery books dropped from 230,700 to 80,100.[1] Membership in the National Union of Mineworkers (NUM), previously the sole union organizing manual workers in the industry, had fallen to fewer than 100,000 at the end of fiscal year 1986–87.[2] Both the NUM and the breakaway union formed in the wake of the 1984–85 strike, the Union of Democratic Miners (UDM), faced continuing pit closures, which they were unable to influence or halt, though in a few cases the NUM delayed closure by

I wish to thank Miriam Golden and Jonas Pontusson for their assistance with this essay. Conversations with Pete Gibbon in summer 1987 were also extremely valuable. My research was partly funded by a University of Michigan–Flint Faculty Research Grant and a University of Michigan Rackham Faculty Research Grant. This essay draws on a long period of work on the British coalfields and mining unionism; over ten years, many working miners, union officials, and others close to the coalfield generously shared their insights and experiences with me.

1. British Coal Corporation/National Coal Board, *Report and Accounts 1988/9*, pp. 28–29.
2. British Coal Corporation/National Coal Board, *Report and Accounts 1986/7*, pp. 18–19.

invoking review procedures set up after the strike. The unions in general were unable to influence the pace, nature, or terms of industrial restructuring, including closures, reorganization of existing sites, and pay. Although restructuring meant improved environmental conditions and pay for many miners, the high rate of redundancy was accompanied by the deterioration of many working conditions and an erosion of job control in general. Overall wage movements are extremely difficult to characterize and of limited significance, because of the fragmentation and complexity of new wage structures. For the first four years after the 1985–85 strike, there were no national wage negotiations, and NUM members had UDM-negotiated wage settlements unilaterally imposed on them by the British Coal Board.[3]

An important reason for the inability of organized labor to participate in national collective bargaining and win concessions at a time when restructuring exacted high costs from labor was the poststrike institutionalization of a preexisting regionalism in the coalfield. The NUM continued to organize the large Yorkshire coalfield and the majority of smaller coalfields. But the large Nottinghamshire coalfield, most of whose miners continued to work in 1984–85, was mainly organized by the UDM. These two national unions, both recognized for negotiating purposes by British Coal, did not, however, cooperate with each other. They were antagonists, organized on the basis of different principles and in competition with one another. The Nottinghamshire-based UDM cooperated with restructuring initiatives. The NUM, on the other hand, declared a policy of opposition but was in a weak position to resist successfully, both because of demoralization in its coalfields and because of the continuity of production ensured by Nottinghamshire.

In this essay, I argue that the failure of the NUM, the majority union in the British coalfields, to maintain the unity of its organizational base, the size of its membership, and favorable terms and conditions of work in the late 1980s must be understood as the product of three related factors. First, it was the result of a government determined to, and capable of, changing the basic framework in which the nationalized coal industry operated. The government's strategy was to subject the industry to market forces by encouraging competing sources of supply, diminishing guaranteed demand, and withdrawing

3. British Coal Corporation/National Coal Board, *Report and Accounts 1986/7,* pp. 8–9, *Report and Accounts 1988/9,* pp. 14–16.

subsidies to the industry. The severe consequences of this strategy for labor also required the disorganization of the union. Second, the weakened condition of unionism was the result of a managerial strategy designed to comply with the more market-oriented framework imposed on the coal industry by the government—a strategy centrally concerned with cost minimization, labor flexibility, and internal labor competition. Finally, union weakness and fragmentation resulted from union inability to design an effective strategy of resistance, especially in view of the preexisting regionalization of the coalfields.

I emphasize government and management political-economic restructuring *strategies* rather than a given or inevitable economic decline of the British coal industry as the key to union weakness and fragmentation. One version of the argument from economic necessity is that the British coal industry was uncompetitive in view of the lower cost of other energy supplies, such as internationally traded steam coal and nuclear energy, and therefore was bound to contract severely. This argument fails to note, however, that energy policy decisions heavily structure energy markets and energy prices, and it obscures the problematic nature of energy supply costs. For example, the British government had clearly made a decision to increase the proportion of electricity supplied by nuclear power and to increase imports of coal. At the same time, much internationally traded steam coal was being dumped at below-cost prices, and the real cost of nuclear power in social as well as economic terms was controversial.[4]

Another version of the argument for the economic inevitability of contraction focuses on the finances of British Coal, the nationalized corporation, itself. The corporation was accumulating large operating deficits and required large government subsidies; the overall operating loss was £358 million in fiscal year 1983–84, and the total government subsidy was £1.34 billion. The British government and others argued that it was therefore imperative to undertake significant economic restructuring, close large numbers of uneconomic pits, and contract employment. But the subsidy to the British coal industry in

4. See, for example, the following essays in *Debating Coal Closures: Economic Calculation in the Coal Dispute 1984–5*, ed. David Cooper and Trevor Hopper (Cambridge: Cambridge University Press, 1988): David Cooper and Trevor Hopper, "Introduction: Financial Calculation in Industrial and Political Debate," pp. 1–24; Stephen Fothergill, "Nuclear Power and the Coal Industry," pp. 225–52; G. Davies and D. Metcalf, "Pit Closures: Some Economics," pp. 25–45; and G. Kerevan and R. Saville, "The Economic Case for Deep-Mined Coal in Scotland," pp. 119–60.

the early 1980s must be regarded as less a matter of fact than a financial situation that was the product of certain legal and accounting conventions and price negotiations between the Coal Board and its largest customer, the nationalized Central Electricity Generating Board (CEGB). Similarly, the Coal Board's calculation of costs of production and profitability of individual pits has been subject to criticism. In addition, it was not clear that pit closures were more economic, that is, that they involved fewer costs to the treasury or to society as a whole, than operating pits at a certain level of loss.[5]

If my argument refutes the view of economic necessity, it also differs from one that suggests that the weakness and fragmentation of unionism was simply due to the failure of union strategy and in particular to "Scargillism," a strategy personally masterminded by Arthur Scargill, the NUM president, which saw the miners as class warriors who could defeat the state through traditional industrial tactics of the strike and mass picketing. Instead, I put considerable emphasis on how government and management created conditions in the industry with severe consequences for union membership, eliminated strategies of effective negotiation, and exaggerated the regionalization of labor. In addition, militant oppositional unionism was not the personal creation of the NUM's president but a regional tradition. The practices of the Yorkshire miners did, however, enter into the 1984–85 dispute and the poststrike period in a manner guided by Scargill and the national leaders of the union. Although it is not appropriate to ascribe union weakness and fragmentation mainly to Scargill, his regionally based strategy of militant mobilization and poststrike leadership may have contributed to them.

THE POLITICAL FRAMEWORK OF THE COAL INDUSTRY

The changing political framework of the coal industry reflected a larger transition in the British political economy from an earlier postwar social democratic compromise to a neoliberal monetarist economic order. The initial postwar political economy was characterized by a variety of collectivist measures and arrangements; the state employed Keynesian macroeconomic techniques to maintain full employ-

5. A. J. Berry, T. Capps, D. J. Cooper, T. M. Hopper, and E. A. Lowe, "NCB Accounts: A Mine of Misinformation?" in ibid., pp. 95–106; Cooper and Hopper, "Introduction," pp. 1–24.

ment, and the economy comprised both private and public industry. Corporatist modes of economic decision making brought capital and labor into the arena of state policy formation. The need for working people to organize into strong unions with roles in both the labor market and party politics was recognized by political elites of both major parties as well as by the business and financial establishments.

From 1979, however, successive Conservative governments undertook a systematic, state-led restructuring of the British economy away from Keynesian and corporatist arrangements toward monetarist and market-oriented economic practices. While the Thatcher governments of the 1980s subscribed to monetarism in the narrow sense of controlling the money supply to influence the rate of inflation, they also undertook to create conditions in which market forces could operate according to principles of laissez-faire and uninhibited competition. The Conservative government worked to remove the state from the economy and to restore market forces through deregulation of the private sector, privatization of much of the substantial public sector, and commercialization of residual state activity. In addition, the government put special emphasis on labor supply as a crucial factor determining the level and cost of production. It worked to restructure labor markets toward cheaper, more flexible, and less organized labor supply. The labor strategy involved a concerted attack on unions, whose industrial and political influence was undermined through the dismantling of corporatist institutions and the reassertion of market discipline in a period of recession and longer-term structural economic change.[6] The coal industry was a site on which many of these developments not only occurred but also were significantly focused.

The Postwar Period to 1980

For most of the postwar period prior to the 1980s, the coal industry was subject to a mix of political and economic determinations in which the government modified or tempered market discipline to varying degrees. The first decade of coal industry nationalization,

6. Andrew Gamble, "The Free Economy and the Strong State," in *Socialist Register 1979*, ed. Ralph Miliband and John Saville (London: Merlin Press, 1979), pp. 1–25; Andrew Gamble, *Britain in Decline* (London: Macmillan, 1981); Andrew Gamble, *The Free Economy and the Strong State: The Thatcher Government* (Durham: Duke University Press, 1988); Peter Riddell, *The Thatcher Experiment* (Oxford: Martin Robertson, 1983); William Keegan, *Mrs. Thatcher's Economic Experiment* (London: Penguin, 1984); Bob Jessop, Kevin Bonnett, Simon Bromley, and Tom Ling, *Thatcherism: A Tale of Two Nations* (Oxford: Polity Press, 1988); Patricia Fosh and Craig Littler, *Industrial Relations and the Law in the 1980s* (Aldershot: Gower, 1981).

1947–57, was a period of coal shortage and economic reconstruction and growth. Government, industry, and unions were united by an emphasis on the maximization of output, provided that revenue as a whole could be maintained near breakeven. The industry was also enjoined from charging high prices in a period of scarcity and so prevented from accumulating reserves.[7]

After 1957, as demand for coal fell, there was more attention to the commercial viability not only of the industry as a whole but of individual areas and pits, and there was considerable contraction of capacity. Though tensions between management and union mounted, a conciliatory industrial relations climate was encouraged by the government and supported by its continued though very limited intervention in the market.

Following the oil price rises of the mid-1970s, the government, management, and unions agreed on the long-term Plan for Coal, to reconstruct capacity in a long-term energy market expected to be more favorable to coal than that of the 1960s. Finance was subordinated to production considerations; all parties agreed that reconstruction would be impossible without substantial deficit financing.[8] The employment implications of the Plan were also regarded as positive, though the Plan addressed capacity rather than employment.

The 1980s

From the early 1980s, the government imposed strict financial targets on the industry and reintroduced an emphasis on the profitability of areas and units. It also took measures to increase other competing sources of energy supply and to decrease certainty of demand and to support management's decision-making power and weaken the power of labor in the industry. The coal industry was subjected to intense commercial pressures fairly late in the Thatcher period, after many other nationalized industries had already been privatized or rationalized and there had been a substantial shift of power toward management in the private and public economy. The most intense commercial pressure on the industry developed after the defeat of the NUM in a year-long strike, which saw an extraordinary mobilization of state power against the striking miners and their families.

7. William Ashworth, *The History of the British Coal Industry*, vol. 5: *1946–82: The Nationalized Industry* (Oxford: Clarendon Press, 1986), chap. 5.
8. Ibid., chap. 7.

From its election in 1979, the Thatcher government began to withdraw the state from financing the industry's operation. The Coal Industry Act 1980, the first coal act under the Thatcher government, replaced the production targets toward which the industry had been working with narrow financial objectives. The 1980 act was subsequently modified as a result of pressure, including industrial action by the NUM, but it was widely understood that the government's longer-term intentions toward the industry remained. These intentions were amply demonstrated in succeeding years by a variety of official reports and documents from the Ministry of Energy, the House Select Committee on Energy, and the Monopolies and Mergers Commission, all of which emphasized the importance of the industry as a whole breaking even and individual pits showing economic results. In March 1987, it was announced that British Coal was to achieve financial breakeven, after payment of interest and accrual of social grants, no later than fiscal year 1988–89 and thereafter to generate an increasing surplus on revenue account and contribute increasingly to self-financing.[9] Although British Coal succeeded in making an operating profit of £498m and a profit of £66m after interest in 1988–89, its overall result, due largely to restructuring costs, was a loss of £203m, and the industry received substantial government grants.[10]

At the same time the industry was directed to break even, the government encouraged competing sources of supply, particularly for electricity generation. The most highly publicized aspect of this policy was the repeated endorsement and practical development of an expanded nuclear power program. The government's public rationale shifted between an argument that nuclear power was cheaper than coal-fired generating capacity and one that it was essential to diversify supply, particularly in order to remove control of energy supply from organized miners and transport workers. Opencast coal had traditionally been used to supplement deep-mined coal in order to meet output targets. In the 1980s, however, the proportion of opencast coal was increased and was justified as a contribution to cost savings. The government also took measures, and expressed further intentions, to

9. National Union of Mineworkers, "The Miners and the Battle for Britain" (NUM, n.d.); United Kingdom, Monopolies and Mergers Commission, *National Coal Board, Report*, vols. 1 and 2 (London: HMSO, 1983); United Kingdom, House of Commons Energy Committee, *The Coal Industry, Report* (London: HMSO, 1987); British Coal/National Coal Board, *Report and Accounts 1986/7*.

10. British Coal/National Coal Board, *Report and Accounts 1988/9*, pp. 7–8.

increase the penetrability of the national economy to imported coal, as an international trade in steam coal based on low-cost supplies developed in the 1980s. The increase in permission to import was especially important in electricity generation.[11]

The only continuously increasing demand for coal in the postwar period has come from power stations. By the 1970s, power stations were using more coal than all other users combined, and coal became dependent on sales to two large customers, the CEGB and the South of Scotland Electricity Board, which together made up the large electricity industry. By 1983, power stations accounted for 75 percent of sales by British Coal, and the CEGB was 85 percent coal fired. In recognition of the importance of this relationship, especially in conditions of deepening recession, power station purchases were regulated by a joint understanding between the coal industry and CEGB after 1979. The terms of the understanding were, however, gradually eroded to the disadvantage of the coal industry. Whereas the original agreement provided for 75 million metric tons per year at prices based on British Coal's industrial coal price structure, the revised understanding of 1986–87 specified three tranches of purchases: 52 million metric tons at production cost, 12 million at a price geared to international steam coal prices, and a further 10 million at a price reflecting the increase in oil prices and certain delivery costs. But there was considerable pressure to decrease prices further and if possible to dispense with the understanding in order to allow increased imports of cheap traded coal. The privatization of the CEGB constituted a considerable threat to the agreement and to the power station market for British coal; it was unlikely the government would direct a private company to purchase British Coal's output, and certain power stations would have both cost incentives and physical facilities to rely on increased quantities of imported coal.[12]

The 1984–85 coalfield strike can be seen as a decisive government and management attempt to defeat union opposition to this new market-oriented framework and its employment consequences. The

11. United Kingdom, House of Commons Energy Committee, *The Coal Industry,* vols. 1 and 2: *Minutes* and *Minutes of Evidence* (London: HMSO, 1986); Stephen Fothergill, "Nuclear Power and the Coal Industry," in *Coalfield Communities Campaign Working Papers,* vol. 3 (Barnsley: Coalfield Communities Campaign, n.d.), pp. 17–28; and Colin Sweet, "Why Coal Is under Attack: Nuclear Powers in the Energy Establishment," in *Digging Deeper: Issues in the Miners' Strike,* ed. Huw Beynon (London: Verso, 1985), pp. 201–16.

12. Andrew Holmes, John Chesshire, and Steve Thomas, *Power on the Market: Strategies for Privatizing the UK Electricity Industry* (London: Financial Times Business Information, 1987); Energy Committee, *Minutes* and *Minutes of Evidence;* and Ashworth, *History,* chap. 7.

government's attempt to restructure material relations and attitudes toward capitalist market competition and its special concerns with the nationalized industries, including coal, had already been strategically conceived while the Conservative party was in opposition. The nationalized industries had been identified as key targets of the restructuring strategy not only because they represented an overextension of the state into the economy but also because they harbored strong unions. An internal Conservative party document, the 1978 Ridley Report, suggested that unions might resist the commercialization or privatization of nationalized industries and saw the coal industry as a likely battleground. Nicholas Ridley recommended that the government take several strategic measures such as building up stocks in power stations, developing plans for the import of coal, and equipping a large mobile police squad to contain picketing.[13] All these measures were taken prior to the miners' strike, when the state's strategic and coercive capacity, coordinated at cabinet level, was used to defeat the miners' union. The government's waging of the strike itself indicated a strategy of exploiting the preexisting regionalization of labor; the working Nottinghamshire coalfield was protected by police and publicly praised by the government. With the coalfield internally divided and in a setting of high unemployment, other sections of organized labor were also reluctant to demonstrate solidarity with striking miners.[14] The government needed to defeat the miners not because of the economic necessity of contracting the coal industry but because of its political commitment to restructuring nationalized industries and the economy in general and to ensuring that labor resistance and solidarity did not interfere. The strike embodied not only themes of market discipline for the coal industry but also Conservative party concerns about disorganizing labor supply and making it more flexible.

MANAGEMENT STRATEGY IN THE COAL INDUSTRY

Some observers have suggested that in the 1970s coal industry managers were eager to commercialize further the operations of the Coal

13. "Appomattox or Civil War?" *Economist* 272 (May 27, 1978): 21–22.

14. Huw Beynon and Peter McMylor, "Decisive Power: The New Tory State against the Miners," in *Digging Deeper*, ed. Beynon, pp. 29–45; Geoffrey Goodman, *The Miners' Strike* (London; Pluto Press, 1985); Peter Wilsher, Donald Macintyre, and Michael Jones, *Strike: Thatcher, Scargill and the Miners* (London: Hodder & Stoughton, 1985).

Board and to increase their control over the production process, but that the corporatist framework of the Labour government stood in their way.[15] This argument, for which there seems to be little empirical evidence, implies that the commercialization strategy was management driven and that the Thatcher government merely removed an external obstacle to the implementation of aggressive, market-oriented management. Yet, it seems more appropriate to stress that government restructuring of the state-industry relation destroyed the existing management-labor compromise within coal. In fact, the publicized conflicts between Ian MacGregor, appointed chairman of the Coal Board in 1983, and other board members and managers during the strike suggest that the appointment of a U.S. financier and company executive was meant to repoliticize the coal industry toward new and aggressive free market practices and away from older corporatist managerial ones.[16] Management strategies moved in the mid-1980s from conciliatory relations with the unions toward more aggressive and unilateral practices, from productivity strategies tied to output to productivity strategies driven by cost lowering.

The Postwar Period to 1980

The corporatist labor-management compromise within the industry prior to the 1980s may be understood not only as actually negotiated compromises but also as management decisions and rules that produced outcomes not only in the interest of management but also in the interest of labor, such as relatively high levels of employment, good working conditions, and an institutionalized role for the union. In addition, that compromise permitted a degree of job control at pit level, though this was exercised unevenly across areas and from pit to pit. The coincidence of management and labor interests was not simply a matter of government support for the industry; it also reflected favorable market conditions. When the market weakened and the state refused to intervene in a major way, the conditions of the compromise were substantially though not entirely undermined. In the 1960s, the

15. John Lloyd, "Address," in *Coalfield Communities Looking Forward: Proceedings of the National Conference of the Coalfield Communities Campaign 1986* (Barnsley: Coalfield Communities Campaign, 1986), pp. 100–109.

16. Beynon, "Introduction," in *Digging Deeper*, ed. Beynon, pp. 1–26; and Ian MacGregor, *The Enemies Within: The Story of the Miners' Strike* (London: Fontana, 1986).

NUM accepted a market-determined industrial rundown—but one cushioned by managerial gradualism and welfarism as the NUM continued to exercise important consultation and conciliation functions at national and local levels. In general, the compromise involved an emphasis on production with a relatively secure demand for coal; acceptance of an element of cross-subsidization of units within the industry; and maintenance of conciliatory industrial relations. But it also involved a series of productivity strategies, including investment and modernization measures, wages structures, and certain supervisory and managerial functions. Productivity tended to be emphasized in connection with achieving high levels of physical output rather than being driven primarily by cost considerations.

In the early postwar period, management tried to maximize output though the industry was obsolescent and heavily undercapitalized, with little mechanization. For much of the period, payment, especially for faceworkers (direct production workers engaged in taking coal from the face, the section of the coal seam being worked) was based on a degenerated payment-by-results scheme. Price lists were negotiated for specific tasks and additional allowances were paid in special circumstances. In general, price lists and allowances did not constitute stable and consistent remuneration-for-effort exchanges, and labor exercised a fair degree of control over compensation as well as other aspects of work.[17]

As more costly and productive machinery was introduced into the industry, and in particular as powerloading was increasingly introduced on faces, management and union negotiated the National Powerloading Agreement in 1966. Powerloading represented an important phase of mechanization in the pits; one machine both cuts the coal from the face and automatically loads it onto conveyer belts, which take the coal out of the mine. For management, this agreement offered the prospect of greater control over and easier administration of wage payment. Time-based pay would also sever the connection between production and wages, increasing workforce flexibility and efficiency and managerial control.[18] It was assumed that supervisors

17. Joel Krieger, *Undermining Capitalism: State Ownership and the Dialectic of Control in the British Coal Industry* (Princeton: Princeton University Press, 1983); L. J. Handy, *Wages Policy in the British Coal-Mining Industry: A Study of National Wage Bargaining* (Cambridge: Cambridge University Press, 1981).

18. Krieger, *Undermining Capitalism;* R. Heath, "The National Powerloading Agreement in the Coal Industry and Some Aspects of Workers' Control," in *Trade Union Register 1969,*

would oversee day-to-day operations at the face, deploying workers and increasing their control over labor now that the self-acting discipline of the piecerate was removed. Supervisors were not, however, trained in such management, and mineworkers were not willing to tolerate such oversight.[19] In part, the resistance to control over labor took the form of reassertion of distinctive local work relations in new forms.[20] In addition, union strength increased as wages were standardized among faceworkers. National daywage structures beyond the 1966 powerloading agreement were introduced and a single, consolidated, multigrade wages structure, bargained nationally by the union, resulted. There was little reconstruction of capacity in the 1960s, and the industry was overtaken by a severe rundown due to the increasing use of cheap imported oil.[21]

In the mid-1970s, as reconstruction proceeded under the Plan for Coal, a rationalized, nationally determined group incentive scheme was introduced alongside the daywage structure. Local union officials and management negotiated performance standards for each production unit or installation at the pit. Performance of work groups against standards determined the incentive earnings of faceworkers and development workers (those who drive headings and roadways in the mines but do not actually take coal from the face). Nonproduction workers' bonus pay derived from the earnings of production workers. The scheme produced higher earnings in pits and areas where the geology was favorable. At the same time, this new wage system involved less direct supervision of labor, and the supervisor devoted more time to planning and managing materials. Management attention was directed more toward costs of production, for the incentive scheme was supposed to be self-financing. "Waiting time" provisions, which provided that stops of more than 20 minutes (assumed to be beyond the control of the workers) should be paid on the scheme, drew attention to losses incurred by idle equipment and led to a determination to increase machine available time.[22] Yet, in this period, considerable management-

---

ed., Ken Coates, Tony Topham, and Michael Barratt Brown (London: Merlin Press, 1969), pp. 185–200; Handy, *Wages Policy.*

19. Edmund Heery, "Group Incentives and the Mining Supervisor: The Effects of a Payment System on First-Line Management," *British Journal of Industrial Relations* 21 (1984): 333–45.

20. Krieger, *Undermining Capitalism.*

21. Ashworth, *History,* chap. 6.

22. Heery, "Group Incentives"; Ben Fine, Kathy O'Donnell, and Martha Prevezer, "Coal

union negotiation and collusion over earnings occurred. The incentive scheme was implemented in the context of broadly conciliatory industrial relations, with well-organized pit-level unions whose officials were linked to faceteam leaders (informal leaders of the work group at the face). The late 1970s was also a period of recession, however, and management and workers were aware of the pit's "ability to pay" in the given economic conditions. In this period, both the scheme and the reconstruction led to increased productivity. The incentive scheme also refragmented union wage interests, reopening differentials between areas as well as between pits within areas. The Nottinghamshire area miners especially seemed to benefit from the incentive scheme.[23]

The 1980s

In the 1980s, management strategy was no longer oriented toward considerations of productivity tied to maximizing output within a system of conciliatory industrial relations in which management worked with national and local unions to secure mutually satisfactory outcomes. Management's strategy was directed more exclusively toward cost lowering so that British coal could compete without subsidy in an uncertain and changing energy market. Maintaining production at approximately 90 million metric tons a year, down from 211 million in 1955 and 115 million in the mid-1970s, management worked toward cost reduction at the level of the industry as a whole as well as at pit level. Rather than planning the industry on the basis of fixed output targets within some cost parameters, the Coal Board adopted a flexible planning strategy based on cost minimization. The key cost parameters involved closing pits operating above £1.65 per gigajoule and aiming at costs of £1.50 per gigajoule at existing operating pits; new investment was required to meet a criterion of marginal cost of £1.00 per gigajoule.[24]

These cost parameters were established as a result of managers' assessments of market conditions and in particular the cost of

after Nationalisation," in *The Peculiarities of the British Economy*, ed. Ben Fine and Lawrence Harris (London: Lawrence & Wishart, 1985), pp. 167–202.

23. Fine, O'Donnell, and Prevezer, "Coal after Nationalisation"; Handy, *Wages Policy.*

24. United Kingdom, House of Commons Energy Committee, *Coal Industry* (London: HMSO, 1986); British Coal, *Report and Accounts 1984/5, Report and Accounts 1986/7*. A gigajoule is a measure of heat output; in costing coal, the use of £ per gigajoule, rather than £ per ton, measures quality as well as quantity of coal produced.

internationally traded steam coal. The importance of the latter as a competitor to British deep-mined coal increased substantially in the 1980s. Investments in mining capacity in the United States, Australia, and Canada, as well as in South Africa and developing countries, followed the 1970s oil crisis; and with the relative stabilization of domestic demand in large producing countries, a great expansion in internationally traded coal occurred. Although a significant portion of this coal was mined at low cost, some of it was traded at low prices producers were unlikely to sustain. Economists argued that very large purchases in this market by the electricity-generating industry would drive up the price of traded coal. In addition, considerable expenditure on handling facilities was necessary to this increased reliance on imports.[25] Nevertheless, managers used international prices as references, particularly in view of the clear intention of the electricity industry, supported by the government, to increase imports from their mid-1980s contribution of about 5 percent to as high as 30 percent.[26] British deep-mined coal was also threatened by other alternative energy sources and the changes in demand encouraged by the government. Falling and uncertain demand was a result not only of specific planned measures of electricity privatization but also of the recession of the 1980s and a structural movement away from energy-intensive industry in Britain.

The key to management's cost minimization efforts appeared to be a strategy of selective capital intensification of the industry, with more continuous and intensive use of capital assets. Eliminating the high-cost tail of the industry through accelerated pit closures was the terrain on which the 1984–85 strike was fought. Management strategy after the strike focused, however, on selective capital intensification and changing working practices at both existing and new pits. More particularly, management worked to create lower costs of production through a series of measures affecting existing pits and directed toward work at the coalface. Throughout the coalfield there was a con-

25. Energy Committee, *Coal Industry* (1986); Gerard McCloskey and Suzan Randle, *International Coal Report's Coal Year 1984* (London: Financial Times Business Information, 1985), *International Coal Report's Coal Year 1985* (London: Financial Times Business Information, 1986), and *International Coal Report's Coal Year 1986* (London: Financial Times Business Information, 1987).

26. Energy Committee, *Coal Industry* (1987). The 30 percent figure, cited by the electricity-generating industry, was regarded as high by many observers. It was seen as an electricity board effort to put additional pressure on British Coal to lower the price of domestic coal.

traction in the geography of working pits to fewer faces more geologically favorable and more heavily capitalized. Face reorganization was seen as the key to productivity improvements not only on the face itself but also elsewhere below ground. In the British coalfield as a whole, there was a reduction from 429 faces in 1986, to 334 faces in 1987, to 251 in 1989, with daily output per face raising from 845 to 1,044 to 1,419 metric tons.[27] Improvements in productivity and cost per ton and per gigajoule seemed to be closely related to face contraction. Reduction in the number of faces improved results by concentrating production where the return was greater. It was a risk-averse form of planning which resulted from the demand for consistent short-term performance. It also abandoned, and sterilized, large reserves.

The requirement of labor in this context was that it operate capital more intensively and continuously and that its cost be reduced as capital costs increased. Management attempted to require miners to work the machinery at the faces both more intensively and more continuously. Intensification of work was the object primarily of new incentive schemes introduced in the coalfield. In general, these schemes tied incentive pay to actual production, measured either in terms of task or saleable output, and rewarded specific groups of producers for their own efforts. Continuity of production and maximum utilization of machinery were the object of the move toward three-shift coaling and no-strike and attendance bonuses, as well as discussions and agreements regarding 6-day, rather than 5-day, coaling, longer shifts, and more variable holidays.[28]

As capital costs increased, not only did management try to increase the productivity of capital but it made reduction of labor costs a priority. Labor constituted approximately 40 percent of total costs in the 1980s; the Coal Board aimed for capital costs of 20 percent and labor costs of 30 percent at reconstructed pits, and the most advanced sites were projected to have capital costs of 60 percent and labor costs near 10 percent.[29] Labor was shed rapidly through a policy of voluntary

27. British Coal, *Report and Accounts 1986/7*, p. 22; *Report and Accounts 1988/9*, p. 31.

28. In September 1988, the Framework Agreement for Mineworkers' Working Time Wages and Conditions Under Six Day Coal Production at new mines was concluded with the UDM. It was subsequently agreed with the UDM that the new agreement would apply to the Asfordby New Mine and the Margam new mine development in South Wales; British Coal, *Annual Report and Accounts 1988/9*, p. 15.

29. Albert Wheeler, "Frontiers and Forward: Colliery Production and Productivity,"

redundancy, opportunities for which were offered especially to workers over age 50. Employment in the industry fell from over 190,000 in 1984, to 125,000 in 1987, to 105,000 in 1989.[30] In addition, there was a crackdown on absenteeism and an apparent increase in disciplinary actions. Where possible, jobs were eliminated or combined. Management moved to eliminate customary practices that shortened working time or commanded additional pay, declaring they were not willing "to buy industrial peace." There was consistent and widespread pressure on managers to use outside contractors for particular but diverse jobs.

For managers to implement the strategy of selective capital intensification and reduction of labor costs, it seemed necessary for them to break the power of national and pit-level unionism to resist these processes. On the one hand, negotiated agreements that stood in the way of restructuring needed to be bypassed or abrogated. On the other hand, management had to remove pit-level resistance, expressed through unofficial stoppages, local negotiating strategies, and local work practices.

At the national level, a key management strategy was to build on the legacy of the 1984–85 strike to further deepen and institutionalize the division between the UDM and the NUM. In 1986, the Coal Board won legal recognition of the UDM as the sole bargaining agent for Nottinghamshire miners, and the government took further steps to grant the union legal recognition and standing. The restructuring strategy was facilitated by the UDM in several ways: it gave early consent to an increasing emphasis on incentive pay and a new incentive scheme, accepted 6-day coaling in principle, agreed to a new disciplinary code for the industry, and cooperated with and organized consent to pit closures and manpower reductions.

The Coal Board also deepened divisions within the NUM, by trying to negotiate on national matters with area unions in coalfields where unemployment was high and board investment was relatively low. The Coal Board, for instance, opened negotiations with the South Wales area of the NUM over a new development at Margam, winning

---

Mining Engineer, September 1986, pp. 152–60; Ken Moses, "New Mines in the United Kingdom," *Mining Engineer,* September 1986, pp. 185–91; C. T. Massey, "Barriers to the Future," *Mining Engineer,* September 1986, pp. 117–83.

30. British Coal, *Report and Accounts 1986/7,* pp. 18–19, *Report and Accounts 1988/9,* p. 14.

tentative agreement to negotiate a form of 6-day working, and there were other informal area and pit-level discussions over changes in working time.

At pit level, the board, with great variation from site to site, worked to weaken the power and legitimacy of the branch-level union. Within areas, the board isolated stronger pits by gradually introducing new working practices into weaker sites first. There was a consistent de-unionization of work life, especially with respect to labor at the face, where increasingly management tried to exercise direct control by offering new incentive schemes, meeting directly with the workers, and breaking traditional practices of labor control. Management initiated various new means of direct communication with the workforce, from informational pit newsletters to letters sent directly to miners' homes. Some pit managers talked openly about breaking miners' loyalty to the union and substituting for it a loyalty to the company that paid their wages. The "American model" was most important to pit managers for the sorts of worker attitudes and practices it represented: identification and cooperation with management's need to win in the marketplace. Management made use of the union's defeat in the 1984–85 strike to reassert its right to manage and reshape working practices. In its refusal to compromise with the union and allow it to exercise control in the pit, it in many cases actively delegitimated the union for a younger workforce that had no real memory of working life prior to the 1980s and little analysis of why the union was powerless.

The new cost-driven management strategy, therefore, represented an interesting contrast to the managerial strategy represented by the National Powerloading Agreement of 1966 and in general to management strategy in the 1960s and 1970s. First, the strategy in the 1980s embodied a more single-minded devotion to financial objectives than did the powerloading agreement, which was also a managerial strategy for efficient production. The 1966 agreement not only represented a management effort to control wages and the deployment of labor but also embodied union objectives of national wage solidarity, which fused the interests of both equity among workers and union power. Second, although the agreement represented a national bureaucratic reform from above, which assumed that increased productivity would follow from a new standardized set of rules about pay and production, it failed to attend to the informal capacities of management to supervise and labor to control the labor process. The new cost-reduction pressures required managers to address custom and practice as well as more formal arrangements. Third, management strategy became more decentralized and internally competitive in the 1980s. There was a considerable devolution of responsibility to areas and pits, and the notion of cost containment was shifted more decisively to pit level. Areas and pits were engaged in competition for investment based on cost performance, and managers' own jobs were tied to the cost performance of their pits. Due to the devolution of responsibility for cost reduction, managers were free to identify regional and pit-level opportunities and obstacles to cost lowering, and they were compelled to address particular regional and local traditions of work and unionism. Management competition also structured labor competition within the industry: miners were in competition for a diminishing numbers of jobs in lower-cost pits, and the area was a key unit of this competition. The labor market pressures inside the industry were increased by the high level of unemployment outside.

UNION STRATEGIES

Union responses to the state-led managerial restructuring of coal in the 1980s were largely region-specific. The fracturing of union activity was precipitated by state and management strategy that emphasized the breaking of labor solidarity and labor constraints on management decisions and practices; management structures and rules that emphasized decentralization and the economics of individual areas and pits; and a central union strategy lodged in a tradition of one major coalfield (Yorkshire), stressing militant mobilization rather than the maintenance of organizational unity or incremental bargaining for improved terms and conditions. Underlying these developments, however, was the long-term regionalization of the British coalfield.

The British coalfield was the product of a long and uneven historical development. From the late nineteenth century, regional coalfields had characteristic markets, the nature of which were often central to the regularity of employment and the level of wages. Regional coalfields also varied geologically, enjoying different levels of productivity and different cost structures. Labor relations in the pits and the culture of work and unionism also came to vary regionally. Even after the 1947 nationalization of the industry, management and union structures reflected this regionalization, and the NUM continued to organize largely autonomous constituent area unions. These constituent area unions were the most important sites for the representation of particular political tendencies in the union. The politics of the regions were carried to the national level of the union by both full-time and area representatives who sat on the national executive committee. The importance of the area as a production and union unit meant that the politics of the national union was often a process of coordination and conflict among areas.[31] The two largest regions for most of the postwar period, Yorkshire and Nottinghamshire, represented contrasting coalfields, and they remained the center of the restructuring coal industry.

The Nottinghamshire area continued in the postwar period to exhibit deference to market determination of employment and to management control of the work process, emphasis on wages rather than job control demands, and reluctance to undertake industrial action. These traditions have been attributed to various historical developments in the coalfield. Several writers point to the evolution of the labor process in the Nottinghamshire pits and the special importance of the butty system, a hierarchical system of subcontracting, in generating work relations. Others emphasize social relations of paternalism in mining communities, the reliance of Notts mines on a relatively stable internal market, and the relatively favorable geology of Notts pits.[32]

31. The structure of the NUM has remained basically unchanged since 1944. The national level of the union, to which certain powers such as the power to call official industrial action are reserved, comprises the national executive committee and three national offices—president, general secretary, and a part-time vice president. These three officials implement the policy set by national conferences. The NUM also comprises constituent area unions, which represent both coalfield regions (such as Yorkshire, Nottinghamshire, Scotland, and South Wales) and occupational groups in the coalfield (such as the colliery officials and staff area and the power group). The constituent unions have considerable autonomy. The preponderance of membership has been contained within the coalfield areas. Within each area, the membership is organized into branches, usually representing members at a particular production site, for example, a pit or a workshop. NUM areas have not always coincided with Coal Board administrative areas; some NUM areas have been governed by more than one Coal Board area and, more recently, a Coal Board area governed more than one NUM area. The UDM has a similar structure, with the preponderance of its membership in Nottinghamshire. See Jack Eaton and Colin Gill, *Trade Union Directory* (London: Pluto Press, 1981).

32. Krieger, *Undermining Capitalism;* Alan Griffin, *The Miners of Nottinghamshire, 1914–1944* (London: Allen & Unwin, 1962); R. Page Arnot, *The Miners, 1881–1910: A History of the Miners Federation of Great Britain* (London: Allen & Unwin, 1949); Robert Waller, *The Dukeries Transformed* (New York: Oxford University Press, 1983).

The importance in the postwar period of these traditions of work and unionism is illustrated by the participation of the Notts miners in the 1972 and 1974 national wage strikes. In 1972 and 1974, Nottinghamshire struck as a result of wage grievances. Notts miners' wages had been held down disproportionately in the movement from area-based and individual-based contracts to nationally uniform time-based wages established by the National Powerloading Agreement. In addition, the changing energy market of those years made it possible for those who accepted the market as the arbiter of wages and conditions to engage in strike action and hope to win. The national ballots that preceded the national strikes of 1972 and 1974 also procedurally bound the Notts area into strike action. But in the widespread unofficial actions of 1969 and 1970, Notts miners were reluctant to withdraw their labor. In the late 1970s, the Notts area was also the first to support and pursue a separate area incentive scheme as a way of attaining local wage increases; this position represented an early and somewhat defiant break with the then decade-old practice of wage solidarity across areas. Notts separatism, which had also been clear in the area's interwar support for district rather than national wage negotiations and for the breakaway "nonpolitical" Spencer union, was based not only on political conservatism but also on the area's favorable geological and economic position. Work relations in the postwar period continued to demonstrate cooperation with management to raise productivity, combined with demands for high wages. In the postwar period, then, the Notts area union maintained an often aggressive wage orientation but conceded control over levels of employment and workplace practices to market and management and demonstrated reluctance to engage in industrial action.

Especially after the late 1960s, the Yorkshire area union reflected coalfield traditions of labor solidarity, orientation toward control of employment and the work process, oppositional pit politics, and willingness to resort to industrial action in defense of wages, jobs, and conditions. In the late 1960s and early 1970s, Yorkshire area activists led unofficial widespread strikes against the area union leadership, as well as the Coal Board, over issues of surface hours and wages. And both officials and activists from Yorkshire were important in pushing the national union into official strikes over wages in 1972 and 1974. The Yorkshire area also resisted the introduction of area incentive schemes, which refragmented national and area wage structures, in the late 1970s. In addition, for much of the postwar period the Yorkshire area, especially in Doncaster, had traditions of worker control in the pits: in most Doncaster pits, the union controlled deployment to the face; in some pits, workers rotated jobs at the face. In addition, Doncaster pits showed a high level of unofficial rank-and-file activity. But even outside Doncaster in the South Yorkshire area there was a tradition of solidarity and opposition to management. The strong unevenness of pit-level work and union traditions within the Yorkshire area may be due to the size and marked uneven development of the Yorkshire coalfield itself over a long period of time.[33]

The outlying coalfields, finally, such as Durham, South Wales, and Scotland, were older and less geologically favored coalfields, or coalfields that produced special qualities of coal that appeared under difficult geological conditions. They tended to have militant pit-level traditions, and South Wales, Scotland, and Kent were centers of left-wing unionism. These outlying coalfields underwent the most severe contraction in the postwar period. From the 1970s, however, the regionalization of the coalfields and the issue of national reconciliation of area differences focused on the two major coalfields of Yorkshire, now the main region of the NUM, and Nottinghamshire, the base of the breakaway UDM.

The Postwar Period to 1980

The early postwar period saw the enlistment of the miners' union, the NUM, in the postwar social democratic settlement partly due to nationalization itself. Nationalization standardized and improved conditions of employment while creating institutional arrangements that granted the union an important role in the affairs of the industry. Across areas the union cooperated with government and management to "make nationalization work" by striving to increase production, maintain industrial peace, and restrain wage demands.[34]

33. Frank Machin, *The Yorkshire Miners: A History* (Barnsley, 1958); Pat Spaven, "Main Gates of Protest: Contrasts in Rank and File Activity among the South Yorkshire Miners, 1858–1894," and James MacFarlane, "Counter-Offensive for a South Yorkshire Mining Community," in *Independent Collier: The Coal Miner as Archetypal Proletarian Reconsidered*, ed. Royden Harrison (London: Harvester Press, 1978), pp. 201–31, and 180–200; and John Benson and Robert Neville, eds., *Studies in the Yorkshire Coal Industry* (Manchester; Manchester University Press, 1976).

34. Tony Hall, *King Coal: Miners, Coal, and Britain's Industrial Future* (Harmondsworth:

The period of severe industrial contraction beginning in 1957 also produced a largely acquiescent union; cooperation in this period was due less to a positive attachment to the arrangements of nationalization than to the severely weakened market position of the coal industry. The union tried unsuccessfully to persuade the Labour party and the Trades Union Congress through political-bureaucratic channels to prevent the industry's contraction by enacting a national fuel policy based on a central role for British coal. Industrial action was likely to be ineffective given both the high level of coal stocks and the market framework to which both political parties, Conservative and Labour, seemed committed. In addition, the rundown affected areas of the coalfield and individual pits differently, and the national union was concerned about unity in industrial action. The late 1950s and 1960s was a period of insecurity, uncertainty, forced mobility, and depressed wages in which the union worked to manage the employment consequences of the severe industrial rundown in a period of full employment in the economy as a whole.[35]

Between 1969 and 1974 the coalfields erupted in a series of strikes, which marked the end of conciliatory and cooperative industrial relations and a turn toward strategies of mobilization and industrial action. Initiated in Yorkshire, Scotland, and South Wales, traditionally militant areas, the unofficial strikes of 1969 and 1970 were the result of accumulated grievances. The strikes of 1972 and 1974, however, were successful official national strikes over wages. By 1974, the energy market had clearly turned in favor of coal. The Conservative government of 1970–74, which did not break decisively with postwar corporatism and collectivism, was succeeded by a Labour government sympathetic to the coal industry and miners. The determination and unity of the miners owed a great deal to wage developments. The 1966 powerloading agreement had unified the wage interests of members of the face teams. In the transition to uniform time-based wages, the wages of the higher-paid areas such as Nottinghamshire were held down. The 1972 and 1974 strikes therefore represented a combination of the wage resentment of the traditionally highly paid conservative areas and the traditional militancy of areas such as Yorkshire. The changing energy market of the early 1970s also made it possible for those who accepted the market as the arbiter of wages and conditions

---

Penguin, 1981), pp. 67–105.

35. Ibid., pp. 106–48.

to demand improved terms and conditions and to hope to succeed in strike action. In addition, in this period a nationally organized, broad left grouping had emerged in the union; this group pressed the union into strike action and played an important role in the waging of the strikes, particularly in the organization of picketing in 1972. The strikes represented an extremely important episode for the whole union; substantial wage increases and other concessions were won.[36]

The later 1970s represented a period of general compliance with successive Labour governments and the Coal Board, as a limited process of reconstruction and modernization was undertaken. In this period, however, a national incentive scheme was introduced alongside the national daywage structure. It was above all in Nottinghamshire, led by the right and with a strong wage orientation and a tradition of separatism, that the incentive scheme was argued for: it would increase the pay of the most productive pits and avoid confrontation with the Labour government's income policies. The left, based in Yorkshire, resisted the reintroduction of incentives on the grounds of union and labor movement solidarity, arguing that the Labour party's income policy should be opposed directly and jointly by the union movement rather than evaded through incentive pay for some. Nevertheless, the incentive scheme, supported also by the national officials of the union, was introduced throughout the coalfield, with the resultant development of wage differentials among areas and pits. In this period, the left continued to consolidate its leadership in the Yorkshire area.[37]

The 1980s

The developing national union response to the restructuring initiatives of the 1980s was, first, a failed attempt to develop unified large-scale industrial militancy; second, a Yorkshire-led strike (1984–85) that struggled to become national but remained regionalized; and then, the institutionalization of regionalization in the poststrike period. Whereas the Yorkshire regional tradition of militancy and solidarity was able to lead and unify the entire NUM in the conditions of the early 1970s, it was clearly unable to do so in the conditions of the

36. Peggy Kahn, "'Coal Not Dole': The British Miners' Strike of 1984–5," *Socialist Review* 17 (1987): 57–90; Hall, *King Coal,* pp. 149–221.

37. Hall, *King Coal,* pp. 222–38.

1980s, as government and management worked deliberately to fragment union solidarity and overcome labor resistance in contracting industrial and recessionary economic conditions.

In the early 1980s, the national leaders of the NUM were aware of the threat to labor in the coalfields from the political economy of Thatcherism. Arthur Scargill, elected president of the NUM after a long period as Yorkshire president, particularly worked to generate a national strike to resist the power of management to restructure. The union was facing an accelerated pit closure program that would disproportionately affect the peripheral coalfields. Scargill concluded that the union leadership of the 1960s had betrayed the membership by not fighting pit closures, despite the terrible market conditions. In addition, he saw the institutional channels of the Trades Union Congress and the Labour party as too reformist and insufficiently class conscious to challenge Thatcherism. Other national leftist leaders represented the peripheral coalfields of Scotland and Wales, which were being run down at a faster rate than the central coalfields of either Yorkshire or Nottinghamshire. Scargill in particular but other leftist leaders as well had been at the fore of the successful national strikes of the 1970s, which had given them considerable prestige and organizational experience.[38]

In Yorkshire and at the national level, industrial resistance was in preparation from the early 1980s. Rank-and-file miners and activists in Yorkshire became restive as management practices became more aggressive. Under Scargill's presidency, Yorkshire had balloted in favor of area resistance to pit closures; in effect, members approved strike action in advance of a strike being called. But between 1981 and 1984, as pits seemed to close ever more rapidly and changes in management style became apparent, the membership of the NUM as a whole and the Nottinghamshire area union in particular failed to back three national calls for strike action: in January 1982 on the question of wages, in October on pay and pit closures, and in March 1983 on supporting South Wales's industrial action and nationally resisting pit closures.[39]

When in March 1984 two developments triggered a Yorkshire strike, the national leadership, by then under the control of the left, took a clear decision not to ballot the membership but to let Yorkshire strikers try to "roll" the strike through other areas by picketing. The

38. Kahn, "Coal Not Dole"; Goodman, *Miners' Strike*.
39. Goodman, *Miners' Strike*.

national executive of the union subsequently made several area strikes official, and a special delegate conference declared the strike national and official, though whether this procedure conformed with union rules was controversial. Yet, this strategy did not succeed in enlisting the Nottinghamshire area in the strike action; these methods of trying to consolidate the strike did not overcome the more favorable economic conditions in the Nottinghamshire coalfield as a whole or the conservative work and union traditions that conceded management's right to manage and rejected industrial action. The sustained mass picketing of Notts by striking miners from other areas called forth the centralized, authoritarian, and brutal policing that had been prepared by the state.[40] A strike strategy intended to overcome the regionalization of the coalfield in the end exposed and intensified regional differences.

The breakaway UDM was founded on the strike experience and subsequent developments, and it seemed to represent a more highly institutionalized expression of Notts union and work traditions in the conditions of the 1980s. Its establishment was especially conducive to the Coal Board's strategy of creating a more managerial union and of breaking national agreements. The UDM accepted nearly all the Coal Board's restructuring initiatives and their consequences.

The UDM conceded managerial prerogative to restructure the industry as a whole and at pit level; its orientation was to cooperate with management initiatives to make the industry more competitive. It did not work to resist pit closures by collective means, nor did it resist restructuring at pit level—for example, the selective capital concentration or the implementation of the new incentive schemes. The UDM also cooperated with management's union-breaking strategies and as an organization was the prime beneficiary of union splitting. While conceding managerial prerogative, the union tried to win good pay for its members. If the union had a job protection strategy, it was one of protecting the jobs of its own members who wished to remain in the industry by competition with the NUM for recognition at new and established sites and in lowering costs of production.[41]

40. Ibid.; Wilsher, Macintyre, and Jones, *Strike;* Martin Adeney and John Lloyd, *The Miners' Strike, 1984–5: Loss without Limit* (London: Routledge & Kegan Paul, 1986); John McIlroy, "Police and Pickets: The Law against the Miners," in *Digging Deeper,* ed. Beynon, pp. 101–22.

41. *Nottinghamshire Miner* (newspaper of the Nottinghamshire area UDM), 1985–1987.

At pit level, among the membership, there was considerable informal resentment toward aspects of the restructuring process, yet the UDM had neither commitment to opposition nor strategy for resistance. Branch officials were integrated with the area leadership but also faced pressure from the rank and file. Confronted with pressures from above—to comply without resistance—and from below—to defend working conditions—individual branch officials responded differently.

After the strike, the Yorkshire area, and the national leadership with which it was closely integrated, developed another set of responses consistent with its longer tradition of work and unionism and its participation in the strike. Yorkshire before and after the strike opposed pit closures and regarded maintenance of employment levels as an important and legitimate demand; it opposed the overall restructuring strategy, which was clearly oriented toward market competition. It favored opposition to closure and restructuring by collective means. It insisted on national agreements and national negotiation rather than area or pit-level bargaining on appropriate issues. Long strikes did not appear a realistic or effective policy, but the area supported the prospect of nationally organized industrial action, for example the NUM overtime ban against the new disciplinary code. Within the Yorkshire area there were numerous small, short-term unofficial strikes beginning in fiscal year 1986–87, and the summer 1987 strike over the new disciplinary code began in Yorkshire. The rate of unofficial militancy in 1986–87 seemed to indicate a recovery from poststrike exhaustion, though local militancy was uneven and related to several different pit-level practices. The area also encouraged and supported pit opposition to closure by taking cases through the pit closure review procedure, urged pits to organize community campaigns for coal, and looked to the politics of the Labour party to maintain employment in the coal industry and the rights of labor generally.[42]

The opposition to closure at area level, however, did not translate into successful pit-level resistance. At pit level, a demoralized membership sought to leave the industry with redundancy pay, and much restructuring was accepted, especially where no closure was involved. The lack of resistance was due to the fact that some restructuring was favorable to sections of the workforce; in addition, there was no avail-

42. *Yorkshire Miner* (newspaper of the Yorkshire Area NUM), 1985–1987; "Cost of Strikes," *Coal News*, February 1987, p. 20.

able effective strategy of resistance. In Yorkshire, branch officials seemed torn between the attempt at area level to sustain a principled oppositional unionism and the lack of effective means within the industrial setting to resist. The Yorkshire area exhibited a response comprising declaratory opposition and unofficial pit-level militancy over a variety of practices. The militancy was not directed against selective capital intensification but against new forms of management control, labor discipline, and pay. In Yorkshire as well as Nottinghamshire, the restructuring strategy continued steadily and without serious negotiation over its implementation.

THATCHERISM, FORDISM, AND THE RESTRUCTURING OF THE COAL INDUSTRY

The British coal industry was propelled into restructuring by a succession of neoliberal Conservative governments. Required to break even by fiscal 1988–89 and to finance investment by 1990, managers in the coal industry decided to minimize the cost of production at a capacity of approximately 90 million metric tons. They decided to do so through a policy of rapid, selective capital intensification and labor reduction and reorganization, which at the same time necessitated a diminution of union coordination and resistance. Especially because there was from the early 1980s a militant national leadership with a base in the large Yorkshire coalfield, management encouraged an alternative union center based in the central Nottinghamshire coalfield, which it used to spearhead its restructuring strategy. Although distinctive traditions and different conditions would have remained significant without the establishment of the UDM, the Notts tendency would have been expressed within the political process of the national union, and some compromise but unified position that limited managerial initiatives or won exchanges for managerial initiatives and maintained the unity of the union might have been the result. The institutionalization of the division between Nottingham and Yorkshire created extremely favorable conditions for management's strategy of capital intensification and labor reduction. Nottinghamshire's enthusiastic embrace of management's restructuring initiatives and the disengagement of Yorkshire and the national union from coordinated negotiation over terms of restructuring meant that resistance in the coalfield was localized, informal, and directed to issues of job control rather than coordinated against restructuring initiatives. A central difficulty for unionism in the coalfield therefore was the exaggeration and institutionalization of regional difference in this period. Although it is unlikely that a unified NUM could have reversed the strategy of restructuring, regional differences in the coalfields might have been resolved through a decision-making process inside the union that would have allowed national negotiations over perhaps (a) the timing of certain restructuring measures, (b) marginal concessions on issues not central to the restructuring, such as terms and conditions of retirement, and certain pay issues, and (c) maintenance of a unified organizational base within a contracted and restructured coal industry.

Two somewhat different concepts have provided a focus for debate on economic change and changes in unionism in Britain in the 1980s: Thatcherism and post-Fordism. Theorists of Thatcherism have argued that the development driving economic change was a complex political response to the long-term structural decline of the British economy and the collapse of social democratic consensus and the Labour government of the 1970s. Thatcherism has been interpreted as a project to rebuild the political dominance of the Conservative party, to establish a new social ideal of a free market order, and to develop economic policies to restore conditions for profitable capital accumulation in Britain. These policies included withdrawing the state from the economy, restoring management's right to manage, restoring sound money and combating inflation, and creating a more flexible, cheaper labor force with weakened union protection.[43] Thatcherism has focused on a politically led restructuring of class relations and emphasized cultural and ideological as well as material change.

Theorists of Fordism and post-Fordism, on the other hand, have located the response to economic crisis in new capitalist strategies themselves. In the narrower sense, Fordism refers to the combination of semiskilled, machine-paced labor processes and scientific management (assembly line production) to produce standardized commodities for the mass consumer market. Post-Fordism (or in a weaker version, neo-Fordism) is described as the production of specialized commodities for luxury or niche markets through more flexible and specialized work processes, often with more worker autonomy and control; it is

43. Stuart Hall and Martin Jacques, *The Politics of Thatcherism* (London: Lawrence & Wishart, 1983); Gamble, *Free Economy;* Jessop, Bonnett, Bromley, and Ling, *Thatcherism.*

argued that flexible specialization is made possible by the application of microelectronics and information technology. In their broader usage, Fordism and post-Fordism are patterns of institutional regulation of economic growth and social conflict. Fordism involves regularized and centralized state supervision of a fully employed and welfare-oriented economy, with generally high levels of consumption and regularized and centralized collective bargaining. Post-Fordism suggests a decline in the role of the state in guaranteeing full employment, ensuring a prominent role for unions, and maintaining social welfare benefits; a decline in the scope, effectiveness, and centralization of collective bargaining; and the exacerbation of social dualism, often along regional, ethnic, and gender lines.[44]

These two conceptualizations of economic change in the 1980s have different focuses, but both emphasize a material restructuring of class relations. The restructuring is away from relations of class compromise—often mediated by large organizations of capital, labor, and the state—and toward relations of exchange and capital accumulation that are increasingly market- or management-determined. Thatcherism emphasizes the political determinations of restructuring strategies and a cultural-ideological, as well as material, project. Fordism focuses primarily on the development of new strategies in the economic sphere. The relative prominence of the Thatcherism thesis in British discussion may well correspond to a more politically determined and culturally powerful response to the economic difficulties of the 1970s and 1980s than has occurred in other Western European and North American societies.

Thatcherism, rather than Fordism, seems better to capture the political impetus behind the restructuring of the British coal industry in the 1980s. In coal, an altered political framework forced management to develop new strategies that would allow coal to compete in the market. Management weakened and disciplined unions in the interests of "management's right to manage" and cost minimization, with considerable direct and indirect support from the state. The state not only used its strategic capacity to assist management during the strike but also, in the early 1980s, fostered a climate of opinion hostile to

44. Stephen Wood, "The Transformation of Work?" in *The Transformation of Work? Skill, Flexibility, and the Labour Process*, ed. Stephen Wood (London: Unwin Hyman, 1988), pp. 1–43; Michael Piore and Charles Sabel, *The Second Industrial Divide: Possibilities for Prosperity* (New York: Basic Books, 1984).

effective unionism, changed the framework of employment and industrial relations law to weaken unions, and abandoned any commitment to full employment.

There is little evidence that the coal industry has become post-Fordist. There have been few changes in production technology and no increased labor autonomy; there have, however, been several changes in the social regulatory institutions in the industry.

Even after it became fully mechanized in the 1960s, the British coal industry was never a classic locus of Fordism; it was obviously not a sector involving assembly line production, where a fixed, product-specific machine dictated an invariant process of work that turned out a standardized product for mass consumption. Coal mining continued to be skilled work in an extractive industry where environmental conditions were constantly changing. Some analysts have emphasized the development of microelectronic information technology in the industry, but no one has suggested that the technology fundamentally changed the process of mining or increased worker autonomy.[45] On the contrary, the application of technology was an attempt to increase managerial control over a production process that was always difficult to supervise. The most consequential changes seem not to have been related to information technology itself, but to the more widespread application of certain kinds of standard mining methods and the introduction of heavy-duty machinery; these technologies were supported by information technology. Management, however, used labor more flexibly to win a higher return on more intensively capitalized pits. Some of the most striking changes in the use of labor entailed the appearance of more extensive and variable shifts and variable holidays. Labor use was also intensified through various changes in incentive schemes, an increased emphasis on incentive pay, and an apparent increase in discipline.

The national coal industry was, however, a bureaucratic organization with substantial central planning in finance, marketing, and production. At the end of the 1980s, a substantial degree of nonmarket organization remained. For example, the industry remained in the

45. Jonathan Winterton, "The Crisis in British Coal Mining," *Insurgent Sociologist* 13 (1985): 53–62; Alan Burns, Dave Feickert, Martin Newby, and Jonathan Winterton, "The Restructuring of the British Coal Industry," *Cambridge Journal of Economics* 9 (1985): 93–110; and Alan Burns, Dave Feickert, Martin Newby, and Jonathan Winterton, "The Miners and the New Technology," *Industrial Relations Journal* 14 (1983): 7–20.

public sector though there appeared to be intentions to privatize it, and as of 1990 the industry still retained its marketing agreement with the CEGB. As both the Thatcherism and Fordism analyses suggest, however, there was considerable withdrawal of state finance. The industry became a less bureaucratic enterprise, with more internal competition and entrepreneurship. By the end of the 1980s, there was no longer a single national union, union power to resist restructuring was limited and exercised unevenly throughout the coalfields at pit and area levels, and management was deunionizing many aspects of pit life.

Two characteristics of the economy and its institutions identified in the Fordism debate do appear to be central to the diminished capacity of coal-mining unionism: the dissociation between production growth and employment and the fragmentation of union structures. Traditionally, growth and expansion of the coal industry, as well as much of the rest of manufacturing, were associated with a steady growth of employment. But in the 1980s the coal industry began to develop the capacity to increase its production with a declining workforce. There was a sharp decline in the absolute number of miners, in labor relative to capital costs, in miners as a proportion or local and regional workforces, and in NUM members as a proportion of the labor movement. The steep fall in mining employment was a reflection of the decline in labor intensiveness in coal, a product of the decline of Britain's manufacturing base and a cyclical downturn in the economy. In these circumstances, the power of the mining unions was greatly attenuated.

In addition, the Fordist or social democratic forms of the national coal industry and union had previously contained the localism and regionalism of British miners. It can be argued that in Britain in general localizing tendencies, historically created or reinforced by Britain's early, decentralized industrialization, were barely contained by the corporatist form of the 1960s and 1970s. The local and shop-floor orientation of the labor movement limited the effective functioning of corporatist institutions and social democratic politics. The coal industry, partly due to industry-specific factors, experienced until the early 1970s a great deal of local militancy, which was moderated by the development of national wage structures in the 1960s and 1970s; but underlying local characteristics of work and labor relations continued to assert themselves. In coal, the dismantling of organized capitalist forms released the localism of labor, and management found ways of using preexisting differences to develop its new managerial strategy. This fragmentation of institutional and social relations among workers in a period of increased economic and labor competition and increased managerial capacity was certainly another key element in the decline of the capacity of mining unionism.

Part 3

LOCAL UNIONS AND CHANGES AT THE FIRM LEVEL

6 The Politics of Flexibility in the German Metalworking Industries

Kathleen Thelen

Widespread agreement prevails among students of labor in the advanced capitalist countries that the context and problems facing labor unions have shifted dramatically since the 1970s. Persistent unemployment, massive restructuring at both the industrial and plant levels, accelerated introduction of new microelectronics-based production technologies, and a variety of employer attempts to inject greater flexibility into their operations are all among the most commonly cited factors contributing to the current crisis in unionism.[1] Although no labor movement has been exempt, most observers agree as well that these developments present a special challenge to national labor unions that organize workers in different industries and with different

This essay draws on and contains excerpts from chaps. 7, 8, and 10 of Kathleen Thelen, *Union of Parts: Labor Politics in Postwar Germany* (Ithaca: Cornell University Press, 1991). I wish to thank the participants in the 1986 Cornell workshop at which this paper was originally presented for their valuable suggestions, and especially Peter Katzenstein and Michael Goldfield, who commented on this essay. Special thanks are due to Jonas Pontusson for his careful readings of earlier versions. This article has also benefited from comments by Christopher Allen, Gary Herrigel, Horst Kern, Richard Locke, Ben Schneider, and Lowell Turner. The German Academic Exchange Program (D.A.A.D.) funded the research on which this work is based. All references to Germany before unification refer to West Germany.

1. See, for example, Peter Gourevitch et al., eds., *Unions and Economic Crisis: Britain, West Germany and Sweden* (London: Allen & Unwin, 1984); Scott Lash and John Urry, *The End of Organized Capitalism* (Cambridge: Polity Press, 1987); several of the essays in *Order and Conflict in Contemporary Capitalism*, ed. John H. Goldthorpe (London: Oxford University Press, 1984), among many others.

skills who have been unevenly affected by the economic crisis and industrial restructuring. Employers often play on differences in workers' market positions, and such fragmentation strategies complicate the already formidable task these unions face of maintaining unity.

In this essay I trace the response of the German metalworkers' union, IG Metall, to these changes and challenges. An examination of the strategic options the union has faced and the choices it has made over the course of the 1980s illuminates the distinctive features of adjustment politics in Germany's "dual system" of industrial relations.[2] In addition, an assessment of IG Metall's relative successes and failures can serve as the basis for a reexamination of the more general question of union success in the 1980s and 1990s.

Specifically, I argue that the plant level has become an increasingly important locus of conflict (and cooperation) in German labor relations. IG Metall has been both pushed and pulled to incorporate works councils into national union strategies. On the one hand, plant representatives have been drawn into national level conflicts (such as that over the 35-hour work week) as part of an industry-wide compromise that traded working-time reduction for greater flexibility in plant personnel policy. On the other hand, recent union initiatives on skills and new technologies reflect attempts by IG Metall to use the legal rights of works councils to go beyond its more traditional emphasis on central collective bargaining to play a more active role in work reorganization at the plant level.

Contemporary labor politics in Germany are thus characterized by strategic maneuvering on the part of both labor and capital within the dual system.[3] This pattern of politics implies elements of both stability

2. An extensive literature exists on the "dual system," a term that refers to the coexistence in Germany of overarching industrial unionism and a statutory system of plant-level works councils. Although works councils are formally independent of Germany's industrial unions, they are in reality overwhelmingly dominated by union members. On the dual system generally, see Joachim Bergmann et al., *Gewerkschaften in der Bundesrepublik* (Frankfurt: Campus Verlag, 1979); Wolfgang Streeck, "Codetermination: The Fourth Decade," in *International Yearbook of Organization Democracy,* vol. 2 (New York: Wiley, 1984); Kathleen Thelen, *Union of Parts: Labor Politics in Postwar Germany* (Ithaca: Cornell University Press, 1991); and Andrei Markovits, *The Politics of the West German Trade Unions* (Cambridge: Cambridge University Press, 1986).

3. My use of the term "strategic maneuvering" is not meant to imply that behind individual union actions and policies lies a single grand and unified plan. The union's policies are sometimes reactive and even stopgap. "Strategic maneuvering" is meant to capture this notion of a union reacting to employer initiatives where it must but also of seizing opportunities as it can.

and change. One important source of stability is the union's strong presence in most works councils. The legal rights unions command through the works council system have shored up central union strength and provided stable institutional bounds for evolving relations among works councils, employers, and the central union. But such structures only constrain; they do not determine political outcomes. Thus, I emphasize as well political conflict and choice within these institutional constraints. Indeed, previous political battles within and over the dual system forged the institutions and practices of German labor relations in their present form, and the outcome of current politicking may also leave an institutional imprint.[4]

My interpretation counters the view that works councils exacerbate problems of central union control by encouraging and facilitating the expression of "plant egoism" and "cooperative syndicalism" that undermine central union power.[5] The danger of the development of some sort of enterprise unionism is quite real, and not only in Germany. Some analyses of this phenomenon, however, paint an overly dichotomous and zero-sum picture of relations between the central union and plant works councils.[6] It is true that the logic of labor representation at the industrial and workplace levels can be conflicting and contradictory. For instance, national unions have an interest in a low unemployment rate but not necessarily in saving particular jobs, whereas the reverse is true for labor representatives at the plant level. But one cannot simply apply a sort of mechanical "stress analysis" and deduce political trends from such structural tensions. To do so yields deterministic and somewhat misleading conclusions about how

4. Elsewhere I examine the political conflicts that helped forge the dual system in its present form. The institutionalization of politically fought outcomes at crucial junctures in the development of the dual system shaped the structure of labor relations in Germany as it now stands; see Thelen, *Union of Parts,* especially chaps. 3–4.

5. The concept of "plant egoism" is perhaps most closely associated with Wolfgang Streeck, because of his important article, "Neo-Corporatist Industrial Relations and the Economic Crisis in West Germany," in *Order and Conflict,* ed. Goldthorpe, pp. 291–314. However, Streeck's treatment of the relationship between works councils and central unions is in fact much more nuanced than that of many others who have picked up on his original insight. See, for example, Streeck, "Industrial Relations in Germany: Agenda for Change," Discussion Paper IIM/LMP 87-5 (Wissenschaftszentrum Berlin, 1987) and "Successful Adjustment to Turbulent Markets: The Automobile Industry," in *Industry and Politics in West Germany: Toward the Third Republic,* ed. Peter J. Katzenstein (Ithaca: Cornell University Press, 1989), pp. 113–56.

6. See especially Hans-Willy Hohn, *Von der Einheitsgewerkschaft zum Betriebssyndikalismus* (Berlin: Sigma Rainer Bohn Verlag, 1988).

centrifugal tendencies within national labor movements are pulling the two levels apart.[7]

While acknowledging these built-in structural strains, my different emphasis—on politics and political strategies within the institutions of the dual system—reveals a somewhat less zero-sum game. By focusing on the interaction of the central union and works councils, my analysis uncovers sources of resiliency that help account for the continued stability of centralized bargaining and the dual system even in the face of new pressures. It thus helps explain why German labor relations have tended to confound theories predicting growing instability in the system and a loss of strategic capacity on the part of its leading unions. Furthermore, the present analysis also helps explain why German unions would far rather continue to live *with* the dual system and works councils—even "egoistic" ones—than do without them.

My analysis of the politics within Germany's dual system also points to more general conclusions regarding union viability and success since the 1980s. In the past, union strength was often measured in terms of centralization and organizational unity. All indications are that central union power is still the sine qua non for labor strength generally. Central union strength may, however, no longer be enough. In light of the changes in labor's political and economic situation, what is increasingly important is labor's organizational resiliency and flexibility, and this implies a combination of central and decentralized strength.[8]

Strong central coordination will remain crucial to the long-term viability of national unions such as IG Metall, but central union strength alone is no longer sufficient. The distinction between central union defenses and plant-level negotiations is not only being undermined by employer strategies; it is also being blurred by the new issues and bargaining situations unions increasingly face. National labor unions will have a difficult time resolving these new problems within the frame-

7. Much of the literature on the decentralization of bargaining and the "breakdown" of neocorporatism, I would argue, leans toward a certain structural determinism.

8. Measuring labor strength in terms of union centralization is in part the legacy of corporatism theory of the 1970s; see, for example, Philippe Schmitter, "Interest Intermediation and Regime Governability in Contemporary Western Europe and North America," in *Organizing Interests in Western Europe,* ed. Suzanne Berger (Cambridge: Cambridge University Press, 1981), pp. 285–327; David Cameron, "Social Democracy, Corporatism, Labour Quiescence, and the Representation of Economic Interests in Advanced Capitalist Society," in *Order and Conflict,* ed. Goldthorpe, pp. 143–78, among many others.

work of industrial relations that proved so successful at regulating wage issues in the 1970s. The continued viability of centralized labor organizations increasingly hinges on the successful integration of plant-level bargaining into central union strategies.

The essay is divided into three parts. The first situates my analysis in a broader set of theoretical issues by sketching out two different perspectives on the current crisis and its implications for labor. In the second part I examine IG Metall's strategies and policies in the 1980s, focusing on the role works councils have assumed in the union's interactions with employers in collective bargaining and technology policy. The third part returns us to the general issue of union success in the 1980s and 1990s, drawing out the broader implications of my analysis of IG Metall.

TWO VIEWS OF THE CRISIS

The current crisis for labor in the advanced capitalist countries is widely perceived as a crisis of neocorporatism and typically characterized in terms of two trends. The first is a decline in class capacity due to the growing fragmentation of labor interests. The second is a decentralization of bargaining which is both symptom and cause of the present weakness of national unions. Beyond the shared terminology, however, different theoretical vantage points yield different interpretations of what lies behind the crisis and how unions ought to respond to it.

Volker Schneiders draws a useful distinction between two different interpretations of the crisis of neocorporatism, one attributing it to a "neoliberal offensive" by employers and the other linking it to broader, structural changes associated with the breakdown of the mass production paradigm.[9] In the neoliberal-offensive interpretation, high unemployment has undermined labor's economic position and diminished

9. Volker Schneiders, "Krise der Massenproduktion, Technologischer Wandel und Gewerkschaftspolitik in der Bundesrepublik: Eine Skizze" (University of Osnabrück manuscript, January 1987), pp. 50–60. Schneiders bases this distinction on an insightful juxtaposition of the work of Wolfgang Streeck and Charles Sabel. My analysis draws on Schneiders's basic insight and extends it a step farther. Schneiders emphasizes the significance of the two perspectives for relations between unions and employers, but what he does not draw out fully—and what I wish to emphasize here—are the implications of the two

employers' interest in centralized collective bargaining.[10] From this perspective, the crisis of neocorporatism stems from employers' desire to decentralize bargaining in order to respond more flexibly to market cues, for example, enabling weaker firms to obtain concessions from labor or allowing stronger firms more freedom to reward their workers or certain groups of them. Employers often combine this national-level strategy of decentralization that weakens central unions with overtures of greater participation and cooperation with labor in their own factories and shops. Workers trying not to join the growing ranks of the unemployed have strong incentives to cooperate with employers in the interest of their own firm's competitiveness, and the resulting "cooperative syndicalism" at the shop-floor level can further undermine centralized bargaining.[11]

The second theoretical perspective links the crisis of neocorporatist bargaining to deeper and more fundamental shifts in the economies of the advanced capitalist countries.[12] This view is closely associated with the work of Michael Piore and Charles Sabel, who argue that a deeper crisis of the mass-production paradigm is what lies behind the crisis of a whole system of regulation (including neocorporatist bargaining and Keynesianism) on which the prosperity of the 1950s and 1960s was premised.[13] The role national unions played in that system, for example, participating in macroeconomic steering to maintain a balance between demand and production capacity, no longer fits with an emerging, alternative paradigm premised on "permanent innovation" (or what Piore and Sabel call "flexible specialization"). Indeed, in this

views for relations *within* unions, between the central leadership and shop-floor representatives.

10. Schneiders, "Krise," pp. 52–53. Schneiders's rendering of the neoliberal-offensive position is based on Streeck, "Neo-Corporatist Industrial Relations," but in fact none of Streeck's work since that article really fits this description (see footnote 5). I nonetheless find the category useful, as it does apply to a rather large literature that emphasizes neoliberal politics and employer strategies in explaining the difficulties labor now faces; see, for example, Gourevitch et al., *Unions and Economic Crisis;* Peter Lange et al., eds., *Unions, Change, and Crisis: French and Italian Union Strategy and the Political Economy, 1945–1980* (London: Allen & Unwin, 1982); Werner Sengenberger, "West German Employment Policy: Restoring Worker Competition," *Industrial Relations* 23: 3 (Fall 1984): 323–43.

11. Hohn, *Von der Einheitsgewerkschaft*, passim; and Paul Windolf and Hans-Willy Hohn, *Arbeitsmarktchancen in der Krise: Betriebliche Rekrutierung und soziale Schließung* (Frankfurt: Campus Verlag, 1984), passim.

12. See Schneiders, "Krise," pp. 55–57.

13. Charles Sabel and Michael Piore, *The Second Industrial Divide* (New York: Basic Books, 1984); and Charles Sabel, "Struktureller Wandel der Produktion und neue gewerkschaftliche Strategien," *Prokla 62* (March 1986): 41–60.

view, for unions to attempt to defend their old role in macroeconomic steering would only undermine their own goal of creating the productive basis necessary to achieve their redistributive goals.[14]

For Schneiders, what is key is how these two perspectives highlight the strategic dilemmas unions now face. Whereas the neoliberal-offensive interpretation stresses employers' attack on neocorporatist bargaining, the crisis-of-mass-production interpretation emphasizes the need for unions to conform to a regime of flexible specialization.[15] Thus, Sabel and others argue that unions must reorient their strategies away from sole attention to distributional issues and toward production issues.[16] Indeed, Sabel contends that unions need to seize the initiative from employers in the emerging flexible-specialization paradigm and turn it to their own advantage.[17] It is only in clearing a place for themselves in the new production paradigm that unions can begin to shape the process of change itself.

Moreover, even as current developments undermine the previous bases of union influence and control, flexible specialization opens up opportunities for new sources of labor influence such as over production organization. The basis of power for industrial unions under mass production was not the skills of their members—which in fact were continuously eroded by mass production—but rather the role unions themselves played in macroeconomic steering and stabilization.[18] Flexible specialization reintroduces the importance of skills and thus rejuvenates a source of union power that mass production had eliminated.

These two perspectives are not necessarily mutually exclusive, but emphasizing one or the other gives a different meaning to the decentralization of bargaining and implies a different response by unions to it. The neoliberal-offensive interpretation draws attention to the dangers of decentralization as an attack on class solidarity, fragmenting worker interests along industry, plant, or skill lines. To the extent that decentralization is seen as part of a broader trend that weakens unions

14. Schneiders, "Krise," p. 58.

15. Schneiders, "Krise," esp. pp. 55–56.

16. See also Horst Kern and Michael Schumann, *Das Ende der Arbeitsteilung? Rationalisierung in der industriellen Produktion* (Munich: Verlag C. H. Beck, 1984); Christopher Allen, "Trade Unions, Worker Participation, and Flexibility: Linking the Micro to the Macro" (Paper presented to the 1987 Conference of Europeanists, Washington D.C., October 30–November 2, 1987); and Thelen, *Union of Parts,* esp. chaps. 8–9.

17. Sabel, "Struktureller Wandel," p. 42.

18. Sabel, "Struktureller Wandel," p. 54.

by strengthening market forces, then the continued viability of central unions seems to hinge at least in part on their ability to resist "a 'downward' transfer of bargaining issues to the work-place"[19] and defend centrally bargained, uniform standards for all workers.

The second interpretation leads to somewhat different conclusions. Sabel alludes to a decentralization of bargaining and warns of the danger of enterprise unionism.[20] For Sabel, however, decentralization seems to imply not just dangers but also opportunities for labor. For example, his emphasis on skills points to new sources of power for labor at the shop-floor level which for him appear partly to compensate for the declining power of national unions in neocorporatist bargaining. Sabel's analysis is vague on the character and organization of labor interests under flexible specialization. He argues that unions should forge links among workers in plants connected by flexible specialization (for example, workers in core plants and their suppliers), as well as across regions.[21] But the overarching organization of labor interests seems to be something of a dependent variable that depends on how flexible specialization itself develops.

For the present analysis, the differences between these two perspectives are decisive. The neoliberal-offensive interpretation emphasizes the changed *context* of bargaining, and especially labor's current market weakness. To the extent that decentralization is associated with a growing fragmentation of working-class interests, labor's fate seems to depend on the ability of unions to resist flexibilization and to control plant egoism. The flexible-specialization perspective, in contrast, stresses the changing *content* of bargaining. From this perspective, unions must redefine their role by launching their own offensive on production issues, not so much to resist flexibilization but to define on whose terms flexibility is to be achieved. The former perspective stresses the pitfalls of decentralization (fragmentation and the growth of enterprise unionism), whereas the latter points to the opportunities (for example, worker influence over production organization).

Although my analysis of IG Metall confirms the central insights in both perspectives, it also suggests the need for a more synthetic interpretation. The problem with the neoliberal-offensive thesis is that it is

19. This was one of Streeck's conclusions in the 1984 article; see Streeck, "Neo-Corporatist Industrial Relations," p. 297.

20. Sabel, "Struktureller Wandel," p. 56.

21. Sabel, "Struktureller Wandel," pp. 57–58.

often overly deterministic, treating unions as relatively passive victims of market forces and employer strategies. Changes in labor's political and economic environment certainly call for strategic innovation on the part of national unions, but their decline is not as inevitable as this line of argumentation sometimes implies. Moreover, this interpretation often rests on a misleading zero-sum conceptualization of the relationship between central unions and the shop floor, equating any decentralization with union weakness.

The flexible-specialization thesis, in contrast, often seems overly sanguine and overstates the room for maneuver unions currently enjoy, given high unemployment and the unsympathetic (if not openly hostile) governments they often face. In addition, although Sabel and others appear to assign a prominent role to plant-level (or subnational) labor representatives to influence the restructuring process, they leave quite ambiguous what role—if any—national unions are to play in the transition.[22]

Thus, the neoliberal-offensive thesis tends to understate the strategic capacities of national unions, and the flexible-specialization thesis tends to exaggerate the ability of local unions to cope with (let alone capitalize on) the shop-floor changes currently under way. Neither comes directly to terms with the critical question of the *interaction* between central union strategies and shop-floor politics. Those versions of the neoliberal-offensive thesis that reduce this interaction to a question of centralization or decentralization miss an important point: whereas in the 1970s the viability of central unions hinged on the passive support of the shop floor, since the 1980s it increasingly depends on its active support. And this is true not only because central unions must defend against employers' fragmentation strategies but also because of the kinds of challenges labor now faces.

The effect of technological change on wages is a case in point. In Germany, the introduction of new technologies often blurs the distinction between central and decentralized bargaining. The widespread "analytic" system of wage determination compensates workers rather generously for such factors as physical exertion and exposure to dust and fumes. New technologies often decrease physical strain and eliminate hazardous jobs through automation. For the affected workers,

22. It is not at all clear that the linkages unions may be able to forge among workers connected by flexible specialization in different plants and regions can simply be summed into an overarching program for the labor movement as a whole.

the reclassification of jobs or relocation in the plant can have an immediate and dramatic effect on income.[23] For them, the works council's defense of income against erosion via qualitative changes in production organization is as important as the quantitative gains the union makes in central wage negotiations.

Moreover, the kinds of problems technological change raises in Germany point to a more general issue, namely, that some union demands are objectively hard for central unions to negotiate.[24] Elsewhere I have made a distinction between quantifiable and nonquantifiable demands and argued that the latter pose problems of central control.[25] Wages and even some qualitative (nonwage) issues such as working time and income guarantees can be negotiated centrally precisely because they can be quantified. But translating nonquantifiable demands such as job enrichment into concrete outcomes is something that by its very nature must be accomplished in the plants where new technologies are being introduced and applied. Åke Sandberg makes a similar point and adds that central union influence over technology is further complicated by the fact that technological change is an ongoing process and thus difficult for unions to address in the context of periodic and relatively short negotiating situations.[26]

One measure of a central union's strength is its ability to define a national agenda and to mobilize its membership around that agenda. This kind of central coordination should not, however, be confused with central bargaining per se, for labor strength at the plant level is also critical in determining how unions weather the current transition. Whether a decentralization of bargaining allows employers to circumvent and weaken unions, as the neoliberal-offensive theorists fear, and the extent to which it affords labor the opportunities to influence restructuring, as the flexible-specialization theorists hope, depends on labor's strategic response to the dangers and opportunities of

23. For a discussion of the impact of technological change on skills and income based on a survey of plants in the metalworking industries, see IG Metall, ***Rationalisierung in der Metallwirtschaft*** (Frankfurt: IG Metall, 1983), pp. 71–76.

24. A central bargain can, for example, stipulate that downwardly classified workers be paid at their previous wage level for a specified transition period, but it cannot directly regulate the skill content of particular jobs.

25. Thelen, *Union of Parts,* chap. 8.

26. Åke Sandberg, "Trade Union Strategies in Production Issues: Some Swedish Experiences" (Paper presented to the Eleventh World Congress of Sociology, New Delhi, August 1986).

decentralization. This in turn depends critically on the organizational and political resources unions command and can mobilize at the plant level.

In the next section I trace how the tensions and opportunities of the present period have been played out in the West German metalworking industries. Like other studies, my analysis documents new pressures on the dual system. But it also points to the sources of resiliency that help explain why the system has proved more durable than other theories predict.

THE POLITICS OF FLEXIBILITY IN THE GERMAN METALWORKING INDUSTRIES

The 1980s were a difficult decade for West German labor. Unemployment began running at post–World War II highs in 1981, sapping unions' power in collective bargaining. For the first time since reconstruction, West German workers took a loss in real income in 1981 and 1982. In 1982 as well, the coalition between the Social Democratic and Free Democratic parties collapsed, and the new conservative-liberal government explicitly embraced a supply-side economic approach that gave priority to monetary stability and fiscal austerity. This government saw the solution to West Germany's economic stagnation in a rejuvenation of market incentives and sought especially to ease rigidities in the labor market, for example by making it easier for employers to hire part-time, fixed-contract, and temporary workers.[27]

Unlike triumphant conservatives elsewhere, however, the government of Chancellor Helmut Kohl has by and large not engaged in an assault on labor's organizational status nor on the institutions (such as codetermination) that give unions broad legal anchoring throughout

27. The centerpiece legislation in the government's labor market policy was the 1985 Beschäftigungsförderungsgesetz (employment promotion act). For a text of this law and commentary, see Michael Kittner, *Beschäftigungsförderungsgesetz* (Cologne: Bund Verlag, 1985). The conservative government's general economic program and labor market policies are discussed in greater detail in Werner Sengenberger, "West German Employment Policy: Restoring Worker Competition," *Industrial Relations 23* (Fall 1984): 323–43; Gerhard Bosch and Hartmut Seifert, "Das geplante Beschäftigungsförderungsgesetz: Ein arbeitsmarktpolitisches Notstandsgesetz," *WSI Mitteilungen 10* (1984): 581–87; and a special issue of *WSI Mitteilungen* on "Deregulierung und Flexibilisierung der Arbeit," August 1988.

the German economy.[28] This difference has significance, since the current combination of high unemployment and the government's market-reinforcing predilections have meant that now, more than ever, IG Metall has been thrown back to a reliance on its own resources, collective bargaining but also the legal levers of codetermination.

Contemporary trends in union collective bargaining and technology policy illustrate the character of the challenges unions now face and document the kind of maneuvering currently under way in Germany's dual system. In both areas, flexibility figures prominently as a theme and point of conflict between union and employers. Since this concept has assumed many meanings and connotations—both in the scholarly literature and in its more popular usage—it is important here to be clear on the concrete challenges and choices flexibility presents for the union.[29]

In the area of employment, flexibility means the ability of employers to adapt the size of the workforce to changes in demand. This issue has been especially contentious in Germany, since works council rights make it difficult for employers to lay workers off. In the 1984, 1987, and 1990 collective bargaining rounds on working-time reduction, this kind of flexibility played a key role in negotiations. The union and employers ultimately reached settlements that delegated new responsibilities to works councils to negotiate with employers over the specific extent and form of such flexibility but within parameters set down in the central contract.

In the area of technology and work organization, the kind of flexibility employers want comes down to their ability to arrange and rearrange production as they please. Such issues are related to employers' interest in reducing inventories, minimizing machine down times, and improving quality through early detection and timely correction. In Germany this second kind of flexibility dovetails with the employment and working-time issues as employers seek to delink machine times

28. A partial exception to this is the revision in 1986 of paragraph 116 of the Arbeitsförderungsgesetz (work promotion act), which affects the legal status and claims on the government of some locked-out workers. This new legislation is expected to impinge on IG Metall's strike strategy. Its effects, however, have yet to be tested. See Stephen Silvia, "The West German Labor Law Controversy: A Struggle for the Factory of the Future," *Comparative Politics 20* (January 1988): 155–74.

29. The two kinds of flexibility outlined below correspond to Cohen's and Zysman's two types of production flexibility; see Stephen S. Cohen and John Zysman, *Manufacturing Matters: The Myth of the Postindustrial Economy* (New York: Basic Books, 1987).

and working times in order to exploit fully their investments in new technologies.

On both kinds of flexibility, the particular tactics German employers have adopted, as well as the character of the issues themselves, make plant-level negotiations crucial to the success of central union strategies. Plant bargaining has become central to IG Metall's strategy, both as part of a defense of its ability to set an agenda for labor as a whole and resist flexibilization on employers' terms, and as part of an effort to mount its own offense to participate in productive restructuring at the shop-floor level. In short, works councils have emerged as critical actors as plant bargaining becomes an increasingly important locus of conflict and compromise in Germany's dual system.

Employment and Working-Time Reduction

The fact that IG Metall has become a vanguard union in the advanced countries on working-time reduction through collective bargaining says as much about the union's political weakness as it does about its industrial self-confidence and strength.[30] Repeated calls by organized labor for government action on unemployment had for years brought virtually no results. Thus IG Metall faced a dilemma: since political pressure was getting them nowhere, they could address the unemployment issue through collective bargaining or not at all.[31]

The union had first proposed a reduction of the 40-hour week in 1978, and specifically for the steel industry. At the time, this demand was conceived as a way of alleviating the employment crisis in the country's steel-producing regions.[32] As overall unemployment grew in the subsequent years, the union made working-time reduction the

30. For an elaboration of this argument and a more detailed analysis of the conflict over working-time reduction, see Kathleen Thelen, "Neoliberalism and the Battle over Working-Time Reduction in West Germany," in *The Politics of Economic Adjustment: Pluralism, Corporatism, and Privatization,* ed. Richard E. Foglesong and Joel D. Wolfe (Westport, Conn.: Greenwood Press, 1989), pp. 65–85 and Thelen, *Union of Parts,* chap. 7.

31. Critics of the union asserted (largely correctly, as it turns out) that working-time reduction would not have the significant employment effects IG Metall was predicting. The point, however, remains that the union's leaders felt the union had to assume a leadership role in putting the country's unemployment problem on the political agenda. For a somewhat different interpretation of the causes behind the union's campaign, see Peter Swenson, *Fair Shares* (Ithaca: Cornell University Press, 1988), esp. pp. 216–22.

32. Andrei Markovits and Christopher Allen, "The 1978–79 Steel Strike: German Unions at a Crossroad" (Unpublished manuscript, 1979).

cornerstone of its national agenda. The first real test came in 1984, when the union struck for a general reduction of the work week to 35 hours, and the issue of working-time reduction continued to dominate labor politics in West Germany through the 1980s. The compromise employers and the union ultimately reached is indicative of the strategic maneuvering that has come to characterize labor relations within the dual system.

In 1984, IG Metall's demand for working-time reduction provoked the largest and most intense industrial conflict in the history of the Federal Republic. The union began the strike in its stronghold of Nord-Württemberg/Nord-Baden. Employers responded immediately and aggressively, locking out workers in unprecedented numbers. The so-called cold lockout played an especially important role in the strike.[33] Indeed, the number of workers affected by the cold lockout (310,000) far exceeded the number of locked-out workers (150,000) and workers on strike (60,000) combined.[34]

Employers' adamant opposition to any reduction of the regular work week, and intransigence on both sides at the beginning of the conflict, made it look as if this might be a fight to the death. In the end, however, employers and the union agreed to a compromise that traded working-time reduction with flexibility in its application at the plant level. This compromise involved a shift in the balance within the dual system and the delegation of important new responsibilities to plant works councils. Concretely, the union and employers settled on a 1.5-hour reduction of the work week (2 hours in the steel industry) in a contract with an opening clause that provided for flexibility in the implementation of the agreement.[35] In a second round of plant-level bargaining, works councils and employers could adapt the agreement to their plant's particular circumstances as long as they stayed within parameters laid down in the central agreement.

The contract allowed two kinds of working-time flexibility, which in Germany are known as *Flexibilisierung* (flexibilization) and *Differenzierung* (differentiation). The flexibilization clause allowed for

33. A cold lockout occurs when employers in a nonstruck bargaining region halt production as a result of a strike in another district, for example, for lack of parts or supplies.

34. Ingrid Kurz-Scherf, "Tarifpolitik und Arbeitskämpfe," in *Gewerkschaftsjahrbuch 1985*, ed. Michael Kittner (Cologne: Bund Verlag, 1985), p. 113; see also Silvia, "Labor Law Controversy," p. 165.

35. The terms of the agreement are laid out in Kurz-Scherf, "Tarifpolitik und Arbeitskämpfe," pp. 76–81.

working-time flexibility over time; works councils and managers could implement the 1.5-hour reduction on a daily or weekly basis, or they could opt to cumulate the reduced hours into larger blocks of time, for example, into free days. Such clustering was permissible, but the contract also specified that plant agreements had to maintain an average of 38.5 hours per week within a two-month time frame.

The contract's differentiation clause allowed plant negotiators to distribute working-time reduction unequally across the workforce. The *plant* average had to equal 38.5 hours per week, but that did not have to mean 38.5 hours per week for each worker. Again the central contract established bounds for this kind of flexibility. Working times could vary within parameters ranging from 37 hours per week for some workers to 40 hours per week for others, as long as workers with longer regular hours were balanced by workers with shorter hours to achieve the 38.5-hour plant-wide average.

Opening clauses negotiated by works councils are not unprecedented in IG Metall contracts, and plant agreements that supplement central contracts are certainly not new. But the 1984 contract broke new ground by delegating to works councils new responsibilities on the working-time issue.[36] Moreover, the character of the second round of plant-level bargaining in 1984 was different. Instead of establishing a minimum baseline for works councils to improve on if they could, the 1984 contract was not only upwardly flexible but downwardly flexible as well, albeit bounded by the centrally negotiated parameters. In the second round of plant-level bargaining, considerable variety emerged in terms of flexibility over time (flexibilization), but in an overwhelming number of cases plant agreements did not allow for different working times for different workers (differentiation).[37]

In 1987, IG Metall and Gesamtmetall (the employers' association for the metalworking industries) reached a second agreement on working-time reduction which further lowered the regular work week in two steps to 37 hours. The highly centralized 1987 negotiations

36. Works councils have always controlled certain aspects of working times such as weekly working schedules and overtime, but a standard, uniform work week set by national collective bargains had been the rule until 1984.

37. A union research institute, the WSI (Wirtschafts- und Sozialwissenschaftliches Institut des DGB), reports that some form of differentiation was agreed on in 13 percent of all plants. Within those plants, however, differentiation usually affected only a small minority of the total workforce. All told, 5.7 percent of all workers in the metalworking industries ended up with a regular work week of something other than 38.5 hours. See WSI, "Informationsblätter Arbeit, Gesundheit, Humanisierung" (Düsseldorf, November 1986).

were remarkable for their relatively soft tone, particularly compared with the vitriolic exchanges during the 1984 strike. From the outset, employers expressed their willingness to discuss further working-time reductions, as long as further working-time flexibility was part of the package.[38] Meanwhile, IG Metall president Franz Steinkühler signaled that the union was willing to discuss arrangements involving further flexibilization of working times, though it would fight differentiation and employers' attempts to continue to exclude apprentices from working-time reduction.[39]

The 1987 agreement (achieved without a strike) followed the same formula as the 1984 settlement: further working-time reduction but with decentralized negotiations over its implementation at the plant level.[40] The 1987 contract restricted employers' ability to hire workers with different regular working times (the differentiation clause) but extended the parameter on working-time flexibilization from two to six months.[41] Again, an opening clause left it up to works councils to adapt the central bargain to plant conditions in a second round of bargaining.

In May 1990, IG Metall and Gesamtmetall reached a third agreement to reduce weekly working times to 35 hours, thus ending the conflict that had dominated labor politics in West Germany for over a decade.[42] The contract calls for a two-step reduction, to 36 hours beginning in April 1993, and to 35 hours in October 1995. Since the agreement will give German workers, who already enjoy among the longest vacations in Europe, the shortest regular work week as well, union leaders were justified in claiming a "historic success."[43] But, as in both the previous two contracts on this issue, the key concession on

38. See *Handelsblatt*, February 23, 1987; and *Nürnberger Nachrichten*, December 31, 1986.

39. *Nürnberger Nachrichten*, November 7, 1986.

40. For the terms of the agreement, see Ingrid Kurz-Scherf, "Tarifpolitik und Arbeitskämpfe," in *Gewerkschaftsjahrbuch 1988*, ed. Michael Kittner (Cologne: Bund Verlag, 1988), pp. 88–89.

41. The explanation for the union's greater willingness to compromise on flexibilization than differentiation can be traced to the more profound fragmenting tendencies of the differentiation clause, which explicitly creates different categories of workers for whom different rules apply; see Thelen, "Neoliberalism," p. 75.

42. For the terms of the agreement, see *Handelsblatt*, May 10, 1990; or IG Metall, "Tarifbewegung 1990: Metallindustrie" (Frankfurt: Vorstandsverwaltung, Abteilung Tarifpolitik, July 1990). The latter also contains a summary of the negotiations and a breakdown of the results by bargaining district.

43. *Der Gewerkschafter*, July 1990, p. 6.

which the 1990 compromise hinged was the flexible application of working-time reduction at the plant level.

The union resisted employer demands to expand the flexibilization clause in the 1987 contract from six to twelve months, but employers scored a crucial victory on the issue of differentiation. According to the new agreement, up to 18 percent of all workers in a plant[44] can—on a strictly voluntary basis—agree to continue with a regular 40-hour work week. Those who opt to do so are entitled either to be paid their regular wage for the extra hours or to accumulate free time, which can be taken in one or more blocks within a twenty-four-month period.

This new differentiation clause differs in important ways from those in the 1984 and 1987 contracts it replaces. Differentiation under the old agreements required such complicated personnel calculations and maneuvers that most employers found it too cumbersome to be useful as an instrument of personnel planning.[45] The new provision in the 1990 contract simplifies matters by allowing employers to conclude individual agreements directly with selected workers and by eliminating the need to shorten the hours of some workers in order to lengthen those of others. Works councils' only formal function in terms of the new differentiation clause is to ensure that employers not exceed the 18 percent quota. The contract requires employers to present the works council with the names of all workers who agree to longer working hours (in some regions, before they conclude such arrangements with the workers; in others, only later).[46] Beyond this, the union has charged works councils with informing workers of the options available to them and especially with ensuring that all agreements are truly voluntary. Above all, the union wants them to persuade workers affected by the new clause to opt for free time rather than monetary compensation.[47]

44. In some districts 13 percent, depending in part on whether certain white-collar employees are counted in the base figure.

45. See Peter Ellguth, Rudi Schmidt, and Rainer Trinczek, "Trends betrieblicher Arbeitszeitgestaltung in der Metallindustrie," *WSI Mitteilungen 3* (March 1990): 170–80, especially p. 175.

46. IG Metall, "Das Ziel ist erreicht! Umsetzungshilfe für das Tarifergebnis 1990" (Frankfurt: Vorstandsverwaltung, Abteilung Tarifpolitik, June 1990), p. 23.

47. *Der Gewerkschafter,* July 1990, pp. 36–37; see also IG Metall, "Das Ziel ist erreicht!" It is too early to tell how the new clause will actually be used, but early indications are that at least some works councils are advising workers not to agree to longer regular working times on the grounds that they will simply lose overtime payments for the extra hours (in-

With the important exception of the 18 percent clause, however, the implications of the new agreement for relations between works councils and the union are in many ways the same. As with the previous two agreements, the regulation of many aspects of the contract is still up to the works council, which continues to negotiate collective rules for the majority of workers in the plant. Thus, for example, new plant-level agreements have to be concluded in 1993 and 1995 when the hourly reductions in working times take effect. In addition, works councils still negotiate over working-time flexibility within the six-month parameters carried over from the 1987 contract. And because they have codetermination rights on related issues such as daily working schedules and the distribution of working times across the days of the week, works councils are still on the front line on those issues on which IG Metall and employers did not reach new agreements. These include weekend work, the length of the working day, and the highly contentious issue of overtime.[48]

The new working-time arrangements clearly involve a measure of decentralization and illustrate how plant works councils have been drawn into the central union's conflicts with employers over working-time reduction. For some, this decentralization of bargaining spells "desynchronization" and signals possible "disintegration" on the labor side.[49] But such conclusions are one-sided, for the results of this struggle speak as much to the resiliency of centralized bargaining and the continued strength of the union as they do to its weakness. After all, IG Metall had mobilized its membership on a national level in a major confrontation with a formidable opponent and came away with a 35-hour work week. Furthermore, the union accomplished this under what have arguably been the most difficult economic and political conditions it has faced in the postwar period. British miners, Italian autoworkers, and U.S. air controllers were doing much worse in the same period (for example, see Chapters 5 and 7 in this volume).

In comparative perspective, what stands out is IG Metall's relative strength and continuing capacity for leadership, despite the more dif-

---

terviews, 1990). Encouraging workers to turn down differentiation in favor of overtime is not what the IG Metall leadership had in mind, but this kind of argumentation could affect the overall number of workers affected by the new differentiation clause.

48. IG Metall, "Das Ziel ist erreicht!" pp. 5, 8–9.

49. Hajo Weber, "Desynchronisation, Dezentralisierung—und Dekomposition? Die Wirkungsdynamik des Tarifkonflikts '84 und ihre Effekte auf das System industrieller Beziehungen," Arbeitsberichte und Forschungsmaterialien, no. 19 (University of Bielefeld, 1986).

ficult political and market context. In making unemployment its main target and working-time reduction its main goal in collective bargaining, the union leadership faced resistance not only from employers but also from important parts of its own constituency. The campaign for the 35-hour work week required some sacrifices on the part of the union's strongest districts, where unemployment is low and workers are more interested in higher wages than more leisure time. The fact that the union's national leaders were able to deflect pressures from within the organization and rally the membership behind the campaign for weekly working-time reduction testifies to the continued organizational and political capacities of the central union, though concessions to these strong districts have been part of the package.[50]

Furthermore, one of the reasons the conflict over working-time reduction did not deteriorate into an all-or-nothing battle over centralized bargaining itself is that, contrary to most characterizations of the crisis of neocorporatism, the core conflict in Germany was not between central rigidity and plant-level flexibility. To be sure, the outcomes of these conflicts—working-time reduction with decentralization and flexibility—have been controversial within IG Metall. But what is striking about the flexibility debate within the union is how it has evolved since 1984. At that time, the controversy was whether to allow flexibility into the central contract.[51] Since then, the core controversy within the union has shifted; the question is no longer whether to accept flexibility, but what kind, how much, and under what conditions. The new differentiation clause in the 1990 contract has provoked so much criticism because it moves away from collectively bargained flexibility (through works councils) to individually bargained flexibility. But flexibilization through the delegation of bargaining to works councils has in the meantime gained acceptability.

50. For example, after the 1984 bargaining round, which reduced the work week by 1.5 hours, Baden-Württemberg and other strong districts successfully demanded that the next bargaining round be over wages, thus delaying further reductions of the work week until 1987. More generally, IG Metall's insistence on working-time reduction *with full pay* reflects the union leadership's recognition that, to maintain the support of its membership, working-time reduction could not come at the direct expense of wages. See Karl Hinrichs and Helmut Wiesenthal, "Arbeitszeitverkürzung als Klassenstrategie: Die Arbeitskämpfe des Jahres '84 als Versuch einer Verbesserung der Klassenposition" (University of Bielefeld manuscript, May 1985), esp. pp. 19–21.

51. More precisely, the issue was the extent to which works councils could be trusted to act in the interest of the national organization in implementing the contract (interview with Hans Mayr, then president of the union, 1989).

Indeed, top union officials are now explicitly advocating an "à la carte" collective bargaining policy that would allow works councils to negotiate locally, choosing among a menu of options laid out in central contracts.[52]

In sum, the outcome of the union's recent struggles with employers over working-time reduction has involved a shift in the balance within the dual system. Plant-level bargaining has become increasingly important for the union's overall success. The campaign for working-time reduction demonstrated that the union is still capable of defining a national agenda and mobilizing its membership behind that agenda. The conflict and its outcome reveal sources of strain in the dual system, but at the same time they resoundingly confirm its resilience as well. The shift in the balance within the dual system accommodated both the union's demand for working-time reduction and employers' demand for flexibility in the deployment of labor. Given German employers' absolute opposition to any working-time reduction at the beginning of the conflict, it is perhaps not farfetched to suggest that this compromise within the dual system may have averted an attack on it.

Technology and Work Organization

Technological change and employers' experimentation with new forms of work organization are also contributing to the growing importance of plant labor representation. As noted above, changes in the organization of production blur the line between centralized and decentralized bargaining to the extent that percentage wage gains negotiated centrally by the national union can be eroded at the plant level through job reclassification. Moreover, technology and work reorganization touch on issues that do not easily lend themselves to quantification and thus regulation through centralized bargaining.

52. The advocates of such a policy include both the union's president, Franz Steinkühler, and the executive board member in charge of collective bargaining policy, Klaus Zwickel; see *Kölner Stadt Anzeiger*, August 27, 1988; Klaus Zwickel's speech in IG Metall, *Tarifpolitik im Strukturwandel*, Materialband no. 6 der Diskussionsforen "Die andere Zukunft: Solidarität und Freiheit" (Köln: Bund Verlag, 1988), pp. 11–28 (especially p. 18); and Steinkühler's remarks at IG Metall's conference on technology in IG Metall, *Technologieentwicklung und Techniksteuerung*, Materialband no. 4 der Diskussionsforen "Die andere Zukunft: Solidarität und Freiheit" (Köln: Bund Verlag, 1988), pp. 126–28. Also IG Metall, "Die Andere Zukunft: Solidarität und Freiheit: Leitlinien der IG Metall zur gesellschaftlichen und gewerkschaftlichen Reform," materials sent to all union locals, district offices, and educational facilities (IG Metall Vorstand: Frankfurt, April 1989), especially p. 50; and *Der Gewerkschafter* 9a, September 1988, pp. 112–13.

Unlike unions in other countries whose demands focus more exclusively on "bread and butter" issues, IG Metall has long been interested in questions of *Gestaltung* (roughly, the organization of work and technology). Indeed, the union demanded and even struck for changes in work organization such as job rotation and group work in the early 1970s, long before employers began experimenting with these in the interest of higher productivity and greater plant flexibility.[53] The pace of technological change and employers' new initiatives for reorganizing production have thus given new life and urgency to the *Gestaltung* issue.

Although the decentralization/flexibilization debate is generally characterized in terms of employer pressures and union givebacks, recent developments in union policy on skills and technology show how the changing character of union demands on these qualitative issues has also contributed to the growing importance of plant-level bargaining. Two trends—recent union initiatives in collective bargaining on skills and the adoption of a new, more plant-oriented technology policy—illustrate this point. In both cases, plant-level bargaining has gained prominence as the union searches for a more differentiated approach to confront the problems of skills and technology in the particular form they take in different plants.

A recently concluded Wage and Salary Framework Agreement (LGRTV-I) in Nord-Württemberg/Nord-Baden illustrates the union's growing reliance on works councils in the area of skills. This contract, which is widely viewed as a model for the metalworking industries as a whole, addresses the connections between workers' wages and skills. The union's primary goals have been to promote a continual upgrading of skills and to link workers' pay to the skills they possess rather than to the jobs they perform.[54] The LGRTV-I makes works

53. In 1973, the union waged a strike in Nord-Württemberg/Nord-Baden on these issues under the banner of "humanizing working life." The resulting framework agreement established a minimum cycle time for assembly tasks of 90 seconds. By lengthening cycle times, the union wanted to promote job enrichment and encourage the introduction of group work. See IG Metall, *Werktage werden besser: Der Kampf um den Lohnrahmentarifvertrag II* (Cologne: Europäische Verlagsanstalt, 1977).

54. IG Metall's current initiatives in collective bargaining strive for precisely the kind of pay-for-knowledge system that U.S. unions often view with such skepticism; see Klaus Lang, "Thesen zum Stand der gewerkschaftlichen Diskussion," in *Tarifpolitik im Strukturwandel*, Materialband no. 6 der Diskussionsforen "Die andere Zukunft," ed. IG Metall (Cologne: Bund Verlag, 1988); and especially the collective bargaining department's proposal for such a system, IG Metall Abteilung Tarifpolitik, "Entgeltrahmentarifvertrag der Zukunft: Interner Entwurf zur Diskussion mit den Tarifsekretären," April 6, 1989.

councils the vehicle for addressing the skill issue. It mandates yearly negotiations between works councils and management to assess the skill requirements for the plant and to plan and implement retraining programs to meet them.[55] The idea behind the agreement is that the best way to protect workers against deskilling and income loss is for labor to push for an ongoing upgrading of workers' skills.

What is important in the present context is that the works council is the crucial intermediary in the union's strategy on the wage-skill question. Works councils have for years been improvising and jury-rigging plant wage structures to compensate for changes in technology and production organization that have rendered obsolete the wage determination methods developed in the 1950s and 1960s.[56] But plant-level bargaining over these issues has been stopgap and has depended more on works council initiative than formal rights. The collective agreement in Nord-Württemberg/Nord-Baden strengthens and, most important, institutionalizes the role of works councils in promoting ongoing retraining and encouraging a closer wage-skill fit.

In some ways, the goals of this 1988 agreement overlap with those of another agreement between IG Metall and employers of a decade earlier. In negotiations in 1978 over a new wage framework contract—also in Nord-Württemberg/Nord-Baden—the union sought a provision that would freeze plant wage levels to prevent the deskilling (and downward classification) of workers when new technologies were introduced. The resulting contract fell far short of this goal. In the end, what the union got was eighteen-month income guarantees for individual workers in the event of deskilling and downward classification.[57]

Two differences between the 1978 and 1988 negotiations are important for the present argument. First, the union took wages as the point of departure in the earlier agreement. By freezing the plant wage level, IG Metall hoped to maintain workers' skills indirectly by holding their wages up. The final agreement, which compensates workers

55. The new agreement does not establish a pay-for-knowledge system, but it does ensure that the wages of workers who receive training are adjusted upward for a bridge period even if they cannot be placed in jobs requiring the acquired skills (which would have entitled them to a higher wage rate on a more permanent basis).

56. Interview with Klaus Lang, head of the IG Metall's collective bargaining department, June 1988.

57. IG Metall Bezirksleitung Stuttgart, *Arbeitsmaterialien zum Tarifvertrag zur Sicherung der Eingruppierung und zur Verdienstsicherung bei Abgruppierung* (Stuttgart: IG Metall, July 1978).

financially for deskilling, reflects the logic of this strategy, but because it freezes the wages of downwardly classified workers for only eighteen months the effect on skills is lost. In contrast, the new agreement turns the wage-skill problem around by putting the skill issue first. Its premise is that maintaining and upgrading skills is ultimately the union's best defense against income loss through technological change. The logic here is that, if you continually upgrade the skills of workers, high wages follow.

The second difference between the two agreements is the more important role of plant-level bargaining in the second agreement. Whereas in 1978 the union sought a uniform, blanket regulation that would apply to all plants, the 1988 contract calls for negotiations between works councils and individual employers to decide measures tailored to individual plant conditions. The second agreement is thus less "top down" in its conception and involves greater decentralization and variability in its implementation. Indeed, the flexibility of the 1988 contract may ultimately account for why employers found it more palatable than its predecessor. In contrast to the 1978 agreement, employers and the union reached a compromise in 1988 without industrial strife. That this was possible—and under worse market conditions—seems to bode well for its becoming a pattern for other bargaining districts.[58]

Works councils also figure prominently in the union's new "action program" on technology, "Arbeit und Technik," which was unveiled in November 1984. This new technology program marks a shift away from central solutions toward a centrally directed but plant-oriented strategy to counteract the negative effects of rationalization and new technologies. The program assigns an important role to plant-level representatives and attempts especially to exploit more systematically the legal rights of works councils to achieve union technology demands.[59]

The goals sketched out in the program are quite ambitious, and the results have been uneven. The strategy, however, goes beyond the purely defensive goal of compensating workers adversely affected by technological change (through employment and income guarantees,

58. See, for example, Harald Maurer, "Metall-Tarif: Qualifizierung der Mitarbeiter," in *Der Arbeitgeber* 5/40, 1988.

59. IG Metall, *Aktionsprogramm Arbeit und Technik: Der Mensch Muß Bleiben!* (Frankfurt: IG Metall, 1984). For a more detailed analysis of the evolution of IG Metall's technology program and of the 1984 action program, see Thelen, *Union of Parts,* chap. 8.

for example). The goal is to develop a more offensive *Gestaltung* strategy to address the organization of production itself by developing alternative, worker-oriented production designs. In particular, the union favors various forms of group work and job rotation, both to boost workers' skills and to achieve previous "humanization of working life" goals such as reducing job stress and work intensity.[60] The central union's department of automation and technology coordinates the program and provides expertise and support for works councils, but ultimately the weight of responsibility for translating this assistance into lasting influence over production organization lies with the plant representatives themselves.[61]

Union technology advisers have been working with selected plants to develop concrete models for worker-oriented production concepts and also to produce a set of written materials to guide works councils in their own negotiations with employers. For example, the union's general demands for group work have been premised on bargaining experiences at firms such as Hoesch and Volkswagen. The technology department has also produced a general methodology for evaluating employers' technology and rationalization plans, along with guidelines to help plant labor representatives develop their own alternatives (the *Zehn-Schritte Programm*). Such aids are meant to provide works councils with "help to help themselves" on the technology issue.[62]

IG Metall's current technology policy aims to avail itself of the rights works councils already command to participate in plant restructuring. The Betriebsverfassungsgesetz (works constitution act) of 1972 does not grant plant labor representatives particularly strong rights on technological change per se (only consultation rights), but production reorganization affects a range of other issues—wage structures, manning levels, and working times—where the rights of works councils are quite substantial. Such linkages provide opportunities for works councils to use their stronger rights in these areas as levers to gain influence on the work organization question. In the union's model cases, such linkages have been crucial bargaining tools in negotiations over work organization. The introduction of group work in

60. See, for example, Manfred Muster, "Eckpunkte zur Gruppenarbeit," Abteilung Automation/Technologie/HdA, June 20, 1988; and Manfred Muster, "Zum Stand der Gruppenarbeit in der Automobilindustrie der Bundesrepublik Deutschland," Abteilung Automation/Technologie/HdA, January 28, 1988.

61. IG Metall, *Aktionsprogramm*, esp. pp. 9–10.

62. IG Metall, *Aktionsprogramm*, esp. pp. 32–35, 39–40.

the cylinder head assembly department at Volkswagen in Salzgitter provides an example.[63] Management's original plan for reorganizing the department was to use a small number of skilled workers to monitor the new, highly automated production equipment and a somewhat larger number of unskilled workers to keep the machinery stocked with parts. The works council rejected this two-tiered organization; although the final deal involved some compromises on their part, they achieved a system of work organization premised on uniform (and uniformly high) skills and wages for all affected workers.[64]

Because of the relatively strong rights of works councils, German unions are in a better position to participate in the kind of plant-level productive restructuring currently under way than are unions in many other countries. Harry Katz and Charles Sabel have noted an important difference between union power embedded in narrow rules (as in the United States) and that expressed in broader rights (as in Sweden and Germany).[65] American unions are more skeptical about employer-initiated pay-for-knowledge systems, job rotation, and group work (the very goals IG Metall is pursuing), but not out of any greater affection for Taylorism. Their defense of rigid job classifications and traditional work rules grows out of the way union rights have been institutionalized at the plant level—piggybacked, as it were, on the Fordist job structure. Dismantle that structure, and the structure of unions' traditional rights crumbles with it.[66]

Works council rights in Germany are more flexible and adaptable in the face of current developments. For example, a works council's right to negotiate with management over a worker's transfer is a general right and has nothing to do with movement across differently

63. This account is based on plant-level interviews with labor representatives in 1985.

64. The Volkswagen case is somewhat exceptional. The more typical works council does not think in terms of realizing alternative worker-oriented production designs. Still, in a broader range of cases labor can have an indirect impact on work reorganization because of the strong resistance works councils *do* ordinarily put up against the negative consequences (income and skill loss) employers' initial plans may entail. For other examples of labor influence on work organization in the West German automobile industry, see Lowell Turner, *Democracy at Work: Changing World Markets and the Future of Labor Unions* (Ithaca: Cornell University Press, 1991).

65. Harry C. Katz and Charles F. Sabel, "Industrial Relations and Industrial Adjustment in the Car Industry," *Industrial Relations* 24 (Fall 1985): 295–315.

66. For an elaboration of this argument (and a comparison of the politics of work reorganization in Sweden, Germany, and the United States), see Thelen, *Union of Parts,* chap. 9. On the connection between the rights of American unions and Fordism, see also Michael J. Piore, "American Labor and the Industrial Crisis," *Challenge* 25: 2 (March-April, 1982): 5–11.

classified jobs. Consequently, unlike in the United States, doing away with or reducing the number of different jobs poses no threat to labor's bargaining rights. Such differences help explain why German unions are generally somewhat more inclined than American ones to view employer initiatives to introduce greater flexibility on the shop floor in terms of the opportunities these present rather than the dangers they pose. As the head of IG Metall's technology department put it, "employers have traditionally insisted that they exercise unilateral control over work and production organization [*Gestaltung*]. Now suddenly they are willingly giving up a part of their prerogatives in these areas. We have been emphasizing the *Gestaltung* issue all along and encouraging works councils to push in this area."[67]

In sum, beyond national bargains that protect certain groups of workers,[68] it is union shop-floor policy that is the target for developing alternative models for production organization in a way that points to a more aggressive, if also more difficult, approach to the problems posed by new technologies. The strategic approach to technological change that IG Metall's action program maps out assigns a crucial role to works councils and identifies the plant level as a critical locus of conflict and change in the face of the challenges of the current period.

An interesting confirmation of the growing importance of plant-level bargaining, stemming from all the trends cited above, is the revival in some union circles of an old discussion revolving around the concept of on-the-job codetermination (*Mitbestimmung am Arbeitsplatz*).[69] In the early 1970s, *Mitbestimmung am Arbeitsplatz* became the rallying cry for leftist unionists critical of overcentralization and excessive bureaucratization in IG Metall. Their proposals for on-the-job codetermination sought to give individual workers and groups of workers greater rights to negotiate directly with management over issues directly affecting them in the plant. Indeed, the IG Metall leadership played a key role in defeating such initiatives, which had stood

67. Interview with Andreas Drinkuth, June 1988.

68. For example, the rationalization protection agreement of 1968 and income guarantees (in Baden-Württemberg) in 1978.

69. Deutscher Gewerkschaftsbund, *Konzeption zur Mitbestimmung am Arbeitsplatz*, DGB Schriftenreihe no. 7 (Frankfurt: DGB, March 1985), pp. 5–15. See also the special issue of *Die Mitbestimmung* (November 1987) on "Unternehmerische Sozialtechniken," and particularly Gerhard Mogwitz, "Qualitätszirkel und Mitbestimmung am Arbeitsplatz," pp. 683–86; also W. Lecher, "Qualitätszirkel und Gruppenarbeit: Stand und Perspektive von "Mitbestimmung am Arbeitsplatz" (WSI manuscript, n.d.).

a good chance of making it into the revised Works Constitution Act of 1972.[70] At that time, union leaders viewed the decentralized power implied by the concept (at least in the versions espoused by the union's left wing) as a possible threat to their own and works councils' representational monopolies.

The current discussion of *Mitbestimmung am Arbeitsplatz* revolves around different issues, of course, and today's advocates have something very different in mind from those of the early 1970s. In fact, so far the concept remains very vague, but in most of its incarnations it appears to refer to some combination of stronger rights for works councils and greater involvement of individual workers, both of which are seen as important sources of leverage in the face of new employer initiatives on quality circles, technology, and a range of other plant issues. Ambiguity and controversy within the labor movement on what *Mitbestimmung am Arbeitsplatz* should mean, as well as opposition by the conservative government to any extension of works councils' rights, have kept the discussion at a very abstract level. Still, the revival of the debate itself is a somewhat ironic testimony to the fact that the relationship between national and plant-level bargaining is once again on the agenda in Germany.

The Shifting Balance between Centralized and Decentralized Bargaining

The developments sketched out above, in collective bargaining and in questions of technology and production organization, point to important changes in the balance between centralized and decentralized bargaining. In the face of the flexibilization challenge from employers and in the context of labor's political and market weakness, works councils figure increasingly prominently, both in labor-capital relations generally and in IG Metall's strategic response to the crisis. The shift in the balance toward the plant is on the one hand part of the union's defense of central bargaining (the compromise on working-

70. Interview with Hans Matthöfer, who in the early 1970s was the foremost proponent within the union of *Mitbestimmung am Arbeitsplatz* as well as a Social Democratic member of parliament (and later finance minister under Chancellor Helmut Schmidt), June 1989; see also Rainer Zoll, *Partizipation oder Delegation: Gewerkschaftliche Betriebspolitik in Italien und in der Bundesrepublik Deutschland* (Frankfurt: Europäische Verlagsanstalt, 1981); and Eberhard Schmidt, *Ordnungsfaktor oder Gegenmacht: Die politische Rolle der Gewerkschaften* (Frankfurt: Suhrkamp, 1975), esp. pp. 183–92.

time reduction). At the same time, however, the mobilization of resources at that level is also part of a somewhat more offensive strategy, one that attempts to implement a set of centrally defined goals through decentralized mechanisms (LGRTV-I, the union's technology program). This offensive component of the union's current strategy attempts to use more aggressively the union's de facto shop-floor influence and the legal rights and plant-level power of works councils.

The character of current economic trends and the strategies employers have adopted since the 1980s both push and pull IG Metall toward the plant. The union has been pushed to integrate the shop floor more closely into annual collective bargaining rounds first to achieve and then to implement its demands, and in particular its nonwage demands such as working-time reduction. At the same time, IG Metall is pulled to the plant by the nature of the issues it currently faces, which increasingly present themselves at the plant level and in different ways in different plants. The union's approach to skills and technology has responded to the diversity at that level, and in doing so makes works councils active vehicles for achieving union demands.

IG Metall's response to the economic strains of the 1980s has entailed significant strategic rethinking, and debates within the union over virtually all the trends described above reveal that this process is still under way. The response does not, however, involve dramatic organizational restructuring, since the works council system has given labor legal anchoring and rights at the plant level that complement the union's central powers. So far, central bargaining shows no signs of withering away, but the plant level is emerging as a parallel and increasingly important second front in union strategies and in labor-capital relations more generally.

BACK TO THE FUTURE: UNION SUCCESS IN THE 1980s AND 1990s

To the extent that the challenge to central union authority often presents itself at subnational levels, it is also there that central unions must meet the challenge. What workers are going to earn, how many will have jobs, and at what skill levels they will be employed are issues that are in part being decided at the firm- and plant-levels in the course of productive restructuring currently under way. If unions are unable to influence these developments at that level, then no amount of macro-economic steering will help them later on. The issue is not really centralization or decentralization, because unions do not have a choice between the two.

Central unions can ill afford to lose their ability to define labor's overall agenda, but this ability to coordinate and define must not be confused with centralized bargaining per se. A central union may choose (or be forced) to pursue centrally defined goals decentrally. The case of IG Metall demonstrates that what national unions can accomplish centrally is limited both by their market weakness and by the character of the challenges they now face. Organizational depth (rather than central strength alone) and unions' subnational defenses will in large measure determine how labor weathers the economic strains of the current period. The challenge national unions face is that they must fight fragmentation and flexibilization on employers' terms at the same time that they pursue a strategy that addresses the particular situations that workers in different plants face.

IG Metall's strategy is both a defensive and an offensive one. The defense (the campaign for weekly working-time reduction and the second-round implementation of the 1984, 1987, and 1990 contracts) is an attempt to defend the union's ability to define a common agenda for labor as a whole (in the 1980s, above all, unemployment). The offensive component of the strategy (for example, skill and technology policy) attempts to use works councils as vehicles for addressing production issues in the particular form they take in different plants. The ultimate success of this strategy is by no means certain, but in what follows I offer some tentative conclusions based on observations of the union to date.

Thus far, IG Metall's *defensive* mobilization has enjoyed remarkable success in those cases where the union has called its members out in support of a national fight with clearly defined objectives. The 1984 strike for a shorter work week as well as a series of demonstrations in 1985 and 1986 are evidence that the union can successfully mobilize its membership behind its national agenda.[71] These mobilizations, and the decade-long campaign for the 35-hour work week more generally, are evidence of IG Metall's continuing capacity for leadership despite the uneven pressures faced by its diverse membership.

71. The demonstrations were against the conservative government's social policies and changes in the strike law, respectively.

In addition, the outcome of these negotiations, working-time reduction with plant flexibility, points to new strains in central bargaining, but also to its continued resiliency in Germany. Pressures for decentralization were resolved not through a breakdown of centralized bargaining but through the incorporation of flexibility into the central contracts themselves. German employers have not sought a retreat from central bargaining, though the price—5 hours working-time reduction—has not been low. Strategic concessions by the union, but also central union strength itself, have contributed to the continued viability of centralized bargaining in Germany.

The plant-based strategy in the union technology program, in contrast, has so far not generated the "thousand points of light" the union intended. This is not surprising; such a strategy is by its very nature bound to produce more uneven results. Aggressive works councils in strong and well-organized plants are both more likely to take the initiative on questions of production organization and better able to extract more concessions from employers than weaker ones. For these reasons, the union's success in achieving its more aggressive goals on work organization will likely continue to be highly uneven.

By the same token, however, plant labor representatives in Germany have still been better positioned to guard against the negative effects of technology, and such defensive maneuvering has also served as a source of indirect labor influence on work organization on a broader scale.[72] In comparative perspective, the rights works councils enjoy on a range of personnel issues make them better able to cope with the new problems posed by technology and productive restructuring. The recent battle in the United States over organized labor's right to be informed in advance of planned plant closures shows how hard it is for unions that entered the 1980s with tenuous and more limited rights to now try to improve their position. In countries such as Sweden, the unions' political leverage with Social Democratic governments has helped to overcome employer resistance to legislative inroads that encroach on managerial prerogatives. Indeed, Swedish unions were able to secure new and enhanced plant-level powers in the course of the 1970s in response to the growing importance of plant

72. For example, works councils' rights in the area of personnel policy stabilize plant employment, and fluid internal labor markets can encourage a continual upgrading of worker skills; see especially Wolfgang Streeck, "Successful Adjustment to Turbulent Markets."

bargaining.[73] Lacking the same legacy of Social Democratic hegemony, the route to German labor's comparatively strong plant-level rights was somewhat more circuitous.[74]

What is important here is that German labor moved into the 1980s already armed with a set of legal rights that now provide the unions with a relatively stable source of leverage in plant negotiations. Not only are their defenses against employer caprice sturdier; these plant-level rights have become all the more crucial with the growing centrality of production issues in labor-capital relations more generally. As Benjamin Coriat and Philippe Zarifan suggest, the breakdown of Taylorist principles of work organization presents labor everywhere with new opportunities and new dangers.[75] The character of both and the balance between the two, however, depend on the institutional and political context.

To the extent that employers' flexibilization and fragmentation strategies target the plant, it is in the plant that labor's counterstrategy will either succeed or fail. The dual system of labor relations in Germany in some ways exacerbates IG Metall's problems of centralized control. But the union's presence in works councils even in plants with low membership levels also gives it a crucial organizational foothold that enables it to pursue its own plant-level counterstrategy. The German case therefore is characterized by a jockeying for position within the context of a structure that no one—neither employers nor the conservative government—is seriously trying to dismantle.[76]

73. See Peter Auer, "Industrial Relations, Work Organization and New Technology: The Volvo Case" (Swedish Center for Working Life Working Paper, Stockholm, 1985); Andrew Martin, "Sweden: Industrial Democracy and Social Democratic Strategy," in *Worker Self-Management in Industry*, ed. G. David Garson (New York: Praeger, 1977); Bjorn Gustavsen, "Technology and Collective Agreements: Some Recent Scandinavian Developments," *Industrial Relations Journal* 16:3 (1985): 34–42; and Anders Broström, "Industrial and Economic Democracy in Sweden: Approach and Problems" (Swedish Center for Working Life Working Paper, Stockholm, 1982).

74. This argument is laid out in Thelen, *Union of Parts*, chaps. 3–4.

75. Benjamin Coriat and Philippe Zarifan, "Tendenzen der Automatisierung und Neuzusammensetzung der industriellen Lohnarbeit," *Prokla 62* (March 1986): 61–73.

76. The German business community, for example, did not support legislation introduced by the Free Democratic party to enhance the chances of "minority" (non–Deutscher Gewerkschaftsbund union) candidates in works council elections. And, although this bill recently became law, employers are unlikely to use it in their own plants to mount an assault on the union. The explanation is simple. Since works council approval is necessary for many routine matters such as overtime, employers above all want predictability in their relations with their works councils. A factionalized works council can often politicize and even paralyze plant politics, and this makes planning difficult for employers as well (interview with Michael Brunz, collective bargaining department of Gesamtmetall, Cologne, June 1987).

Many current theories of the breakdown of corporatism might lead us to expect growing instability within Germany's dual system and a weakening of the country's central unions. My analysis of evolving relations between works councils and IG Metall points to tensions and strains within the system. But, my emphasis on the dynamics of this relationship offers as well an account of the resilience of the dual system and of the politics within these institutional constraints that helps explain both stability and change in contemporary German labor relations.

The nature of the economic and structural transformations in the current period requires a more nuanced picture of the organizational formula for union effectiveness. Unions need to find new organizational forms that combine centralization and organizational depth and new strategies that combine central coordination with decentralized flexibility. Decentralization without coordination leaves the unions vulnerable to flexibility on the employers' terms—fragmentation. But centralization without strong subnational enforcement and implementation is no longer tenable either. The danger labor faces in the 1990s is not just that central unions grow weak, but rather that weak defenses at the plant level could render their central successes irrelevant.

7 Industrial Restructuring and Industrial Relations in the Italian Automobile Industry

Richard Locke

In this essay I analyze the recent reconfiguration of Italian industrial relations. Through a case study of the automobile industry, I seek to explain how the current period of industrial reorganization is challenging established practices and eroding traditional institutional boundaries. As a result of this challenge, political struggles over the redefinition of these arrangements have erupted both at the local or firm level, between labor and management, and at the industry level, between local and national unions. These political struggles are recasting the strategies of the various actors and, in the process, changing the very essence of Italy's industrial relations system.

The Italian industrial relations system is usually portrayed as highly political, poorly institutionalized, and unstable.[1] This image was reinforced in recent years by radical swings in the balance of power between organized labor and capital. Italian unions emerged from the "hot autumn" struggles of the late 1960s and early 1970s as politically powerful and strategically innovative organizations.[2] Union strength

This argument was developed in earlier, slightly different versions in *Industrial and Labor Relations Review* 45 (January 1992): 229–49, and *Politics and Society* 18 (September 1990): 347–79. For helpful comments on earlier drafts of this paper, the author thanks Miriam Golden, Victoria Hattam, Harry Katz, Peter Lange, Maurice Neufeld, Jonas Pontusson, Sidney Tarrow, and Kathy Thelen.

1. See, for example, Gianprimo Cella, "Criteria of Regulation in Italian Industrial Relations: A Case of Weak Institutions," in *State, Market, and Social Regulation: New Perspectives on Italy*, ed., Peter Lange and Marino Regini, (New York: Cambridge University Press, 1989), pp. 167–86.

2. For more on union strategy in these years, see Pietro Merli Brandini, "Italy: Creating

and initiative were expressed both on the shop floor, where unions regulated production, internal mobility, and dismissals, and at the national level, where they succeeded in promoting social reforms and protecting workers' wages against inflation.

In the 1980s, the balance of power shifted again, this time against labor. Following their defeat in several highly visible strikes (especially the one at Fiat in 1980) and renewed divisions among the three leading confederations over the 1984 referendum on the *scala mobile,*[3] the unions lost considerable power and management regained initiative. As individual firms and entire industries restructured, the unions appeared unable to negotiate, let alone protect their membership against, the consequences of this reorganization. With the emergence of hundreds of thousands of redundant industrial workers, union membership among this core constituency declined, as did their bargaining power in the political arena. How do we account for this shift from previous strength to present disarray?

In contrast to the traditional view, which emphasizes the backwardness or disfunctionality of Italian industrial relations, I argue that the current crisis results from a mismatch between nationally oriented industrial unions and firm-level changes generated by the current wave of industrial reorganization—a problem common to labor movements in all advanced industrial nations. In recent years, the new terms of international competition and technological innovation have radically altered markets and the organization of production. The simultaneous globalization and segmentation of national markets has rendered traditional business practices in all advanced industrial nations less effective. Technological innovations have not only shortened product life cycles but also created opportunities for firms to compete along lines that challenge the supremacy of mass production.[4]

---

a New Industrial Relations System from the Bottom," in *Worker Militancy and Its Consequences, 1965–75,* ed., Solomon Barkin, (New York: Praeger, 1975); and Marino Regini and Gösta Esping-Anderson, "Trade Union Strategies and Social Policy in Italy and Sweden," in *Trade Unions and Politics in Western Europe,* ed., Jack Hayward, (London: Frank Cass, 1980).

3. The *scala mobile* is a cost-of-living adjustment formula designed to protect workers' wages against inflation. This system was held largely responsible for Italy's inability to combat inflation in the early 1980s. As a result, the government proposed to modify the formula, which was resisted by the Italian Communist party and parts of the Confederazione Generale Italiana del Lavoro through a referendum held in 1984. The referendum lost and the system was consequently reformed, but at the expense of union unity.

4. See Michael J. Piore and Charles F. Sabel, *The Second Industrial Divide* (New York: Basic Books, 1984); and Michael Porter, *The Competitive Advantage of Nations* (New York: Free Press, 1990).

The breakup of national markets has spurred individual firms and entire industries to restructure in ways that test or transcend the boundaries of traditional industrial relations practices. While national industrial relations institutions have proven unwilling, or perhaps unable, to respond to or even accommodate these changes, individual firms have experimented with and implemented a variety of solutions that transform their structures, strategies, and relations with labor. This combination of microlevel effervescence and macrolevel paralysis has provoked a series of political struggles both within union locals and between local and national unions over how best to respond to individual firm needs for flexibility while also preserving sufficient organizational solidarity to prevent whipsawing.

To illustrate these dilemmas, I analyze the reorganization of Italy's two leading automobile producers—Fiat Auto and Alfa Romeo. Examination of these cases is interesting for a variety of reasons. First, both firms have historically played major roles in Italy's economy and have often set the pattern of industrial relations elsewhere in the country. The development of work relations and the balance of power in these firms reveals (often in extreme form)[5] the situation elsewhere in the country. Second, in many ways Fiat and Alfa have acted as advanced laboratories for Italian industrial relations. Since the late 1960s, these firms have witnessed several experiments in both the organization of production and the strategy of the union movement. Finally, union experiences with industrial adjustment at these two firms have been radically different. Whereas Fiat reorganized by asserting managerial control and repressing the unions, Alfa experienced a more negotiated process. Moreover, whereas both firms emerged more competitive as a result of the reorganization, the outcomes for the two unions differed sharply : Alfa's unions managed to preserve if not enhance their strength, whereas Fiat's unions lost membership and practically all influence on the shop floor. This divergence is especially interesting given that both firms share the same ownership, their workforces are organized by the same unions, their plants possess similar technologies, and they operate within the same national setting.

To explain these different outcomes, I argue that two factors are key: local socioeconomic conditions that shape the strategies of unions and management in firms undergoing adjustment, and the choices

5. Aris Accornero, "Torino da laboratorio a caso limite," *Politica ed economia*, no. 1 (January 1988):14–16.

unions make in reallocating responsibilities between local and national structures. Given that adjustment is not uniquely associated with one set of choices but that a range of alternative strategies are possible, what determines the choice of one solution over another? I propose that local historical traditions shape the strategic choices of individual firms and unions. Given that industrial development occurred in different ways and at different times in the various localities and regions of all national economies, local firms and unions developed divergent organizational resources and attributes that reflect the particular context in which they are embedded. These differences were latent or perhaps less noticeable during the hey-day of national industrial unionism, but they have recently reemerged to fill the vacuum left open by anachronistic industrial relations practices and regulations. This accounts for the increasing divergence in industrial politics manifest not just across but also within industrial sectors, sometimes even between plants within the same firm.

In short, the renewed importance of local socioeconomic contexts and diverse microlevel patterns of industrial adjustment necessitates a different way of understanding national industrial relations systems. Historical legacies may shape the organizational attributes of firms and unions, but patterns of industrial relations are not simply set in stone from the beginning and immutable thereafter. Rather, at certain critical conjunctures, industrial actors endowed with different organizational resources and worldviews struggle with one another over their competing strategic choices. The outcome of these struggles, whether in the form of complete victory of some actors over others or compromises and alliances among them, reshapes their own organizations, their context (that is, the subsequent structure of the local industry), and their future relations. In other words, political struggles define and redefine the set of viable strategic choices available to local actors.

Since this process of microlevel change is to a certain extent subterranean, it is often overlooked by conventional analyses that focus on national institutions and arrangements. Yet, the accumulation of these microlevel developments appear to be transforming the substance (if not the form) of the relationship between local and national industrial relations actors. The monolithic and hierarchical relations that existed (or were assumed to exist) between these two levels of the industrial relations system are increasingly being called into question by all this microlevel dynamism. The division of labor between these two vertical structures is also being renegotiated as local unions begin to assume certain responsibilities and functions previously relegated to the national industry federations.

To better explain these developments, I first lay out my theoretical approach and contrast it with more traditional explanations. Then I describe in highly stylized terms the demise of the national union in Italy. Finally I illustrate this approach with an analysis of industrial restructuring in the Italian automobile industry. The automobile industry is an interesting case since it has long served as an example of the Fordist system of production and work organization. With recent changes in markets and technologies, automobile manufacturers in all advanced industrial nations have begun to experiment with new strategies based on greater product diversity, more flexible methods of production, and new relations with labor. As a result, this industry provides an excellent setting to study the relationship between industrial restructuring and industrial relations. I conclude by discussing the more general issues raised by this case study and their implications for the future of the labor movement in Italy and elsewhere.

EXPLAINING THE CURRENT CRISIS

Since the early work of John Commons, industrial relations theory has stressed the importance of national institutional structures and regulations.[6] This literature seeks to account for national patterns of industrial relations by showing how particular laws, regulations, and organizational arrangements shape the behavior of firms and unions in different countries. Given divergent structures and patterns of arrangements, typologies have been developed that classify industrial relations systems according to whether they are organizationally centralized or not, whether they defend narrow job classification schemes or encourage broad skills, whether their allied political parties are in power or in opposition, and whether their ideologies are revolutionary, reformist, or, as in the United States, "businesslike." The peculiarities of these institutional arrangements reflect the particular

6. John R. Commons, *Institutional Economics: Its Place in Political Economy* (New York: Macmillan, 1934), p. 311.

national histories of these different states. In fact, these institutions are the organizational legacy of past struggles between industrial relations actors.

From this classification scheme, industrial relations systems are organized along a continuum, with the United Kingdom and the United States on one end, due to their fragmented union structures and emphasis on collective bargaining between labor and management, and Austria and Sweden on the other end, with their centralized structures and peak-level bargaining. French and Italian unions are situated somewhere in between because of their weak structures, highly politicized strategies, and dependence on the state.

These typologies are not merely descriptive. They are also normative and imply that certain systems are more mature or stable than others. For instance, following the economic crisis of the 1970s, numerous scholars argued that nations with centralized interest organizations, peak-level bargaining, and social democratic governments were better able to weather the crisis since they were capable of implementing neocorporatist polices that traded wage moderation and labor peace for increased investment and price freezes. These neocorporatist arrangements, it was argued, were responsible for the lower inflation and unemployment rates and more stable economic growth of these countries.[7]

Viewed in these terms, the current crisis in Italian industrial relations is the natural product of its poorly designed institutions. Because the Italian bureaucracy is inefficient and unable to implement reforms, and the unions are organizationally incapable of enforcing concertative arrangements, neocorporatist deals like those negotiated by labor movements in certain northern European nations are impossible. Even attempts to create functionally equivalent arrangements are bound to fail in Italy.[8]

Yet, this conventional interpretation rests on serious empirical flaws and theoretical simplifications. For instance, even in nations with

7. See, for instance, David Cameron, "Social Democracy, Corporatism, Labor Quiescence, and the Representation of Economic Interest in Advanced Capitalist Society," and Peter Lange, "Unions, Workers, and Wage Regulation: The Rational Bases of Consent," both in *Order and Conflict in Contemporary Capitalism*, ed., John H. Goldthorpe (Oxford: Clarendon Press, 1984), pp. 143–78, 98–123.

8. Marino Regini, "The Conditions for Political Exchange: How Concertation Emerged and Collapsed in Italy and Great Britain," in *Order and Conflict*, ed. Goldthorpe, pp. 124–42.

the supposedly correct mix of institutions, unemployment rates have soared, economic performance has plummeted, and unions have come under increasing attack by both private business and the state. Moreover, corporatist-like arrangements were, in fact, achieved in several industries and in various regions in Italy.[9] The conventional approach also rests on a set of problematic assumptions about microlevel developments and their relationship to macrolevel regulatory arrangements. In essence, it portrays firms and unions as isomorphic, national institutions as static, and the relationship between these two levels as hierarchically unidirectional and monolithic. As a result, it underestimates the degree of change occurring within these national industrial relations institutions and is blind to the wide array of diverse labor-management patterns obtaining at the industry and firm levels in all advanced industrial nations, not just Italy. Recent work by Horst Kern and Charles Sabel for Germany, Kristina Ahlen and Nils Elvander for Sweden, and Thomas Kochan, Harry Katz, and Robert McKersie for the United States all suggest that similar patterns of decentralization and redefinition of industrial relations practices are taking place in these countries as well. [10]

In short, what we are witnessing in Italy (and elsewhere) is not a crisis of a particular set of institutional arrangements or of any individual labor movement but rather the unraveling of all industrial relations systems with nationally oriented industrial unions at their core. The present crisis, in other words, is an organizational crisis of vertical sectoral unions. Because of the changes outlined above, these industrial federations are no longer capable of aggregating the diverse interests of the many locals within their sector or of acting as an effective conduit between the national confederations and the firm-level unions. As a result, union policy at all three levels is in disarray.

9. In all fairness, one must note that Regini has subsequently shifted his attention to analyze these more regional and sectoral corporatist experiences, see Marino Regini and Charles Sabel, "Le strategie di riaggiustamento industriale in Italia: Uno sguardo d'insieme in chiave comparata," in *Strategie di riaggiustamento industriale,* ed. Marino Regini and Charles Sabel (Bologna: Il Mulino, 1989).

10. See Horst Kern and Charles Sabel, "Trade Unions and Decentralized Production: A Sketch of Strategic Problems for the West German Labor Movement," *Politics and Society* (forthcoming); Kristina Ahlen, "Swedish Collective Bargaining under Pressure: Inter-Union Rivalry and Incomes Policies," *British Journal of Industrial Relations* 27 (November 1989): 330–46; Nils Elvander, "Incomes Policies in the Nordic Countries," *International Labour Review* 129, no. 1 (1990): 1–21; and Thomas A. Kochan, Harry C. Katz, and Robert B. McKersie, *The Transformation of American Industrial Relations* (New York: Basic Books, 1986).

THE DECLINE OF THE NATIONAL UNION

National unions arose throughout the West in response to the emergence of the modern corporation and the creation of national markets. These national industrial unions were characterized by two basic features: organizational hierarchies in which vertical industry structures dominated local and regional union bodies and national contracts standardized wages and working conditions throughout the industry, and firm-level functionalism in which managerial authority was respected and unions merely grieved or negotiated the impact of managerial decisions.

These two basic features were mutually reinforcing. For example, in response to the growth of national markets, national unions standardized wages and working conditions across plants and industrial sectors. These practices, in turn, helped sustain the consumer demand that created national markets based on mass production of standardized goods. Similarly, as industrial production became centered around large firms employing semiskilled workers to produce standardized commodities according to a strict division of labor within the plant, national industrial unions increasingly focused their organizational strategies around these workers, often at the expense of other segments of the working class. Union contracts also sought to regulate rather than transform the emergent division of labor within plants.

The recent transformation of national markets and consequent proliferation of diverse business practices not only across but also within the same industries have rendered void the organizational rationale for the supremacy of national industrial unions. In fact, these vertical structures appear unable to adapt to the variety of corporate structures and strategies emerging within their sectors. The union's place within the firm is also changing. Functional distinctions between different kinds of jobs or between labor and management more generally are becoming blurred in firms where new technologies require broadly skilled workers capable of performing a variety of jobs.[11] This transformation of work combined with the increased participation of new types of workers (women, youth, part-time) in the labor market has shrunk the traditional power base (semiskilled male workers) of most

11. Katherine Van Wezel Stone, "Labor and the Corporate Structure: Changing Conceptions and Emerging Possibilities," *University of Chicago Law Review* 55, no. 1 (1988): 73–173.

industrial unions. And even these traditional workers have become disgruntled with national union structures that appear unable to represent, let alone defend, their interests. In short, both constituent elements of the postwar industrial relations system—the supremacy of national industrial unions and firm-level functionalism—have been swept away by the current wave of industrial restructuring.

In Italy, this pattern is unfolding in slightly different ways due to the peculiarities of Italy's postwar industrial relations system, in which national industrial unions developed somewhat later and as creatures of the national confederations. The Italian labor movement emerged from the destruction of twenty years of fascism and World War II as a highly politicized, centralized, and unified organization, the Confederazione Generale Italiana del Lavoro (CGIL). The union movement, like Italy's first postwar governments, consisted of a broad coalition of antifascist resistance forces: Communist, Socialist, Republican, and Catholic currents coexisted within the trade union confederation.

The union movement was the creation of these political parties. Because the postwar labor movement had to rebuild more or less from scratch, union structures at all levels were creations of the central confederations in Rome. Rank-and-file workers and prefascist trade unionists had little to do with the reconstruction of the Italian union movement. Indeed, many of the CGIL's initial union leaders were recruited directly from political parties, and often they had little previous union experience.[12]

With the advent of the cold war, both government and labor coalitions dissolved. The Catholic current of the CGIL eventually established itself as the Confederazione Italiana dei Sindacati Lavoratori (CISL), and the Republican and Social Democratic trade union leaders set up the Unione Italiana dei Lavoratori (UIL). Throughout the 1950s and 1960s, the politics and strategies of the three union confederations were shaped by their political affiliations and rivalries.

Increased collaboration during the "hot autumn" led to a form of reunification in 1972 with the signing of a federative pact. Within the Federazione Unitaria CGIL-CISL-UIL, each confederation retained its autonomy at all levels of the union hierarchy, but new joint

12. See also Sergio Turone, *Storia del sindacato in Italia* (Bari: Laterza, 1976); Joseph La Palombara, *The Italian Labor Movement: Problems and Prospects* (Ithaca: Cornell University Press, 1957); and Joseph A. Raffaele, *Labor Leadership in Italy and Denmark* (Madison: University of Wisconsin Press, 1962).

structures aimed at coordinating decisions among these existing organizations were also created. The federation dissolved in 1984, due to disagreements between the Communists in the CGIL and the rest of the labor movement over a referendum sponsored by the Italian Communist party which sought to abrogate a government decree revising the *scala mobile*. Since then, the three confederations have continued to cooperate in contract negotiations, notwithstanding increasing levels of antagonistic rhetoric over such issues as working hours and labor flexibility.

Each confederation has both vertical and horizontal structures. The vertical structures are based on industries or branches of industry. Thus, each confederation has a national chemicalworkers', textileworkers', and metalworkers' federation. The three confederations are also organized geographically, in what are called horizontal structures (for example, the Camera del Lavoro of Turin or Milan). During the 1950s, when the union movement was fragmented, weak, and politically isolated, these horizontal structures, especially the confederations, were predominant. But with the increase in collective bargaining at the industry and firm levels during the 1960s, the national industrial unions became ascendant.[13] Following the "hot autumn" struggles and the federative pact in 1972, factory councils, elected by and composed of union and nonunion workers alike, were established at the shop floor. These are the official workplace organs of the three confederations, replacing the earlier *commisione interne* (factory grievance committees).

Because of their role in negotiating the *contratti collettivi nazionali di lavoro*, triennial industry-wide collective bargaining agreements over minimum wages, work hours, and job classification schemes, the national industrial unions remained extremely powerful throughout the 1970s, notwithstanding other (not necessarily coordinated) accords being negotiated at the confederal and plant levels.[14] Among these in-

13. Ettore Santi, "L'evoluzione delle strutture di categoria: Il caso Cisl," *Prospettive Sindacale*, no. 48 (1983): 102–22.

14. During the 1970s, the national confederations negotiated with employers' organizations and the government over economy-wide agreements while factory councils, in conjunction with the provincial unions, bargained over a wide range of issues including wages and working conditions. Confusion and conflict among these three levels of the union hierarchy ensued. For more on this general process, see Tiziano Treu, "Centralization and Decentralization in Collective Bargaining," *Labour* 1 (1987): 147–75. For more on the disruptive influence these multi-level negotiations had at Fiat, see Tom Dealessandri and Maurizio Magnabosco, *Contrattare alla Fiat* (Rome: Edizoni Lavoro, 1987).

dustry federations, the metalworkers' unions—the FIOM, FIM, and UILM, associated respectively with the CGIL, CISL, and UIL—were traditionally Italy's largest and most powerful national unions.[15] The metalworkers often served as strategic and political innovators for the rest of the union movement, leading the way for the other industrial federations and even for the three national confederations.[16] For example, it was the metalworkers who instigated the resurgence of working-class militancy and promoted renewed unity among the three competing confederations in the 1960s. The metalworkers also spearheaded most innovations in collective bargaining, often setting the pattern to be replicated by national unions in other industrial sectors. Their leadership role was so pronounced that the most assured way of climbing the union hierarchy was within the metalworkers' unions; almost all confederal secretaries came from these national industrial unions.

This leadership role has, however, been seriously challenged by the massive industrial restructuring that took place in Italy throughout the 1980s.[17] As individual firms and even entire industries reorganized their plants, invested in new technologies, and reduced their workforces, national industrial unions like the metalworkers' found themselves suddenly outflanked. With each firm embarking on a different adjustment strategy, it became increasingly difficult for the national unions to negotiate, let alone coordinate their responses to, the reorganization under way in the industry. Attempts to do so through various industry plans failed miserably.

Even the triennial industry-wide collective bargaining negotiations, the institutional basis of the metalworkers' power, began to elude their control as individual employers and local unions resisted national accords that continued to standardize working conditions, work hours, and job classifications throughout the industry. These microlevel

15. A note of clarification: the three metalworkers' unions united as the FLM in the early 1970s and continued in this form through most of the 1980s; workers, however, can be members of either the individual unions or the FLM.

16. For more on the importance of the metalworkers, see Miriam Golden, *Labor Divided: Austerity and Working-Class Politics in Contemporary Italy* (Ithaca: Cornell University Press, 1988).

17. An interesting analysis of this process is presented in Fabrizio Barca and Marco Magnani, *L'industra fra capitale e lavoro* (Bologna: Il Mulino, 1989). See also Maurizio Ferrera, "Politics, Institutional Features, and the Government of Industry," in *State, Market, and Social Regulation*, ed. Lange and Regini, pp. 111–28; and CER-IRS, *Quale strategia per l'industria?* (Bologna: Il Mulino, 1986).

Table 7–1 Metalworkers' national contract renewal dates (1973–87)

Signature	Date of contract's initiation	Date of contract's expiration	Vacancy period (months)
1.8.70			
4.19.73	1.1.73	12.31.75	
5.1.76	5.1.76	1.1.79	5
7.16.79	7.16.79	12.31.81	7
9.1.83	9.1.83	12.31.85	21
1.18.87	1.1.87	12.31.89	13

Source: Based on a review of national and firm-level contracts made available by Fiat Auto and the CGIL.

Note: Vacancy period is time that elapsed between the expiration of the prior contract and the signature of the subsequent contract.

actors argued that these nation-wide contracts were overly rigid and unresponsive to their particular needs. As a result, both the sequencing and the content of these industry agreements began to change in ways that further eroded the leadership role of the national industrial unions. For example, these master agreements had once been negotiated every three years and renewals were essentially automatic. Negotiations by union locals at individual firms were mere addenda to these more standardized national contracts and usually took place within one year of the signing of the national agreements. During the 1980s, this pattern completely broke down. Examination of the metalworkers' contracts indicates that time lags between the expiration and renegotiation of national contracts as well as between the signing of national accords and their integration at the firm level have increased substantially (see Table 7–1). We must be careful not to overinterpret these developments, but it seems safe to infer that these trends suggest that the national metalworkers' union suffers substantial difficulties in developing, let alone implementing, contracts capable of covering the wide array of experiences prevalent within the same industry.

The content of collective bargaining agreements also appears to be shifting in favor of local unions. Recent research on collective bargaining in Italy reveals that, contrary to past practice, local union contracts seem the most innovative and important agreements covering workers in industry.[18] At both Fiat and Alfa, in fact, negotiations over work

18. See Raul Nacamulli, Giovanni Costa, and Luigi Manzolini, *La razionalita contrattata* (Bologna: Il Mulino, 1986); and Arnaldo Camuffo, "Relazioni industriali e performance d'impresa: Alcune implicazioni delle transformazioni del sistema di relazioni industriali"

time, work rhythms, bonuses and profit sharing, new technologies, and redundancies all appear to be negotiated at the firm level.[19] Even the sequencing of contract negotiations has shifted in favor of local unions. Before, national contracts were negotiated first and local agreements later, often with a prescribed lag period, today, many local unions negotiate their own contracts first, with the national agreement emerging later more as an aggregation and ratification of prior local deals.[20]

INDUSTRIAL ADJUSTMENT AND INDUSTRIAL RELATIONS: A TALE OF TWO COMPANIES

Fiat Auto

Fiat was founded in 1899. After a few years, its founder and chairman, Giovanni Agnelli, began to pursue a strategy aimed at the transformation of automobile production into large-scale industry. This change in strategy was the result of Agnelli's visit to the United States and his decision to "produce like Henry Ford."[21] This plan by Agnelli to develop large-scale industry in Turin made Fiat not only a major actor in the local economy but also the main architect of Fordism in Italy. Fiat, like Ford, began to pay higher wages as a way of attracting skilled workers away from other firms. After the recession of 1907, it took over several of its suppliers as well as its competitors. As a result, Fiat managed to simultaneously increase its productive integration and reduce local competition.

Factory work also began to change. Production was organized by sequence and American semiautomatic single-purpose machine

(Tesi di Laurea, Facoltà di Economia e Commercio, Università Degli Studi di Venezia, 1984).

19. See also Richard Locke and Serafino Negrelli, "Il caso Fiat Auto," in *Strategie di Riaggiustamento,* ed. Regini and Sabel, pp. 61–94.

20. Daniella Guidotti, *Strategia generale e azione decentrata* (Milan: Franco Angeli, 1986); and Giovanni Provasi, ed., *Il gioco negoziale* (Milan: Franco Angeli, 1987).

21. This section draws heavily on Duccio Bigazzi, "Management Strategies in the Italian Car Industry, 1906–1945: Fiat and Alfa Romeo," in *The Automobile Industry and Its Workers,* ed. Stephen Tolliday and Jonathan Zeitlin (Cambridge: Polity Press, 1986), pp. 76–96; Valerio Castronovo, *Giovanni Agnelli: La Fiat dal 1899 al 1945* (Turin: Einaudi, 1977); Angelo Michelsons, "Turin between Fordism and Flexible Specialization: Industrial Structure and Social Change, 1970–85" (Ph.D. dissertation, Cambridge University, 1986); and Simonetta Ortaggi, "Padronato e classe operaia a Torino negli anni 1906–1911," *Rivista di storia contemporanea* 3 (1979): 321–66.

tools were introduced. Interestingly enough, the metalworkers' union, FIOM, not only agreed to these changes (in return for increased piecerates) but also reorganized its structures to match the emergent Fordist order.[22]

Although two world wars and the autarkic economic policies of the fascist regime delayed the realization of Agnelli's plans for about forty years, by the late 1950s Fiat had succeeded in creating and servicing a mass market for automobiles in Italy. By the late 1960s, Fiat had one of the largest automobile production facilities in Western Europe, from which it dominated the Italian market and exported abroad. In short, over the course of the postwar period, Fiat became Italy's leading automobile producer and largest private enterprise.

By the late 1970s, however, Fiat, like most automobile producers in Western Europe and the United States, met serious organizational and financial problems. In many ways, Fiat's troubles were related to the more general crisis of the auto industry. A variety of factors, including increased international competition, the rise of fuel costs, changing consumer tastes, more stringent government health, safety, and environmental protection regulations, and increased labor costs all contributed to the crisis of the automobile industry in the West.[23] Yet, because of insufficient capital investments and extremely conflictual and rigid industrial relations practices throughout the 1970s, Fiat's productivity, profitability, and plant utilization rates were all lower than its major competitors.

Fiat's crisis became visible when the automobile division acquired a separate balance sheet for the first time in 1979. Suddenly, Italy's largest privately owned firm appeared to be on the verge of bankruptcy. As a result, the firm launched a restructuring process that included the massive introduction of new process and product technologies, a reorganization of its supplier and sales networks, and a radical break with the industrial relations practices of the 1970s.[24] As part of its

22. See also Giuseppe Berta, "Dalla manifattura al sistema di fabrica: Razionalizzazione e conflitti di lavoro," in *Storia d'Italia annali,* vol. 1 (Turin: Einaudi, 1978). The union leadership's own explanation for this shift can be found in Bruno Buozzi, "Per l'organizzazione dei metallurgici a Milano," published originally in *Il Metallurgo,* February 20, 1910, and reprinted in *I Metalmeccanici: Documenti per una storia,* ed. Gianfranco Bianchi and Giorgio Lauzi (Bari: De Donato, 1981), pp. 13–17.

23. Giuseppe Volpato, *L'industria automobilistico internazionale* (Padova: CEDAM, 1983).

24. For more on the reorganization of Fiat, see Locke and Negrelli, "Il caso Fiat Auto."

reorganization plan, Fiat proposed to place 24,000 workers in *cassa integrazione,* a state-financed redundancy fund, during the autumn of 1980.

The local union rejected this reorganization plan and broke off relations with the firm. Fiat, in turn, declared its intention to fire 15,000 workers, beginning on October 6. Things heated up as the union blockaded the firm and Fiat sent out letters of dismissal. The ensuing strike lasted 35 days, but rank-and-file participation was low. Finally, on October 14, Fiat foremen and supervisors organized a successful demonstration calling for a return to work: 40,000 people marched against the union, among them many blue-collar workers.[25] That very night an agreement was signed which represented a major defeat for the union. The agreement met with resistance from the more militant factions of the local union but was signed and pushed through for approval by the national industrial federations. Despite initial attempts by the local labor movement to claim victory in this strike, it marked a major defeat from which the unions never recovered.[26]

With the union out of the way, Fiat embarked on a major reorganization of its production processes. Its products were rehauled so that many new models with greater differentiation in design but more common components were introduced. The modular design of these new models permitted the automaker to reap greater economies of scale as well. Fiat also invested heavily in new technologies like computer-assisted design and manufacturing and industrial robots. Finally, it rationalized and upgraded its network of component suppliers. This increased collaboration between Fiat and its suppliers both enhanced the quality of its components and stimulated continuous product innovation.

The consequences of this reorganization have been positive for the firm. Profits rose from 324 billion lire in 1981 to 1,764 billion in 1988.[27] Productivity, as measured by the average number of cars

25. For more on this episode, see Alberto Baldissera, "Alle origini della politica della disuguagliaza nell'Italia degli anni '80: La marcia dei quarantamila," *Quaderni di sociologia* 31 (1984); and Giuseppe Bonazzi, "La lotta dei 35 giorni alla Fiat: Un analisi sociologica," *Politica ed economia* 11 (1984): 33–43.

26. It is interesting to note that the union already possessed information suggesting its lack of rank-and-file support; see A. Accornero, A. Baldisera, and S. Scamuzzi, "Ricerca di massa sulla condizione operaia alla Fiat," *Bolletino CESPE* 2 (February 1980).

27. I obtained these and other figures on Fiat's restructuring during field research in Turin in 1986–87 which included interviews with company managers, union officials, and local and national government leaders, see Richard M. Locke, "Local Politics and Industrial

produced by single worker, also increased from 14.0 in 1979 to 31.2 in 1989. As a result of these and other improvements, Fiat has increased its market share and now rivals Volkswagen as Europe's premier auto producer.

If the results of Fiat's restructuring have been positive for the auto firm, the consequences for the union have not. Immediately following the rupture in relations with the unions in 1980, the firm asserted a hard line with the labor movement. Within the factories, this amounted to a re-creation of traditional hierarchies and control on the shop floor, the expulsion of numerous union activists, and the reduction of the workforce by tens of thousands of workers.[28] Ongoing antagonism between the local unions and Fiat management foreclosed all possibilities of labor participation in the adjustment processes. In many shops, traditional union rules and practices were rendered obsolete by the introduction of new technologies and the reorganization of production. Three examples concerning informal accords over piecerates and pauses, job classification schemes, and sourcing decisions illustrate this point. During the 1970s, factory delegates and the job analysis offices of Fiat's plants engaged in extremely meticulous, time-consuming negotiations over individual and group work effort levels *(livelli di saturazione)*, piecerates and new piecework times, and working conditions.[29] As a result, numerous informal accords were reached regulating piecerates and breaks in different parts of the assembly line, and hazardous work sites (for example, paint shops) were restructured. Later, with the introduction of new technologies in chassis welding, engine construction, and the paint shops, work was reorganized in a variety of different shops and these previous accords were rendered obsolete, if not entirely unnecessary.

Adjustment: The Political Economy of Italy in the 1980s" (Ph.D. dissertation, Department of Political Science, MIT, February 1989) for more details. See also Fiat, *Relazioni e bilancio al 31 Dicembre, 1988* (Turin: Fiat, 1989), p. 69.

28. This figure was taken from Giuseppe Bonazzi, "Lasciae la fabbrica: Cassa integrazione e mobilità hegli anni oltanta," in *Laciltà dopo Ford. Il caso Torino,* ed. Arnaldo Bagnasio (Turin: Bollati Boringhieri, 1990), p. 31. For more on the expulsion of union activists, see figures in A. Becchi Collida and Serafino Negrelli, *La transizione nell'industria e nelle relazioni industriali: L'auto e il caso Fiat* (Milan: Franco Angeli, 1986).

29. See also Giovanni Contini, "The Rise and Fall of Shop-Floor Bargaining at Fiat, 1945–80," in *Automobile Industry and Its Workers,* ed. Tolliday and Zeitlin, pp. 192–218; and the interview of Cesare Cosi in Gabriele Polo, *I Tamburi di Mirafiori* (Turin: RIC Editore, 1989).

These new technologies also transcended traditional job classification schemes as they simultaneously rendered certain traditional jobs redundant and created new positions for people capable of both operating and servicing these new process technologies. Since the skill requirements and responsibilities for these new jobs did not fit nicely into traditional job classification schemes, the unions found themselves with an anachronistic classification system. As increasing numbers of workers began to occupy these new jobs, the unions faced a dilemma. They must either antagonize these new workers by not fully appreciating their skills or anger their traditional constituency of semi-skilled workers by appearing to favor these new workers with the extra bonuses and privileges associated with higher classification levels.

The reconceptualization of the automobile as a composite of modular macrocomponent systems also overhauled prior production and sourcing arrangements; engines, brake systems, dashboards, and seats could now be produced by specialized suppliers working in collaboration with Fiat. Since these make-or-buy decisions seemed to be continuously renegotiated by the firm, and given that many of these suppliers were also organized by the metalworkers' union, it became increasingly difficult for the union to develop a viable position on these issues.

Perhaps more damaging for union practices than the actual changes in production was the way these changes were implemented by the firm. For the first half of the decade, Fiat management circumvented the unions, negotiating directly with workers over issues concerning retraining, flexible work hours, and modifications of their jobs. These modifications were significant enough to match the changes under way in the organization of production, but they were not so dramatic as to necessitate formal renegotiations of job classification schemes, which would have legally required union participation. This blurring or bending *but not breaking* of already established contractual rules and boundaries was very characteristic of Fiat industrial relations policies over the course of the 1980s.

A 1986 study on the way Fiat workers perceived the technological changes in the firm suggests that those workers most vulnerable to being replaced by automation were extremely anxious about their positions and diffident toward the union. Unions were shunned not only because of their failure to protect these workers but also because of fears that union contacts would result in company reprisals in the form of dismissals or *cassa integrazione*.[30] Union membership rates reflected these feelings: at Fiat's various Turinese plants, membership in the local metalworkers' union, the FLM, fell from 32,898 in 1980 to 11,589 in 1986.[31]

If the situation was precarious for workers within the firm, it was even more dismal for those workers expelled from the factories. The most evident sign of the severe dislocation resulting from Fiat's restructuring and the defeat of the union was the existence and fate of the *cassintegrati*—the redundant workers supported by the special fund. Fiat alone placed 30,590 full-time workers in *cassa integrazione* while also using this mechanism to lay off other workers during periodic downward shifts in demand. During the first half of the 1980s, tens of thousands of local workers found themselves under- or unemployed, though the exact number of people placed in *cassa integrazione* by Fiat and related firms is difficult to determine precisely (figures are calculated in terms of hours, not individuals).

The majority of *cassintegrati* were middle-aged, unskilled, poorly educated workers of southern origin. Many of the handicapped and women workers hired during the latter half of 1970s (because of union enforcement of national hiring policies) were also removed from the factory during these years. Many *cassintegrati* had tremendous difficulties adjusting to their new lives outside the factory. With the loss of their jobs, their identities—very much associated with the workplace, work group, and productive activity—were thrown into question. Removed from the shop floor, these workers also lost their political affiliations and social relations. Workers in *cassa integrazione* found themselves in a state of limbo—no longer active in the factory but still legally dependent on the firm for survival. The costs of this exclusion are high. Among these workers, rates of suicide, divorce, substance abuse, and psychological illness have reached alarming proportions.[32]

Needless to say, serious tensions have developed between this group and the unions, which are held responsible for their sad state. Loss of

30. Vittorio Reiser, "Immagini del progresso tecnologico e del lavoro," *Ex macchina,* no. 2 (1986).

31. Figures from FLM, Turin, December 31, 1986.

32. See Roberto Cardacci, "Gli effetti sociali della ristrutturazione: La cassa integrazione a Torino Dopo il 1980," in *Tre incognite per lo sviluppo,* ed. Angelo Michelsons, (Milan: Franco Angeli, 1985), pp. 341–62.

support among the rank and file has been matched by other problems, including continued strategic confusion, factional in-fighting and purges, and persistent paralysis vis-à-vis firm initiatives. In sum, the local union's policy of militant confrontation and intransigence in the face of the firm's need to restructure not only failed but also threatens to destroy the union.

Alfa Romeo

Alfa Romeo was founded in 1906 but did not concentrate its production on automobiles until after World War II.[33] Instead, alongside its automobile production it also manufactured a variety of more or less profitable items such as munitions, railroad stock, and aircraft engines.

Following World War I, market limits, financial problems, and management errors constrained Alfa Romeo's car output. This occurred during the same period in which Fiat began to reorganize its production along the lines of mass production. In contrast, Alfa management drew on the firm's experience with racing cars and concentrated on the manufacture of high-quality, expensive automobiles. In the field of industrial relations, the firm stressed workers' skills, cooperation, and loyalty to the firm. Even after the company's takeover by the state during the depression, Alfa continued to be characterized by this model of industrial development.

This triad of high-quality production, skilled workers, and cooperative industrial relations continued to underpin the firm's industrial strategy in the postwar period. In fact, Alfa did not really embark on the mass production of autos until the early 1960s, when it opened its Arese plant outside Milan and doubled its productive capacity. Even then, it continued its tradition of high-quality production through technical innovation (Alfa was famous for its technically advanced product development and design) and labor-management cooperation. The results were impressive: over the course of the decade, Alfa tripled its sales, doubled its workforce, and became an internationally recognized leader in sportscars.

The success of this model, however, was fully appreciated only after it was abandoned for Fordism. In 1972, Alfa Romeo opened its

33. For more on the early years at Alfa Romeo, see Duccio Bigazzi, *Il Portello: Operai, tecnici e imprenditori all'Alfa-Romeo, 1906–1926* (Milan: Franco Angeli, 1988).

Pomigliano plant outside Naples and thus sought to break from its past and embark on a new path of development. With the Pomigliano plant, Alfa intended to change its traditional product differentiation-based strategy and instead manufacture a new product, the Alfasud—a small, economy car for a mass market (which the firm knew little about since its traditional products were extremely expensive and catered to a small niche of clients)—in a new way (using unskilled workers and highly automated and dedicated equipment).[34] That the firm sought to change its strategy exactly at the moment when the European automobile industry began to suffer from overcapacity, increased fuel and labor costs, and greater international competition may explain the disastrous results. That these two productive poles were operated more or less as two distinct companies, with separate managements and autonomous design, purchasing, and marketing offices, may also account for the poor results during the 1970s. In fact, following the opening of Pomigliano, Alfa never again turned a profit; what was once seen as the pride and joy of Italian state enterprise languished for over a decade before it was finally restructured.

To further exacerbate the firm's troubles, labor relations at Alfa (both in the north and the south) became extremely conflictual in the 1970s. Like Fiat, Alfa experienced an especially militant wave of strikes and worker mobilization during the "hot autumn". Although instigated and for the most part controlled by older union militants, here too southern migrant workers were active in the strikes.[35] In fact, unions at Alfa became so powerful that they were often able to achieve their goals with no more than the threat of strikes. Absenteeism and hours lost to work stoppages increased dramatically over the decade, and productivity and product quality plummeted.[36] The climate of industrial relations at the Pomigliano plant became so horrible that

34. Gianni Geroldi and Antonio Nizzoli, *L'Alfa Romeo: Il mercato, la struttura, le risorse d'azienda, le prospettive* (Milan: FIM-CISL, 1986).

35. See Emilio Reyneri, "Maggio Strisciante: L'inizio della mobilitazione operaia," in Alessandro Pizzorno et al., *Lotte operaie e sindacato: Il ciclo 1968–1972 in Italia* (Bologna: Il Mulino, 1978); Massimo Roccella, "La composizione dei conflitti di lavoro nella grande impresa: Il caso dell'Alfa Romeo di Arese," *Giornale di diritto del lavoro e di relazioni industriali*, no. 14, (1982): 251–73; and Martin Slater, "Migration and Workers' Conflicts in Western Europe" (Ph.D. dissertation, Department of Political Science, MIT, October 1976).

36. See Giovanni Costa and Claudio Gradara, *Impresa e relazioni industriali: Alfa Romeo, Italsider, e Olivetti* (Padora: LEDAM, 1984).

Table 7–2 Work hours lost to union actions and absenteeism at Alfa Romeo (1980–86)

	1980	1981	1982	1983	1984	1985	1986
Hours lost to union actions	785	669	1,071	778	565	152	365
Hours lost to absenteeism	9,152	6,423	3,927	3,147	2,664	1,936	2,585

Source: Marco Frey, "Ristrutturazione ritardata e consequenze occupazionali: Il caso Alfa Romeo," *Economia e politica industriale,* no. 59 (1988): 67.

industrial sociologists dedicated volumes to understand this case of "anomalous conflictuality."[37]

Yet, the way Alfa sought to deal with its troubles was radically different from Fiat's. For example, in the early 1980s, the local union and Alfa's management negotiated a series of accords aimed at both increasing the firm's productivity and enriching workers' skills. Out of these agreements emerged the homogeneous production group, teams of ten to twenty workers assigned to different segments of the production line. Within these groups, workers rotated various jobs as a way of eliminating monotony and increasing skills. Quality control and maintenance work were also relegated to these groups. As a result of these changes, productivity increased 35 percent within a year, product quality improved, and several indirect and supervisory jobs were eliminated from the factory.[38] The success of this experiment appeared so great that one of Alfa's personnel managers argued that one could "forget Turin" in this new phase of "negotiated restructuring."[39] In fact, both absenteeism and strikes decreased significantly following these accords (see Table 7–2).

A variety of factors—increased militancy of the local FIM and the subsequent dissolution of union unity at Alfa, a breakdown of Alfa's logistic system (making it nearly impossible to maintain production schedules, let alone product quality), a series of management turnovers, and persistent underinvestment, especially in new product and process technologies—combined to undermine the production

37. See, for instance, Dario Salerni, *Sindacato e forza lavoro all'Alfasud: Un caso anomalo di conflittualità industriale* (Turin: Einaudi, 1980).

38. Marco Frey, "Ristrutturazione ritardata e consequenze occupazionali: Il caso Alfa Romeo," *Economia e politica industriale,* no. 59 (September 1988): 51–96.

39. Giuseppe Medusa, *L'impresa tra produttività e consenso: Il caso Alfa Romeo* (Milan: ETAS Libri, 1983).

Table 7–3 Unionization rate at Alfa Romeo Arese plant

	May 1987		April 1988	
FIOM-CGIL	4,462	(30.5%)	3,300	(26.6%)
FIM-CISL	2,211	(15.0%)	1,200	(9.7%)
UILM-UIL	655	(4.5%)	513	(4.1%)
FLM	708	(5.0%)	450	(3.6%)
Total	8,036	(55.0%)	5,463	(44.0%)

Source: Based on an elaboration of data presented in Marco Frey, "Ristrutturazione ritardata e consequenze occupazionali: Il caso Alfa Romeo," *Economia e politica industriale*, no. 59 (1988): 85.
Note: Figures in parentheses indicate the percentage of all employees belonging to the unions.

group experience.[40] But the more cooperative spirit of Alfa's labor-management relations continues, even now that Alfa belongs to Fiat and is run by Fiat managers. Illustrative of this continuity is the May 3, 1987 agreement between Fiat and the unions over the restructuring of Alfa Romeo. In this accord, Fiat agreed to increase production by investing 55 billion lire in new process technologies, restyling several existing Alfa models, and transferring production of various Lancia models (Y-10 and Thema) to Alfa's plants. In return for these investments, the union abandoned what remained of the production groups, agreed to more early retirements and the use of *cassa integrazione,* and relaxed its norms regulating internal labor mobility. In essence, the unions traded labor flexibility in return for job security for the vast majority of Alfa's workforce. The radical faction of the local FIM at Alfa in Milan rejected this restructuring plan and mobilized the local workforce against it. Claiming that the national metalworkers' union and the local FIOM and UILM had sold out to Fiat, this faction demanded a referendum on the restructuring plan. This took place in the late spring of 1987, with a victory for the more cooperative forces. Moreover, with the unions involved, the costs of the reorganization in terms of *cassa integrazione* or union membership were much lower than anticipated. Although the plan envisioned the continued use of this instrument through 1990, most workers placed in *cassa integrazione* were back at their jobs by 1989. And although all unions suffered a slight reduction in membership following the accord with Fiat (much of it due to early retirements), the more cooperative unions fared much better than the militant FIM (see Table 7–3). With the success

40. Geroldi and Nizzoli, *L'Alfa Romeo.*

of the 164 model, Alfa has once again become profitable and is regaining market share in both Italy and abroad.[41]

ALTERNATIVE EXPLANATIONS CONSIDERED

We have two cases, one of apparent success and the other of failure. How do we account for these differences in union experiences with industrial restructuring? One's first instinct is to attribute them to economic factors; because the two firms occupied different market segments, they faced different challenges, and thus the processes and outcomes of their respective reorganizations diverged. But, although it is true that Alfa and Fiat have traditionally pursued different strategies, it is also true that during the 1970s (with Fiat's acquisition of Lancia and Alfa's construction of Pomigliano) their strategies and product ranges began to converge. If anything, Alfa's financial difficulties were much more serious than Fiat's. Moreover, other foreign companies competing with Fiat in exactly the same market segments appear to have restructured in vastly different ways.[42] Thus, competitive strategy alone can not explain the observed differences.

Another explanation commonly offered to account for the divergent patterns of industrial relations at these two firms focuses on the fact that Alfa (until 1986) was a state-owned firm, and thus that its management could be more relaxed about economic goals like efficiency and sales, permitting it to be easier on the unions. But, Alfa's management during these years was no more benevolent toward the unions than Fiat's management, and at times it was even more aggressive.[43] That labor relations at Alfa continue to be significantly different from those at Fiat, even now that they share the same ownership and management, also casts doubt on this assertion.

An alternative explanation of the diversity of union experiences with corporate restructuring focuses on two basic features: local socioeconomic factors that shape union behavior at the firm level, and the

41. Ibid.

42. See Wolfgang Streeck, "Industrial Relations and Industrial Change: The Restructuring of the World Automobile Industry in the 1970s and 1980s," *Economic and Industrial Democracy* 8 (1987): 437–62.

43. Giuseppe Medusa, "Condizioni di impiego nella grande impresa: Il caso Alfa Romeo–Arese," *Osservatorio sul mercato del lavoro e sulle professioni*, nos. 11–12 (1979): 54–78; and Raffaela Montini, "Il caso Alfa Romeo: Anni settanta" (Unpublished manuscript, Camera del Lavoro di Milano, 1986).

institutional linkages between local and national union structures. Building on the work of Arnaldo Bagnasco, Carlo Trigilia, and Mark Granovetter, which illustrates how local sociopolitical arrangements and resources influence the strategic choices of such economic actors as firms and unions, I argue that three local features shape the type of strategies developed by local unions: the organizational strength of the local union, the ideological outlook or worldview of its leadership, and the degree of social and political development of the surrounding context.[44]

But the story of Italian industrial relations in the 1980s is not simply a collection of local stories. In fact, to fully understand how diverse models of local industrial politics have proliferated over this decade, we must also examine the institutional linkages between local and national union structures. What we observe is that the ability (or lack thereof) of particular national unions to articulate a new division of labor within their organizations, one that provides local unions with increased autonomy over their firm-level strategies while preserving for themselves a minimum degree of control and coordination over such basic issues as wages and working conditions, also influences union experiences with industrial change. A reexamination of our two cases illustrates the importance of these two sets of factors in shaping contemporary industrial relations patterns in Italy.

Shaping Union Politics: Local Patterns of Industrial Relations

The development of Fiat along the lines of Fordism had significant effects on both the firm and its workforce, as well as on the history of Turin.[45] The expansive development of the firm made it not only the biggest, but in many ways the only show in town. Fiat is referred to as *la mamma* by local residents. The local economy has historically revolved around the firm, and the majority of the local labor force is employed at either Fiat or one of its numerous suppliers.

44. Arnaldo Bagnasco, "La eostruzione sociale del mercato (Bologna: Il Mulino, 1988); Mark Granovetter, "Social Structures and Economic Action: The Problem of Embeddedness," *American Journal of Sociology* 91 (November 1985): 481–510; and Carlo Trigilia, *Grandi partiti e piccole imprese* (Bologna: Il Mulino, 1986).

45. See Valerio Castronovo, *Impresa ed economia in Piemonte dalla "grande crisi" ad oggi* (Turin: UTET, 1979); and Michelsons, "Turin between Fordism and Flexible Specialization."

Due to its hegemonic position, Fiat was able to dominate local government, control local business and cultural associations, and thus more or less determine the development of the city. Fiat management cultivated an extremely authoritarian, hierarchical vision of its role; from the early years of the firm, through the long tenure of Vittorio Valletta, and continuing to this day, it has sought to control the firm's development unilaterally.[46] It promoted pro-business political forces and company unions. It also sought to tame its workforce through a combination of repression and paternalism and undermined all attempts at alternative bases of power (such as the postwar comanagement councils, *consigli di gestione*) within its plants.

The local labor movement's development reflects this particular model of development.[47] For instance, peculiar to the local labor movement are its frequent spontaneous worker upsurges, regularly followed by the politicization of industrial relations. This occurred in 1913, when the rank and file supported anarcho-syndicalist positions and prevented the local union from negotiating with the firm, and similar events have continued throughout the local union's history. The political development of the local labor movement was such that it created weak organizations with strong ideologies. Antagonism toward the firm combined with a radical, almost maximalist vision of politics to create a local union that perceived itself (and at times sought to act) as the vanguard of the Italian labor movement.[48]

As a result of the particular way industry developed in Turin and the peculiarities of the local labor movement, stable relations between the firm and its workforce never developed. The result was a continuous struggle between these actors in which no long-lasting compromises were possible. Defeat by one meant its almost complete subordination to the other. The wounds of past battles were nourished as the loser prepared for revenge in the next round of struggles. Since the factory occupations in 1920, and continuing through the rise and fall of fascism, the restoration of private capital in the 1950s, the "hot autumn"

46. See Castronovo, *Giovanni Agnelli;* and Piero Bairati, *Valletta* (Turin: UTET, 1983) for the specific case of Fiat.

47. For more on the labor movement at Fiat, see various essays in Aldo Agosti and Gian Mario Bravo, eds., *Storia del movimento operiao, del socialism e delle lotte sociali in Piemonte* (Bari: De Donato, 1980); Renzo Gianotti, *Trent'anni di lotte alla Fiat, 1948–1978* (Bari: De Donato, 1979); and Miriam A. Golden, "Historical Memory and Ideological Orientations in the Italian Workers' Movement," *Politics and Society* 16, no. 1 (1988): 1–34.

48. See Vittorio Reiser, "Come si riproduce un avanguardia," in Aris Accornero and Vittorio Reiser, *Il mestiere dell'avanguardia* (Bari: De Donato, 1981), pp. 7–26.

struggles in the late 1960s, and the 35-day strike in 1980, labor and management in Turin have been engaged in an all-or-nothing battle.

Furthermore, Turin does not possess the sociopolitical resources necessary to mediate the type of conflictual labor relations characteristic of Fiat. Because of the simplicity of Turinese society—composed essentially of two groups, an industrial bourgeoisie and a proletarian working class—organized interest groups and political parties never fully developed in Turin. Membership figures and participation rates in these political institutions are especially low in Turin.[49] Even in the union, which has historically been more of a movement than an institution, membership rates have always been below the national average. What other interest groups exist are dominated by either the firm or the union movement. The only institutions that are autonomous of these two protagonists are the local churches. But due to their own historical development even they are quite radical and actually enhance rather than hinder antagonisms between labor and management at Fiat.[50] In sum, the local union at Fiat is a highly political but organizationally weak structure located in a city lacking potential mediators of industrial conflict. It is no surprise, therefore, that repeated attempts by groups within the local union and firm to construct a more negotiated and stable form of industrial relations at Fiat have failed repeatedly.[51]

The contrast with Alfa is striking. As we have seen, Alfa developed in a way that preserved workers' skills and reinforced local union organizations through much of this century. Unlike that at Fiat, the union at Alfa was never seriously repressed during the postwar period. Thus, throughout the 1950s and 1960s, as well as after the "hot autumn," the union at Alfa consisted of a sizeable group of disciplined old-guard unionists who promoted shop-floor bargaining. This group was active in all debates over union politics and played a major role in the negotiated restructuring of the firm in the 1980s.

The local union in Milan was always a stronger and more complex organization than its equivalent at Fiat and thus less subject to the vicissitudes of the more movement-oriented union in Turin.[52] More-

49. Arnaldo Bagnasco, *Torino: Un profilo sociologico* (Turin: Einaudi, 1986), chap. 4.

50. Luigi Berzano et. al., *Uomini di frontiera: "Scelta di classe" e trasformazione della coscienza Cristiana a Torino dal concilio ad Oggi* (Turin: Cooperative di Cultura L. Milani, 1984).

51. Deallesandri and Magnabosco, *Contrattare alla Fiat.*

52. For more on the unions at Alfa and how they differed from those at Fiat, see Carol Anne Mershon, "The Micropolitics of Union Action: Industrial Conflict in Italian Facto-

over, the auto industry is only one of many industries in the area, and although Alfa is the largest factory in Milan the metalworkers are not hegemonic as they are in Turin.[53] Textile and chemical unions—two unions with much experience in technological innovation and firm restructuring—are also strong in Milan and thus counterbalance the particular interests or strategies of the more militant wings of the local metalworkers' unions. Unlike Turin, Milan possesses strong and well-organized interest groups and political parties, which have served historically as mediators between labor and management and thus have helped avoid the development of the zero-sum scenario that exists between labor and management at Fiat.

Thus, local socioeconomic factors shaped the divergent models of union politics we examined. But they alone can not explain the different outcomes, especially since the resurgence of local patterns of industrial politics has also redrawn the boundaries between local and national unions. To fully understand the different outcomes at Fiat and Alfa, we must also examine the changing relations between the national metalworkers' union and the two locals in question. What we find is that, whereas the metalworkers' federation was unable to develop a new, mutually agreeable division of labor between it and the locals at the time of the Fiat restructuring, seven years later and partially as a result of what it had learned from the Fiat experience, a redistribution of responsibilities was achieved and the two levels of the union hierarchy could work together during the reorganization of Alfa.

In the late 1970s, the two levels of the union competed with one another for the strategic leadership of the union, often at the expense of its membership. The debacle at Fiat in 1980 best illustrates the negative consequences of this internal union struggle. For instance, before the 35-day strike at Fiat, the national leadership of the metalworkers' union sought to negotiate the reorganization of Fiat with the firm's management. Unwilling to include the local union leadership (for fear that it was too radical), national union leaders began these negotiations in secret. When these meetings were discovered, the local union, unwilling to relegate the power to negotiate the new firm-level contract to the national leadership, rebelled against these negotiations and

ries" (Ph.D. dissertation, Department of Political Science, Yale University, May 1986).

53. Amalia Fumagalli, "Lo sviluppo dell'area metropolitana milanese," in *Grandi città e aree metropolitane*, vol. 1, ed. R. Mainardi and C. Tombola (Milan: Franco Angeli, 1982).

insisted that a new platform, including more radical language and various nonnegotiable demands, be presented instead. Unable to impose its will on the local (recall that we are dealing with the largest firm in Italy), the national union acquiesced and negotiations subsequently broke down.[54] Thus, because of internal rivalries between the different levels of the metalworkers' union, and given that a clear division of labor was not established between the local and the national over bargaining procedures and issues, contractual negotiations were blocked. The 35-day strike and the eventual demise of the local union soon followed.

The situation at Alfa was different. Notwithstanding the existence of a strong and militant group within the local FIM which opposed the accord with Fiat over the restructuring of the company, the local FIOM, UILM, and FLM, along with the regional CGIL, CISL, and UIL, all supported the agreement. Not only did these other union groups outnumber the opposition but, more important, the national union, having learned from its prior mistakes, organized a referendum over the accord in order to rally rank-and-file support. It eventually even censured Claudio Tiboni, the leader of the FIM opposition, for his continuing agitations against the agreement. In short, seven years later the national union had learned how to work with reform-oriented groups within the local union to prevent the type of showdown that had occurred in Turin.

CONCLUDING CONSIDERATIONS: REDRAWING THE BOUNDARIES OF UNION POLITICS

I have argued that the current wave of industrial restructuring in Italy has provoked a reconfiguration of industrial relations in ways that promote the renewed importance of local unions. Yet, the resurgence of local unions is not simply an Italian phenomenon. Although local patterns of industrial politics may be especially salient in Italy because of its peculiar political-economic development,[55] they none-

54. For more on this episode, see Fabrizio Carmignani, "Il 'sindacato di classe' nella lotta dei 35 giorni alla Fiat," *Politica ed Economia*, no. 11 (1984): 43–48.

55. See, for instance, Percy A. Allum, *Italy: Republic without Government?* (New York: Norton, 1973); Perry Anderson, "Italy," in *Lineages of the Absolutist State* (London: Verso, 1979); Derek Beales, *The Risorgimento and the Unification of Italy* (London: Longman, 1981).

theless appear to be emerging (perhaps in different ways) in other countries with very different political-economic histories as well. What is happening in Italy is not exceptional but rather reflective of more general trends sweeping across all advanced industrial nations.[56] Clearly, unions mean different things to different groups of workers within sectors and within nations, not just across them. These different conceptions shape union behavior and help explain the divergent responses to a common challenge (industrial restructuring) observed throughout the West.

The reemergence of these differences, especially at a time when the unity of the labor movement could determine its future viability, is the most significant feature of labor politics today. The reconfiguration of industrial relations in favor of local unions not only creates opportunities for unions to become more responsive to local needs but also poses several risks for the labor movement as a whole. How does the labor movement prevent whipsawing or the exploitation of workers in firms or in regions with weaker local unions? How do unions (with or without allied political parties) reaggregate the increasingly divergent interests of their rank and file (and of the majority of workers who do not belong to unions) into an organizationally coherent labor movement capable of promoting social and political reforms at the national level?

Maintaining unity amid the increasing diversity of the labor movement will not be easy. While some unions appear to be able to achieve this balance, others have failed. As the Italian metalworkers' case illustrates, maintaining traditional structures and strategies in the face of radical economic change simply does not work. Times have changed and unions must change accordingly. The transformation of the union away from its previous vertical, highly bureaucratic structures and toward a more horizontal, perhaps more democratic, organization has begun to take shape, but only after much internal debate and several setbacks. Perhaps it is safe to say that it took the defeat at Fiat for the metalworkers to respond differently at Alfa.

The reconstruction of the labor movement along more horizontal lines—as a federation of locals firmly embedded in their regional economies—may be a viable solution for the entire labor movement.

56. For an interesting discussion of the concept of exceptionalism in labor history, see Aristide R. Zolberg, "How Many Exceptionalisms?" in *Working Class Formation*, ed. Ira Katznelson and Aristide R. Zolberg (Princeton: Princeton University Press, 1986).

Just as the national union was the appropriate organizational solution in the previous era of national markets and large, bureaucratic corporations, the federation of strong locals could be most adept at representing the interests of workers in this period of market fragmentation and continuous industrial change. Whether this alternative arrangement is possible and, if so, whether it is sufficient to save organized labor, can not be answered at present. These questions are the focus of future research. Nonetheless, if this essay is at all convincing, it should stimulate others to explore organizational transformation of the labor movement along these lines.

8 Unions, New Technology, and Job Redesign at Volvo and British Leyland

Jonas Pontusson

It is commonplace to observe that car makers and other mass producers in the advanced capitalist countries are seeking to diversify their product range, to improve product quality, and to deploy labor and capital more flexibly. While changes in product markets have made flexibility necessary, the revolution in microelectronics has made it possible by reducing the costs of machinery that can be programmed to perform several different operations.

The significance of recent manufacturing innovations has been a subject of considerable debate. At the same time, most contributors to the literature on post-Fordism (or neo-Fordism) agree that neither technology nor market forces suffice to explain changes in working practices and work organization. Technology is plastic in the sense that it can be deployed in different ways, and there is more than one path to regain or maintain competitiveness in the new world economy. By this line of reasoning, we end up with the proposition that "politics" or the "balance of social forces" shape corporate choices

This chapter is a longer version of an article in *Economic and Industrial Democracy* 11 (August 1990): 331–36. It contains new data (on absenteeism and labor turnover) that strengthen my argument. My research was made possible by a fellowship from the German Marshall Fund of the United States. For comments on previous drafts, I am indebted to Christian Berggren, Richard Hyman, Harry Katz, Peter Katzenstein, David Soskice, Peter Swenson, Mike Terry, Lowell Turner, and especially to Miriam Golden, Wolfgang Streeck, and Stephen Wood. Special thanks to Christian Berggren, David Buckle, and Kajsa Ellegård for sharing their research and experience so generously.

about technology and work organization.[1] The vagueness of such formulations is often striking. What are the political or social institutions and actors that matter in the process of industrial innovation at the firm level? And exactly *how,* or why, do they matter? To get a better handle on these questions, we need to compare different experiences, within and across national boundaries, in a more systematic fashion. The following analysis, intended as a contribution to this enterprise, compares the "micropolitics" of reorganizing car production at Volvo and British Leyland (henceforth BL) in the 1970s and 1980s.[2]

Whereas Volvo represents a prototypical case of industrial innovation through bargaining and collaboration between management and labor, BL represents a prototypical case of innovation conceived by management and imposed on labor. Two basic questions arise. First, how do the technological and organizational changes introduced by Volvo differ from those introduced by BL, and to what extent can the differences be attributed to union influence? Second, why was organized labor included in the process of innovation at Volvo but excluded at BL?

My discussion is divided into three parts. In the first I demonstrate that Volvo represents a case of labor inclusion and BL a case of labor exclusion by describing the interaction of unions and management in the process whereby technological and organizational changes were conceived and implemented. My characterization of BL is accurate only for the period since 1979; in the mid-1970s, BL management and unions tried to find a collaborative, Swedish-style formula for industrial innovation.

1. See for example, Michael Piore and Charles Sabel, *The Second Industrial Divide* (New York: Basic Books, 1985); Arndt Sorge and Wolfgang Streeck, "Industrial Relations and Technical Change," *New Technology and Industrial Relations,* ed. Richard Hyman and Wolfgang Streeck (Oxford: Basil Blackwell, 1988), pp. 19–47; Steven Tolliday and Jonathan Zeitlin, "Introduction: Between Fordism and Flexibility," in *The Automobile Industry and Its Workers,* ed. Steven Tolliday and Jonathan Zeitlin (Cambridge: Polity Press, 1986), pp. 1–26; and Stephen Wood, "The Transformation of Work?" in *The Transformation of Work?* ed. Stephen Wood (London: Unwin Hyman, 1989), pp. 1–43.

2. I refer to my two cases as "BL" and "Volvo" for the sake of simplicity. Actually, my analysis deals only with the volume-cars divisions of these companies, that is the Austin Rover Group, previously known as Austin Morris, and the Volvo Car Corporation. A state-owned company since 1975, BL changed its name to become the Rover Group in 1986 and has subsequently been dismembered and privatized. The Austin Rover Group was sold to British Aerospace in 1988. See F. H. M. Blacker and C. A. Brown, *Job Redesign and Management Control: Studies in British Leyland and Volvo* (New York: Praeger, 1978) for a comparison of work reorganization efforts in the these two companies in the first half of the 1970s, focusing empirically on truck assembly.

In the second section I describe the technological and organizational changes introduced by Volvo and BL. It should be stressed that the case of BL, as I understand it, diverges from the familiar British story of a company failing to undertake innovative measures due to management incompetence or union resistance. Like Volvo, BL has introduced far-reaching changes at the shop floor since the early 1980s, but the thrust of innovation is markedly different.[3] To anticipate, I argue that BL's innovation strategy has emphasized flexible automation and tighter management control of the work process while leaving assembly work essentially unaltered. Volvo has also pursued greater automation and technological flexibility, but its innovation strategy has pivoted on job redesign and teamwork.

My third section is an exploration of the reasons for the observed differences with respect to outcomes as well as processes of innovation. It is tempting to explain the worker-centered orientation of Volvo's innovation strategy in terms of union influence in the process of innovation; I argue that this is not an adequate explanation. For the most part, the initiative behind innovative measures at Volvo has come from management. It was not until the 1980s that the Volvo unions began to develop a coherent conception of the kind of workplace reforms they wanted, and indeed they developed such a conception in response to management initiatives. The unions had some direct influence over the design of Volvo's most recent final assembly plant (in Uddevalla), but this influence took the form of tipping the balance in favor of one management faction over another. At no time can the Volvo unions be said to have prevailed over management.

Arguably, this assessment rests on too narrow a conception of union influence. Rather than asking whether the unions have prevailed when their preferences have conflicted with those of management, we should perhaps ask whether the unions have influenced management preferences in the course of an ongoing process of industrial innovation. Instead of pursuing this line of inquiry, I suggest that a great deal of explanatory leverage may be gained by looking at the broader political and economic parameters of direct interactions between unions and management. I argue that Volvo's innovation strategy can be seen

3. The extent to which these changes account for the turnaround in BL's (Austin Rover's) financial performance in the 1980s is complicated question that lies beyond the scope of my analysis; see Karel Williams, John Williams, and Colin Haslam, *The Breakdown of Austin Rover* (Leamington Spa: Berg, 1987).

as a management response to Swedish labor market conditions, and specifically as an attempt to reduce labor turnover. Volvo confronts a more serious labor turnover problem than BL because of the Swedish government's commitment to full employment, and because the unions' commitment to solidaristic wage policy constrains Volvo's ability to raise wages. At the same time, Volvo has been more sensitive to labor turnover because of its up-market product strategy.

Let me immediately point out that this argument is *not* intended as an explanation of why firms innovate. Confronting very different labor market conditions, BL and other car makers have also engaged in innovations, including the introduction of teamwork. The basic impetus behind innovation would seem to derive from product markets. My argument about labor market conditions is meant to explain why firms pursue different kinds of innovation in response to similar product market pressures—for instance, why BL and Volvo conceive and practice teamwork in very different ways.

To clarify further, I am convinced that unions do matter to the process of industrial innovation. My point is that the influence they exercise through direct interaction with management is contingent on their ability to influence the "external" environment of the firm. This argument is consistent with and inspired by the approach set forth by Wolfgang Streeck, but I disagree with Streeck on the precise mechanisms whereby macroconditions shaped by labor have in turn shaped corporate strategies. Streeck's thesis that political constraints on layoffs have forced Swedish and West German car makers to invest in training their workforce, and to seek more flexible production methods, ignores the high rates of labor turnover in the Swedish case. Had Volvo wanted to shed labor, it could simply have allowed turnover to become attrition.[4]

PROCESSES OF INNOVATION: THE ROLE OF ORGANIZED LABOR

My first task is to establish that Volvo represents a case of labor inclusion and BL a case of labor exclusion. Whereas in subsequent parts

4. Streeck, "Industrial Relations and Industrial Change: The Restructuring of the World Automobile Industry," *Economic and Industry Democratic* 8 (1987):437–62. Assuming that Streeck is right about the West German case, the question arises whether there might be significant differences between the manufacturing strategies and workplace reforms introduced by Swedish and West German car makers.

of this essay I compare the two cases more directly, I here treat the micropolitics of innovation as two separate stories; but let me first make some preliminary observations on the organization of labor (narrowly understood as manual labor) in the two cases.

Backgrounds: Unions at Volvo and BL

At BL as well as Volvo, close to 100 percent of manual workers were union members during the entire period covered by this analysis. At Volvo, all manual workers belong to the same metalworkers' union, Svenska metallindustriarbetarförbundet (Metall, for short). At BL, by contrast, workers belong to no less than eleven different unions. Most assembly operators and other unskilled workers belong to the Transport and General Workers Union (TGWU). Skilled workers belong to various craft unions, which also organize some unskilled workers. The largest of the craft unions at BL is the Amalgamated Union of Engineering Workers (AUEW). Whereas British unions are organized strictly on a geographic basis, the organization of Swedish unions includes plant locals (*verkstadsklubbar*) as well as a branches (*avdelningar*).[5]

The unions at BL belong to the Confederation of Shipbuilding and Engineering Unions. Until 1980, BL itself belonged to the Engineering Employers Federation, which bargains with the confederation over benefits and minimum wage rates. While part of industry-wide bargaining, BL also engaged in bargaining over pay, work pace, and working conditions with shop stewards at the plant or subplant level. At the same time it withdrew from this bargaining, BL introduced a system of centralized, company-wide negotiations.

British shop stewards are elected by the members of a particular union within some plant area and have traditionally enjoyed a great deal of autonomy vis-à-vis national and regional union officials. Their power at BL, and throughout much of British industry, was based on piecerate bargaining. As W. Lewchuck points out, BL relied on pay incentives rather than mechanization and management supervision to achieve productivity growth in the 1950s and 1960s.[6] Indeed, one

5. On the structure of unions and collective bargaining, see Peter Enström and Klas Levinson, *Industrial Relations in the Swedish Auto Industry* (Stockholm: Swedish Center for Working Life, 1982); and Paul Willman and Graham Winch, *Innovation and Management Control: Labour Relations at BL Cars* (Cambridge: Cambridge University Press, 1985), chap. 4.

6. Lewchuck, "The British Motor Vehicle Industry," in *The Decline of the British Economy*, ed. Bernard Elbaum and William Lazonick (Oxford: Clarendon, 1986), esp. pp. 149–

might argue that BL did not become a Fordist mass producer until the 1970s. The first step in this direction was taken when piecerates were replaced by hourly pay rates in the early 1970s. The shop stewards managed to retain a powerful position through the 1970s, however. To get the unions to agree to hourly pay rates, BL management conceded the principle of "mutuality." Written into plant-level procedural agreements, this principle required management to secure the agreement of shop stewards prior to the implementation of any change in working practices.

The Volvo unions gave up the kind or job control exercized by BL shop stewards in the 1950s. The introduction of methods-time-management at this time gave management the right to determine work pace more or less unilaterally and shifted the locus of piecerate bargaining to the plant level.[7] At Volvo, union officials alone have the authority to bargain with management; at best, shop stewards (*förtroendevalda*) serve as a two-way "transmission belt" between rank-and-file members and union officials. Plant-level bargaining occurs within the parameters set by national industry agreements, which broadly conform to recommendations agreed by the Lardsorganisationen (LO) and Svenska Arbetsgivarföreningen (SAF), the powerful and well-known peak organizations of labor and employers.

In sum, Volvo and BL confronted the challenges of the 1970s and 1980s with two very industrial relations systems. Having achieved a stable Fordist bargain with its unions, Volvo could respond to these challenges only by pursuing innovations that departed from the traditional Fordist model. By contrast, BL management could blame shop steward power for its problems and seek flexibility within the framework of a "belated attempt . . . to move towards a Fordist managerial system."[8]

Volvo

We can distinguish three stages in the workplace reform movement at Volvo—three reform waves, as it were. The famous Kalmar assem-

153. See also Steven Tolliday and Jonathan Zeitlin, "Shopfloor Bargaining, Contract Unionism and Job Control" in *Automibile Industry,* ed. Tolliday and Zetlin, pp. 99–120.

7. See Per Sundgren, "Införandet av MTM-metoden i svensk verkstadsindustri, 1950–56," *Arkiv för studier i arbetarrörelsens historia* (1978): 3–33.

8. Lewchuck, "Motor Vehicle Industry," p. 137.

bly plant, which came on line in 1974, can be said to represent the first stage. The design of the Kalmar plant was far less innovative than Volvo management and outside observers made it out to be at the time. The use of computer-guided platforms, auto carriers, instead of a conveyor belt made longer job cycles possible, but assembly work remained machine-paced. Also, there was little attempt at job enrichment, as distinct from job enlargement, at Kalmar.

The Kalmar plant and other Volvo plants experimented with stationary dock assembly on a small scale in the mid-1970s, but these experiments were abandoned as the world economic crisis hit Volvo. More generally, management retreated from reformist ambitions articulated earlier and tightened its control over the work process at Kalmar in the second half of the 1970s. Among other things, workers were no longer allowed to take an auto-carrier out of the main flow without prior authorization of a foreman.[9]

Three new plant facilities that began operations in 1980–81 represent the second stage of workplace reform. Two of these facilities were associated with a new car model, the 700 series, and were located on the premises of Volvo's main plant complex at Torslanda, just outside Gothenburg. In addition to a new body plant (known by the acronym TAÖ), Volvo constructed a small assembly facility (TUN) at Torslanda to handle the initial phase of production and to train operators for the main line. This facility now specializes in station wagons. Also, Volvo opened a new assembly plant for heavy trucks at Tuve in 1981. These three plant facilities were conceived to operate on teamwork principles that went beyond the Kalmar model by providing work teams with more collective responsibilities and decision-making autonomy.

The new assembly plant at Uddevalla, which began production in 1988, goes beyond the Kalmar model by linking the new conception of teamwork to dock assembly. At Uddevalla, teams of eight to ten workers are supposed to build an entire car. The third stage of workplace reform also involves the modernization of the main final assembly facility at Torslanda (TC), which until recently operated along completely conventional lines. It remains to be seen how far the

9. Christian Berggren, *Det nya bilarbetet: Konkurrensen mellan olika produktionskoncept inom svensk bilindustri* (Lund: Arkiv, 1990), pp. 179–90. For a propagandistic account of the first reform wave at Volvo, see Rolf Lindholm and Jan-Peder Norstedt, *The Volvo Report* (Stockholm: Swedish Employers' Confederation, 1975).

Torslanda modernization scheme will go in the direction of the Uddevalla model. Given the secrecy of the process and the uncertainty of the outcome, let us leave the TC modernization scheme aside. In so doing, we must keep in mind that the workplace reforms discussed here pertain only to a fraction of Volvo's total output of cars.[10] Nonetheless, the three stages of workplace reform involve a cumulative process of innovation, with a trajectory that adds up to a more or less definitive break with Fordism.

The ideas behind the Kalmar plant were almost completely a product of management thinking. In no way did the unions participate in decisions pertaining to plant design and technology.[11] They were consulted in matters of work environment and organization, but even here their role seems to have been quite limited and essentially passive. This reflected the attitudes of the unions as well as management. At the time that the Kalmar plant was designed, Metall and its Torslanda local had yet to begin to think seriously about work organization and job redesign.[12] Rather, the attention of organized labor focused on institutional arrangements for codetermination at the firm level. At least initially, the unions feared that teamwork and other innovations associated with Kalmar were conceived and would serve as an alternative to codetermination.

Organized labor played a more important role in the planning of the TUN, TAÖ and Tuve facilities, which came on line in 1980–81.[13] Two factors account for this activation of the unions. First, the codetermination law of 1976 required management to negotiate with unions over any issue that would affect the work force if the unions requested such negotations. Second, two of these new plant facilities

10. In 1986, the Torslanda plant produced some 164,000 cars, the Kalmar plant produced 31,000 cars, and the TUN plant produced 13,000 cars. Together these three Swedish final assembly plants accounted for slightly more than two-thirds of total output of the Volvo Car Corporation, with its plant facilities in Ghent, Belgium, accounting for most of the remainder. The Uddevalla plant is designed to produce 40,000 cars per year.

11. There exists no comprehensive treatment of the role of codermination and the unions' influence in the process of industrial innovation at Volvo. In addition to the (plant-specific) sources cited below, the following discussion draws on interviews with Ingemar Göransson at Metall's research department and with local union officials at Torslanda (carried out in May 1988).

12. Kajsa Ellegård, "Utvecklingsprocessen: Ny product, ny fabrik, ny arbetsorganisation" (Department of Human and Economic Geography, University of Gothenburg, 1986), pp. 21–22.

13. See ibid.; Christian Berggren, "Hur formas monteringsarbetet?" (Royal Institute of Technology, Stockholm, 1985); and Anna Holmgren, "Hur formas monteringsarbetet?" (Royal Institute of Technology, Stockholm, 1985).

were located at Torslanda, where there already existed a strong trade union organization and ongoing relations between management and unions.

The unions were not brought in until rather late in the game, however. At Volvo as well as BL, the conception and construction of new plant facilities typically involves three stages. First, a "red book" sets out the objectives and parameters of the project. Its approval by the board of directors leads to the appointment of a team that will draft a "blue book," providing basic specifications for the plant to be built, including the type of technology to be used and cost estimates. A project group is then appointed to plan in detail and to supervise the actual construction of the plant. The red book for each of the plants inaugurated in 1980–81 had already been approved before consultations with the unions began, and so prior management decisions constrained the scope of such consultations and negotations. Once the unions were brought in, they were represented on the project group as well as its various subcommittees. Specific decisions by the project group were also a subject of formal codetermination bargaining.

In accordance with a codetermination agreement previously reached at Torslanda, the unions were involved in the planning of the Uddevalla plant from the time the board of directors commissioned a red book.[14] The steering committee (*styrnigsgrupp*) established at this time to supervise the planning and development of the Uddevalla plant included two presidents of Volvo locals of Metall (and representatives of white-collar unions as well). In addition, three Torslanda union officials worked full-time on the Uddevalla project for nearly three years (1985–87), participating in the deliberations of the main working party (*projektledningsgruppen*) and its subgroups. Formalized codetermination negotiations were in this case avoided; according to union officials, consensual decision making by the working party and steering group rendered such negotiations superfluous.

The working party's initial proposals were inspired by the Kalmar model. To begin with, the union officials included in the working party did not object, but discussions among union officials, including

14. For a detailed account of the metalworkers' union's role in the Uddevalla project, see Kajsa Ellegård, "Metalls medverkan i projekteringen av Volvos Uddevallafabrik" (Department of Human and Economic Geography, University of Gothenburg, 1989). More generally on the planning of the Uddevalla plant, see Berggren, *Det nya bilarbetet*, pp. 223–49; and Kajsa Ellegård, Thomas Engström, and Lennart Nilsson, *Principer och realiteter vid förnyelse av industriellt arbete* (Stockholm: Arbetsmiljöfonden, 1989).

Metall's central research department, subsequently led to the articulation of a series of demands that ran counter to the working party's proposals. At this juncture, Volvo's top management prevailed on the steering committee to pursue alternative schemes, and academic consultants and industrial engineers committed to more far-reaching industrial innovation were given the opportunity to develop their ideas. Only slowly did management and union officials acknowledge the notion that machine-paced assembly might be abandoned altogether.

British Leyland

British Leyland became a subsidiary of the National Enterprise Board in 1975. The decision to save the company from bankruptcy by nationalizing it was based on the findings of an investigation headed by Sir Don Ryder. The so-called Ryder report argued that industrial relations reforms were an essential component of any attempt to turn the company around. Alongside other recommendations, it set out a detailed organizational scheme for union participation in corporate decision making to which BL management and union subsequently agreed. The Ryder participation scheme provided for the establishment of joint management councils at the divisional level as well as joint management committees at the plant level and at the departmental level within plants. At least formally, it provided labor with as much involvement in corporate decision making as did the Swedish codetermination law of 1976 and subsequent collective agreements on codetermination.[15]

From the beginning, participation at the divisional level seems to have been essentially a rhetorical exercise, staged by management for the benefit of the National Enterprise Board and the government. Whereas the unions quickly came to view the Cars Council as irrelevant, they valued the experience of participation at the plant level. One of the most meaningful participation exercises involved the planning and construction of the facilities that would produce the company's new small car, the Metro, at the Longbridge plant in Birmingham.

15. Sir Don Ryder et al., *British Leyland: The Next Decade* (London: HMSO, 1975). On the politics surrounding the nationalization of BL, see Stephen Wilks, *Industrial Policy and the Motor Industry* (Manchester: Manchester University Press, 1984), chap. 5. Willman and Winch, *Innovation and Management Control,* chap. 5, provide the most comprehensive discussion of the structure and experience of participation at BL.

The Longbridge joint management committee established a subcommittee to discuss the Metro project in 1976, and this subcommittee met frequently over the next three years. The red book for the Metro project had already been drafted and approved by the time participation got under way. Paul Willman and Graham Winch argue that the scope of participation was severely constrained by prior management decisions about technology and productivity targets, but management choices at the red book stage still left open a wide range of possible solutions in the realm of working practices and work organization. According to Derek Robinson, the senior shop steward at Longbridge, the Metro subcommittee allowed the unions to "look objectively at some of the changes that were required outside of being in a bargaining position." And, according to Jack Adams, Robinson's successor as senior shop steward at Longbridge, the Metro subcommittee was "the most successful participation exercise that we took part in. . . . [It was] less abstract than other exercises."[16]

Along with Willman and Winch, Harry Scarbrough stresses that the Longbridge shop stewards welcomed the company's commitment to a high level of automation on the Metro body line and were quite willing to discuss more flexible working practices, including teamwork. Perhaps the shop stewards thought that they had little choice in the matter. Be that as it may, the participation scheme fell apart in 1979 because management and unions failed to agree on the "macrodimensions" of corporate strategy, *not* because they failed to agree on workplace reforms.

The whole point of the Ryder report was that management and unions were to collaborate to improve industrial relations, productivity, and product quality and that government was to provide the funds necessary to modernize and expand BL's plant facilities. As far as the unions were concerned, participation was premised on expansion. The corporate strategy adopted by Michael Edwardes, the new chief executive appointed in 1977, ran directly counter to this line of thinking. Unwilling to assume coresponsibility for the massive workforce reductions Edwardes insisted on, the unions formally withdrew from the participation scheme in September 1979.[17]

16. Both quotations appear in Harry Scarbrough, "The Politics of Technological Change at British Leyland" in *Technological Change, Rationalization and Industrial Relations,* ed. Otto Jacobi et al. (London: Croom Helm, 1986), p. 103.

17. From 1978 to 1982, roughly Edwardes's tenure as chief executive, the BL cars divi-

Against the resistance of the TGWU and the shop stewards, but with the support of the AEUW and some other craft unions, Edwardes successfully imposed centralized, company-wide wage negotiations in 1978–79. Along with the breakdown of the participation scheme, this victory set the stage for a direct management assault on the power of shop stewards. In November 1979, the company dismissed the senior shop steward at Longbridge (Derek Robinson) on the grounds that he had publicly criticized its recovery plan. In the ensuing wage negotiations, management insisted that wage increases presupposed the removal of restrictive practices and the unions' acceptance of industrial engineering techniques. Furthermore, it asserted its right to implement new working practices unilaterally, thus rejecting the principle of mutuality.

Without the support of the AUEW, the shop stewards' resistance to this offensive failed, and management unilaterally eliminated a wide range of restrictive practices in the two or three years following the confrontation of 1980. At the same time, it withdrew facilities from shop stewards. From 1980 to 1982, management reduced the number of full-time stewards from eight to two at Longbridge and from nine to two at Cowley (Oxford), its other major plant complex, and reduced the time other shop stewards could spend on union activities.

As Willman puts it, the management offensive should be seen as "an attempt to mould trade-union organization to fit the radically restricted scope of collective bargaining." The new procedure agreement of 1982 reaffirmed the company's commitment to "constitutional unionism" and stated that consultative committees were to be established at the corporate level and at the plant level "so that the views of the Unions may be taken into account in the management decision making process."[18] In contrast to the Ryder participation scheme, this was clearly to be an exercise in consultation rather than joint decision making. In any case, the plan does not appear to have gotten off the ground. The Cowley shop stewards I interviewed in the spring of 1988 certainly did not think they were being consulted by manage-

sion cut its workforce from 86,000 to 48,000, according to Williams, Williams, and Haslam, *Breakdown of Austin Rover,* p. 23. In addition to the published sources, my treatment of industrial relations at BL draws on a series of extensive interviews with David Buckle (Oxford district official of the TGWU from 1966 to 1987) and interviews with former and present shop stewards at Cowley in the spring of 1988. For the management perspective, see Michael Edwardes, *Back from the Brink* (London: Collins, 1983).

18. Paul Willman, "Labour-Relations Strategy at BL Cars," in *Automobile Industry,* ed. Tolliday and Zeitlin, p. 314.

ment and maintained that they had played no role whatsoever in the planning and developing of plant facilities since 1980 (both the Longbridge and Cowley plants have been largely reequipped as four new car models have come on line since 1980).

BL's approach to industrial relations has become less confrontational since 1982. While at least paying lip service to the idea of consultation with unions, BL has engaged in a series of initiatives designed to improve communications between management and employees and to promote employee identification with the company.[19] Still, BL clearly qualifies as a case of industrial innovation without the participation of organized labor.

OUTCOMES OF INNOVATION: AUTOMATION, JOB REDESIGN, AND TEAMWORK

BL and Volvo have pursued two different strategies to achieve greater efficiency, quality, and flexibility in production. Whereas BL's strategy has centered on automation, Volvo's strategy has centered on job redesign. I hasten to add that Volvo's innovation strategy has also involved automation; the point is that, for Volvo, technological change forms part of a larger reform project.

The differences between the two strategies are revealed by their differential impact on different stages of production and different segments of the workforce. Because of the vast number of components involved, final assembly does not lend itself well to automation and remains, at BL and Volvo alike, highly labor intensive. Although BL has introduced far-reaching changes in engine machining, body assembly, and body painting, its final assembly lines are set up almost exactly as they were ten to fifteen years ago. By contrast, Volvo's innovation strategy has focused on final assembly.

To the extent that BL has engaged in job redesign, it is skilled, machine maintenance jobs that have been redesigned. At Volvo, by contrast, "job redesign" refers first and foremost to assembly work—body

19. See Dennis Smith, "The Japanese Example in South West Birmingham," *Industrial Relations Journal* 19 (1988): 41–50. See also Stephen Wood, "Some Observations on Industrial Relations in the British Car Industry, 1985–87," in *Die Zukunft der Arbeit in der Automobilindustrie*, ed. Ben Dankbaar, Ulrich Jürgens, and Thomas Malsch (Berlin: Edition Sigma, 1988), pp. 229–48.

assembly as well as final assembly. Teamwork figures in both innovation strategies, but the conception of teamwork is fundamentally different.

The Automation of Body Assembly at BL and Volvo

The Metro project pioneered a new era of automated body assembly at BL. Relative to existing body lines at BL, the Metro line involved the displacement of up to 80 percent of direct labor in some areas. With the Metro designed as an inexpensive, large-volume car, BL management was not particularly concerned with being able to accommodate product variations. Consequently, it chose to rely heavily on multiwelders rather than robots, making for a very rigid line. Unable to show that a high level of automation would be more economical, the authors of the red book on the Metro line appealed to its "unquantifiable advantages." Management saw automation as a means to improve the precision of welding, but also as a means to shed labor and to gain better control of the production process—that is, as a solution to its industrial relations problems.[20]

As a result of automation, the percentage of the Metro workforce engaged in skilled machine maintenance tasks was higher than on existing body assembly lines at BL. At the same time, however, the Metro line represented a further fragmentation and degradation of direct assembly work. In the words of Willman and Winch, "welding robots appear to have been used not to relieve workers of tedious jobs but in situations were reliability of a weld was particularly important, and where robot-welding does take place, apart from the ABF line, it results in workers having extremely short-cycle unskilled jobs feeding the machines."[21] Subsequent body assembly lines designed by BL have used more robots and a more flexible combination of workers and machines than the Metro line, but they do not seem to represent any significant improvement as far as the nature of assembly work is concerned.[22]

20. See Willman and Winch, *Innovation and Management Control,* pp. 50–61.

21. Ibid., p. 157. See also Arthur Francis, *New Technology at Work* (Oxford: Clarendon Press, 1986), pp. 97–102.

22. See David Marsden et al., *The Car Industry: Labour Relations and Industrial Adjustment* (London: Travistock Publications 1985), pp. 49–53; and Williams, Williams and, Haslam, *Breakdown of Austin Rover,* chap. 3.

Beginning operations in 1980, Volvo's new body plant at Torslanda, TAÖ, provides a useful point of comparison with the Metro line.[23] Like BL, Volvo rejected the "line-out system" of parallel body assembly previously introduced by SAAB. Volvo decided that parallel assembly was incompatible with its desire to gain flexibility by substituting robots for multiwelders; it would simply have been too expensive to duplicate robotized assembly. The decision to go with a single line severely restricted the extension of on-line job cycles, most of which are set at 90 seconds. In contrast to BL, however, Volvo invested heavily in the automation of machine feeding and largely eliminated this, the most repetitive type of on-line work. Furthermore, the situation of assembly workers at TAÖ is different in that they rotate among work stations and spend some part of their day doing off-line work. This is a characteristic feature of teamwork as practiced in numerous Volvo plants. What distinguishes TAÖ from the Metro line has more to do with work organization than with the nature of automation.

Job Redesign and Teamwork at Volvo

The redesign of assembly work at Volvo encompasses several distinct, though closely related, features.[24] The two most basic, least "advanced," features are job enlargement and job rotation. With job enlargement, assembly workers are asked to perform a larger number of assembly operations (doing more welds or adding more parts to each body). Whereas the average job cycle at BL's final assembly lines is about 2 minutes, job cycles at Volvo's Kalmar plant range between 20 and 25 minutes, and job cycles at the Uddevalla plant might turn out to be as long as four hours. The extension of job cycles at Uddevalla is linked to the elimination of machine pacing, but job enlargement need

23. The following observations are based on Kajsa Ellegård's description of TAÖ in "Lägesbeskrivning av verksamhet: TAÖ 1985," and "Utvärdering av verksamhet, production, and organisation i TAÖ 1985" (Department of Human and Economic Geography, University of Gothenburg, 1986).

24. In addition to the sources cited in notes 9, 12–14, and 23, this section draws on Pehr Gyllenhammar, *People at Work* (Reading, Mass.: Addison-Wesley, 1977); Stefan Augurén et al., *Volvo Kalmar Revisited* (Stockholm: Efficiency and Participation Development Council, 1985); Peter Auer, "Industrial Relations, Work Organization, and New Technology: The Volvo Case" (Wissenschaftszentrum, Berlin, 1985); and Christian Berggren, "'New Production Concepts' in Final Asssembly: the Swedish Experience," in *Transformation of Work?* ed. Wood, pp. 171–203.

not entail such far-reaching innovation. The design of the Kalmar plant made the extension of job cycles possible by having assembly operators work on moving auto-carriers. At the TUN facility, job cycles were extended simply by having fewer workers and a slower line.

Job rotation within work teams figured prominently in the Kalmar model. Though the twenty teams that make up the Kalmar line (each with fifteen to twenty members) are said to be collectively responsible for materials handling, quality control, and rectification work as well as for direct assembly, these indirect labor tasks are in fact assigned to individual team members, based on seniority and special qualification. There is plenty of opportunity for assembly workers to rotate tasks among themselves, but not much rotation across job classifications, at Kalmar.

Job enrichment emerged as a central feature of Volvo's efforts to redesign assembly work with the new plant facilities launched in 1980–81 (TAÖ, TUN, and Tuve). At these facilities, the range of tasks assigned to work teams has been extended to include administrative tasks previously carried out by foremen, routine machine maintenance, and housekeeping in the team area. The performance of certain tasks, such as machine maintenance, requires special qualification, but the official goal is that all team members should be able to perform all team tasks. Training programs are provided to workers who wish to gain the necessary qualifications. At the TAÖ plant, for example, there are now four grades of machine operators; each step in this ladder requires formal training as well as experience and is rewarded by extra pay.

Closely linked to the new emphasis on job enrichment, a new conception of the organizational status of work teams was developed at the plant facilities launched in 1980–81. As originally conceived, the teams at Kalmar had no shared tasks to perform or any decision-making authority. By contrast, the teams at the newer facilities allocate their collective responsibilities among their members (within the constraints of qualification requirements set by management). They are also responsible for scheduling vacation time and other personal leaves, and they participate in the hiring and training of new workers. Each team has a formally recognized *ombud,* who organizes team meetings, handles administrative matters, and represents the team vis-à-vis management. This position is supposed to rotate, on a weekly or monthly basis, among team members with the necessary qualifications.

If we consider job enrichment and teamwork as the third and fourth features of job redesign at Volvo, the fifth is the introduction of self-paced assembly work. It is on this score that the Uddevalla plant represents a radical departure from established principles of car manufacturing. As indicated above, the Uddevalla plant essentially combines the conception of teamwork introduced in the early 1980s with the ideal of dock assembly. Without abandoning machine pacing, previous workplace reforms at Volvo used buffers to introduce an element of self-pacing. By filling up their buffers, teams might create an extra break for themselves.

Teamwork at BL

The Metro project pioneered teamwork as well as highly technological automation at BL. Management conceived teamwork almost entirely as a means to achieve greater flexibility in the deployment of labor. Teams were to be organized around foremen and to include material handlers, quality controllers, and workers trained in routine machine maintenance as well as assembly operators. Within the teams, job rotation was to take place, and it would be possible for workers to advance from material handling to assembly to quality control to machine maintenance. As originally conceived, assembly workers were to do rectification work as well as direct assembly work, but management retreated from this unitary conception of assembly work when the unions demanded that assembly operators on the Metro line be assigned a higher pay grade than regular assembly operators.[25]

Initially, the workforce on the Metro line consisted mainly of newly recruited workers, which facilitated the implementation of teamwork. When management tried to introduce the same teamwork principles at Cowley in 1982–83, shop stewards and workers resisted; it was primarily in work areas where there were no shop stewards that management was able to realize its intentions. It is difficult to assess the extent to which BL actually practices teamwork today. According to Willman, teams do not exist in all BL plants,[26] and where they do exist, under the label "production zones," it may be in name only.

As we have seen, the introduction of teamwork at Volvo was closely linked to the redesign of assembly work. At BL, by contrast, manage-

25. Willman and Winch, *Innovation and Management Control,* pp. 100–102, 118–21.
26. Willman, "Labour-Relations Strategy," p. 317.

ment tried to superimpose teamwork on a largely unchanged system of production. Equally important, the two conceptions of teamwork differ with respect to the internal organization of teams and their relationship to management. As Willman points out, the teams at BL are hierarchical and center on the disciplinary function of the foreman.[27] The foreman is, of course, appointed by management; indeed, he or she is part of the management hierarchy. By contrast, work teams at Volvo have their own leaders and some degree of collective decision-making authority. Whereas the introduction of teamwork has been accompanied by a redefinition of the role of foreman at Volvo, one that emphasizes their coordinative rather than their disciplinary functions, it appears to have reinforced the traditional role of foremen and augmented their power at BL.

The introduction of quality circles, known as "zone circles," in 1986 can be seen as an attempt by BL management to enhance the meaning of teamwork.[28] The idea was that workers from a given production zone would, on a voluntary basis, join a circle, chaired by a foreman, to discuss production problems in their zone and to take on problem-solving projects. Some twenty-one zone circles were established at Longbridge in 1986, but less than 200 workers (out of a total workforce of about 10,000) participated in them. The shop stewards were, from the beginning, skeptical or hostile to zone circles and discouraged workers from participating. The shop stewards' opposition stiffened in the spring of 1987, and by May only one zone circle remained active.

The shop stewards resisted the introduction of zone circles in particular, and teamwork more generally, because they viewed these innovations as part of a management strategy to displace the unions as the representatives of the workforce. Shop stewards could not prevent management from designating certain work areas as production zones, but they could, and effectively did, dissuade workers from participating in zone circles. This experience illustrates the limits of the labor-exclusive approach to industrial innovation adopted by BL. Although management was able to eliminate many working practices that interfered with efficiency and flexibility, the way it accomplished this precluded the union cooperation required to achieve effective teamwork.

27. Ibid., p. 316.
28. See Smith, "Japanese Example."

ELEMENTS OF AN EXPLANATION

Responding to market pressures, both Volvo and BL have pursued innovations designed to improve product quality as well as production efficiency and flexibility. What distinguishes our two cases is that Volvo has also pursued work humanization alongside these market-driven corporate goals, and BL has not. It is tempting to attribute this distinctive feature to the participation of organized labor in the process of innovation at Volvo. I here spell out several union-centered explanatory arguments and then develop a more management-centered approach to the contrast between our two cases. Without denying that the unions have influenced the outcomes of innovation at Volvo, I argue that union demands alone cannot explain why Volvo management opted for an innovation strategy so markedly different from that of BL.

Union-Centered Explanations

In the planning of Volvo's Uddevalla plant, Metall advanced four basic demands pertaining to production methods: first, assembly should be done on stationary objects; second, job cycles should be at least 20 minutes; third, there should be no machine pacing; and, fourth, all workers should perform indirect labor tasks as well as direct assembly work. Confronted with these demands, management abandoned its initial, Kalmar-inspired plan for Uddevalla. The plan it ultimately adopted pretty much satisfied the unions' four demands.

The Uddevalla project might thus be invoked to support the notion that the direct influence exercized by organized labor through codetermination accounts for the distinctive orientation of Volvo's innovation strategy. As indicated above, however, the unions played a much less active role in the conception of earlier workplace reforms; yet the Uddevalla plant clearly represents an extension of these reforms. In the planning of the Uddevalla plant, the unions essentially demanded that the company be more systematic and ambitious in its approach to workplace reform; the precepts behind their demands were implicit in previous experiments initiated by management. It must also be noted that the Uddevalla project brought out latent divisions between innovators and traditionalists within Volvo management. The unions certainly did not impose their vision for Uddevalla on management;

rather, management was split, and union demands tipped the balance in favor of the innovators.

We have seen that an elaborate system of union participation in management decision making existed at BL from 1976 to 1979, but in this case participation did not yield any sustained or far-reaching work humanization effort. If Volvo's approach to workplace reform is to be attributed to union participation in the process of innovation, why did union participation not have similar consequences in the case of BL? At this point, it seems useful to distinguish between union-centered arguments couched in terms of union *power* and union-centered arguments couched in terms of union *strategy.*

Arguably, the Ryder participation scheme did not empower labor to the same degree as the Swedish codetermination act of 1976. Apart from the fact that it was not mandated by law, two features that distinguish the BL participation scheme from the Swedish system of codetermination might be invoked to support this argument. First, the BL scheme relied exclusively on representation by shop stewards—that is, company employees—and did not involve union officials. Second, the BL scheme rested on the separation of participation and collective bargaining. According to Willman and Winch, "areas traditionally subject to collective bargaining were not typically the concern of Joint Management Committees, and the unions could not respond to management initiatives by seeking to bargain within the scheme."[29]

The limits of Swedish codetermination must be emphasized in this context, however. The codetermination act of 1976 requires management to negotiate with the unions over any issues that affect the workforce, but it does not require management to reach agreement with the unions. On the other hand, the Ryder scheme did provide the BL unions with extentive participation rights. The contrast between out two cases would seem to support the thesis, advanced by Evelyne Huber Stephens and John Stephens, that formal participation arrangements are of secondary importance to the actual degree of union influence in corporate decision making, the crucial determinant being

29. Willman and Winch, *Innovation and Management Control,* p. 90. In both these respects, the BL participation scheme was more akin to German than to Swedish codetermination. It should also be noted that the BL scheme, in contrast to both Swedish and German codetermination, did not include board representation.

whether unions mobilize to take advantage of the opportunities any participation scheme provides.[30]

One might argue that the unitary structure of the Swedish labor movement enabled the Volvo unions to use participation rights more effectively than did the BL unions. As indicated above, the ability of BL management to impose its solutions to the problem of competitiveness rested on divisions among the unions. Specifically, BL management was able to play the interests of skilled workers (AEUW) off against those of unskilled workers (TGWU).[31] Presumably, this would not have been possible at Volvo, but then Volvo management never perceived the need for a "right-to-manage" offensive.

It is perhaps more useful to think of the contrast between our two cases in terms of different union strategies. From this perspective, two questions arise. First, under what circumstances do unions want to participate in industrial innovation? And, second, what goals do they pursue through participation?

To repeat, the BL participation exercise broke down over the issue of plant closures and layoffs. Arguably, management never excluded the BL unions from participation in the process of industrial innovation; rather, the unions chose not to participate because they could not (or would not) share responsibility for the workforce reductions.[32] In other words, the BL participation exercise might have evolved into something akin to the Volvo experience had it not been for BL's profitability crisis in the second half of the 1970s. This notion suggests that the sales performance of the two firms explains their divergent innovation strategies. Though Volvo's car division struggled in the 1970s, even its darkest hour was bright by comparison to BL, and profits soared in the first half of the 1980s. Volvo's commercial success should be seen a necessary but not sufficient condition for the process

30. Evelyn Huber Stephens and John Stephens, "The Labor Movement, Political Power, and Workers' Participation in Western Europe," *Political Power and Social Theory* 3 (1982): 215–49.

31. The craft unions at BL were willing to go along with centralized wage bargaining because they saw it as a means to establish parity among workers of the same skill level across plants and thus eliminate a source of internal disunity. At the same time, management made it quite clear to the craft unions that it shared their concern with the compression of wage differentials between skilled and unskilled workers that had occurred in 1970s.

32. Compare Harry Katz's argument that worker/union cooperation in the introduction of more flexible working practices presupposes the promise of enhanced employment security; Katz, *Shifting Gears: Changing Labor Relations in the U.S. Automobile Industry* (Cambridge: MIT Press, 1985).

and outcomes of innovation described above. A broader comparative perspective immediately brings out the limits of this explanation, for other commercially successful car makers have pursued very different innovation strategies.

Turning to the question of the goals unions pursue when they do participate in industrial innovation, it should be stressed that the unions at BL never developed a coherent set of demands pertaining to the reorganization of production. To the extent that they worried about BL's competitive problems, their solution was couched entirely in terms of the need to expand capacity in order to achieve economies of scale.[33] By contrast, Metall and its Volvo locals had by the mid-1980s developed a strategic approach to the reorganization of production, linking job redesign to competitiveness, as well as a great deal of technical competence in this field.[34]

The BL unions' lack of strategy or vision might be invoked to explain their lack of influence in the process of industrial innovation. This line of argument is suggestive, but the obvious question arises, why do unions develop different strategic orientations or capacities? I do not attempt an adequate answer to this question here. Let me simply make two points. To begin with, the strategies unions pursue are related to their organizational structures.[35] At BL, the craft unions strenuously resisted the assignment of machine maintenance tasks to assembly workers and any other innovations that might dilute the distinction between craftsmen and assembly operators. Having used the craft unions to defeat the TGWU and the shop stewards, management could not very well turn around and ask the latter to support it against the craft unions. The situation at Volvo is completely different, for here the "winners" and "losers" in the reallocation of manual labor tasks belong to the same union. The rhetoric of Metall displaces this internal conflict by arguing that job enrichment benefits manual workers at the expense of foremen and white-collar employees, but in pushing for job enrichment the union can be said to have pursued the interests of its unskilled members at the expense of its skilled members.

33. See TGWU, *British Leyland: The Next Decade* (1980).

34. See *Rewarding Work* (Stockholm: Swedish Work Environment Fund, 1987) for the metalworkers' general approach to job redesign. See also Svenska Metallindustriarbetarförbundet, *Solidarisk arbetspolitik för det goda arbetet* (report to the 1989 Congress).

35. See Harry Katz and Charles Sabel, "Industrial Relations and Industrial Adjustment in the Car Industry," *Industrial Relations Journal* 24 (1985): 295–314.

The second point is that union strategies can to some extent be treated as derivative of management strategies. To repeat, union officials at Volvo did not have a clear conception of what kind of workplace reforms they wanted in the 1970s; they developed such a conception in response to various management initiatives.

Management-Centered Explanations

The contrast between our two cases hinges on choices made by management, and union demands do not seem to provide an adequate explanation as to why Volvo managers opted for a different innovation strategy than their BL counterparts. What other variables must be considered to explain divergent management strategies? Differences in corporate and societal culture are undoubtedly significant, but they are difficult to pin down. Leaving aside such considerations, I suggest that labor market conditions, shaped by national government and union policies, constitute a critical variable in explaining the divergent choices of Volvo and BL management. My argument is that high rates of absenteeism and labor turnover have impinged on Volvo's efforts to improve efficiency, flexibility, and product quality. For BL, problems of absenteeism and turnover have been much less pronounced.[36]

Measured as a percentage of available work hours, the rate of absenteeism among blue-collar workers at Torslanda, Volvo's main plant complex, increased markedly, and quite steadily, in the course of the 1970s. From 1972 to 1980, absenteeism due to illness increased from 13.4 to 17.3 percent, and total absenteeism, including personal and educational leaves as well as absenteeism due to illness, increased from 22.3 to 29.1 percent. In 1980–87, the figure for absenteeism due to illness hovered around 15–16 percent and, in 1988, management estimated total absenteeism at Torslanda to be 27 percent.[37] The figures for BL are of an entirely different order. In 1987–89, the rate of absenteeism due to illness averaged 5.6 percent at Cowley and 4.6

36. This line of argument is suggested by Walter Korpi, *The Working Class in Welfare Capitalism* (London: Routledge & Kegan Paul, 1978), p. 140; and Eric Einhorn and John Logue, *Democracy on the Shop Floor?* (Kent, Ohio: Kent Popular Press, 1982), pp. 12–13.

37. Data for the 1970s from Enström and Levinson, *Industrial Relations*, p. 36. The 15–16 percent figure comes from Berggren, *Det nya bilarbetet*, p. 291; and the later 1980s estimate was obtained on a plant visit in May 1988.

per cent at Longbridge. The figures for total absenteeism were 7.9 percent at Cowley and 6.7 percent at Longbridge.[38]

Longitudinal studies show that the rate of absenteeism tends to decline as the rate of unemployment rises, and the sharp contrast between Sweden and Britain with respect to rates of unemployment in the period since the mid-1970s explains some of the discrepancy between rates of absenteeism at Volvo and BL. But there are clearly institutional factors at work here as well.[39] Volvo's higher rate of absenteeism due to illness reflects the fact that the Swedish welfare state provides virtually full sick pay even for one-day illnesses. Equally important, legislative provisions must be invoked to explain the prominence of other forms of absenteeism in the Swedish case. Under Swedish law, immigrants are entitled to paid leaves for language instruction, and parents are entitled not only to lengthy parental leaves but also to personal leaves if their children are ill. The extension of such entitlements would appear to account for most of the increase of the rate of absenteeism in the 1970s. It should also be noted in this context that the codetermination agreement signed by LO and SAF in 1982 extended the right of workers to take leaves for purposes of further education and training.

Turning now to labor turnover, Table 8–1 provides annual rates of labor turnover for all of Volvo's Swedish operations, for its Torslanda facilities, and for its final assembly plant at Torslanda since 1973. BL does not do as good a job keeping statistics or is less willing to share them, but I have been able to obtain figures for the final assembly plant at Cowley for 1984–88. As Table 8–2 shows, the rate of labor turnover was in this period, on average, nearly twice as high at Volvo's final assembly plant at Torslanda.[40]

The reasons Volvo has had a much a higher rate of labor turnover seem quite straightforward, having to do with the aggregate demand

38. Calculated on the basis of data provided by the personnel department of the Rover Group. These data may include white-collar personnel, but since blue-collar workers account for more than 80 percent of total personnel at both Cowley and Longbridge this would not significantly affect the discrepancy relative to Volvo–Torslanda. The figures presented here tally with aggregate data for The Swedish and British manufacturing industries. According to *The Economist,* March 3, 1990 ("Survey of Sweden," p. 16), the average Swedish industrial worker was absent from work due to illness 29 days in 1988, as compared to 11 days for the average British industrial worker.

39. According to Blackler and Brown, *Job Redesign,* pp. 61–62, the rate of absenteeism at Volvo's Lundby truck plant was twice as high as that of a comparable BL truck plant in west London in 1972–73 (14.9 and 7.0 percent, respectively).

40. The differential was even greater in the two truck assembly plants studied by Blackler and Brown in the earlier 1970s. For 1970–72, the annual rate of net turnover of manual

Table 8–1 Net turnover of manual labor at Volvo, 1973–88

	Sweden(%)	Torslanda(%)	Torslanda final assembly(%)
1973	20.0	28.1	—
1974	18.0	25.0	—
1975	15.7	19.5	23.8
1976	12.6	15.9	20.5
1977	8.2	10.6	13.5
1978	7.2	10.5	14.0
1979	11.7	17.7	23.2
1980	13.5	20.6	24.9
1981	9.6	15.0	18.4
1982	6.1	11.3	12.0
1983	5.4	8.6	13.2
1984	6.4	10.7	16.3
1985	7.9	12.2	16.1
1986	8.8	14.5	19.7
1987	9.9	15.6	21.6
1988	—	—	25.2
1989	—	—	27.3

Sources: The first and second columns are based on data provided directly by Volvo; the third column on Christian Berggren, *Det nya bilarbetet* (Lund: Arkiv, 1990), p. 292.

Note: The first and second columns include noncar operations. All three columns exclude internal transfers.

for labor and wage differentials. With respect to demand, it is well known that Sweden is one of the few advanced capitalist countries that did not allow the economic crisis of 1974–83 to result in mass unemployment. The rate of unemployment in Sweden crept up to a postwar peak of 3.5 percent in 1982 and has since dropped well below 2 percent. By contrast, the rate of unemployment in Britain had already reached 6 percent by the time Thatcher came to power in 1979, and it rose as high as 13 percent in the early 1980s. The contrast between Sweden's and Britain's employment performance can be explained in terms of the greater power of Swedish labor at the societal level, as measured by workforce unionization and electoral mobilization, but also, less tangibly, by social democratic control of the political agenda.[41]

labor average 26.5 percent at Volvo–Lundby and 9.6 percent at BL–AEC (west London); ibid., p. 62.

41. See Stephen McBride, "The Comparative Politics of Unemployment: Swedish and British Responses to Economic Crisis," *Comparative Politics* 20 (1988): 303–24; and Jonas Pontusson, *Swedish Social Democracy and British Labour* (Occasional Paper no. 19, Western Societies Program, Cornell University, 1988).

Table 8–2 Net turnover of manual labor at Volvo and British Leyland final assembly plants, 1984–88

	Volvo–Torslanda(%)	BL–Cowley(%)
1984	16.3	12.6
1985	16.1	9.1
1986	19.7	9.3
1987	21.6	12.0
1988	25.2	20.1
average	19.8	12.6

Sources: Volvo data from Christian Berggren, *Det nya bilarbetet* (Lund: Arkiv, 1990), p. 292; BL data provided directly by BL.

Full employment implies a labor recruitment problem for Volvo because the solidaristic wage policy pursued by the LO unions since the 1950s has constrained Volvo's ability to attract and retain assembly workers by offering higher wages than other employers. Traditional Fordist mass producers need this kind of wage flexibility because the jobs they offer are especially boring, stressful, and physically straining. In particular, Volvo and other Swedish firms complain that solidaristic wage policy has undermined differentials between industrial and public-sector jobs. This problem took on serious proportions as the government increasingly relied on public-sector expansion as a means to maintain full employment from the mid-1970s onward.[42]

In a sense, work humanization can be seen as a functional equivalent of wage drift. Because its wages have been determined entirely through company-level bargaining, BL has not faced the same constraints as Volvo with regard to labor recruitment, and hence it has not needed to engage in work humanization. The longitudinal data presented in Table 8–1 provides further support for this interpretation. I argued earlier that we can distinguish three waves of workplace reform at Volvo: one in the early 1970s (when the Kalmar plant was conceived), a second in 1979–81 (TUN, TAO, Tuve), and a third in the mid-1980s (Uddevalla). Table 8–1 shows that these reform waves broadly coincide with cyclical increases in the rate of labor turnover.

To the extent that the rate of absenteeism is unpredictable, Volvo is forced to employ more workers than it strictly needs. Thus absenteeism may lead to higher labor costs, and higher administrative costs as

42. See Fritz Scharpf, "Economic and Institutional Constraints of Full-Employment Strategies," in *Order and Conflict in Contemporary Capitalism*, ed. John Goldthrope (Oxford: Clarendon Press, 1984), pp. 257–90.

well, but it is not obvious why it should adversely affect efficiency, quality, or flexibility. Arguably, high rates of labor turnover present more serious problems in this regard. Leaving recruitment and training costs aside, there is some evidence to suggest that a kind of collective knowledge is built up in a plant over time, and that this knowledge contributes significantly to productivity and flexibility. It also seems plausible, and Volvo management certainly believes, that a more stable and older workforce is more likely to identify with the company and to take pride in the quality of its product. As developed in the 1980s, job redesign and teamwork are meant to lengthen the tenure of assembly workers not only by providing them more meaningful work and a better working environment but also by providing them with a career ladder of sorts (emphasizing continuous training, this strategy actually increases the rate of absenteeism).

One might go further to argue that Volvo has not only had to contend with higher rates of turnover than BL, but that it has also been more sensitive to the problem of labor turnover because of the kind of product it sells. Quality and product customization are more important to Volvo's ability to compete than to BL's because Volvo competes at the upper end of the market, and these would appear to be the aspects of competitiveness that are most directly affected by labor turnover. Volvo's up-market strategy makes its reliance on a skilled, well-paid work force both possible and necessary; possible by virtue of the high value added per car, and necessary by virtue of the importance of quality and customization.[43]

It should be noted that Volvo's up-market product strategy is of relatively recent origin. Volvo certainly was not a "craft producer" of customized cars when the Kalmar plant was conceived in the early 1970s; on the contrary, its product and production strategies typified the Fordist model. Volvo began to customize in response to the collapse of world demand in the mid-1970s, and this new product strategy did not become firmly established until the launch of the new 700 series in 1980. As Volvo's product strategy has evolved alongside its efforts to reorganize production, it is difficult to establish a simple causal relationship between these two aspects of corporate strategy.[44] The causal

43. Alan Altschuler et al., *The Future of the Automobile* (Cambridge: MIT Press, 1984), pp. 217–18.

44. It should also be noted that Streeck's notion of a high-volume specialist producer (elaborated in Streeck, "Industrial Relations and Industrial Change") captures Volvo's new

link between labor turnover and Volvo's emphasis on work humanization seems more straightforward.

The up-market product strategy pursued by Volvo since the mid-1970s is closely related to its dependence on exports, and hence its exposure to international competition—in particular, competition from the Japanese at the lower end of the market. Volvo was already more export oriented than BL in 1970, and it has become increasingly export oriented while BL has become less so since 1970. In part, this divergence of corporate strategies is attributable to government policy. Whereas successive devaluations by Swedish governments in 1977–82 promoted Volvo's export orientation, the exchange rate policies pursued by the Thatcher governments of the 1980s effectively confined BL to the home market. Here again, macropolitics created a very different structure of constraints and opportunities for corporate management.

THE MICRO AND MACRO POLITICS OF JOB REDESIGN

In sum, my comparative analysis of industrial innovation at Volvo and BL brings out the importance of management choices. To restate the argument most boldly, Volvo management included organized labor in the process of industrial innovation and BL excluded it because they had already opted for different innovation strategies.

Arndt Sorge and Wolfgang Streeck criticize the common tendency to treat management strategy and technical change as a *deus ex machina*, entirely exogenous to the industrial relations system.[45] Although I agree with the thrust of their argument, I would formulate it somewhat differently, for my point is that, to explain management strategies in terms of the relationship between labor and capital, we must conceive this relationship more broadly than the notion of "industrial relations" permits. Our explanation of Volvo's distinctive approach to the reorganization of production must begin with the

profile much better than the notion of a craft producer. Though BL produces more cars than Volvo, it also produces more models, and even its bets-selling model in 1984, the Metro, fell far short of the production volume Volvo had achieved for its 200 series (145,000 car per year, as compared to 206,000).

45. Sorge and Streeck, "Industrial Relations and Technical Change"; Streeck, "Industrial Relations and Industrial Change."

constraints and opportunities implied by three core features of the political economy of class compromise in Sweden: full employment, compressed (intersectoral) wage differentials, and export dependence. While these constraints and opportunities made management sensitive to union demands for work humanization, the inclusion of labor in the process of innovation encouraged the unions to articulate such demands.

To repeat, I do not wish to deny that the unions have influenced Volvo's innovation strategy; the point is rather that the direct influence exercized by the unions through codetermination has been predicated on a certain congruence of management and union interests. To the extent that full employment, compressed wage differentials, and exports dependence are a result of policies introduced or supported by the labor movement, we might conclude that labor's direct influence over management is secondary to—and perhaps derivative from—its influence over the external environment of business. It is noteworthy that Volvo's assembly plant in Ghent, Belgium, remains an entirely conventional plant, more like a BL plant than like Uddevalla or even Kalmar. From the perspective adopted here, this should come as no surprise: in a slack labor market, and in the absence of wage solidarity, Volvo has been able to improve efficiency and enhance flexibility without engaging in work humanization.

It should also be noted that the Swedish system of wage bargaining has undergone major changes in 1980s.[46] Volvo and other export-oriented engineering firms have taken the lead in a sustained employers' campaign to decouple public- and private-sector wage bargaining and to decentralize wage bargaining within the private sector. The logic of my analysis holds that these developments threaten the workplace reform movement in Sweden to the extent that they enable profitable firms such as Volvo to reduce labor turnover by means of above-average wage increases. But it may be that full employment outweighs solidaristic wage policy as a determinant of labor turnover. My data do not allow us to assess the relative importance of these variables. Also, we should not assume that firms will always opt to deal with turnover problems by increasing wages if this option is available. This option is preferable in that management retains more complete

46. See Scott Lash, "The End of Neocorporatism?" *British Journal of Industrial Relations* 23 (1985): 215–39; Nils Elvander, *Den svenska modellen* (Stockholm: Publica, 1988); and Peter Swenson, Chapter 1 this volume.

control of the work process, but beyond a certain point considerations of cost competitiveness may lead management to pursue work humanization instead.

Perhaps the widespread pursuit of workplace innovation in the world car industry can be explained by corporate efforts to reduce relative labor costs. As I indicated at the outset, however, I believe that the basic impetus behind industrial innovation derives from changes in the character of demand and the terms of competition in product markets. To repeat, my argument about labor turnover is meant to explain why firms pursue different kinds of innovation in response to similar product market pressures.

One might invoke variations among firms within a single country to argue that the micropolitics of industrial innovation are more important than my analysis suggests.[47] Although the case of BL is certainly not representative of the entire British auto industry, and the Volvo experience differs from that of SAAB in important respects, I do think that there are certain broad national patterns at work here.[48] Also, labor market conditions vary within as well as across national boundaries and may help explain some of the variations in processes and outcomes of industrial innovation which we can observe among firms within a single country. In the end, my defense against the argument that each firm is different comes down to this: the micropolitics of industrial innovation surely matter, but we cannot know how much they matter—or when and in what respects they matter—unless we specify the broader political-economic parameters within which unions and management interact over issues of new technology and work organization.

47. See, for example, Richard Locke's discussion of the different experiences of Fiat and Alfa Romeo in Chapter 7 of this volume.

48. See Marsden et al., *Car Industry;* and Berggren, *Dat nya bilarbetet.*

Conclusion: Current Trends in Trade Union Politics

Miriam Golden

The essays collected in this volume offer an abundance of materials on contemporary trade unionism and labor politics. Covering fourteen unions distributed across eight Western European and North American countries, written by eight young scholars working largely independently of one another, they address a range of empirical issues and analytical concerns. At first glance, they may even appear somewhat disparate. This apparent fragmentation, however, accurately captures the increasingly fragmented state of organized labor in contemporary advanced capitalism. Indeed, the very disparity of the essays collected here offers a window onto the various ways labor movements have become divided against themselves under the economic pressures of recent decades. For the main effect on labor movements of current international economic changes has been to breed new kinds of intraclass conflicts, conflicts that divide workers and hence unions. It is with the nature and extent of these conflicts that this concluding essay is concerned.

The case studies in this volume allow two substantive observations. First, whereas investigations into the effects of the economic crisis on organized labor in Western Europe that were carried out during the

For helpful comments on an earlier version of this essay, I thank Jeffry Frieden, Geoffrey Garrett, Michael Goldfield, Peter Lange, Ruth Milkman, George Tsebelis, Michael Wallerstein, and especially Jonas Pontusson.

1970s, the first decade of recent international economic disruption, found surprisingly little impact on labor politics, the contributions included here demonstrate that union politics subsequently underwent substantial transformations. By the 1980s and 1990s, trade unions were responding to new external pressures in genuinely new ways. Sheer novelty did not, of course, guarantee success. But, as Jonas Pontusson notes in his introductory essay, it did raise the question of whether trade unionism in advanced capitalism would ever be the same again.

Second, our case studies suggest something about the nature of the changes affecting organized labor. If these studies are correct, the general pattern of intraclass conflict has shifted. In the 1960s and 1970s, according to much available literature, the politics of organized labor in the advanced capitalist countries were typically characterized by conflicts between national and local union offices, leaders and led, union elites and the rank and file. Such conflicts turned on the extent of the centralization of authority within organized labor. The more recent period analyzed by our contributors is painted instead as one characterized by increasing vertical lines of division within labor, divisions pitting worker against worker, plant against plant, union against union, and confederation against confederation. These are what we may call interorganizational conflicts, which turn on the degree of the concentration (or fragmentation) of organized labor. The essays in this book suggest that in the 1980s and 1990s labor movements are experiencing a process of deconcentration, as a series of centrifugal pressures intensify rivalries among wage earners.

The substantive issues dividing workers and propelling these conflicts are delineated in the Introduction. International economic interdependence and capital mobility increased markedly as of the 1980s. Firms responded to new competitive pressures with changes in structures of production as well as by elaborating new political agendas and coalitions. As the scope and nature of the markets in which they interacted changed, so did the interests and strategies of entrepreneurs and enterprises.

For a variety of reasons, these changes have tended to favor capital at the expense of labor. First, from the point of view of employees and their unions, capital has become increasingly unpredictable in its behavior. New international alliances and competition have meant sudden, unexpected domestic changes in production. Typically unable to anticipate such changes, labor has tended to be unprepared in its responses and thereby thrust onto the defensive. Second, although capital has become more mobile and less attached to specific locations and assets, labor typically has not. With more ties to specific skills and locations, labor cannot move as easily as capital, and this too has placed labor at a disadvantage. It may not matter much to a large, diversified multinational if it invests in Scottish woolens or Belgian glass, but it matters considerably to Scottish workers if textile factories remain in Scotland, relocate elsewhere, or cease operations entirely. For Scottish woolen workers cannot the next day become Belgian glassworkers. Capital can flee demands from labor which it considers too costly, but labor may have few other employment options. Finally, new investment opportunities for capital have changed aggregate employment opportunities for workers. Continuing trends long in evidence, vast transformations of occupational structures have occurred in the advanced capitalist countries. In most of them, core manufacturing industries now provide relatively few jobs. These are the industries in which the organization of labor has historically been strongest, and their decline has entailed a concomitant (even if only relative) decline of the strongest and oldest industrial unions. At the same time, in most of the Western European countries (although not in the United States) job creation has ceased altogether, while at the same time relatively high unemployment levels have obtained for more than a decade. High unemployment too has tended to diminish labor's bargaining power vis-à-vis capital.

Although the causes are more complex than pointing only to increases in the costs of raw materials would suggest, the international economic transformations that we can, for convenience, date from the first and then the second oil shocks of 1973–74 and 1979 have induced new lines of cleavage in the political orientations and interests of organized labor as much as among capitalists. For instance, political divergences among internationally oriented and domestic capitalists have become visible, even in those countries where such conflicts were previously largely absent; likewise, they have become more intense in those smaller export-oriented economies where such lines of cleavage were historically central. The essays collected here demonstrate that among workers, attention has shifted from conflicts between members and officials to conflicts among groups of wage earners and their organizational representatives.

Below I describe the ways these conflicts are portrayed in the essays collected here. But first a caveat is in order. The essays are more attentive to conflicts among unions and groups within unions than to conflicts between leaders and led. The latter theme dominated work on the politics of organized labor for much of the twentieth century. Although such a shift may reflect changes in the real world, this volume cannot itself demonstrate that such a shift has indeed been genuine rather than simply a change in intellectual fashion and interest. If work on organized labor is today more concerned with interplant competition than with grass roots rebellion, this may not be because the incidence of the latter has fallen but rather because the former has become, for whatever reasons, more interesting to analysts.

Still, it seems likely that the changes in concerns demonstrated by our contributors are products of genuine changes in the political economy of advanced capitalism and not just trends in intellectual fashion. The new international economic conditions I briefly noted a moment ago have fragmented domestic markets and producer groups sectorally and regionally. This clearly has an impact on domestic political cleavages. Although it would surely be an exaggeration to argue that class-based cleavages have been wholly displaced by new sectoral and regional divisions that pit domestic producer groups against internationally oriented coalitions of labor and capital, it is undeniable that competitive pressures today generate new kinds of cleavages within organized producer groups. Eventually it may be possible to derive policy orientations among different groups within organized labor from their position in the international economy, as it is proving possible to do for capital.[1] Our aspirations for this volume are more modest, however. We examine the new conflicts and cleavages within labor movements empirically and seek to distill some general patterns.

The studies collected here are distinctive in the degree to which they articulate a shift in the fault lines of the internal politics of organized labor. The research is marked by systematic attention to the internal politics of organized labor and to the nature and extent of intraclass conflict. It thus represents a third wave of labor studies undertaken by political sociologists and political scientists in the twentieth century. Under the title of political sociology, the first focused on issues of union bureaucracy and democracy. The second wave of attention di-

1. See Jeffry Frieden, "Invested Interests: The Politics of Economic Policies in a World of Global Finance," *International Organization* 45 (Autumn 1991): 425–51.

rected at trade unionism was undertaken within the confines of political economy and focused on the relationships between trade unions, governments, and the economy. Both treated organized labor as a unitary (or aggregate) actor, one that interacted either with a rank and file or with external economic and political elites. Here, we move beyond these earlier conceptualizations to consider trade union movements as complex organizations rather than unitary or aggregate actors. Largely directed at the substantive concerns of political economy, and in that sense consciously within the second of these two earlier approaches to labor, our essays are nonetheless distinctive in their concern with interactions among unions and union groups.

Such a perspective resonates with the literature on preference aggregation. The major weakness of the unitary actor fiction—whether used to analyze trade unions or national parliaments—is that decision making in groups or organizations generates outcomes that fail to correspond to the sum of the preferences of the individuals constituting the collectivity.[2] To treat trade unions as unitary or aggregate actors—essentially as big individuals—whose behavior is a function of interactions with the external political and economic environment is to ignore the internal sources of decision making and behavior. Such internal sources of decision making include interactions among unions and among groups within unions, all of whom compete for resources and influence within the labor movement. With its sensitivity to the importance of rules governing institutional interactions, the literature on preference aggregation suggests by extension that the rules that govern interactions within labor movements bear on the decisions that emerge. It points to the importance of the internal politics of organized labor in accounting for the policies labor adopts.

In union movements, organizational demarcations are highly nation-specific. And although it is true that the most common organizational form in trade unions in the advanced capitalist countries is the industrial (as opposed to the craft or the general) union, the number and nature of industrial unions vary widely, as do the various formal and informal rules regulating relations within and among unions. So too the number of peak organizations with which unions affiliate differs, with countries exhibiting anywhere from one to as many as half a

2. Kenneth J. Arrow, *Social Choice and Individual Values*, 2d ed. (New Haven: Yale University Press, 1963).

dozen different national confederations. Although the economic pressures to which Western European and North American unions have been subjected in recent decades are relatively similar, national differences in the preexisting organization of labor affect the responses unions muster, as Pontusson explains. Below I use evidence provided by our case studies to explore this point in greater detail.

The contributors to this book engage in what Eckstein once called *heuristic case analysis,* that is, case studies "deliberately used to stimulate the imagination toward discerning important general problems and possible theoretical solutions."[3] These case studies identify intraclass conflict as a major empirical issue in the field of political economy; moreover, they draw attention to how organizational and institutional parameters affect such conflict. Later in this chapter I use the information provided in these studies to assess and classify forms of intraclass conflict affecting contemporary organized labor. Doing so allows me to draw some provisional conclusions about general trends across Western European and North American countries. I also place these findings in intellectual context by describing how the work undertaken by our contributors contrasts with earlier studies of labor politics. To set the stage for that comparison, I begin with a review of the earlier literature.

POLITICAL SCIENCE AND THE STUDY OF UNION POLITICS

Because I want to place the essays in intellectual context, the literature I review here is somewhat narrow. I examine the sources to which I believe contemporary political scientists working on labor have most likely been exposed and to which they are most indebted. I thus exclude some important areas of work on trade unions, most notably that conducted by specialists in industrial relations. Political scientists have turned primarily to sociology and to political economy in their study of organized labor; I discuss what I believe they have taken from these two perspectives. Moreover, since my main concern here is to assess the intellectual background of work recently undertaken by

3. Harry Eckstein, "Case Study and Theory in Political Science," in *Strategies of Inquiry,* vol. 7 of *Handbook of Political Science,* ed. Fred I. Greenstein and Nelson W. Polsby (Reading, Mass.: Addison-Wesley, 1975), p. 104.

North American political scientists—the category to which our contributors belong—after a brief discussion of the most important twentieth-century sources on labor politics which have influenced contemporary American political science, I concentrate exclusively on relevant work by North American political scientists.

For political scientists and political sociologists, interest in labor politics during the first half of the twentieth century was almost exclusively a matter of the twin themes of trade union bureaucracy and democracy. The classic studies were those of Robert Michels and then, nearly fifty years later, of Seymour Martin Lipset, Martin Trow, and James Coleman.[4] Concerned with the degree to which unions were able to represent the interests of their members as opposed to the claims of their leaders, the sociological approach concluded that, in trade unions, bureaucracy and democracy generally were inversely related. Trade unions, at least those of any size and stability, were usually not very democratic. They operated in ways that tended to promote the narrow, careerist interests of their bureaucrats rather than the broader, social interests of their members.

These studies of labor politics asked questions generated by democratic theory, analyzing trade unions as if they were private governments whose main purpose was to represent and regulate their members. To the degree that these studies were concerned with internal union politics, these had to do with relations between leaders and led, members and officials. Thus, these studies generally considered single unions or national confederations and the efforts of those who staffed them to free themselves from rank-and-file controls. Their main concerns were classically sociological, in that they examined issues of power and authority within formal organizations.

After some years of relative neglect, the wave of industrial unrest that swept the advanced capitalist countries in the closing years of the 1960s prompted a new flurry of studies of organized labor. Trade unions were reintroduced into the political imagination, acquiring a degree of scholarly interest, certainly in North America, hitherto unknown. Once again, the twin sociological themes of bureaucracy and democracy initially proved central for political scientists and political

4. Robert Michels, *Political Parties: A Sociological Study of the Oligarchical Tendencies of Modern Democracy* (New York: Free Press, 1962); Seymour Martin Lipset, Martin Trow, and James Coleman, *Union Democracy: The Inside Politics of the International Typographical Union* (New York: Free Press, 1956).

sociologists, as the two most important sets of studies of the wave of militancy, the first coordinated by Alessandro Pizzorno and the second by Colin Crouch and Alessandro Pizzorno, demonstrated.[5] At the same time, however, new issues were introduced into the political study of organized labor, issues that fell under the scope of political economy. Pertaining to relations between organized labor, political institutions, and markets, the new political economy approach shifted the intellectual agenda in the study of labor.

The Crouch and Pizzorno volumes bridged the transition from sociology to political economy, for most of the essays were intellectually indebted to the sociological tradition while taking up substantive concerns of political economy. Illustrative is that of David Soskice, perhaps the most successful explanation for why high levels of industrial action took place more or less simultaneously in most of the Western European countries at the end of the 1960s and why it tended to come from the grass roots acting against or without central labor elites.[6] According to Soskice, governments sought to cope with declining profitability in the recession of the mid-1960s by asking central union confederations to approve incomes policies. At the same time, enterprises reacted to the recession by extensive rationalization. Whether formal or merely informally subscribed to by labor, income policies effectively held wage increases below what the market could have borne. Faced with increasing rates of exploitation on the shop floor and a national leadership co-opted into standing agreements over wage moderation, workers rebelled toward the end of the 1960s. They did so with grass roots action—semiofficial at best, often entirely nonofficial—aimed at reclaiming the wages lost to incomes policies and at reversing the speedups and worsening working conditions characteristic of the 1960s.

Soskice's study illustrates two themes characteristic of much work on labor politics in the period following the mobilization of the late 1960s, including most of the essays collected by Crouch and Pizzorno. First, true to the sociological tradition that saw organized labor as fundamentally caught between the bureaucratic tendencies of its leaders

5. Alessandro Pizzorno, ed., *Lotte operaie e sindacato in Italia: 1968–1972,* 6 vols. (Bologna: Il Mulino, 1978); and Colin Crouch and Alessandro Pizzorno, eds., *The Resurgence of Class Conflict in Western Europe since 1968,* 2 vols. (New York: Holmes & Meier, 1978).

6. David Soskice, "Strike Waves and Wage Explosions, 1968–1970: An Economic Interpretation," *Comparative Analyses,* vol. 2 of *Resurgence of Class Conflict,* ed. Crouch and Pizzorno, pp. 221–46.

and the democratic aspirations of its members, these scholars identified conflicts between central labor elites and the rank and file (or possibly the rank and file in conjunction with grass roots activists and peripheral union officials) as the central lines of division within labor movements. Second, and related, the contributors to these volumes, including Pizzorno himself as well as Soskice and others such as Leo Panitch, argued that these conflicts stemmed from the co-optation of central union officials into national incomes policies, or what would later come to be termed corporatist agreements.[7] Both themes surfaced in most of the studies collected by Crouch and Pizzorno, and they more or less defined the tenor of work, especially that undertaken by Western Europeans themselves, on labor and labor militancy in the 1960s and 1970s.

The literature on the heightened industrial militancy characteristic in advanced capitalist countries between the mid-1960s and mid-1970s thus bridged the older sociological concern with union democracy with the interest in political economy that was to emerge fully in the 1970s and 1980s. The phenomenon of income policies displayed this dual focus. Incomes policies directed attention at the relationship between union officials and other economic and political elites while also inspiring continued interest in the interaction between union officials and the rank and file. Union leaders were increasingly seen as caught between the conflicting pressures emanating from their members, on the one hand, and from governments and capitalists, on the other. This second set of interactions was to acquire even greater importance after the oil shock of 1973.

It was really only after the wave of industrial unrest of the late 1960s that many American political scientists turned their attention to labor. Indeed, by the time most arrived on the scene, the novelty of militancy had been overshadowed by the claims of economic crisis.[8] Earlier, Anglo-American studies of interest groups and of functional

7. Pizzorno, "Political Exchange and Collective Identity in Industrial Conflict," in *Comparative Analyses,* vol. 2 of *Resurgence of Class Conflict,* ed. Crouch and Pizzorno, pp. 277–98; Soskice, "Strike Waves and Wage Explosions"; Leo Panitch, *Social Democracy and Industrial Militancy: The Labour Party, the Trade Unions and Incomes Policy, 1945–1974* (Cambridge: Cambridge University Press, 1976). Here I ignore some important differences among these various authors regarding the sources and nature of the conflicts they all observe between the rank and file and union elites.

8. An exception is the study of John R. Low-Beer, *Protest and Participation: The New Working Class in Italy* (Cambridge: Cambridge University Press, 1978).

representation included a concern with trade unions,[9] but the discipline as a whole considered trade unions as such to be the province of sociologists, economists, and industrial relations specialists. Only in the 1970s and 1980s did the study of organized labor begin to acquire intellectual legitimacy within political science. And if the motivating questions of earlier research had placed political scientists at the intersection of sociology—Michels, Lipset, and Pizzorno were, after all, political sociologists to a man—given the centrality of economic pressures on unions in the 1970s, when American political scientists began work on organized labor it occurred instead at the intersection of economics. The general questions driving inquiry were those of political economy: how political institutions interacted with markets and economic agents, the impact of economic phenomena on political decisions and processes.

The first wave of union studies by American political scientists, which we can date from the late 1970s, came in two distinct methodological types. First, researchers undertook intensive national case studies of labor confederations, their economic and political orientations, their involvements in the policy process, and their responses to the pressures engendered by the first oil shock. Representative of this kind of work was the influential comparative study known as the Harvard Center for European Studies Project on European Trade Union Responses to Economic Crisis, eventually associated with Peter Gourevitch and others for Britain, Sweden, and the Federal Republic of Germany and Peter Lange, George Ross, and Maurizio Vannicelli for Italy and France.[10] In these volumes, union responses to the economic changes of the 1970s were investigated.

9. Henry W. Erhmann, *Interest Groups on Four Continents* (Pittsburgh: University of Pittsburgh Press, 1958); Stein Rokkan, "Norway: Numerical Democracy and Corporate Pluralism," in *Political Oppositions in Western Democracies,* ed. Robert A. Dahl (New Haven: Yale University Press, 1966), pp. 70–115; Samuel H. Beer, *Modern British Politics: Politics and Pressure Groups in the Collectivist Age* (New York: Norton, 1965); Suzanne Berger, "Introduction," in *Organizing Interests in Western Europe: Pluralism, Corporatism, and the Transformation of Politics,* ed. Suzanne D. Berger (Cambridge: Cambridge University Press, 1981), pp. 1–23; and Gabriel Almond, "Corporatism, Pluralism, and Professional Memory," *World Politics* 35 (January 1983): 245–60.

10. Peter Gourevitch et al., *Unions and Economic Crisis: Britain, West Germany, and Sweden* (London: Allen & Unwin, 1984); and Peter Lange, George Ross, and Maurizio Vannicelli, *Unions, Change and Crisis: French and Italian Union Strategy and the Political Economy, 1945–1980* (London: Allen & Unwin, 1982). A convenient way to date American interest in the topic is with the original Workshop on Comparative Labor Movements, sponsored by the Center for European Studies of Harvard University and the Council for European Studies, Cambridge, Mass., October 14–16, 1977. This workshop eventually gave birth to the two volumes of comparative study of trade unions cited here.

A second kind of research, running parallel to the first but usually employing the methods of cross-sectional aggregate statistical analysis, was carried out under the corporatist rubric.[11] These studies investigated the relationship between such variables as union strength and centralization, national economic performance, industrial militancy, and governmental partisanship.[12] Not strictly concerned with trade unionism as such, this second line of research incorporated unions into the more general study of contemporary political economy.

Despite displaying methodological differences, these two clusters of researchers bespoke a common intellectual and normative agenda. Both were concerned with the interactions between organized labor and the national political economy. And working in a political context increasingly unsympathetic to organized labor, in which trade unions were suspected of damaging markets and economic performance, both were interested in assessing whether unions were as bad for capitalism as was increasingly believed to be the case.

Their methodological differences allowed them to view these problems from complementary perspectives. Whereas practitioners of the statistical approach used characteristics of labor movements as independent variables to explain national economic performance, researchers using case study analysis took characteristics of the national economy as independent variables and sought to assess their impact on labor's strategy and performance. The direction of causality—whether, that is, labor was used as the independent variable in an analysis of national economic performance or national economic performance was used as an independent variable in analyzing labor—varied with the method of analysis. Statistical methods were required for the former; historical case analysis was more suitable for the latter.

Both kinds of researcher treated labor as a unitary or aggregate actor. Neither exhibited much interest in lower levels of organization or

11. An exception is the work of Peter J. Katzenstein, which, because it involves five countries, clearly transcends the single case study approach without, however, principally using statistical methods; see Katzenstein, *Small States in World Markets: Industrial Policy in Europe* (Ithaca: Cornell University Press, 1985); and Katzenstein, *Corporatism and Change: Austria, Switzerland and the Politics of Industry* (Ithaca: Cornell University Press, 1984).

12. David R. Cameron, "Social Democracy, Corporatism, Labor Quiescence, and the Representation of Economic Interest in Advanced Capitalist Society," in *Order and Conflict in Contemporary Capitalism: Studies in the Political Economy of Western European Nations*, ed. John H. Goldthorpe (Oxford: Oxford University Press, 1984), pp. 143–78; Walter Korpi and Michael Shalev, "Strikes, Power and Politics in the Western Nations, 1900–1976," in *Political Power and Social Theory*, vol. 1, ed. Maurice Zeitlin (Greenwich, Conn.: JAI, 1980), pp. 301–34; Peter Lange and Geoffrey Garrett, "The Politics of Growth: Strategic Interaction and Economic Performance in the Advanced Industrial Democracies, 1974–1980," *Journal of Politics* 47 (August 1985): 792–827.

in internal organizational demarcations and interactions. Concern with the traditional sociological themes of bureaucracy and democracy had not entirely vanished,[13] but it was more often replaced by attention to the role of organized labor in the political economy. And in depicting labor's place in the political economy, scholars held that organized labor ought to be viewed as an actor. This conception drew on a formulation originally proposed by Pizzorno, who sought to delineate the conditions that made trade unions capable of strategic action: "The union is an actor in its own right, not only developing its specific interest, but being capable of carrying out a strategy, that is a succession of intertemporal decisions in which present action is evaluated in terms of its consequences for future goals."[14] Such an idea provided an essential analytic underpinning for studies of national union confederations conducted in the 1970s. For instance, it constituted the thrust of the two companion volumes published under the auspices of Harvard's Center for European Studies, the purpose of which was to investigate why different union confederations adopted different strategies despite similar environmental challenges. The answer, the authors of these studies argued, was that each union movement had a distinctive history—even when (as in the French and Italian cases, for instance) they appeared superficially similar.[15]

The essays collected in the present volume all substantively fall very much within the confines of political economy, but they attend to organizational conflicts and cleavages within and among unions instead of conceptualizing labor as a unitary or aggregate actor. Heavily influenced by the corporatist paradigm, our contributors merge some of the substantive issues found in the statistical work characteristic of that line of inquiry with the focus on union strategy found in the national case studies. But the work represented here is distinguished from earlier work in four other ways along with this methodological breach.

First, unlike their predecessors, most of our contributors use fieldwork techniques of inquiry and, second, in so doing, they tend to

13. As demonstrated by Peter Lange, "Union Democracy and Liberal Corporatism: Exit, Voice and Wage Regulation in Postwar Europe" (Western Societies Program, Cornell Studies in International Affairs, Occasional Paper no. 16, n.d.).

14. Pizzorno, "Political Exchange and Collective Identity," p. 281.

15. Peter Lange and George Ross, "Conclusions: French and Italian Union Development in Comparative Perspective," in *Unions, Change and Crisis*, pp. 207–91.

investigate levels of union organization below the confederation—particular industrial unions, for instance, or specific localities. The two features are obviously related: the lack of public source material on subconfederal levels of trade unionism means that fieldwork constitutes the only viable method with which to collect information—information, it should be said, virtually unknown to the scholarly community prior to this wave of research.

Third, extending the concern with economic crisis exhibited in the research carried out after the first oil shock, researchers in the 1980s and 1990s paid more attention to the details of the daily routines of trade unionism. Collective bargaining, shop-floor politics, the plant, the enterprise, and the industry in which they are located, industrial organization and reorganization, technology and technological change, were all brought under scholarly scrutiny. The essays collected here reflect this increased sensitivity to the industrial and economic contexts in which trade unions are embedded. They are part of a shift of attention from macroeconomic issues characteristic, for instance, of the earlier corporatist literature, to microeconomic issues, including those associated with the industrial restructuring so common to the 1980s.

Finally, our contributors also share a cohort characteristic. Young political scientists turned in increasing numbers to the study of organized labor in the 1980s. While students of underdeveloped countries, including those in Africa and Latin America,[16] occasionally looked at labor and labor politics, the bulk of interest among younger scholars was shown by those concerned with the advanced capitalist countries. Dissertations were written on American labor and labor history[17] and, as exemplified by the work of Charlotte Yates included here, on Canadian labor too. But the thrust of the interest younger political scientists have displayed in trade unionism has come from those working on the Western European countries. Besides our contributors, all of whom have completed dissertations on organized labor, numerous

16. For instance, Glenn Adler, "Labor Organization under Authoritarian Industrialization: Black Trade Unions in the South African Motor Industry, 1968–83" (Ph.D. dissertation in progress, Columbia University); and Margaret E. Keck, *The Workers' Party and Democratization in Brazil* (New Haven: Yale University Press, 1992).

17. For instance, Victoria Hattam, *Changing Conceptions of Class and American Political Development, 1806–1896* (Princeton: Princeton University Press, forthcoming); and Michael Goldfield, *The Decline of Organized Labor in the United States* (Chicago: University of Chicago Press, 1987).

other young scholars have looked at various Western European countries and occasionally at more than one.[18]

All these features lend the studies collected here a natural intellectual cohesion. But the main innovation our contributors offer is a skepticism of the notion that organized labor constitutes a unitary actor. By focusing on particular industrial unions, localities, and firms, they implicitly reject such a conception, proposing instead that trade unions be studied as complex organizations. With this move, they acquire a distinctive analytic voice. It is a voice that incorporates the strengths of earlier studies—the sensitivity to local case histories, the concern with unions as important vehicles for both mass representation and economic interest, the attention to the reciprocal connections between organized labor and the political arena—while at the same time adding a new dimension of analysis. That dimension involves the increasing organizational conflicts among and within unions.

EMPIRICAL FINDINGS OF THE RESEARCH

Students of organized labor in the advanced capitalist countries during the 1970s stressed the behavioral and ideological stability leaders

18. For instance, Michael Contarino, "The Politics of Industrial Change: Textile Unions and Industrial Restructuring in Five Italian Localities" (Ph.D. dissertation, Harvard University, 1984); Robert Fishman, *Working-Class Organization and the Return to Democracy in Spain* (Ithaca: Cornell University Press, 1990); Chris Howell, "Regulating Labor: The State and Industrial Relations Reform in Postwar France" (Princeton: Princeton University Press, 1992); Steven C. Lewis, "Unions and Socialism: The CFDT and the Reconstruction of the French Left" (Ph.D. dissertation, MIT, 1988); Carol Anne Mershon, "The Micropolitics of Union Action: Industrial Conflict in Italian Factories" (Ph.D. dissertation, Yale University, 1986); Stephen J. Silvia, "Jobs, Trade and Unions: The Politics of Employment and Protectionism in West German and American Unions" (Ph.D. dissertation, Yale University, 1990); and W. Rand Smith, *Crisis in the French Labour Movement: A Grassroots Perspective* (New York: St. Martin's 1987). Cross-national studies include Stephen Bornstein, "States and Unions: From Postwar Settlement to Contemporary Stalemate," in *The State in Capitalist Europe: A Casebook*, ed. Stephen Bornstein, David Held, and Joel Krieger (London: Allen & Unwin, 1985), pp. 54–90; Gary Marks, *Unions in Politics: Britain, Germany, and the United States in the Nineteenth and Early Twentieth Centuries* (Princeton: Princeton University Press, 1989); and Michael Wallerstein, "Working Class Solidarity and Rational Behavior" (Ph.D. dissertation, University of Chicago, 1985). Both of these latter studies are unusual, the first because it is one of the very few that is exclusively historical rather than contemporary, the second because it uses formal methods of inquiry. See also Wallerstein, "Centralized Bargaining and Wage Restraint," *American Journal of Political Science* 34 (November 1991): 982–1004; and Wallerstein, "Union Organization in Advanced Industrial Democracies," *American Political Science Review* 83 (June 1989): 481–501.

exhibited in responding to changed economic conditions.[19] Their responses, the Harvard Center for European Studies Project reported, for instance, were by and large drawn from existing ideological repertoires and constructed along historically established, nationally specific lines. The general picture that emerged was that, although shaken, trade union leaders did not believe the economic crisis demanded fundamentally restructuring their own organizations or policies.

The direct and measurable effects of economic change on trade unions were, in fact, still relatively modest. The twin pressures of inflation and recession placed incomes policies high on the political agendas of most advanced capitalists countries, but in many ways trade unions were still largely unaffected by economic crisis.[20] Indeed, as Pontusson notes in his introductory chapter, the political influence of organized labor actually expanded during this period, thanks to the requirements for union cooperation in incomes policies. Membership levels generally continued to increase in most Western European countries throughout the 1970s;[21] and although incomes policies may have held down the rate of wage increases employees enjoyed, their standards of living were still generally protected.

Our studies convey the flavor of a very different, and a much more difficult, context. During the 1980s, trade unions were seriously and perhaps irreversibly affected by economic change. These changes were no longer filtered through government policy and political pressures on confederal leaders. Rooted instead in international changes in markets and structures of production, often involving restructuring and changes in the actual processes of production as well, they touched unions directly by changing the labor market and work situations in which employees found themselves. In addition, unemployment remained persistently high across Western Europe, and real wages and standards of living declined in the advanced capitalist countries. So too did strike rates and union membership.

19. Gourevitch et al., *Unions and Economic Crisis;* Lange, Ross, and Vannicelli, *Unions, Change and Crisis;* and Richard Edwards, Paolo Garonna, and Franz Tödtling, eds., *Unions in Crisis and Beyond: Perspectives from Six Countries* (Dover, Mass.: Auburn House, 1986).

20. See Robert J. Flanagan, David W. Soskice, and Lloyd Ulman, *Unionism, Economic Stabilization and Incomes Policies: European Experience* (Washington, D.C.: Brookings Institution, 1983).

21. Jelle Visser, "Trade Unionism in Western Europe: Present Situation and Prospects," *Labour and Society* 13 (April 1988): 125–82; see especially p. 127.

All of our essays are set within this context, in which trade unions contend with apparently irreversible transformations of the structures of production and often of the processes of production as well, transformations for which they are unprepared, about which they are often ill informed, and to which they have little ready response.[22] Such a context has naturally taken a toll on organized labor. This toll is particularly evident as a kind of internal paralysis of union behavior and decision making, and I propose that this paralysis, in turn, is a result of a change in the main lines of division within labor movements. Whereas classic sociological conflicts between leaders and led propelled union politics in the 1960s and 1970s, by the 1980s these conflicts were increasingly displaced by another set of divisions, divisions that pitted worker against worker, plant against plant, union against union, and confederation against confederation. These divisions, in turn, because they undercut the abilities of central confederations to delineate general lines of union policy, generate an overall impression of strategic disarray. This disarray is evident in a centrifugal fragmentation of collective bargaining and of trade union organizations.

During the 1960s and 1970s, a wealth of studies on labor politics and industrial relations suggested that union movements in the advanced capitalist countries were experiencing pressures toward decentralization: that the powers of confederations and of national industrial federations were being undermined by the grass roots militancy of the shop floor. Particularly as a result of the strike wave that overtook most of the advanced capitalist nations during the closing years of the 1960s and into the 1970s, the central challenge to labor's ability to coordinate its own activities across organizational boundaries came from below. I have already discussed why this was so; the essays collected by Pizzorno and by Crouch and Pizzorno represent a whole body of literature concerned with center-periphery conflicts within organized labor during the 1960s and 1970s.

The present essays suggest that the 1980s and 1990s, in contrast to the preceding two decades, are increasingly characterized by growing conflicts of interest within organized labor among similarly positioned groups. Center-periphery and top-bottom conflicts have not vanished since 1979, but they have been increasingly displaced by sectional and centrifugal conflicts among groups of workers and their or-

22. See Wolfgang Streeck, "The Uncertainties of Management in the Management of Uncertainty," *International Journal of Political Economy* 17 (Fall 1987): 57–87.

ganizational representatives. These conflicts are driven by the material fragmentation of working-class interests and the more acute competition for wages and jobs that characterizes the advanced capitalist economies in the 1980s and 1990s.

Peggy Kahn and Charlotte Yates tell similar stories of increasing trade union fragmentation in the 1980s. Both the North American United Auto Workers (UAW) and the British National Union of Mineworkers (NUM) experienced splits in the middle of the decade: the UAW in 1984, when the Canadian section broke off to establish itself as an autonomous trade union (CAW) representing auto employees in Canada, and the NUM in the aftermath of the debacle of the 1984–85 strike, when the Union for Democratic Mineworkers (UDM) was established. Both cases illustrate that the increasing fragmentation of worker interests in the 1980s, driven by a growing heterogeneity of market conditions, generates in its wake an increasing fragmentation of and competition among unions. As workers in the same industry experience heightened competition for jobs and wages in an era of economic distress, this competition feeds latent organizational rivalries and eventually leads to open organizational schisms. The establishment of new trade unions through a process of schism mimics the increasing fragmentation of rank-and-file interests.

The outcomes identified by Yates and Kahn, however, are extreme, and probably atypical. A general trend toward the establishment of new (and often rival) unions where single unions once existed is probably not under way. Good comparative data do not exist, but what longitudinal data are available regarding the number of unions in different countries suggest that the increasing fragmentation of worker interests in the 1980s was only occasionally met with explicit organizational fragmentation. Indeed, trade union movements generally seem to have responded to new economic difficulties by consolidating their levels of concentration, not fragmenting even further. In other words, at least in some countries, a wave of union mergers has occurred. These have been driven by two related sets of causes. Some have resulted from the vast changes in occupational structures I have already mentioned. Given the virtual disappearance of the British coal industry in the 1980s and 1990s, for instance, the NUM is now set to merge with a large general union. Very small unions attached to industries undergoing permanent decline have often undertaken to merge with more powerful organizations. Other union mergers in the

1980s have been part of an ongoing process of organizational rationalization. The Italian union movement, for example, has seen the number of industrial federations fall substantially as part of a package of mergers aimed at consolidating and rationalizing the collective bargaining structure. More research would be required to know whether these mergers have effectively increased union concentration—the proportion of members organized by the largest affiliated unions.

If there is no general trend toward increased organizational fragmentation, why, in the two cases explored by Yates and Kahn, did actual organizational schisms occur? Their evidence suggests that, when workers organized by the same industrial union experience severe divergences in market positions, organizational fragmentation occurs where established regional or national cleavages overlay and reinforce these market distinctions. Both the North American auto industry and the British coal industry had been undergoing increased competitive pressures, especially from abroad; both industries were facing substantial job loss and possible degenerations of pay or working conditions. But these economic factors differentially affected different regions represented by the two original unions, placing different groups of North American autoworkers and British miners in substantially different market situations. Canadian autoworkers, thanks to the exchange rate of the Canadian dollar compared with the American dollar, found their products more competitive than identical products from just across the border and resented pressures from their American counterparts to undertake concession bargaining not necessarily required by Canadian market conditions. Nottinghamshire miners, the core of the breakaway UDM, worked a particularly prosperous group of pits, pits less threatened with closure than those in other regions of the country. So in both cases the breakaway unions represented employees in stronger market positions than most members of the parent union.

Both Kahn and Yates show that region-specific union leadership groups were threatened by members enjoying market positions strong enough to repudiate their leaders unless the latter distinguished themselves from the weaker parent union. This repudiation assumed different forms in the two contexts: in Canadian autos, the threat was of wildcats; in the Notts mines, of continuing to work during the 1984–85 strike. But, in both cases, region-specific leadership groups, confronting potential rank-and-file discontent based on greater-than-average market power, exploited the opportunity to mobilize their constituents on the basis of region-specific identities and loyalties.

Richard Locke's and Kathleen Thelen's analyses of the new tensions characterizing relations between national union officials and their plant-based counterparts in the Italian and German metalworking industries highlight that interorganizational conflicts do not necessarily imply organizational schisms. The thesis of both authors is that in the 1980s the increased heterogeneity of the material interests of workers, even workers within the same industry, generated severe strains between local union representatives and their national leaderships. In the case of the Italian automobile industry, Locke argues that the increasing diversity among plants made it more difficult for the national industrial union to reconcile the bargaining process across them. His is a story in which a national industrial union virtually loses control of the bargaining process. It does so because of increased centrifugal tendencies in the industry. The outcome, although not a region-specific schism of the type identified by Yates and Kahn, is otherwise similar. Regional units of the same union diverge strategically and begin to compete in the bargaining process.

Thelen's account of similar pressures in the German metalworking industry shows that IG Metall, the metalworkers' union, has been more successful than its Italian counterpart in retaining a coordinated bargaining process and handling similar centrifugal strains of the 1980s. She argues that, although the fragmentation of market opportunities places workers in different plants at cross purposes, IG Metall has successfully incorporated the works councils into its general bargaining strategy, thereby containing centrifugal pressures. So, while the material pressures on German and Italian engineering workers have been similar, placing them into increasing plant-specific and regional competition, the responses of their unions have been different.

Why this difference in the abilities of the German and Italian engineering federations to respond to the fragmentation of worker interests? Yates's and Kahn's evidence shows that national industrial unions experienced schisms in the 1980s because of overlapping and reinforcing market and regional cleavages: both the CAW and the UDM took advantage of preexisting regionally defined organizational identities. If the organizational boundaries within the UAW and the NUM had not already delineated the CAW and the UDM as distinct subentities and hence potentially separate unions, regional officials would probably not have been able to mobilize effectively around regional loyalties. A variant of this explanation can be extended to account for the relative degrees of success encountered by the national metalworking unions in Germany and Italy in responding to similar centrifugal pressures. The cases analyzed by Locke and Thelen suggest that preexisting organizational demarcations may exacerbate internal organizational conflicts and rivalries as market pressures put groups of workers in the same industries into increasing competition with each other.

In particular, the German metalworking industry is organized by a single organization whereas the equivalent Italian federation actually comprises three distinct, ideologically rival unions. The latter's lack of success in managing its relations with the factor councils and local union officials at Fiat and Alfa Romeo has been closely linked, I would hazard, to preexisting organizational fragmentation. Historical organizational divisions, which had been largely papered over in the years between the mid-1960s and the early 1980s, became increasingly important in the 1980s for both the national union and its local counterparts. The ability of the national union to monitor and coordinate local activities dropped in the 1980s as national officials found themselves devoting increasing resources to managing their relations with their parent confederations and to preserving a semblance of internal unity. This gave local officials considerably more independence than they had once exercised. And in a context of increasing market differences among plants and firms in the same industry, local officials developed greater incentives to exploit the absence of central authority and, as Locke recounts, more or less to go their own way. This situation contrasts sharply with the German, where, as Thelen presents it, a unified and cohesive national leadership dealt relatively effectively with plant-based organizations even as these, like their Italian counterparts, clamored for increased plant differentiation on the basis of a growing market fragmentation of worker interests.

A similar attention to the importance of preexisting organizational demarcations in accounting for variations in the degrees of success of different union movements in responding to growing market fragmentation could arguably be sustained on the basis of Jonas Pontusson's comparison of trade unionism in the Swedish and British auto industry and Peter Swenson's analysis of confederal unionism in Sweden and Germany. Ostensibly a workplace study, Pontusson's argument, like Swenson's, invokes characteristics of the national political economy to explain differences in industrial relations in the years since 1979. He argues that whether industrial restructuring has been carried out with or against organized labor has been a function of the degree to which the national political economy includes a historically powerful labor movement. The historical unity and cohesiveness of the Swedish union movement, especially compared with its internally divided British counterpart, thus play important roles in the explanation Pontusson constructs. In the events he recounts, the more limited ability of the British to respond to restructuring and technological innovation at British Leyland compared with the Swedes turns on the greater degree of interorganizational conflict characteristic of the former. With eleven trade unions competing for influence among British Leyland employees, the unions' response to restructuring—itself not the thrust of Pontusson's story, but recounted as part of his explanation for the degree to which management included trade unions in technological reorganization—was hampered by internal division. The Swedes, by contrast, were better able to take advantage of the opportunities afforded by restructuring. Here, too, preexisting organizational demarcations exacerbated fragmented responses to an increasing diversification of market interests among workers in the years since the second oil shock.

Organizational conflicts among unions are central to Peter Swenson's analysis of confederal unionism in Sweden and the Federal Republic of Germany; he refers to them as intraclass distributional conflicts. The conflicts he analyzes occur among blocs of trade unions in single confederations. In Sweden, these conflicts have pitted private-sector unions against their public counterparts in open and extremely divisive rivalries over the privileges according employees in the latter sector as regards pay, job security, and benefits. The catalyst for the open emergence of these conflicts lay with the persistent economic pressures of the 1980s, as Swenson describes it. The emergence of increasingly zero-sum conflicts over shares of the national income eventually fragmented established alliances between private- and public-sector unions. These conflicts were, moreover, adroitly exploited by business organizations, who capitalized on labor's problems to fragment collective bargaining, thereby hoping to restrain the pay growth of the public sector. In Germany, by contrast, conflicts have occurred between high-pay and low-pay unions, cutting across the private-public barrier. Swenson argues that the relative size of the state sector explains why the lines of division differed in the two cases. But, in both, declining economic resources have provided the basic terms of interorganizational conflict.

The Swedish case is especially illuminating of the current state of trade unionism in advanced capitalism. Historically, the union movement in Sweden ranked as one of the most centralized and cohesive in the world, but by the early 1990s peak-level collective bargaining had been severely eroded there. Swenson provides an analytical context for understanding that erosion. As he indicates, it involved increasingly bitter conflicts among rival blocs of unions. The end of Swedish corporatism did not occur because of a breakdown in relations between leaders and led or center and periphery, as sociologists concerned with union democracy would have led us to expect.[23] Because of their lack of attention to interorganizational rivalries, this earlier approach to trade union studies would not easily have been able to account for the demise of peak-level collective bargaining in Sweden in the 1990s.

Both Anthony Daley's and Jeannette Money's essays on industrial relations in the U.S., French, and Belgian steel and coal industries echo these themes of the fragmentation of collective bargaining. Daley describes an industry which, already declining in the 1970s, literally collapsed in the 1980s. Job reduction and the loss of wages and benefits were so severe in the U.S. steel industry after the second oil shock that industry-wide pattern bargaining collapsed in 1983. Since then, bargaining has proceeded instead on a plant-by-plant basis, generating what Daley refers to as competitive concessions. In fact, the 1986 contract renewals took place at company level. The fragmentation of workers into rival bargaining units has thus been virtually complete.

Likewise, in France, twenty years of industrial action collapsed in 1980s as the various ideologically defined rival unions in steel found themselves unable to reach agreements. The presence of a Socialist government undoubtedly contributed to this outcome, as political differences among unions were reactivated by economic and labor market distress. As is suggested by various other essays as well, where preexisting organizational demarcations exist they exacerbate the frag-

23. Such as Leo Panitch, "Trade Unions and the Capitalist State," *New Left Review* 125 (January-February 1981): 21–43. For an argument related to that made here, see Miriam Golden, "The Dynamics of Trade Unionism and National Economic Performance," paper presented at the Midwest Political Science Association, April 9–11, 1992.

mentation of union responses to the growing material difficulties of workers in the post–oil shock era.

Jeannette Money's contribution, too, stresses the increased organizational fragmentation affecting unions. Using evidence from three countries—the United States, France, and Belgium—Money observes a decentralization of industrial relations in the 1980s that began in the 1960s, with a displacement of confederal by industrial level bargaining. This change has been followed more recently with the displacement of industrial unions by bargaining agents in specific plants. Her argument echoes a large literature that describes the growing fragmentation of industrial relations in the 1980s in terms of decentralization.[24] What has been less often noted, however, is the degree to which the decentralization of bargaining involves increasing interorganizational conflicts among unions and union groups.

Money's evidence from the United States, for instance, shows that the decentralization of industrial relations and collective bargaining there entailed heightened interorganizational conflicts. The American coal industry achieved national bargaining in the 1930s. The 1970s and 1980s witnessed a regional fragmentation of bargaining, as the United Mine Workers became increasingly confined to Appalachia while preexisting rival unions enacted their own agreements covering the western states. The American story Money tells is thus one of intensified rivalries among competing regional unions not unlike that characteristic of British coal and North American automobiles.

Money's French story argues that the decentralization of collective bargaining in the 1980s was a function of the 1982 Auroux legislation, which finally forced employers to negotiate with unions at the level of the firm. This, too, involved increasing interorganizational conflicts among unions. As Money tells it, the Auroux laws were a result of competition among ideologically rival confederations in which more militant unions sought to counter "unrepresentative" national agreements by enacting firm agreements. The Socialist government's support for the legislation enforcing firm agreements was in part designed to alter the balance of forces among competing unions. So here, too, the decentralization of collective bargaining in the 1980s was the result of just the kinds of competitive pressures among rival unions which I have argued are characteristic of the period.

24. Characteristic is Visser, "Trade Unionism in Western Europe," p. 171.

The findings reported across our eight studies are outlined below. I classify the outcomes observed as involving either decentralization within or deconcentration among union organizations. The eight studies allow me to classify twelve cases (one case, that of Swedish autos, I consider unclassifiable in terms of these outcomes).

Decentralization within unions

Bargaining shifted from industry to company or plant level

- French coal (Money)
- U.S. steel (Daley)
- German engineering (Thelen)
- Belgian coal (Money)

Deconcentration among unions

Conflicts between regional unions in the same industry

- North American autos (Yates)
- Italian autos (Locke)
- U.S. coal (Money)
- British coal (Kahn)

Conflicts among competing unions in the same industry

- French steel (Daley)
- British autos (Pontusson)

Conflicts among unions in different industries

- Swedish LO (Swenson)
- German DGB (Swenson)

Of these twelve cases, eight involve various kinds of deconcentration. It is worth noting that in none of the cases of apparent decentralization do the kinds of grass roots pressure stressed by the sociological approach appear relevant. Even where a decentralization of bargaining has occurred in the 1980s and 1990s, it has been a decentralization in which competition among groups of workers generates increasingly competitive relations among rival unions and groups of unions.

The findings reported in this volume can be synthesized as four distinct patterns of union fragmentation and interorganizational conflict. First, what I class as deconcentration occurred along three distinct lines in the years since the second oil shock. In some cases, a regionalization of bargaining has occurred in which an industrial union has seen regional subunits thrust into intensified competition and rivalry with each other. These situations have sometimes even resulted in outright organizational schisms. A second kind of deconcentration has involved heightened conflicts among competing unions in the same industry, unions distinguished along either ideological or craft lines. A third kind, finally, concerns heightened conflicts among unions or blocs of unions across different industries. Examples include public-private conflicts or high-pay/low-pay conflicts. The fourth pattern I call, with some reservations, decentralization. In these cases, it appears that collective bargaining has shifted from the industrial to the company or plant level in the 1980s. This shift, however, has often been driven by conflicts among groups of workers in the same industry.

One conclusion of these studies is that market forces alone are inadequate predictors of how unions respond to economic pressures. The intensity of competition among workers for wages and jobs appears to vary independently of the severity of interorganizational conflicts. The conflicts of interest between American and Canadian autoworkers, for instance, although serious, were probably not more serious than between autoworkers at Fiat and at Alfa in Italy. Yet, in the first case an organizational schism occurred, whereas in the second one did not.

Instead, the range of outcomes I have described appears linked to prexisting organizational characteristics of various unions. Preexisting organizational demarcations of all types have been exacerbated by the increasing conflicts of interest among workers. On rare occasions, actual organizational schisms have occurred. More often, however, fragmentation and rivalry among workers has been played out with a reactivation of existing lines of organizational identity. And where no distinct regional, ideological, craft, or industrial organizational demarcation existed, bargaining has fragmented by plant. The few cases of apparent decentralization nearly all occurred in situations of monopoly unionism; that is, where there were no preexisting organizational divisions—regional, ideological, or craft-based—in a particular sector. The only place rivalry and fragmentation could go in such a context was to the plant. And in all cases of what I call deconcentration, preexisting lines of organizational division have been reactivated by heightened material conflicts of interest among workers.

ORGANIZATIONAL COMPLEXITY AND INTERORGANIZATIONAL CONFLICT

The general trend that emerges out of the dozen case studies investigated here is that trade unions have experienced increasing organizational tensions in the 1980s and into the 1990s. These have usually not followed earlier patterns that may have pitted rank and file against central elites, or grass roots activists against full-time officials. Rather, these new divisions have pitted full-time officials or groups of organized workers against each other. Union officials organizing the same industry in different regions have fought one another, as have officials in different plants; officials in the public sector have battled their private-sector counterparts. Trade union officials representing whole industries have found themselves at war with other industries for shares of a shrinking pie. Under the strain of economic competition, labor movements have become divided against themselves.

These findings help dispel the fiction of a unitary actor which treats national union movements as single wholes or as aggregates. Instead, they suggest that variations in the institutional rules and organizational structures of trade unions generate variations in the outcomes of decision-making processes, variations that would not be predicted solely on the basis of an examination of the cleavages among workers. Two union movements, representing equally fragmented groups of workers, could elaborate quite different policies depending on their existing organizational structures and institutional rules. The fragmentation and strategic paralysis afflicting organized labor in the years since 1979 is thus not arbitrary. It has occurred along relatively predictable, albeit national, lines. These involve preexisting regional, ideological, craft, and industrial divisions.

Thus, the organizational outcomes examined in our essays depend on the rules and procedures used to count preferences and then to make decisions. By extension, what a union does is a function solely of neither the interests and preferences of the rank and file it represents nor of the pressures management exerts. What a union does reflects how its own internal processes of decision making work on these two external streams of pressure. Class relations are therefore incomprehensible without an organizational map, a map that outlines the institutional parameters and demarcations of class politics.

Although it is certainly true that detailed case-specific knowledge is required to understand the lines along which the increased organizational tensions of the 1980s and 1990s are played out, the essays collected here suggest some ways that contemporary labor studies may in the future advance political scientific theory as well. Investigation of the organizational aspects of intraclass conflict speaks to the growing body of institutionally focused literature, especially important to the study of American politics, which analyzes how variations in the rules governing institutions affect policy decisions. As we accumulate more empirical knowledge about trade unions, the next logical step—and one that directs the study of trade unions in ways theoretically congruent with developments in other parts of the discipline of political science—is to begin using formal tools of analysis.

Contributors

ANTHONY DALEY is Assistant Professor of Government, Wesleyan University.

MIRIAM GOLDEN is Assistant Professor of Political Science, University of California, Los Angeles.

PEGGY KAHN is Assistant Professor of Political Science, University of Michigan, Flint.

RICHARD LOCKE is Assistant Professor, Sloan School of Management, Massachusetts Institute of Technology.

JEANNETTE MONEY is Assistant Professor of Political Science, Louisiana State University, Baton Rouge.

JONAS PONTUSSON is Associate Professor of Government, Cornell University.

PETER SWENSON is Assistant Professor of Political Science, University of Pennsylvania.

KATHLEEN THELEN is Assistant Professor of Politics, Princeton University.

CHARLOTTE YATES is Assistant Professor of Political Science and Labor Studies, McMaster University.

Index

Library of Congress Cataloging-in-Publication Data

Bargaining for change : Union politics in North America and Europe / edited by Miriam Golden and Jonas Pontusson.

p. cm.

Based on papers presented at a conference held in the spring of 1986 at Cornell University.

Includes bibliographical references and index.

ISBN 0-8014-2647-2 (cloth : alk. paper). — ISBN 0-8014-9948-8 (paper : alk. paper)

1. Trade-unions—Political activity. I. Golden, Miriam, 1934– . II. Pontusson, Jonas.

HD8031.U53 1992

322′.2—dc20 91-57901